Naming the Whirlwind

The Renewal of God-Language

Naming the Whirlwind
The Renewal of God-Language

by Langdon Gilkey

"Then answered the Lord unto Job out of the whirlwind, and said,
Gird up thy loins now like a man:
I will demand of thee, and declare thou unto me."
Job 40:6-7

Bobbs-Merrill Educational Publishing
Indianapolis

Acknowledgments

Blackwell & Mott Ltd.—for quotations from *Philosophical Investigations* by Ludwig Wittgenstein, translation by G. E. M. Anscombe. Copyright © 1963 by Blackwell & Mott. Used with permission of the Wittgenstein Trustees.

P. F. Collier, Inc.—for quotations from *Ideas* by Edmund Husserl. Copyright © 1962 by Collier Books, New York, N. Y. Used with permission of Collier and Allen & Unwin, London, England.

Fortress Press—for quotations from *Word and Faith* by Gerherd Ebeling. Copyright by SCM Press. Used with permission.

Harper and Row, Publishers, Inc.—for quotations from Schubert Ogden, *The Reality of God;* Heinrich Ott, *The Later Heidegger and Theology;* and Paul Ricoeur, *The Symbolism of Evil.* Used with permission.

Macmillan Publishing Co.—for quotations from *The Secular Meaning of the Gospel* by Paul van Buren. Copyright © 1963 by Macmillan Co. Used with permission of Macmillan and the Student Christian Movement Press, Ltd.

Sheed & Ward Inc.—for quotations from *Patterns in Comparative Religion* by Mircea Eliade. Copyright © 1958 by Sheed & Ward Inc. Used with permission.

The Westminster Press—quotations from *The Gospel of Christian Atheism* by Thomas J. J. Altizer. Copyright © 1966, by W. L. Jenkins, The Westminster Press. British, Dutch, German, Italian, and Spanish rights courtesy of Wm. Collins Sons & Co. Ltd., Uitgeverij Ambo n. v., Zwingli Verlag, Casa Editrice Astrolabio, and Llibres del Nopal, respectively. Used with permission.

The Bobbs-Merrill Company, Inc.
4300 West 62nd Street
Indianapolis, Indiana 46268
First Edition
Seventh Printing—1976
Library of Congress Catalog Card Number 68-11146
ISBN 0-672-60796-4 (pbk)

*For Mark Whitney Gilkey
and Amos Welcome Gilkey.*

Contents

Preface

This book, like the theological situation to which it addresses itself, has been slowly ripening through various stages. It appeared first in the form of a paper on the radical, or "God is dead," theology, written for the Society for Theological Discussion in the fall of 1963, some time before that fascinating movement hit the headlines, and then in the next summer was revised and enlarged for the faculty retreat in 1964 of the University of Chicago Divinity School. In that form, before the many excellent commentaries on the radical theology had appeared, this paper, entitled "The God-Is-Dead Theology and the Necessity of God-Language," enjoyed a fairly wide, unofficial circulation. In the four years since that time, the thoughts first formulated in that long paper have been steadily enlarged and, it is hoped, clarified and developed, through addresses and lectures at a number of institutions and through a year's course at the University of Chicago Divinity School. The institutions, among others, at which one aspect or another of the steadily maturing and often revised viewpoint represented in this volume was presented, were: Wake Forest College, Crozier Theological Seminary (where, in an abbreviated form, it appeared in print in the Crozier *Voice*), Colgate-Rochester Theological Seminary, Lancaster Theological Seminary, Philips University, Bexley Hall, Queens College in Ontario, Christian Theological Seminary in Indianapolis, Louisville Presbyterian Seminary, the Yale Divinity School, Pomona College, and the Perkins School of Theology. This volume, then, can rightly be regarded as an expansion of these scattered writings and lectures, especially, and in its initial form, the Samuel Robinson Lecture Series at Wake Forest College and then, as it developed and enlarged, the Orin E. Scott Lectures at Philips University, the Easter-Bedell Lectures at Bexley Hall, and the Nathaniel

Taylor Lectures at Yale, the Clark Lectures at Pomona, and the Fondren Lectures at Perkins.

The main efforts of this book, as of those addresses, are to describe the background and character of the present ferment in theology, to assess the importance of this upheaval for contemporary religious thought, to point out some of the more characteristic and perhaps damaging weaknesses of the radical theology, and then, in Part II, to suggest some preliminary answers to the problems for language about God raised by these developments in contemporary culture. I should like to express my gratitude for the hospitality, the appreciation, and the questioning which I have received at the schools named above, and to my students at the University of Chicago Divinity School for their never-failing and vastly helpful criticism of all that is there offered to them. I wish to thank two persons for their help in the preparation of this manuscript: Mrs. Anne Grant for her accurate typing and retyping, and Tyron Inbody for his excellent work on the annotation and for preparing the index. The book is dedicated to my two sons, but I also wish to say here that Sonja, my wife, was creatively there at every stage of its maturing.

—LANGDON GILKEY

University of Chicago Divinity School
May 25, 1969

Part I

The Challenge to God-Language

1 / The Present Ferment
in Theology

ANYONE WHO is at all aware of the intellectual and spiritual goings-on in our present culture knows that there is abroad a ferment in theology. Through reports and articles in the mass media, through public lectures, and through widely read books, he will have gathered that many prominent religious thinkers have begun in the last few years radically to question the traditional beliefs of our culture's major religious faiths. From the same sources, moreover, he knows that even the most stable and unchanging of our religious institutions has openly admitted that its doctrines, as well as its practical structures and many of its basic policies, must be "brought up to date" to meet the demands of the current crisis. And probably either he himself, his son, or perhaps a close friend has at one time or another said, "I just can't believe any longer what my church [or synagogue] teaches; it seems so anachronistic, so unreal, so unrelated to everything else."[1] Whether, that is, we look outside ourselves at intellectual movements in our cultural environment or inside at current changes in our feelings, attitudes, and convictions, we find religious concepts and certainties in upheaval, criticized not only by those outside the religious establishment, but even more by those within.

While such external and internal criticism of traditional

[1] See, for example, the very perceptive article on this experience by Thomas F. O'Dea, "The Crisis of the Contemporary Religious Consciousness," in *Daedalus*, 96, no. 1 (Winter 1967).

Christian notions was, of course, characteristic of nineteenth- and
early twentieth-century liberal religion, by and large it was, in that
period, only rigidly orthodox, fundamentalist beliefs that were
under vigorous attack. The new in the present situation is that
the upheaval inside the religious community has fully as much to
do with liberal or sophisticated religion as with orthodoxy; consequently it seems to question the very roots of any form of religious belief at all. Our task here is to describe the background and
present character of this ferment within religion and its most
fundamental beliefs, to see what major cultural forces make religious affirmations difficult, and so to explore what possibilities
there may be for meaningful theology in our time.

The current ferment spans almost the entire range of religious concepts and concerns. Every familiar Christian doctrine,
from those of the authority of scripture, the trinity, or the deity
of Christ, to the more fundamental question of the reality of God,
has been questioned, in some instances in order to make room for
reformulation, in others in order to abandon the conception altogether. Moreover, many nondoctrinal but nevertheless essential
issues have been made the center of the debate: for example, such
questions as "What does it mean to be a Christian today, what
sort of style of life, of action and attitude in and toward the world
—in matters of sex, of race, of property, of war—characterize
the Christian?" and "How should the Church relate to the world,
to its ways, its ideas, its standards and its needs; is it essentially
separate and autonomous in relation to the world, drawing its life
from elsewhere and leading men to another realm; or is its task
to be in the world serving the world?" And, "If the Church is to
be *in* the world, where does its authority and its message come
from, from the world itself, or from some other source? And if
the latter, then from where, and in that case, how are its message
and its challenge to be understood, appropriated, and so affirmed
by the world?"[2] All of these questions have been the center of

[2] The recent literature on the church's relation to the world is
immense. Especially important at the early stages of this discussion were
Gibson Winter's *The Suburban Captivity of the Churches* (New York:
Doubleday, 1961); the many very influential works of Peter Berger; and
Harvey Cox's *The Secular City* (New York: Macmillan Company,

most of the creative theological debate of the last years. One sees them reflected in the development of new forms and views of the ministry; in the new worldly activism of religious leaders in civil-rights protests and peace movements; in the organization of new training centers for ministry in the cities; in the heated arguments about a new sex ethic and drugs—and also one sees this side of the upheaval more conservatively reflected in most of the documents of Vatican II on the Church, its liturgy, authority, polity, and relation to the world.

There is, then, almost nothing in the life of the churches —from the mode of their practical existence to their theoretical self-understanding—that has not been questioned with the utmost intensity in the last few years. Since a single survey cannot cover this entire debate, we shall concentrate here on what we regard, from the point of view of theology, as the center of the crisis, namely the question of the reality of God and so of the possibility of meaningful language about him. Is faith in God a real possibility for a modern secular man; is it possible to speak meaningfully—to ourselves and to others—of God and what he has done for man, is there a Word and a Presence in scripture, in sacrament, and in the preaching and moral aims of the Church that is not merely human, relative, and fallible? Does our religion, and so its institutions, its ministries, its worship, its obligations and its behavior, relate us to a reality beyond ourselves, or is it only a useful (or useless) activity played out by man in an unresponsive cosmos? Is the God we seek to worship, preach and serve, in church and out of it, in the old forms or in new ways, real or illusory, alive or dead? These are the central issues of the current theological ferment, and it is to clarify the characteristic forms, the present urgency, and the intellectual background of this debate about God that we shall direct our next remarks. We shall concentrate our attention on the developments within Protestantism, where, for various reasons, the debate has largely been carried on. It should be recognized, however, that the same crisis,

---

1965). The present writer has also tried to deal with some of these questions in *How the Church Can Minister to the World without Losing Itself* (New York: Harper & Row, 1964).

albeit in different forms and possibly at different stages of development, is reflected in both present-day Catholicism and Judaism.

The suddenness and the radicalness of the present ferment in theology cannot be overemphasized. For four decades, since 1918 or thereabouts, there had been going on what seemed to the younger generation of theologians an immensely creative and yet firmly based process of theological construction, fashioned by a remarkable group of brilliant minds: Barth, Brunner, Tillich, Bultmann, and the Niebuhrs, to name only a few. Those who stood closer to Barth drew primarily upon Biblical and traditional sources for their constructive work; others reflected more a worldly or cultural wisdom. But all together shared certain common assumptions about the theological task which were communicated to their enthusiastic younger followers: (1) that theology as an enterprise has both substance and integrity since, as a way of reflecting on God, man, and destiny, it stems from a unique and certain source in divine revelation, a source related to in faith and so in direct experience, whereby the validity of this viewpoint was assured; (2) that the reflective language of theology is universally meaningful since, far from being in conflict with legitimate cultural truths, it provides on the contrary the basis for a more intelligible interpretation of the totality of cultural experience than can any secular standpoint. Theological construction thus springs ultimately from faith, where its validity is known, and its implied meanings include those foundational attitudes that form the presuppositions of the furthest reaches of secular human inquiry and knowledge: the natural sciences, the social sciences, philosophy of history, moral studies, psychology, literature, and the arts. Thus did the younger generation of theologians, whatever "school" they followed (Barthian, Niebuhrian, Tillichian, or even Whiteheadian), feel inwardly certain about the possibilities, the validity, and the universal meaningfulness of the theological language they were learning to use—and correspondingly, younger ministers or chaplains, and the theologically involved laymen whom they interested, had confidence that what they preached and expounded in church or college discussion groups had firm validity in and immense relevance to modern life. Theological or doctrinal construction, theological analyses of the bases of culture, application of theological concepts to social affairs, history, psychology, ethics, and literary analysis all seemed to have assured and almost infinite possibilities. Younger men, to be sure, felt critical of certain elements in the vast systems formed by their elders, and saw their own task to be that of improving and strengthening the particular theological structure they had chosen to inhabit by better exegesis, more thorough historical study, clearer and firmer relations to philosophy and science, more insight into its relations to social and psychological studies, and so on. Almost none guessed that, instead of thus finishing off an already constructed building, they would soon be searching for new foundations for a building that had now been almost entirely dismantled.

What has happened in the course of the last five years is that this whole relation to the great theological systems of the recent past has suddenly shifted. Unexpected new problems have arisen, and with their appearance younger theologians have found their own points of view uncomfortably changing, and so almost in an instant all these certainties about the established validity and meaningfulness of theological language have disintegrated.[3] As a consequence, instead of applying a given system of theological thought to new areas or improving its edges by more careful study, today's theologian finds himself wondering whether he can do theology at all in the contemporary world and, if he still feels he can, on what possible basis he might now speak

[3] See especially the perceptive comment of Gordon Kaufman's: "But the historical situation has changed and with it the theological task. The great critical questions posed by liberalism and humanism . . . —questions which could be more or less ignored or overlooked during the crises of recent decades—have come into view once again and are demanding attention. Most notable of all in this respect is the central conception on which the whole theological program rests, the problem of 'God'. What do we mean by 'God'? Is this notion intelligible at all to 'modern man' or does it depend on outgrown mythological patterns of thought?" Gordon D. Kaufman, "Theological Historicism as an Experiment in Thought," in Dean Peerman, ed., *Frontline Theology* (Richmond, Va.: John Knox Press, 1967), pp. 53–54.

about God. Far from living securely within an established theological system, or even hoping to write a new one, he is concerned with whether the most rudimentary theological affirmations are possible or meaningful. Some of the present generation of theologians, as is well known, have in this situation decided that such theological language—and *a fortiori* all theological systems and all implied theologies of culture—is quite impossible. Others do not agree with this radically negative judgment and are seeking in tentative and preliminary ways to discover new bases for theological language. All alike are participating in a situation in which even the most fundamental assumptions of our elders now seem shaky, and so in which theological reflection concerns itself with the foundations of theological language and not its outer implications.[4] In the fall of 1964, this writer described this sudden and radical change in the theological situation in the following terms:

> No more than five years ago the "younger theologians" seemed to have a comfortable basis for their task, fashioned by the great theologians of the 20's, 30's, and 40's. . . . We saw ourselves as a generation of "scholastics" whose function would be to work out in greater detail the firm theological principles already forged for us. We knew from our teachers what theology was, what its principles and starting point were, how to go about it, and above all we were confident about its universal value and truth.
>
> The most significant recent theological development has been the steady dissolution of all these certainties, the washing away of the firm ground on which our generation believed we were safely standing. What we thought was solid earth has turned out to be shifting ice—and in recent years, as the weather has grown steadily warmer, some of us have in horror

[4] Rabbi Richard Rubenstein also expresses well this new theological self-consciousness within the wider Judeo-Christian tradition: "A breach had been made between the mood and the theological perspective of our times and those of our predecessors. There was simply no way in which to escape the fact that the second half of the twentieth century was radically different. Our theology would have to be an expression of the way we, rather than those who preceded us, felt about ultimate questions. It was impossible to renounce this work." Richard L. Rubenstein, *After Auschwitz* (Indianapolis: Bobbs-Merrill Company, 1966), p. 244.

found ourselves staring down into rushing depths of dark water.[5]

The present theological situation, then, is characterized by a radical "shaking of the foundations," and this upheaval has, we believe, been recently experienced by almost all those concerned with Christian belief, with theology, preaching, and religious existence generally. Can we, however, be more precise than this and pinpoint what the foundation is that has been thus shaken, what it is that is now suddenly and in a new way problematic or in doubt? For after all, in the last two centuries almost every fundamental religious belief has at one time or another been regarded as questionable if not downright irrational by the modern secular world, and we are all used to this form of radical doubt about traditional religion. At this point we shall mention three things about the character of the present ferment in theology which distinguish it from its predecessors:

1. This upheaval, this radical questioning of the foundations of religious affirmation and so of the theological language reflective of it, is now taking place *within* and not outside of the Church. Heretofore in this century, the radical questioning of religious beliefs was a characteristic of the secular world outside the Church, and thus rather automatically such doubt signaled the departure of the doubter from the ranks of the faithful, and certainly from the professional enterprises of either the ministry or theology. In the present crisis, however, one finds not only concerned laymen wondering about the usage and meaning of religious language; even more one encounters younger clergy and theologians questioning whether it is any longer possible to speak intelligibly of God. The Church itself, the religious community itself, through the experience and the reflective thought of its official representatives and functionaries, is not so much expounding "faith" to a doubting world as it is itself exploring the depths of its own uncertainty, and itself searching for possible foundations for its language, its worship, and its works. This *is* new, and

[5] Langdon Gilkey, "Dissolution and Reconstruction in Theology," *Christian Century,* February 3, 1965, reprinted in Dean Peerman, *Frontline Theology,* p. 29.

it is radical.[6] One might phrase it that the Church is now recognizing experientially and so reflectively its own extreme "secularity." Consequently, in its self-understanding, it no longer finds itself polarized over against the world with regard to the problems of belief, but fully involved theologically in the world through its own secularity of spirit. As a result, the doubts which the world has long known about the articles of belief are now recognized by the Church to be her own doubts, and the world's problems with her theological language are the theologian's problems. This new realization in theology of the identity in spirit of the Church and the world is, to this writer, the most significant single element in our theological present, and it distinguishes the current theological situation most radically from the immediate neoorthodox past when the Church understood itself as the faithful hearer, if not the firm possessor, of a divine Word, and thus radically distinguished from the world of unbelief and doubt. To me, therefore, any current theology, Continental, English, or American, that does not recognize and seek reflectively to deal with this presence of secularity, of doubt, of skepticism, and so of a sense of the meaninglessness of religious language inside the Church as well as outside, and so inside the theologian and believer, is so far irrelevant to our present situation.

2. Not only is the situation radical because the community of Christians itself is experiencing this upheaval; even more is it radical because it is the most fundamental of all our Judeo-Christian religious affirmations that is under searching and critical scrutiny by all, and forthrightly rejected by many. For it is the reality of what our tradition has called "God" that is now the subject of theological debate, and the question of God is, of course, the most fundamental of all theological questions. As we shall argue throughout this book, all other theological issues are logically secondary to this one. Such issues—as, for example, that of revelation, of faith, of a theological hermeneutics of scripture, of Christology, of law and gospel, of Word and sacrament, of an eschatological view of history, and of eternal life—simply do not

[6] Some of the differences between our present situation and that of questioning liberals in the nineteenth and early twentieth centuries is considered in Chapter 3 below.

exist as *theological* issues if there be no God, if the totality of what is real be devoid of a divine dimension transcendent to the finite, contingent, transient creatures—for then there can be no revelation, no divine word, no incarnation, no revealed gospel, no sacrament, no eschatological "view" in history, and no eternity. The question of the reality of God and so of the possibility, meaningfulness, and validity of any religious faith and of any theological discourse at all, forms the center of our present ferment— which is as fundamental a question as theology can raise. Furthermore, the question of God is radical as well as fundamental. For, in essence, to debate the question of God in theology means that in that debate no theological assumptions can usefully be made, or any theological authorities invoked—since every such assumption or authority presupposes the reality of the divine. One cannot begin, for example, with the presupposition of the presence of the Word of God, if one is asking the question of God—nor, as we shall argue, can one begin with the assumption of a divine Logos which makes metaphysics possible. If the question of *God* is raised, theology literally must begin from the beginning, it must deal with its own most basic foundations. And however much one may be guided by one's great teachers, that means starting as best one can on one's own and at the level of concrete experience. This is an upheaval that has thrown us all quite back to the beginnings of all religious reflection.

The question of the reality of God is an immensely subtle and complex one, and each age discusses it in its own unique manner. That is to say, the question of God arises in relation to the total cultural context of the moment, especially that of philosophy and of religion, and takes its form from that context. Thus, in a confident rationalistic age, it arises as the question of a proof of God in natural theology; in another sort of period, it may arise as the question of the reality of religious experience, or as the question of the meaning of life and of history—as it did in the recent past. For reasons that will become clear as we proceed, in the present situation the question has arisen in connection with that of the possibility or the intelligibility of religious or theological language. Our age, we may suggest, is dominated by a radical adherence to, or confinement in, the immediate and the concrete; it knows little of speculative distances or overarching meanings. Speaking, feeling, and sensing are about all it feels it can talk and so think safely about. And so when it asks about God, about ultimate meanings, characteristically it investigates its *language* about these things, whether such speaking or talking makes sense, communicates, and has reference to reality or not.

Now to be sure, the theological discussions of the recent past had also centered themselves around the question of theological language. Since 1918, the most important debate in theology had concerned itself with the question whether theological language should have as its basis and its form a philosophical metaphysical system, as both Thomistic and Whiteheadian philosophers argued, or whether on the contrary it must derive entirely from faith in relation to revelation, and so be formed solely from the Biblical Word, as the neoorthodox were inclined to insist. In none of this rather heated debate—whose echoes still reverberate on the Continent and among some philosophical theologians—were there from either side serious questions raised whether there was a God to talk about, and so whether theological language of any sort at all was possible or meaningful. These matters of the possibility of theological discourse and the reality of its referent were more or less taken for granted in concern with the character of that discourse, and so, by implication, with the *character* or nature of the God referred to.[7]

At the present, however, the thrust of the question of theological language has significantly shifted. It is not merely the question of what sort religious language should be, but the question whether any talk about God is possible at all; the debate concerns not whether God is known by philosophy or by revelation, but whether he is dead or alive, and so whether any language

---

[7] For an example of this concentration on penultimate rather than ultimate questions in theology, see the remark in an early essay (1963) of Schubert M. Ogden: "But, for my part, the real issue is not *whether* the statement 'God acts in history' makes sense, but *what* sense it makes. Furthermore, it belongs to the very nature of the theologian's work that the possibility of speaking of God's acting in history is not the question he must consider." Schubert M. Ogden, *The Reality of God* (New York: Harper & Row, 1966), p. 164.

about him is empty or meaningful.[8] Consequently, the present form of the question of religious language is such that it drives theological inquiry to the new task of justifying religious discourse as a whole. And that task can be accomplished only by seeking to locate within concrete experience some element, aspect, or being which calls for religious symbolization, for which religious or theological language is necessary, and in relation to which it communicates and so has "meaning." Instead of asking "Is philosophy or revelation the true way to know God?" theologians are now asking the very different question: "Is there in experience any transcendent dimension for which religious or theological language is necessary and in relation to which it makes sense?" The theological debate has moved from the question of the character of God to the more radical question of his reality, and from the question of the nature and form of religious language to the more radical question of its possibility as a mode of meaningful discourse.

An even more illuminating illustration of this radicalization of the debate over theological language is the fact that current questions concern more the *meaning* than the *validity* of theological discourse. This concern of reflective thought with problems of meaning rather than of validity has, of course, been pioneered by the appearance in philosophy in the early years of the century of what Professor Gustav Bergman called "the linguistic turn,"[9] and has diverted most Anglo-American philosophy from

[8] The advent of a new and more ultimate question in theology is again illustrated by Ogden, in a later essay (1966): "One of the obvious conclusions to be drawn from the latest developments in Protestant theology is that the reality of God has now become the central theological problem. . . . Rightly understood, the problem of God is not one problem among several others; it is the only problem there is." *Ibid.*, p. 1.

[9] The development in philosophy of the "linguistic" understanding of philosophy, i.e., the understanding of philosophy as a "second-order discipline," as "talk about talk," is, of course, a very complex affair. The best summaries of it are, to this writer, G. J. Warnock, *English Philosophy Since 1900* (London: Oxford University Press, 1958), and J. O. Urmson, *Philosophical Analysis: Its Development Between the Two World Wars* (Oxford: Clarendon Press, 1956). A very good recent collection on the meaning and importance of this understanding of phi-

concern with "reality" and its characteristics to concern with
words, their meanings and uses. As we shall argue, this skepticism in philosophy about the possibility through reflective reason
of metaphysical knowledge of reality and the skepticism in religious circles about the possibility of theological knowledge of
God parallel each other; in fact, speaking historically, the death
of metaphysics in philosophy preceded the death of God in
theology by roughly half a century. Thus the loss of metaphysics
in philosophy and the loss of God-language in theology are
alike symptoms of what we shall call the "radical secularity" of
our culture. Consequently, as co-sufferers from the same disease,
they can hardly rescue one another, but on the contrary, the foundations of each must be reexplored and rediscovered. One of the
significant consequences of this prior death in philosophy was
that philosophical statements ceased claiming to be cognitive assertions about reality and therefore validatable, and now claim
only to be analyses of the meanings of propositions and language
games. The philosophical shift of concern from the weighing of
validity to the analysis of meaning thus signaled a shift in reflective thought from cognitive discourse about reality to analytic talk
about talk.

Because it is in this way a parallel and even prior symptom of our cultural situation, this new philosophical concentration on meaning has important theological implications in the
field of religious discourse which illumine the precise character of
the crisis in theology. So long as theological debate centered only
on the question of *validity*, on whether or not our statements about
God are true and in what ways we might have certainty of that
validity, no real questions were raised about the possibility of
either Biblical or metaphysical language about God. Each of
these modes of theological discourse (i.e., the Biblical and the
metaphysical) possessed within its systematic structure "built-

---

losophy, with an excellent introduction, is Richard Rorty, *The Linguistic
Turn* (Chicago: University of Chicago Press, 1967). Bergman describes
the "turn" this way: "All linguistic philosophers talk about the world
by means of talking about a suitable language. This is the linguistic turn,
the fundamental gambit as to method, on which ordinary and ideal language philosophies agree." Rorty, p. 8.

in" means of validation for its statements, and also "built-in" grounds for meaning; and thus each form of discourse had in its own terms both meaning and validity to its adherents. Theological affirmations in neoorthodox or Biblical theology were, it was said, known to be true "by faith"; the act or experience of faith itself guaranteed for the believer the truth of a Biblical statement. And correspondingly, the meaning of what was believed in faith came from the whole system of concepts (what we called the "Biblical faith") which was asserted to be valid by faith. Thus an intelligible theological system of discourse, intelligible to those who had faith, could be founded on "what faith knew," or "what faith required," and everyone who both believed it and was familiar with its terms could find it both valid and intensely meaningful. Correspondingly, in a philosophical theology oriented to metaphysical speculation, metaphysical statements about God were validatable according to the criteria recognized by the metaphysical system in question, usually some combination of such criteria as coherence, width or scope of explanatory power, and adequacy to concrete experience. And again, the meanings of the metaphysical terms used to explicate religious beliefs were obtainable from the whole system of concepts in which they functioned, and in terms of which all the others were defined—as "entity" in Whitehead's thought is defined in terms of "prehension," and so on. While, to be sure, only those who believed in the possibility of speculative metaphysics found these criteria of validity useful or convincing, and these meanings intelligible, nonetheless for those with that sort of faith in rational speculation a system of discourse that seemed both valid and meaningful was certainly possible. So, because both revelational and metaphysical systems had their own internal criteria of validity for their own concepts, the recent debate about the adequacy for theological purposes of one or the other of these two types of discourse raised no serious questions about the possibility of God-language as such. Both of them presupposed the reality of the referent of their language, and so the possibility of some form of intelligible discourse about him. While they debated hotly the means through which the divine mystery might be known or described, neither of these theological options questioned that through one or the other the confining limits of the naturalistic and atheistic world of secularity could legitimately be transcended.

When, however, the *meaning*, as opposed to the validity, of a form of discourse becomes the subject of serious discussion, as has occurred in recent years, an entirely different theological situation manifests itself. As numerous philosophers of religion have pointed out, faith cannot guarantee the meaning of the propositions it believes to be true.[10] To hold by faith to the truth of an assertion certainly guarantees that for us its referent is believed to be real; but such indomitable loyalty does not necessarily indicate, even psychologically, that we have any idea where in experience such a referent may be encountered, and consequently the proposition so asserted may not have any meaning for us. In fact, humans apparently can "believe in" something that in no way fits into their experienced world or makes a discernible difference to that world, and may affirm a whole mode of language to be true which has no real use in their own significant discourse. This insight of contemporary analytic philosophy, that a self-consistent system of language can still be said to be "meaningless," is more than reflected, as we shall see, in the character of contemporary Church life, where more frequently than not a system of doctrinal propositions is declared to be true (or at least to be believed) which in no way enters either the real lives or the real discourse of the modern urban churchman who may affirm it. Such doctrinal terms have to their adherents apparently some validity but almost certainly no real or effective meaning. Correspondingly, a system of metaphysical propositions which may be validatable by the criteria inherent in the system itself, may, so it has been persuasively argued by the majority of modern philosophers, nevertheless have no "meaning"—that is to say, the system may float in the mind as an imagined system of concepts,

---

[10] Cf. Ogden: "If the issue is whether assertions about God are even meaningful, it will hardly do to reply . . . that such assertions rest solely on the basis of faith in a special revelation. Obviously, not even faith can assert something as true which is in principle lacking in any genuine meaning." Ogden, *The Reality of God*, p. 26. The reason, of course, is that, in affirming the *content* of a given proposition to be true, faith must presuppose the *meaning* of what it affirms.

consistently self-supporting in its coherence and its scope, and yet not enter at any point as explanatory of any aspect of actual experience, as making any difference to that experience, or as functioning in any way in the language usage with which experience is actually thematized. In both these cases, then, we find systems of abstract propositions which are internally validatable according to their own criteria, but which have no "cash value," no relevance or effectiveness in experience as a whole. Apparently they have validity to us and yet no ascertainable meaning.

To question, therefore, the meaning of a fideistic or a metaphysical theological system is more radical than to question its validity. To say "I understand what you mean by belief in God, but I do not think it is true," is, to be sure, to deny the actuality of the Christian view; but it is at least to grant its *possibility* as one intelligible mode of understanding the world. We seem here to be agreeing that, while the world as we experience it *might* be as Christians describe it, nevertheless, because of such and such, we do not think in fact it is that way. When, however, we question the meaning of the statements of faith or of metaphysics—when we say, "I do not even know what you mean by the word 'God'," or "I find metaphysical propositions meaningless"—we are not merely questioning the actuality or validity of these conceptual systems as explanatory of the experienced world. Rather, we are doubting even that they are intelligible at all as potential modes of understanding the world, we are doubting their *possibility* as explanatory or assertive conceptual systems.[11] That is to say, we are in fact wondering whether, granted the

[11] It is for this reason, despite its outmoded dependence on the verification principle, that Paul van Buren's book *The Secular Meaning of the Gospel* (New York: Macmillan Company, 1963) has been so important in the present situation. As he makes clear, van Buren in this work is not merely raising the older question of the validity of theism; he is raising the more radical question of its meaningfulness. He is wondering if the word "God" has any *use* in ordinary, contemporary discourse, whether it and its associated concepts "fit" anywhere into experience and are thus verifiable, falsifiable, or make any difference there; and since he can find only a negative answer to both questions, he concludes the word is meaningless. Or, as we have argued here, the concept is "impossible" as a mode of understanding the world. Cf. Chapter 4 below for further discussion of this work.

modern view of things, such forms of belief or thought can even be conceived to fit at any point at all into the world as we actually experience it, and so *a fortiori* whether they can parade as modes of understanding that world. The category "Meaningless" has been hard to define and in some quarters even abandoned in modern linguistic philosophy, especially after the demise of the verification principle; but, we believe, this lack of precise definition does not entail either the meaninglessness or the uselessness of the concept. What "meaninglessness" implies, we submit, is a sense of the total disrelation of a given set of concepts or a language game to experience and to life; and it is this total disrelation that is being asserted in the accusation that metaphysics or theology is meaningless—since it is clearly not their self-contradiction for which we are indicting them. Thus it is quite legitimate that, in relation to the question of meaning, there have arisen the various requirements or norms of verification and falsification, of "making a discernible difference," of "counting for or against," of usage in our ordinary discourse, and of relating our symbols to lived experience. All of these are ways, some better and some worse, of seeking to guarantee a relation of our concepts to experience and so to establishing at least a basic part of the *meaning* of the concepts involved.

When, therefore, we assert that viewpoints or conceptual systems are "meaningless," what we are really saying is (1) that these assertions relate at no point to concrete experience, and (2) that therefore they are not possible modes of understanding experience. Rather, are they "impossible," or, perhaps better, not "compossible" with our experienced world, to borrow a word from Leibniz[12]—since the issue is *not* that of self-contradiction. Such systems of symbols may be comprehensible as abstractions, as fantasies, as structured landscapes in the realm of essence, as Santayana would put it. Unlike mathematics and fiction, however,

[12] For Leibniz, monads (existents) were (1) possible if their content did not contain a contradiction, and (2) *compossible* with their world if they fitted to the structure of that world. Monads A and B might both be possible, and yet not be compossible with one another and in the same world. The idea refers to the compatability of an entity or its concept with the system of entities or concepts within which it functions. Cf., Bertrand Russell, *A Critical Exposition of the Philosophy of Leibniz* (London: George Allen and Unwin, 1937), pp. 66–69, 223.

they have, as claimants to be assertions, little interest or value in such a purely abstractive role. If, then, they do in fact (as they do) make the claim to be assertions about "reality," and if they are still quite unrelated to experience, in that case they are not conceivable as even potentially actual, and so we say that, as assertions, they are meaningless.

A most important meaning of the modern question of "meaning" thus reflects a new form of the question of the *possibility* of a symbol, of propositions which include it, and of the conceptual system in which both function. In the older form of the question of possibility, a concept was considered not possible only because inherent self-contradiction prevented the relation of the concept to actuality and so made it meaningless. In the newer form, it is the claim that, because there is a total disrelation of the concept to experienced actuality, the concept and its system are meaningless, or, as we have argued, not possible, impossible, or "not compossible" with our experienced world. It is important to note that this sense of meaninglessness is not identical with self-contradiction, since to show, as philosophers have tended to do, that a concept is not self-contradictory, is by no means yet to answer in a definitive way the charge that it is meaningless. In any case, the question of the *noncompossibility* and therefore the meaninglessness of a concept or a system of language is a more radical question than is that of their *validity* since the former asserts a much more total disjunction of the word game or concept from all that we take to be the case in the world around us.

This digression on the implications of the new debate about the meaning of theological language reveals just how radical, how concerned with fundamentals, the present theological situation is. In a cultural situation in which theological reflection asks, "How do I know the *truth* of religious belief, by faith or by metaphysical speculation?" the possibility for a modern religious, that is, nonatheistic or nonsecular, stance is assumed, and we are inquiring merely about the grounds for the validity of that stance. When, however, theological reflection is discussing the *meaning* of Biblical or metaphysical theological language, it is the very possibility of a nonsecular stance that is under question. We are asking whether for our age religious belief itself, and with it metaphysical speculation, are possibilities at all, and therefore whether there is any way at all by which modern man can transcend the confinements of the secularistic world view.

Again, the reality of God and so of the referent of religious language is the central point at issue, but it is a question that now arises within the context of the question of the meaningfulness to modern experience of religious discourse. Is the world of our experience, the modern *Lebenswelt,* bounded entirely by the secular so that a religious interpretation of it, and thus theological discourse, is impossible or meaningless; or is it not so bounded, and thus is this sort of language a possibility and meaningful? The question of the meaning of theological language therefore involves theological reflection in questions prior to those either of a revelation given to faith or of the structure of a metaphysical theology. It involves the prior delineation of the meaningfulness in a secular age of religious discourse as such, of its possibility as a form of language expressive of modern experience—and hence of the meaningfulness or possibility of the language both of Christian faith and of speculative metaphysics. These questions of compossibility, of potential actuality, are questions of the relations of concepts to experience; and consequently the radical question of meaning drives theological reflection beneath its own accustomed materials and authorities to the examination of ordinary experience. The purpose of such an inquiry is to find there those dimensions or regions of ordinary experience to which the language of religious symbols has reference, and so in terms of which such symbols can be said to have legitimate meaning and real possibility. This is for our age a new theological requirement posed by the radical questions with which we are faced in the contemporary situation of extreme secularity and radical doubt.[13] It

[13] In a strangely similar situation, when traditional Biblical and metaphysical authorities in religion had broken down at the end of the Enlightenment, Friedrich Schleiermacher faced much the same set of difficulties; and in a somewhat similar fashion he sought to show the usage and referent, i.e., the *meaning,* of religious language, by pointing to those "experiences" or "feelings" in ordinary life of which religious language or concepts were, as he put it, the reflections, and so which they "meant." The differences, in character and especially in quality, between his efforts and ours will be obvious; that was a long time ago and he was a very great man; but the similarity of lineage is unmistakable.

is to cope with these new requirements for theology that these present thoughts on the relevance and renewal of religious language have largely been developed.

3. The theological ferment we are delineating, therefore, convulses the Church itself, both in its ordinary lay life and in its more deliberate theological reflection; and it is a ferment which involves the most fundamental religious affirmations of the reality of the transcendent or the divine, and so of the possibility or meaningfulness for modern experience of theological language of all sorts, and thus whether we can speak of God at all. Now, it is in this context that we can best understand the significance of that recent radical movement in theology whose unifying slogan has been "the death of God." In our view, this movement presents us with neither a viable interpretation of Christian faith nor a valid symbolic account of our general human experience, secular or otherwise—and one of the purposes of this book is to point out both of these liabilities. It is, however, also true that the representatives of this movement, much more clearly than any of the rest of us, have discerned and expressed in their thought the anatomy of our present situation. These theologians, in other words, can be regarded as both symptoms and causes of the wider theological situation we have just described: symptoms because they express in theological discourse the deepest tendencies of our cultural epoch, and causes because their clarifying expression in radical form of these tendencies has hastened their realization by the rest of us and their effectiveness on us. In their studied and powerful protest against the theologies of the past—orthodox, liberal, neoorthodox, and metaphysical—these theologians have brought to clear expression every important difficulty with which contemporary Christian faith, and its theologies of all varieties, are faced; and in their denial of the reality of the referent of religious language and so of the meaningfulness of all religious discourse, they have stated flatly and clearly the problems with which every theology must deal. Thus to understand at their deepest level the issues with which a relevant contemporary theology must concern itself, it is obligatory for us to analyze, to understand, and then to answer the significant forms of present-day radical theology.

The clarity with which the radical theology has expressed

the tendencies and the difficulties of the present theological upheaval as we have here described them will be evident if we list
briefly and in an introductory fashion the most significant characteristics, as we see them, of this theology of protest: (1) By making its central affirmation the denial of the reality of God, the
relevance of any relation to him, and even the meaningfulness of
any language about him, this theology expresses in its clearest
form all of the tendencies and the difficulties of our cultural mood
that we have described. It presents, we believe, in terms of *theological* conceptuality, an essential and mortal challenge to the long
tradition of Christian religious and theological discourse—and
while that by no means makes this theology *wrong,* it surely
makes it significant! (2) By this rejection of God, this theology
represents a definite new movement of theological thought, a
new self-consciousness, with a new starting point and something
quite new to say—although what it has to say is less clear than
that it is new. It is a movement in conscious and deliberate repudiation of its total theological past, both liberal and neoorthodox, a
movement designed specifically to fit into what it regards as the
new cultural situation. Its vigor, originality, and creativity are
themselves worth our interest, and its studied attempt to theologize within the present historical moment augurs well for its usefulness in understanding our contemporary situation and its new
problems. (3) It represents an explicit and potent rejection of
the dominant neoorthodox[14] "establishment" in theology that
preceded it. Thus its appearance, its undoubted relevance to the
questions people are asking, and its consequent influence among
seminary students and clergy alike, signalize the demise of neoorthodoxy as the ruling mode of theological discourse, a not inconsiderable event. (4) It represents within the walls of the
Church community, and thus within the circle of Christian faith
and of theology, the mood and viewpoint of our present strongly
secular age, an age that not only finds a traditional faith difficult
if not incredible, but is also metaphysically despairing, or at least
agnostic, although it remains provisionally confident about man's
capacity. This theology has first expressed, then, the undoubted
fact that the Church is permeated by the world's spirit, and thus

[14] The characteristic and subsequent difficulties of "neoorthodoxy" will be more fully described in Chapter 3 below.

no useful distinction for the purposes of theological method can be made between a theological starting point relevant for the Church and one relevant for the world—a point with very radical implications for theological method. (5) These are, furthermore, theologies which are explicitly built on an ontological foundation that is secular or, better, naturalistic in character, which therefore rejects any peculiarly religious means of knowing reality, be it called revelation or religious experience, and thus which finds meaningless or undiscoverable any category of the transcendent, the sacred, the holy, that which is more than the finite realities experienced in our ordinary secular contact with nature and with other persons in community.[15] Thus, while in our view the radical theology does not express faithfully the Christian message, nevertheless it does present to us in theological language and symbols

[15] The naturalistic position here referred to—a position which takes "nature" as known by scientific inquiry to be "all that is the case" in the widest environment of man—will be more fully discussed in Chapter 2 below. The literature of the naturalistic position here referred to is, of course, immense. It begins, probably, in modern European thought with Hobbes, is implied in much of David Hume, but reaches its first major statement in the French physiocrats and in the encyclopedists of the eighteenth century, and then later, in the nineteenth century, in the writings of such important men as Feuerbach, Marx and, still later, Freud. Since then, a host of writers have espoused this naturalistic atheism: representative modern figures are John Dewey, *Experience and Nature* (Chicago: Open Court, 1925), *A Common Faith* (New Haven: Yale University Press, 1934); George Santayana, *The Realm of Matter* (New York: Charles Scribner's Sons, 1930), and *The Realm of Essence* (New York: Charles Scribner's Sons, 1927); Bertrand Russell, *A Free Man's Worship* (Portland, Me.: T. B. Mosher, 1923), and *Why I Am Not a Christian* (New York: Simon and Schuster, 1957); and, in positivist terms, A. J. Ayer, *Language, Truth and Logic* (London: V. Gollancz, 1946). Probably the best summary of this naturalistic position is found in Yervant Krikorian, ed., *Naturalism and the Human Spirit* (New York: Columbia University Press, 1944). For our immediate purposes, it is significant to note that all of these "naturalists" (except possibly Hobbes) assumed that such a view of things "without God" was essentially and necessarily antithetical to Christian faith (though in Santayana's case, not to Christian piety, or in Dewey's, not to Christian virtue), and certainly to any responsible Christian theology. What is therefore new in the present movement is the claim that Christian belief, practice, and theology alike must, and can, establish themselves on this naturalistic base.

the secular mind of modern urban man in the churches as well as
outside them—and this makes its serious study a supremely significant task. (6) By representing this particular mood in modern
life, a mood skeptical about all formulations of ultimate coherence or of ultimate meaning, speculative as well as theological, a
mood that doubts the possibility of both philosophical knowing
and religious faith, it creates an entirely new situation for theological method, making provisionally irrelevant both the metaphysical starting point of liberal philosophy of religion and the
faith starting point of revelationist or neoorthodox theology. (7)
Finally, and perhaps most important, this movement expresses in
powerful theoretical form the most creative aspect of modern contemporary Christian existence, namely its sense that Christianity
is primarily mission and service in the world and for the neighbor,
and consequently that Christian existence is "secular," that is,
worldly, political, and historical in character, seeking to transform
historical existence rather than merely religiously to react to it
and reflect upon it. It is this new conviction that to be a Christian
is not to be "religious," that is, to be worshipful, theological, or
even to "believe" with all one's heart, but to love, serve, and so to
change the world, that has more than anything else made for this
theology recruits among the younger clergy and serious younger
laymen. Thus the radical theology has tended to become the reflective framework within which much Christian participation in
civil rights, in inner-city work, in experimental forms of the ministry, and in peace movements has understood itself. Any theology, therefore, that wishes to speak to and for the most creative
elements of modern Church life, must come to terms with this
mode of theological thinking and, for the integrity of both its
thinking and its mission, speak theologically in secular, political
and historical terms. This book may rightly be taken as an effort to
think out the beginnings of a "secular theology," but one that
nonetheless retains the essential attitudes and symbolic forms of
the historic Christian faith.

The radical theologies have thus expressed in forceful, if
in negative and extravagant, terms the main elements of the present theological upheaval as contemporary churchmen, lay, clerical, and theological, have felt them. For this reason, they provide

a useful context for our further discussion of the present situation in theology, its background, anatomy, and possible cures. Theologians and churchmen of any sort should, we believe, be grateful to these radicals for the courage and the clarity with which they have stated their doubts, problems and convictions. Because they have roused both Church and theological seminary from their dogmatic slumbers, it is they who have made it possible for the rest of us to tackle the real theological issues of our time rather than to rework the traditional questions bequeathed to us by the liberal and the neoorthodox past. If their slogan is "God is dead, and this fact is the starting point for contemporary theology," our own paraphrase might read, "Radical theology may be dead, but its protests and its affirmations set the sole framework for relevant theological discussion today."

In the discussion of radical theology appearing subsequently in this book, we shall omit several figures who, in the view of many, might appropriately be included. First and foremost, there is the thought of Harvey Cox,[16] whose widely read and noted *The Secular City* might seem a prime example of a secular and therefore radical theology. While his book reveals an astounding number of genuinely novel ideas about the relations of social change to religious practices and theological concepts, and offers some very creative suggestions about secular applications of the gospel, and has for this reason been enormously influential, nevertheless the book is on a theological level quite conservative, almost untouched, one might say, by the new mood of secularism. Cox argues very persuasively that the secularization that has come with the rise of the large urban centers has stripped from modern culture all of its mythical, religious, and metaphysical foundations, leaving life pragmatic and profane. This argument might be taken to imply that theology itself should become secular and profane in the sense that the radical theologians propose. But Cox does not draw this conclusion. Rather, to him Biblical religion has been spared this secular devastation: miraculously, while all of man's other myths, religions, gods, and metaphysical systems

---

[16] Harvey Cox, *The Secular City* (New York: Macmillan Company, 1965).

have had to flee the city, irrelevant, unheard, and unpreachable, the Bible's myths, gods, and religions have not, Moreover, not only is Biblical faith intensely relevant to the new world; for Cox, it is in fact the historical basis for secular society and the key to its continued health. Thus this faith is for him as viable, relevant, and convincing today as it ever was—in fact probably more so, since now at last the inherent secular implications of Biblical faith have been realized. Paradoxically, Cox's argument seems almost to say that Biblical faith can be said to be at last "established" in a secular world! To transform Biblical theology on the basis of the secular is, therefore, for Cox an erroneous "secularism" that would reflect an ideology or a world view mortally opposed not only to Biblical faith but also to the real meaning of secularity.

The main thesis of the radical theology with which we are concerned is, however, just the opposite. In its view, the secularization of culture forces drastic changes precisely in theology itself, since secularization has rendered our inherited Biblical faith as irrelevant and empty as are man's other myths and religions. Since to the radical theologians—and here we cannot but agree with them—the secularization of society means the secularization of *all* of man's thinking, this includes his religious and so his Biblical thinking as well—a position Cox seems to agree with in relation to all faiths but the one revealed in the Bible. Thus Cox's fundamental distinction—derived from Friedrich Gogarten—between a "secularization" harmonious to Biblical faith and a "secularism" antithetical to it, itself reflects a "religious" presupposition which would be totally unintelligible to the secular world. This nonsecular presupposition is that Biblical faith has its basis, not, as do other myths and philosophies, in man's developing social context and so in his changing cultural imagination, but in what transcends social change, namely divine revelation. Since this neoorthodox distinction between divine revelation and human religion is itself founded upon Biblical faith, and would therefore be meaningless to the profane man, who by definition knows no revelation, this book hardly reflects in its theology the secular mood it describes so well. Thus it not only represents a very different position from that of the radical theologians, but even more it fails to raise—or even clearly to see—the crucial problems for theology which the radicals pose and with which we here seek to deal.

Much the same reason precludes a discussion of the thought of Gabriel Vahanian.[17] He certainly deserves great credit for being the first to point out the utter secularity of our culture, and many of its inevitable consequences for religion. His analysis of the spirit and religiosity of modern American culture, therefore, is very similar to that of the radical theologians: ours is a secular age for which categories and symbols of transcendence, especially those pertaining to God, are empty, irrelevant, and un-heeded—and thus we can only say that God is dead in our time. Correspondingly, contemporary religion has become man-cen-tered, subjective, flabby, amorphous, and ineffective, reflecting more secular values than Christian ones. Vahanian, however, makes clear that theologically he does not approve of this secular-izing of religion, and that for him only a faith validly based on divine revelation whose source lies therefore in the God tran-scendent to culture—and so invulnerable to all the forces and pressures of secularity—can redeem either secular man or his pro-fanized religiosity. Again, the opposite conclusion from that of the radical theologians is drawn. Effective faith and valid the-ology are here based on a ground in divine revelation transcendent to and untouched by the secularizing process that has twisted and emasculated "religion," and so these writings beg precisely the point the radicals raise for debate—namely the reality of God and so of revelation. Theologically, therefore, both of these men reflect not at all a secular viewpoint, but an untroubled neoortho-dox perspective.

Also omitted from our analysis are the strongly resurgent younger "Whiteheadian" theologians such as John B. Cobb, Jr., and Schubert M. Ogden.[18] There are, to be sure, elements in the

[17] Gabriel Vahanian, *The Death of God* (New York: George Braziller, 1961); *Wait Without Idols* (New York: George Braziller, 1964); and *No Other God* (New York: George Braziller, 1966).

[18] John B. Cobb, Jr., *A Christian Natural Theology* (Philadel-phia: Westminster Press, 1965); and "From Crisis Theology to the Post-Modern World," *Centennial Review* (Spring 1964); Schubert M. Ogden, *Christ Without Myth* (New York: Harper & Row, 1961); and *The Reality of God* (New York: Harper & Row, 1966).

viewpoints of both of these men that could legitimately be called
radical or secular, since they are both embarked on the enterprise
of translating Christian symbols into the categories of a modern
secular philosophy. In this process, such traditional orthodox doctrines as the final authority for theology of revelation and scripture, the absoluteness and aseity of God, and, with Ogden at
least, the ultimacy of the revelatory event of Jesus Christ are
relinquished. Nevertheless, this group belongs no more to the
"God is dead" theology than do its opposite Biblical numbers,
Cox and Vahanian. For despite these strongly "liberal" elements
in their thought, these men still find the symbol of God crucial
to their theology.[19] Though this symbol is based upon and elaborated through a metaphysical analysis of experience—in the place
of the authority of revelation and scripture—still, for them,
God is very much the active and crucial center of their theologies
as that ultimate and, in many ways, transcendant factor explanatory of the coherence and the developing order of process, an
order which gives to both the cosmos and to man's life their purpose and their meaning.

Somewhat ironically, both of these groups regard the radical theologians, and with them the present theological situation,
as having proved the untenability only of the viewpoint of the
other party. Cox and Vahanian are sure that at last secularization
has made impossible the very kind of metaphysical system on
which Cobb and Ogden base their theological discourse—while
leaving, of course, the Biblical God intact. Cobb and Ogden, on
the other hand, regarded secularity as deadly, not so much to a
modern metaphysics, as to man's mythical thinking, and so as a
mortal threat to any naïve form of "Biblical theology" for which
only translation into rational metaphysical discourse can provide

[19] For this same reason, while it certainly reflects much of the
new temper, Bishop J. A. T. Robinson's *Honest To God* (Philadelphia:
Westminster Press, 1963), no more than *Christ Without Myth*, is representative of this radical group. For all its kindredness of spirit and of
concept, it is too Tillichian, it even hints at ontological and metaphysical
definitions of God, and so it refashions rather than disposes of God-
language and with the religion appropriate to it. This judgment is,
moreover, borne out by Bishop Robinson's latest book, *In the End God*
(New York: Harper & Row, 1968).

an antidote. We shall argue that *both* are right about the effects
of secularity on the other's position—but, by the same token, both
are far too sanguine about the invulnerability of their own to
the kinds of attitudes expressed by the radical theologians. To
understand the nature of this attack on each of these forms of
modern theology, we shall have to make a much more thorough
analysis of the secularity that the radical theologians claim to
represent. Meanwhile, let us note one rather amusing fact. In
the midst of the heated argument between Biblical and philosophical theologians, a quite new opponent, disdainful equally
of each of the others, has appeared, and so in consequence these
old antagonists now find it necessary to join together against the
onslaught of this much more radical theology which interprets
our present secular mood as one which makes impossible *any*
view of God at all, be it metaphysical or Biblical, immanent or
transcendent. Thus have the old arguments between these two
groups as to how we are to know and speak of God, whether by
revelation or by philosophy, been completely outflanked and
rendered for the moment uninteresting and irrelevant by the flat
assertion that the word "God" is dead in any of its forms and
only Jesus and the Christian's task in the world are left for us to
ponder.

2/The Cultural Background
of the Current
Theological Situation

THE MAJOR HISTORICAL CAUSE of the current ferment in religious belief lies in the interaction between two important forces in our cultural life, namely the developing "secularity" of our cultural existence on the one hand, and our traditional religious communities, with their convictions, values, shared experiences and loyalties on the other. Thus a large part of the intellectual background of the current situation in theology is the maturation of the secular spirit which almost all present theological commentators, however they may assess that spirit, agree is predominant in our age. Now it is, I think, very important to know what we are talking about when we speak of "secularity," how the word is being used. For it is an ironic fact that the meaning of all significant symbols in philosophical or theological discourse—of which now this is assuredly one—tends, not to become more precise and ascertainable, but, on the contrary, to become more vague and ambiguous the moment they attain important and frequent usage. When words are peripheral to important matters of discourse, they can easily be precisely defined and univocally used. When they begin to bear significant weight in crucial speech—as is evident in current discourse about "democracy"—then mystery and equivocity seem to envelop both their meaning and their usage.

I do not propose to use the word "secular" as a description merely of the "nonreligious" elements of a society's life: the secular as opposed to the religious; political or economic in-

stitutions as opposed to the Church. "Secularity" or "secularization" have been used thus by Friedrich Gogarten and now by
Harvey Cox to indicate the gradual freeing of nonreligious social
institutions from religious control and their establishment in
terms of their own autonomous principles and their own inherent
values.[1] In this usage, the concept parallels the Enlightenment
concept of a secular realm as the larger part of a social order that
in its own eyes enjoys "natural" foundations but that can include
"Biblical faith" as one of its viable spiritual alternatives. Thus, it
is argued, the Bible (surprisingly, as well as *die Aufklärung!*) ap-
proves of secularization in this sense, the desacralizing of nature
and of the structures of ordinary social life, and celebrates both
nature and society as autonomous realms of value recognized and
encouraged by Biblical faith. But to baptize the "secular" in this
way is too easy; theology wins its war with secularity by setting
the latter within the terms of Biblical faith. A *Biblical* definition
of the secular is dependent for its authority and its meaning on
the very categories of "revelation" (and so of religion generally)
which the secular rejects, and so is a definition which, as we saw,
is meaningless to those secular attitudes it wishes to celebrate.

[1] In his usage of the word "secular," Harvey Cox distinguishes
"secularization," as the desacralizing of social institutions and of ordinary
life, from "secularism," as a philosophy derived from that secular mode
of existence. As we noted, Cox argues that, while the process of secularization is compatible with Biblical faith—in fact is the latter's historical
offspring—secularism as a philosophy is the mortal enemy of Christian
faith (*The Secular City* [New York: Macmillan and Company, 1965],
pp. 18–19, 65–86). Thus Cox makes what to me is an unreal division
between a historical process that is liberating and "Biblical" and an inner
philosophy of life (secularism) which he deplores. It is for this reason
that he feels, far too optimistically, that it is not difficult still to "have" the
Biblical faith in the midst of the process of secularization. We are inclined to unite the two aspects into one phrase, "secular mood," because
we feel that both the historical process and the attitude, spirit, or self-
understanding go together. Which is cause and which effect is difficult
to determine; but that a new secular *attitude* is implied in the process of
secularization seems to us undoubted, and even more that that attitude
has threatening implications for Biblical faith as well as for the other
faiths and world views of man seems all too true. By our phrase "secular
spirit," then, we speak of this attitude or mode of self-understanding
which is so important for current problems of theology.

Consequently, it makes its imprint *only* on those already "religious" minds which wish to rediscover their place and role in the world. What is relevant to our *theological* discussion of the secular is another, more profound meaning which relates to the very roots of religion and of theology. This is the secular as descriptive of the spirit of our times, as referent to that fundamental attitude toward existence characteristic of our age. And this spirit is by *no* means simply Biblical, nor does it represent merely a neutral desacralizing of nonchurchly social structures of which Christian faith might approve. On the contrary, the present problem for faith and theology is precisely that the secular in this sense, as a basic spirit we all share, tends to be subversive of any sort of faith and discourse that might be called authentically Biblical.

When we speak, as we just have, of the "spirit," "mind," "mood," or "*Geist*" of our culture, we refer to that deep, preconceptual attitude toward and understanding of existence which dominates and forms the cultural life of any epoch, the way men of a given time characteristically apprehend the world they live in and their place within it; their fundamental self-understanding of their being in the world. Since the end of the eighteenth century, largely under the influence of the development of the study of history and in philosophy of the thought of Herder and Hegel, historians have been increasingly aware that every age does have such a fundamental mood; that it is both possible and important to speak of the Hellenistic mind, the Medieval attitude, the Renaissance spirit, and so on. Consequently, it is now taken for granted in historical studies that, if one is to understand the art, literature, philosophy, religion—or the concrete political, economic, and personal decisions—of an epoch, one must first "set it in its cultural context," and that means to comprehend this general mood within terms of which all aspects of thought and all modes of life arise and are formed. Such a general mood is not *a* philosophy so much as it is the background, the foundation for all the philosophies of the period, that which each philosophical school of an era expresses; it gives to all the cultural creations of an epoch that particular shape which makes them "of that time." Thus such moods are generally prerational, prethematized or conceptualized, since they are *expressed* in the explicit concepts of reflective systems. Their shape, therefore, is unreflected upon and often even unconscious; they are the *pre*suppositions of thought, to be known only by the historian of ideas.[2] A cultural mood, then, is that fundamental attitude toward reality, toward truth, and toward value which characterizes an epoch, and within whose terms every creative aspect of life, including a period's religion and its theology, expresses itself.

Our thesis in this analysis is that "the secular spirit," or "secularity," represents the cultural *Geist* of our time, and that it is the particular character of this mood or self-understanding as dominant in the minds of all of us that creates most of the important problems for belief and for theological reflection which we will discuss here. By the phrase "the secular spirit," therefore, I do not mean to refer merely to the historical process of secularization, although that is clearly related to the referent of our use of the word. Rather, we wish to point to that fundamental attitude toward the world and toward life, slowly developing into the dominant *Geist* of the West since the Medieval period, and so which has been both the cause and the effect of the cultural and social process of secularization. We wish to delineate this attitude or spirit because it is precisely this mood which raises all our contemporary theological problems, and which makes the meaningfulness alike of the Biblical, the traditional, and the philosophical forms of Christian belief so problematic in our time.

Perhaps the most familiar of these cultural moods or spirits to those of us who study theology is that of the Hellenistic Age

---

[2] For perceptive and seminal discussion of the relativity of all cultural forms, and so of all thought, to this *presupposed* cultural self-understanding characteristic of each historical epoch, cf. R. G. Collingwood, *The Idea of History* (Oxford: University Press, 1946); and *An Essay on Metaphysics* (Oxford: University Press, 1940). For Collingwood, therefore, metaphysics is the study of the presuppositions of a cultural epoch. And, making much the same point, but from an entirely different perspective, Claude Levi-Strauss argues that linguistics and its partner anthropology study the *unconscious* foundations of a culture, the former studying the basic structural propensities, in various cultural forms, of man, and anthropology the analogs in social life of these subconscious forces. Cf. Claude Levi-Strauss, *Structural Anthropology* (New York: Basic Books, 1963), pp. 18–23, 55–65.

(200 B.C.–500 A.D.). When we look back upon the religious and philosophical documents of that era, we can see plainly the determinative influence, for good or for ill, of what were probably the unconscious presuppositions of that age on the way both pagans and Christians thought about their respective philosophies or faiths. From these documents a general characterization of that spirit, which we might label "idealistic dualism," can be made. This spirit appears in one form or another in every cultural product, including, of course, theology. Even the theologians who fought those heresies, such as the gnostic interpretations of Christianity, which stemmed directly from this dualistic mood, did so in the Hellenistic terms familiar and relevant to their own age.

This latter fact is significant for any understanding of the relation of theology to the spirit of its own time. Although every early Church theology expressed itself in the categories of the Hellenistic spirit, the most significant theologies did not by any means accept *all* of the implications of that spirit. And so they struggled with what they regarded as the heresies of their time— not because these heresies were "Hellenistic"—for every form of thought was that—but because, in being Hellenistic, they had capitulated too completely to their cultural mood and had given up certain elements of the faith that seemed to the Church to be essential to its life. Interestingly, it was just those elements affirmed by the early Church as a part of the Biblical view which, antithetical to the Hellenistic spirit, were to become the foundations of the modern mood we now call "secular." These elements, defended by the intransigent Church against the innate idealism of their cultural spirit, were (1) the emphasis on the reality and goodness of natural existence; (2) the possibility of an incarnation of the divine into the flesh and into history; and (3) the ultimate meaning of the "worldly" both in ethical action through love and in eternity through the resurrection of the flesh. What resulted from this stretching and transforming of the Hellenistic categories was a "Christian Hellenism" that was, on the one hand, partly Biblical and traditional, because in a measure intransigent to its culture, and, on the other, relevant to its time because Hellenistic. And perhaps it was more relevant than its rival, Gnosticism, precisely because it was *not* completely Hellenistic.

What we are here proposing, then, is that "secularism" is a category descriptive of the general mood of our time much as "idealistic dualism" might define the mood of that earlier one, and that the issues raised for theology in these two periods by its cultural environment are roughly analogous. The expression of the gospel probably always requires that there be no total capitulation to any cultural *Geist;* and yet no formulation of the gospel that is relevant or meaningful can possibly fail to express itself in categories familiar to its hearers. The peril is to let either side dominate: if theology uses *only* traditional or Biblical language, unrelated to contemporary thought forms, then what is said will seem meaningless, empty, and unreal; if, on the other hand, the current spirit dominates entirely, nothing new or significant is said at all. The former peril has certainly been that of neoorthodoxy and of European theology generally; the latter is the clear danger of present-day radical theology, and of most American religious thought.

Let us, however, return to our description of the secularity within terms of which all the living and relevant forms of contemporary cultural expression arise. What is its shape and character? How does it view reality, truth, and value? And, how has it developed? Our description will be a *historical* or *descriptive* and not a constructive enterprise. That is, we are seeking to describe faithfully how modern man in fact apprehends his world, not how he should do so if that apprehension were to be valid; our object is the truth about what the modern mind thinks, not the truth of "what is."

The causes of fundamental cultural change are as baffling as they are complex. Do objective historical, economic, technical, and social developments determine changes in attitudes, beliefs, and values—or do the main determining influences run in the opposite direction? Our own guess is that influences go both ways, and that fundamental attitudes are as determinative for objective social developments as the latter are for the former. Certainly, in any case, objective and subjective cultural changes parallel each other, and so, at the start of our description of the secular spirit, it may be helpful briefly to point to some of the social and institu-

tional changes in our life that have paralleled these transformations of our attitudes and values.

1. As technology and urbanization have slowly pro-
gressed in the West, the setting of man's life has significantly
shifted. He is not dependent any longer on the eternal, changeless,
given order of nature to which he must accommodate himself;
rather, the environment to which he adapts himself is now composed of the ever-changing and relative arrangements of human
enterprise. He seems to have moved from God's world to man's,
from being the participant in an eternal order to becoming the
creator of a relative and fluctuating one.

2. Concurrently, his view of this human world about
him, of the social institutions, traditions, and customs in which he
lives his life, has changed. These institutions—state, church, class,
and even family—are no longer for him "given" unalterably by a
transcendent authority which he must obey; they are no longer
temporal expressions of a divine and eternal order, participation
in and obedience to which give coherence and meaning to man's
fragmentary life on earth—as they were for our Greek and Christian forebears. Rather, man now knows that they are created by
historical, geographical, and above all human forces, that they
are, indeed, relative, temporal, and so "secular" institutions, and
not the sacred orders which God eternally willed for his world.
Consequently, the rulers of these institutions—king, ruler, father,
Pope, schoolmaster—are no longer sacral, unquestioned authorities and models for all that man is and knows.

3. Above all, as modern man has learned to know and
think about his world, he has not found it peopled with spiritual
beings; nor has his present understanding of it seemed to support
the traditional assumption that it was, so to speak, engineered by
"someone" with human purposes and needs in mind. Rather,
insofar as he feels he can know anything with certainty at all, he
realizes he knows his natural environment only through scientific
inquiry, and the picture he finds implied there is that he and his
world are the results of countless, strangely harmonious, but
utterly blind causes whose fortuitous interaction has produced
his relatively benevolent environment and even his own admirable
powers of life, love, and thought. Matter blindly running its

heedless course seems to be God, if by that symbol one means the mystery that produced us, maintains us, and will claim us in the end.

Thus all the dominant factors of modern existence—its social locus, its sense of its historical and institutional environment, and its apprehension of the cosmos around it, in short, the way modern man structures his world and himself within it—have led toward a new secular attitude toward our world and ourselves. This is the sense that our environment, taken even in its widest sense, exhibits neither a holy eternal order, as it seemed to the Greeks, nor one eternally willed by a holy sovereign Lord, as in the Biblical tradition; and our life, therefore, is not dependent on a sacred order or a transcendent divinity for either its existence or its meaning.[3] Rather, what is *real* in our universe is only the profane, the contingent, blind causes that have produced us, the relative social institutions in which we live, the things and artifacts that we can make, and our relations to one another; any other "sacred" realm of existence partakes for our age more of fantasy than it does of deity. Correspondingly, what we can *know* are only these finite, contingent factors we see around us. That is, valid knowing occurs only where we can directly experience, manipulate, test, and verify; any other "knowing" than such a

[3] The historian of religion, Mircea Eliade, to whom many of the thoughts in this book owe their origin, has made clear that primitive man, as we know him through his religious rites and myths, did feel he lived in an eternal, sacred order which was the foundation for both what is real and what is meaningful, and that his religious symbols, myths, and rites were media through which he could by repetition and enactment regain access to this order and so transform the chaos of profane experience into the cosmos of the original order. (Cf. *Patterns in Comparative Religion* [New York: Meridian Books, 1963], pp. 429–431.) Since metaphysics and theology define dialectically or rationally what myth expresses dramatically (*ibid.*, p. 418), we may regard the metaphysical and theological traditions in the West as *in part* rationalizations of this original mythical consciousness of a divine order in which man must participate in order to be man, and the secular spirit as the final dissolution of this age-old consciousness. Whether modern man can thus, by ceasing to be in this sense "primitive," cease to need myth or to reflect some such consciousness, is the basic issue to which this book addresses itself.

radically empirical mode of inquiry, for example, by poetic imagination, by religious vision, or even by rational speculation, severs
its touch with what is "real" and so in fact tells us more about our
own psychological and verbal problems than it does about what
there is. And, finally, what is *valuable* is not some far-off heaven,
or a mystical union with a transcendent reality, but a better life
here and now, among men in this world.

The modern spirit is thus radically this-worldly. We tend
not to see our life and its meanings as stretching out toward an
eternal order beyond this existence, or our fortunes as dependent
upon a transcendant ruler of time and history. We view our life
as here, and our destiny as beginning with birth and ending with
the grave, as confined in space and time to this world in nature
and among men. Consequently, whatever knowing we can achieve
will deal with this limited environment, and whatever meaning
we can find in our short life will, we feel, depend entirely on our
own powers of intellect and will and the relative historical and
communal values we can create—and not on the grace and mercy
of an ultimate heavenly sovereign. Modern man thus feels he has
"come of age" in a contingent, faceless world. He can, and
should, depend on no one or on no other beyond himself to continue in being, to know and to decide about his life. If anyone
is to rule and direct his destiny, it must be man himself alone.
Such, we suggest, is the "secular spirit" which dominates our age
and which, as a fundamental attitude toward reality, truth, and
value, is expressed not only by our own most fundamental reactions to life, but also objectively in the dominant philosophies, the
creative arts, and the most profound literature of our day. Needless to say, not every member—even every creative member—of
present Western culture understands himself and his world in
this way, any more than every man possessed a "Renaissance
spirit" during that period. But that this secular mood characterizes the pervasive and fundamental attitudes of those urban and
semiurban middle classes who participate in and so are domi-
nantly creative of our cultural existence, there can be little doubt.

There are four general characteristics of this secular spirit, the
brief conceptual elaboration of which will help to make its expe-

rienced shape more precise. We shall encounter these four elements of the modern *Geist* throughout our study of the contemporary possibilities for religious discourse.

1. *Contingency.* This is the sense that what is—the world
around us and we ourselves—is the result of causes that are neither
necessary, rational, nor purposive. The flow of events, to be sure,
may exhibit a proximate order sufficient to maintain us and to
allow us to trace out its recurrent habits and so to predict—sufficient, that is, for practical decisions, for science, and for technology. But none of these things that have evolved in time is
necessary or intended; they are accidental, and why things either
are, or are as they are, are thus mysteries which our minds cannot
fathom.

This apprehension of finite reality as contingent, arising
as an end result of seventeenth-century science, has since been extended and further radicalized, especially through Darwin's influence, and now it dominates most of modern philosophy as
perhaps its pivotal concept.[4] It is, we believe, this understanding
or apprehension of our contingency which most directly restricts
modern thought to the immediately given, to the sensory manifold and its traceable interrelations. The essence of this modern
sense of contingency is that the given is ultimately arbitrary,
and consequently beyond the given there lies nothing, no ground,

[4] The influence of Charles Darwin in creating the sense that we
are brought into being by "chance" interactions of blind events is undeniable. More than any other result of modern inquiry, his theory of
origins seemed to displace man from his former setting within an eternal
rational order, or a purposefully willed order, and pictured him as the
product of the *blind* law of selection combined with *random* mutations.
The modern sense of radical contingency, relativity, and temporality—in
which even the fundamental forms of species arise and fall again "because of causes but for no reasons"—has its origin in Darwin. Needless
to say, back of Darwin lies the entire development of post-Galilean science
and philosophy, with its denial that teleology or purpose has any creative
role in the understanding of the habits of nature. What Darwin did was
to enlarge this antiteleological view of nature to cover the question of
the origin of man's form and thus to include all of our relevant environment, and ourselves, within the blind mechanism of matter.

no ultimate order, no explanation, no reason. For this view, finitude does not appear set within a wider order which reason might explore and so know, or faith reveal, and that thus might explain and so temper its arbitrariness. The given just appears; it can be described as it appears, and *that* is all that can be said. Existence and thought alike begin and end with the given. The concept of contingency, so important in modern philosophy, is, in other words, the ontological and logical correlate of the equally central canon of radical empiricism dominant in all modern views of knowing.

This most basic apprehension of the radical limitation of thought to the contingent given is expressed in the insistence of much of linguistic philosophy that all assertions that have to do with what there is, all, as they put it, "factual" assertions, are contingent and therefore empirical or scientific in form. What is crucial here is the identification, first, of assertions about what is with "factual" and contingent statements *alone* (i.e., nonnecessary or "might not have been" statements); and secondly, of contingent statements with empirically verifiable or sensory statements alone. Thus, putting this point in less logical language, the only way we can talk about what is real is through statements based upon and confined to concrete, sensory data: this is our only cognitive contact with what is, and so the only way we can speak about it. Only the immediately given is knowable and intelligible, and nothing else *is* for us; contingency equals the real and limits the knowable. For this view, then, indicative statements as contingent are to be radically distinguished from necessary statements based on the analysis of concepts or words. As contingent, the only meaning that such assertions about what is can have is that of "stating experienceable facts," as "factual" or empirical in that limited sense. Thus the meaning of contingent assertions consists solely in that which sense experience can give them, through their verification or falsification in immediate experience. The confinement of indicative statements to those that are logically contingent and also sensibly verifiable has led to the most radical form of empiricism conceivable. For this view of our contingency, there are and can be no meanings to propositions which are assertive and yet move be-

yond the given, which are (1) *non*analytical, which (2) nevertheless are nonfactual in the sense of nonscientific, and yet which
(3) claim to assert something of what "is the case."

As a result, to most linguistic philosophy, "metaphysical"
statements about an eternal order, an ultimate reality, or a pervasive structure of things, or about the general or universal characteristics even of finite actuality or finite interrelations, being
neither analytic nor strictly scientific in form or in modality of
validation, are thus meaningless. Consequently, the conclusion is
drawn that philosophical statements, being nonscientific, are nonassertive about what is and are, rather, descriptions concerned
with the analysis of the meanings of words: "Philosophical theory has its source in linguistic facts rather than in facts about the
world, and . . . despite appearances, it gives us information only
about language."[5]

This identification of all assertions about what is with
factual or empirical assertions, meaning propositions generated
by and tested in and through scientific methods, common to most
linguistic analysis as well as to positivism, thus radically restricts
reflective thought to the interrelations of the given, that is, to
science, or else to the analysis of the verbal meanings and usages
of ordinary commonsense language and experience. Here the category of "contingency," defined logically as referent to factual and
empirical assertions that may or may not be the case, as opposed
to analytic and necessary statements, expresses powerfully the
modern sense of the meaninglessness of all "cognitive" thought
that moves beyond the given, the consequent limitation of knowing to the things and persons around us, and the confinement of
reflective thought to our conventional words and usages—the assumption clearly being that there is nothing more than the contingent, the immediately given factuality, to talk about.

In the philosophy of empirical naturalism, the category of
"contingency" manifests itself as an ontological rather than a
logical category, but it expresses much the same apprehension of
the relation of thought to reality. As defined by Ernst Nagel, the

[5] Alice Ambrose Lazerowitz, "Linguistic Approaches to Philosophical Problems," in Richard Rorty, *The Linguistic Turn* (Chicago:
University of Chicago Press, 1967), p. 147.

"contingency" of things indicates that, while to be sure there are *causes* for events, there are no *reasons*—and the causes themselves having no reasons, things as a whole just "are," and their being has no explanation.[6] George Santayana expresses the same sense of the radical contingency of all that is with his usual poetry: "Matter is the invisible wind which, sweeping *for no reason* over the field of essences, raises some of them into a cloud of dust: and that whirlwind we call existence."[7] And, "in a contingent world, necessity is a conspiracy of accidents."[8] Again, things merely "are," and for absolutely no reason, so that thought cannot proceed beyond immediate experience to clarify the radical mystery of what is.

Perhaps the strongest assertion of the contingency of whatever is appears in existentialism, for which contingency practically defines the meaning of the word "existence." Here one does not observe contingency from the outside as a phenomenon of things; one grasps it from within as the character of one's own existence. Our being is, says Heidegger, most fundamentally defined as "being there," and he does not mean "being there for this or that reason," but *just* "being there," being posited—for the essence of being there is the experience of being thrown or cast into existence. Our existence is thrown, but there is no thrower and so no reason for the throw.[9] Apparently, for all its proximate orders traced by science, existence comes at modern man as if out of the dark, from no further reality, within no ultimate order and for no ultimate reason. It is brute fact, the absolutely given, the ulti-

[6] Ernst Nagel, *Logic Without Metaphysics* (Glencoe, Ill.: The Free Press, 1956), pp. 7–9.

[7] George Santayana, *The Realm of Matter* (New York: Scribner's, 1930), p. 94. Italics are mine.

[8] *Ibid.*, p. 99.

[9] "As something thrown, Dasein has been thrown *into existence.* It exists as an entity which has to be as it is and as it can be. *That* it is factically, may be obscure and hidden as regards the *'why'* of it; but the *that-it-is* has *itself* been disclosed to Dasein. . . . The caller is Dasein in its uncanniness: primordial, thrown Being in the world as the 'not-at-home'—the bare 'that-it-is' in the 'nothing' of the world." Martin Heidegger, *Being and Time,* trans. J. Macquarrie and E. Robinson (New York: Harper & Row, 1962), p. 321.

mately arbitrary, the merely posited: beyond what is thus starkly given, there is merely a Void. This is what contingency means in our age, and it is in large part this sense of existence as ultimately arbitrary that makes language which moves beyond the given, whether in speculative philosophy or in theology, seem unreal, empty, and irrational to modern man. The antimetaphysical as well as the antitheological bent of the secular spirit finds its deepest roots in this sense of the radical contingency of what we experience, and so of the utter mystery—even the irrationality—in all that lies beyond the immediately given. Our radical empiricism is an outgrowth of the more fundamental ontological vision that all that there is that can be known is exhausted by the proximate patterns of immediate sensory experience. All intelligible language is thus monodimensional, referent to the plane or surface of events in immediate or phenomenal experience. Symbolic language referent to depths beneath the surface reveals for modern man more about our psychological and verbal problems than it does about any transcendent or divine dimension of reality.

It is clear at a glance how different this modern concept of contingency is from what in comparison we might call the "halfhearted" contingency of the classical theological tradition. For the concept of contingency has, of course, been long held in honor by the theological tradition. In Schleiermacher, for example, contingency is a fairly accurate conceptual description of what gives rise, in the realm of finite self-consciousness, to the "feeling of absolute dependence"—namely the sense of being both caused and free, dependent and yet real and effective.[10] But it has been in the tradition of Thomism that the notion of contingency has been especially central. There contingency has meant that which is not self-sufficient, and thus that which exhibits a dependency which points beyond itself precisely to the noncontingent for its own sufficient explanation. Contingency in this tradition has been the springboard from which the mind leaps to the pure air of being. Thus in traditional thought the contingent is not that which has *no* reasons at all; rather, it refers to merely one realm of

[10] Friedrich Schleiermacher, *The Christian Faith*, trans. H. R. Mackintosh and J. S. Stewart (Edinburgh: T. & T. Clark, 1928), paragraphs 4–5, 32–34, pp. 12–26, 131–140.

what is, to that whose "reasons" are not necessary, and it is assumed that the nonnecessary still demands a sufficient reason. The
contingency of the finite is, therefore, for Thomism such that
it implies in itself a movement of the mind beyond the contingent
and so beyond the natural world to that noncontingent reality
which provides the ground or reason that contingency cannot itself
provide. I shall argue that in many respects this notion is a valid
description of the way even modern men *feel* their existence as
they live it. But we should recognize that this view of contingency,
as *logically* implying a more rational, necessary realm beyond itself, makes no sense to modern *thought*, which defines the contingent as precisely the opposite, namely that which, as the purely
factual and therefore as the absolutely and arbitrarily given, does
not and cannot point thought beyond itself for an explanation.[11]
Thus, in the modern situation, to argue philosophically from con-

[11] That to the classical Thomist tradition the contingency of the
world meant merely its nonnecessity, and did *not* mean that there was no
eternal and purposive ground for the contingent, is shown by the fact that
it is of the essence of the Thomist proofs of the existence of God that it is
precisely the contingency of the world which, by the law of sufficient reason and the consequent impossibility of an infinite regress, calls for the being of a first, efficient Cause of that contingent world. To the medieval
mind (and to the Greek), therefore, contingency pointed beyond itself to
the noncontingent, its very "thrownness" necessarily implied a divine
"Thrower." Cf. St. Thomas, *Summa Theologica*, First Part, Question 2,
Article 3, and the excellent commentaries on this proof in E. L. Mascall's
He Who Is (London: Longmans, Green, 1943) and *Existence and
Analogy* (London: Longmans, Green, 1949). Our point is that the modern
sense of contingency implies precisely the denial of this further eternal
and purposive ground; contingent existence means the *merely* "thrown,"
that which has finite causes but no ultimate reasons, that which is accident.
One could phrase this point by saying that contingency so understood
denies the applicability of the law of sufficient reason beyond the sphere
of the contingent itself. Such a refusal to apply the law of sufficient reason
beyond the contingent factors of direct experience is represented in modern naturalistic philosophy, in positivism and language analysis, and in
existentialism, different as each of these modern schools may be on all
other grounds. For the best description of this view of contingency as
the basic characteristic of existence as viewed by modern man, cf. Karl
Löwith, *Nature, History, and Existentialism* (Evanston, Ill.: Northwestern University Press, 1966), and especially the excellent introduction by
Arnold Levison.

tingency to a transcendent and sufficient reason for contingency, is to appear irrational instead of rational, for whether one argues in the linguistic, the naturalistic, or the existentialist mode, the concept of contingency with which one begins the argument simply and essentially will not allow such a movement beyond the given. Perhaps the deepest intellectual difficulty for contemporary philosophical theology is this wall which the modern view of contingency in all its philosophical forms has built around the given. I take it that the near demise of traditional forms of natural theology, in both Protestant and Catholic thought recently, is one reflection of just this difficulty inherent in the modern apprehension of contingency and so the modern spirit of empiricism.

Not only has this wall restricted reflective thought to the given and thus prevented any movement of that thought by rational implication beyond the relative to the transcendent; perhaps even more it has made increasingly difficult the starting point of any natural theology, namely a rational consideration of those universal characteristics of being (the classical transcendentals) which reflect the universal characteristics of things, which are predicates not of this or that subject but of the subjects of all indicative propositions, and which thus delineate the structures of universal experience. As Whitehead insisted, an examination of the given, a "factual" statement, will never reveal these universal structures. Since they are always present in any experience and qualify every statement, they are never noticed when we are looking at the immediate objects of experience.[12] To restrict thought, therefore, to the sensible manifold of immediacy, to what can be verified or falsified in particular concrete experiences, and to what constitutes our ordinary usages of language, is to be unable to think about these general structures of experience which are there as the universal form of all experience and of all language. And, as we shall see, to be unable to speak of the general characteristics of being or of actuality, to be unable to reflect on the pervasive order inherent in the passage of things, to be unable,

---

[12] Cf. Alfred North Whitehead, *Process and Reality* (New York: Macmillan Company, 1929), pp. 6–7; *Adventures of Ideas* (New York: Macmillan Company, 1933), p. 209.

that is, to speak ontologically or metaphysically, is to be unable philosophically to conduct any sort of discourse directly relevant to the task of philosophical theology.

To the optimistic mind of the modern American intelligentsia, the radical contingency of our existence and its consequent, the limitation of our knowledge to what is immediately given, do not appear as threats to life's meaning. The confidence of this class in the intelligence and the liberal motivations of educated middle-class man is such that they are sure that, through empirical inquiry into the structures of contingency, scientific and moral intelligence can create such proximate meanings as to foster and preserve the good life. This same contingency, however, can be experienced in another darker, more European mood. Here the irrationality and the unmanageability of the given, in the form of the heavy hand of blind fate, is felt more sharply, upsetting ruthlessly the frail meanings of men and even eroding inwardly their vaunted powers of intelligence and goodwill. Then, within the terms of the same modern vision of things, we are in the soberer, existentialist world. The emotional differences between these two philosophies are immense and make up a good deal of the most intriguing debate in present-day serious Western philosophy. But let us note that the ultimate vision is the same:[13] man is set within a universe with neither a transcendant source nor an inherent or ultimate order; his context is constituted exhaustively by blind nature or a meaningless Void, not hostile, to be sure, but empty of purpose, indifferent, a faceless mystery. He can talk about it only in terms of the immediately given patterns of his phenomenal experience of it; beyond that he can know and speak nothing meaningful about what is. Thus the meaning, security, and value of man's life cannot come from outside himself at all; they come from his own efforts of knowing and of willing within that given range of contingency. Man may use this wider natural environment for his moral and social purposes, as in the thought of John Dewey; or he may shrink in alienation from it,

---

[13] For a careful discussion of this basic similarity of vision between naturalism and existentialism with regard to man's place in his universe, cf. the introduction by Levison in Löwith, *Nature, History, and Existentialism.*

as with existentialism—but he cannot relate inwardly to it by
mind or heart, and he cannot and should not depend on it. If the
symbol of God represents a cosmic or transcosmic source of security, order, meaning, and purpose to man's life, we can now see
how it is that, in our time, men say God has died for us.

2. The second general characteristic or category of contemporary life, central to all we mean by the secular spirit, is
that of *relativity*, or, in its other context, *relativism*. This sense of
relativity is a product not so much of the cosmology of seventeenth-century science as it is the result of the historical consciousness which developed in the late eighteenth and the early nineteenth centuries, and of the ontologies and then the biology that
grew out of this historical consciousness. The resultant sense of
the relativity of all things to one another in the passage of time—
of the forms of the cosmos itself, of natural life, of our own species, of political and social structures, of the most significant historical events, the noblest of ideas, the most sacred of scriptures,
institutions or creeds—practically defines our era.

For this modern view, all that is is pinioned within the
flux of passage or of history, determined in large part by all that
lies behind it, shaped by all that surrounds it, and to be replaced
by what follows. Nothing in nature or history, and so by implication nothing at all that is, is thus "*a se*," an unchanging and self-
sufficient substance, capable of existing in and by itself and thus
exhibiting an essence underived from and so unrelated to the
other things that surround it. Nothing anywhere in experience,
space, time, or any mode of being is, in that sense, absolute; all
is relative to all else and so essentially conditioned by its relevant
environment. Each entity thus belongs to a nexus or system of
causes or factors which cause its rise, influence its character, and,
for the purposes of understanding its origin, shape, and destiny,
provide the sole grounds or materials for explaining it. The philosophical concept of internal relations—that whatever is, is formed
essentially by its concrete relations to its context—is the ontological expression of this sense of relativism, and it dominates every
form of modern philosophy—idealistic, naturalistic, existentialist,
phenomenological. This assumption, moreover, forms the fundamental presupposition not only of biology and of all of modern

physics, but also of all the social and psychological sciences which seek to understand the individual and his behavior, not in terms of his individual and changeless substance or soul, but in terms of the nexus of social relations out of which he has been formed and so in terms of which he is to be explained.

The implications of this sense of the relativity of all things to one another (i.e., of the doctrine of internal relations) have, of course, been both significant and diverse. On the one hand, in all realms of thought it has tended to emphasize change as opposed to sameness and identity, process as opposed to substance, becoming as opposed to being, and context as opposed to innate individual capacities and powers. If what is is constituted by its relations to its context, its being is a process of becoming in that context, a changing result of the interactions or transactions of things with one another. Most modern ontologies, stemming ultimately from that of Hegel and leading by devious routes to the modern systems of Bradley, Santayana, Dewey, Whitehead, and even of Tillich and Heidegger, have emphasized this relativity of all that is to its changing context.[14]

Another parallel implication is better denominated "relativism" instead of "relativity," since the latter in many of the ontologies just mentioned can connote a metaphysical principle, or metaphysical categories, that are by no means "relative"![15]

---

[14] It should be noted that a doctrine of internal relations, of "relativity" in that sense, has fitted into an absolutist or monist ontology—as in Hegel or Bradley—as easily as into a pluralist ontology—as in Whitehead. That all finite things are relative to one another does not *necessarily* mean, therefore, that God is himself relative—any more than it means in Whitehead that Process is relative to some other process. In monist systems, God *is* the system of internal relations viewed *sub specie aeternitatis* (i.e., metaphysically).

[15] The reference here is primarily to Whitehead's metaphysics. Whitehead has to this interpreter a strange relation to these aspects of the "modern spirit." He expresses most of them elegantly in his thought, and yet in a speculative manner that is far from "contemporary." The ultimacy of contingency in existence is radically defended in his view of the primordial nature of God, and in the ontological principle of explanation according to which *only* actual entities can be reasons. The relativity of all things to each other is vigorously upheld in his doctrine of universal internal relations. And finally, the total becomingness of all things, their "perpetual perishing," the fact that they "never really are" at

Here the consequences of the essential interrelatedness of things appear not so much in space and so ontology as now in the passage of time and so in history, its structures, its events, and the cultural creations of historical man. If all *is* by means of and within its locus in space and time, a product of the forces behind it, relative to what surrounds it, and replaced by what follows, then our deeds, our artistic creativity, even our thoughts, our philosophic categories and our metaphysical systems are formed in part by our historical context and so by the fundamental social and intellectual forces of our era, and thus they are relative to their time and place. The seemingly undeniable doctrine of internal relations, when applied to thought and to history, paradoxically implies the relativity of even its own truth. For if all is relative to its context, then none of these things man has created or thought is absolute, eternal, or transcendent to the flux. Nowhere, therefore, in observable history is there anything permanent or of ultimate authority, for all, being in part human, shares in the relativity of all things creaturely to their context. Any event or creative product in culture, its philosophies, religious beliefs, scriptures,

---

all, provides, along with the principle of autonomy and freedom, perhaps the two most fundamental ontological assertions characteristic of his system. All of this, however, is set within a system of rational speculation in which categories are devised by "controlled and imaginative generalization," and in which those same categories purportedly apply universally and necessarily to all actual entities in whatever relations they are, and in whatever spatiotemporal epoch they appear. As the basis of this metaphysical system of contingency, relativity, and becoming, therefore, Whitehead assumes (1) that there is an order inherent in process which is neither contingent nor relative, and (2) that the philosophical mind can by implication and insight know this order inherent in all occasions, and thus can know the nature of actual entities or a level of concreteness beyond the reach either of direct and immediate experience or of the special sciences, which are both relatively "abstract." Philosophy, therefore, is here a form of knowing comparable to but higher than science and thus capable of making assertions about the concrete nature of the "real" or the "actual" which are universal in scope and necessary in character, and thus which transcend that which is given in immediate, relative experience. Cf. *Process and Reality, op. cit.* For a criticism of Whitehead's speculative rationalism on "naturalistic" grounds, cf. A. E. Murphy, "Whitehead and the Method of Speculative Philosophy," in P. A. Schilpp, ed., *The Philosophy of Alfred North Whitehead* (Evanston, Ill.: Northwestern University Press, 1941), pp. 354ff.

laws, values or practices, is relevant and of immense significance to what surrounds it and shares its general contours; but, by the same token, any historical creation of culture becomes irrelevant to us—if, to be sure, interesting—as it moves away from us in space and time. Can the code of Hammurabi be promulgated in Washington now, or even in Rome?[16] If permanence, universality of value, and ultimacy in authority are essential characteristics of the sacred, can there be anything sacred or any experience of sacrality in this historical flux?

Again the effects on religion, and on theology, of this aspect of relativity have been devastating. If the ontological relativity of all things has cast doubt on the possibility of a transcendent and self-sufficient God, the relativism of all things historical has seemed to make impossible any of those concrete, sacral evidences of his presence to his creatures upon which all religions are founded and on which depends any intelligible usage of religious language. Where are the ultimate events of revelation when all in history swims in the relativity of time; what is the Word of God amidst the welter and variety of historical words in scripture; what is the mind of the Church in this manifold of changing historical minds, each rooted in and so directly relevant only to its own epoch? The divine bases for authority in theology seem to have fled with this historicizing of everything historical, leaving us with only the tatters of merely human authorities—a "Hebrew understanding," an "apostolic faith," a "patristic mind," "Medieval viewpoints," a "Reformation attitude," and even "nineteenth-century cosmologies." And if, correspondingly, all faiths and world views are thus historical, relative to their stage and place in general history, how can any one of them claim our ultimate allegiance or promise an ultimate truth or an ultimate salvation? Above all, as the language analysts ask, where do we get this word "absolute," and what is its possible legitimate usage? Is anything absolute in the nature or history that we experience? What then do we *mean* by these words that point beyond

[16] For an excellent discussion of the character of modern historical relativism in thought and the problems it raises, cf. Gordon Kaufman, *Relativism, Knowledge, and Faith* (Chicago: University of Chicago Press, 1960); also, H. Richard Niebuhr, *The Meaning of Revelation* (New York: Macmillan Company, 1941).

the levels of our ordinary experience and so beyond the ordinary usages of language? How can we ever talk meaningfully of transcendence when all experience is of the relative? The relativity of all things to one another, then, has seemed to destroy any authoritative basis for religious belief in doctrine, any ground in experience for our concepts of the absolute or the sacred, and any intelligible usage to language referent beyond the nexus of relative causes to their ultimate ground or goal. The difficulties which such a view of the relativity of all that we experience makes for a theology based on a divine and therefore absolute revelation in historical events, witnessed to by an authoritative scripture and proclaimed by an authoritative church, are obvious.

A final implication of this relativistic understanding of all things concerns the intelligibility of religious or theological language. If all that is is to be understood in terms of the nexus of causes and factors which give it birth, then explanation—in nature, history, or even psychology—is confined to that interacting nexus of relative causes or factors. It is a basic assumption of such a view that no explanatory factor unrelated to this interlocking system can enter in from the outside[17]: natural events are exhaustively explained by natural causes, not by divine acts; historical explanations are confined to the plane of natural, social, and psychological factors, and no Apollo, no Ares, and no Aphrodite band together to cause the wars of history. Intelligible assertions about reality are, therefore, confined to the plane of finite factors, to the nexus of which the immediate given is composed. Assertive or indicative language, then, is monodimensional, referent only to finitude and its factors. Symbolic or religious language, referent to a sacral or ultimate dimension appearing within the finite media, is *ipso facto* unintelligible to this consciousness, a form of superstitious explanation viable only before the nexus of causal

[17] Cf. A. N. Whitehead, *Process and Reality, op. cit.*, for a metaphysical explication of this naturalistic principle in what he calls the "ontological principle of explanation" (pp. 36–37). In historical studies, this principle of explanation is most naturally associated with the name of Ernst Troeltsch. Cf. his essay *Der Historismus und seine Probleme*, Gesammelte Werke, vol. 3 (Tubingen: J. C. B. Mohr, 1922), and the article on "Historiography" in *The Encyclopedia of Religion and Ethics*, ed. James Hastings, vol. 6 (New York: Charles Scribner's Sons, 1914), pp. 716–723.

factors was discerned and understood. We noted above how the sense of contingency and its correlate empiricism led to this restriction of intelligible language to the immediately given; now we see even more clearly how the modern apprehension of the relativity of all things leads in the same direction. It almost seems as if the modern consciousness could be defined as "antisymbolic" in this sense, and that inevitably for this consciousness the *word* God as well as the *being* God would be dead.

3. Another major theme of the modern consciousness, closely related to the preceding, is that of *temporality* or *transience,* the becomingness and so the mortality of all the things there are. All is in time, and time being in all things, each has its appointed terminus.[18] The Greeks, of course, realized this transience; but, as with the older view of contingency, they never thought of asserting it about reality as a *whole.* Just as to Aristotle and to Thomas contingency pointed beyond itself to a level of necessity and utter rationality, so transience and becoming pointed the Hellenic mind beyond itself to a ground that was eternal being.[19] As in the case of the concept of contingency, however, the meaning of the modern sense of temporality or becoming is precisely the opposite, for here any dependence of that which is temporal on that which is not transient or in passage is denied. What is new, therefore, in the modern sense of transience is its *total*

[18] Nathan A. Scott, Jr., puts this very beautifully in his essay "Mimesis and Time in Modern Literature": "Human life is drenched in time . . . for we are but the merest reeds in nature, feeble at best, and soon withering away: we are not creatures of permanence; nothing stays for us, and there is no escaping what Camus called 'the cruel mathematics that command our condition' . . . for the career of anything that grows and develops is bracketed within the consecutive flow of temporality, and death is the form that finality takes for all living things, whether they be vegetable or animal or human." Nathan A. Scott, Jr., *The Broken Center; Studies in the Theological Horizon of Modern Literature* (New Haven: Yale University Press, 1966), p. 25.

[19] Cf. Aristotle, *The Physics*, Book IV, Chapter 12, 221a, 221b; Marcus Aurelius, *Meditations*, Book II, Sections 14, 17; Book VII, Section 19; Book IX, Sections 14, 28. Cf. also Psalms 39 and 90. For the most acute sense in ancient literature of the passage of all things, and of the unreality of the fleeting present, which is all that "is" for us, cf. Augustine, *The Confessions*, Book XI, Chapter 15, Sections 18–20.

character. For moderns, time is the most fundamental structure of all experienced being.[20] All is becoming, all is changing, all is in passage out of the past and into the future, and so all causes and all effects come and go—and all is mortal—and nothing else is real. There is in direct experience nothing else besides creatures which "never really are"[21]—and death or perishing claims all creatures.

It is no wonder that the traditional category of pure being, combining as it does necessity, absoluteness, rationality, and now eternity, has had rough going in recent times. Almost every significant aspect of the modern spirit—its sense of contingency, of relativity, of temporality, and of transience—moves in exactly the opposite direction from the concept of a necessary, self-sufficient, changeless, unrelated, and eternal being. The result, as many representatives of what is called traditional theism have yet to learn, is that many of the traditional modes of understanding deity—especially that associated with an independent, unrelated, changeless *actus purus*—are quite irrelevant and meaningless to the modern intelligence. The anachronism of these traditional views is not, as some think, the major problem for the idea of God[22]; nevertheless there is no doubt that *this* inherited form of traditional theism is quite irrelevant as a proposal in theology to-

[20] A list of the most significant and influential of modern ontologists establishes this generalization that temporality and change are contemporaneously taken as the main and even the exhaustive traits of "being": Hegel, Bergson, Alexander, Dewey, Santayana, Whitehead, Husserl, and Heidegger.

[21] This is the way that Whitehead, following Plato, characterizes all actual entities: "Always becoming and never really are." *Adventures of Ideas, op. cit.*, p. 209. The reference from Plato is from the *Timaeus*, Section 52.

[22] This is the main theme of Leslie Dewart's stimulating book, *The Future of Belief* (New York: Herder and Herder, 1966), as it is of the continual polemic of process philosophy against traditional theism, namely that the classical metaphysical concept of God is antithetical to the modern consciousness, and thus hinders rather than aids religious belief. While we agree with this critique of traditional forms of theism, we also believe that the current problems for theology lie much deeper than this critique of traditional metaphysics indicates, and include all forms—even modern ones—of metaphysical and theological discussion.

day, and that the quicker this is understood, the more creative traditional theology will be. The fact is that, to the modern mind, every form of logical argument that tries to point toward this traditional Aristotelian or Thomist concept of God seems not rational but precisely irrational or strange. To subscribe to these arguments, therefore, a modern man has in fact to accept this older world view on faith since it is so alien to his own contemporary spiritual world; that is, one has to "believe" first if one is to regard the establishment and the delineation of this Hellenic-Medieval world as philosophy and not as nostalgic fantasy. Because of the vast changes in the Western cultural mood we have outlined, what was in one age a natural theology based in large measure on reason and experience alone, has become in our secular age the last, not even the first, section of a theology founded solely on "faith" in past verities.

This emphasis on becoming, on transience and change, is almost as fundamental a characteristic of the modern spirit as is that of contingency and interrelatedness. It has been expressed in a variety of ways and has had innumerable implications for our spiritual, philosophical, and religious life. As we have indicated, it has, along with the notion of internal relations, made the concept of changeless, self-sufficient being virtually meaningless to our age; and since at least Hegel almost every contemporary theology consequently exhibits a view of deity as essentially dynamic, in relations, and so in process, rather than as essentially unrelated and static. Perhaps even more important, it has focused attention on patterns of development and process in time rather than on the eternally recurrent structures of existence. Modern man thus has tended to find the meaning of his history in patterns of development leading toward a future goal, rather than through his reiterated participation in an eternal order established at the beginning of things[23]—as the modern "myths" of progress and of the Marxist dialectic so well illustrate. Consequently time and history have replaced the eternal order of nature as the loci of human significance, and modern man has become above all conscious

[23] Cf. Eliade, *Patterns in Comparative Religion, op. cit.*, esp. pp. 33, 410, and 429–430; cf. also *Cosmos and History* (New York: Harper Torchbooks, 1959), Chapters 1 and 2.

of his "historicity," of his openness to the future, of the creative
possibilities of his freedom, and so of the importance of the category of hope for the historical future. In theology the influence of
this "temporalism" has been enormous and, making union with
the Biblical emphasis on history, has tended to replace Hellenic
categories of eternity with those of historical activity,[24] and to
understand Christian hope not in terms of a supratemporal end
to time but in the terms of political progress and of eschatological
expectation for a "new" in the continuing processes of time. The
modern secular spirit is thus "time-bound" in a way that no previous age in our culture has been; our life is bounded by birth and
by death, and the relevant environment for our hopes, as for our
fears, is confined to the temporal processes of nature and of history.

    As a result, of almost all the concepts in the theological
tradition that seem meaningless and unreal to the modern mind,
the primary one is surely that of a divine eternity that transcends
temporal passage, and the correlative concepts of everlasting life,
eternal judgment, and eternal salvation. Where on earth, asks the
modern empirical man, except in the abstract and therefore unreal realms of mathematics, logic, and fantasy, does a concept
such as that of eternity find its base in experience? What lodgment has it in reality when all our experience, external and internal alike, knows only transience, the becoming and the death
of all that once had life? Does not all we know come to be and
pass away—and how can we know or experience anything more
than this? Is not all talk of things transcendent to mortal passage
just protective illusion, the product of fears and of hopes—and
even harmful besides, since its comforting but illusory fantasy
dulls the cold shock of the prospect of our own death, that final
term toward which all authentic existence, existence decisively at

    [24] Almost all of recent "Biblical theology" has represented this
temporalist, dynamic mind-set as opposed to the static categories of
changelessness and of eternity of the Hellenic tradition. Most prominent
among them, of course, is Oscar Cullman in his *Christ and Time* (Philadelphia: Westminster Press, 1940), and now, in a new "eschatological"
vein, the thought of Jürgen Moltmann, *The Theology of Hope* (New
York: Harper & Row, 1967), Wolfhart Pannenberg and Johannes B.
Metz, S.J.

grips with its own reality, points? Such are the searching questions facing current theology which the fact of universal transience poses for us—questions which in *un*reflective form each layman's gaze asks of the cleric when the latter tries stumblingly to speak of the Christian answer to the death of some loved one.

There seems to be, then, no direct experience of an eternity that transcends passage for transient men. Characteristically, therefore, modern reflection finds this category meaningless, and as a result discussion of the eternal or transtemporal aspects of eschatology have almost disappeared from contemporary theological reflection. While, therefore, a *historical* interpretation of eschatology (i.e., as the "new" in the continuing process of time) has perhaps become more meaningful to modern than to medieval men, nevertheless the fundamental basis of even such a historical eschatology, namely the whole transtemporal structure of Christian faith, fear and hope, has been rendered radically equivocal if not meaningless to this modern temporalist spirit. For if there be nothing that transcends passage, there can hardly be an "eschatological" interpretation of history that has meaning. Much as the transnatural source of existence in God's being, and the absolute center of history in the Incarnation, have been made empty by the themes of contingency and relativism, so every form of eschatology has been subverted by the exclusive emphasis of the secular spirit on temporal passage. As much as any other factor, the temporalist understanding of reality has rendered equivocal and empty any relevant notion of God and of the permanence and stability of his promises for salvation, individual or historical.

4. *Autonomy.* The three faces of the modern secular spirit so far portrayed—contingency, relativism, and temporality—might seem grim indeed were it not for the fourth, which is the source of whatever optimism and courage the modern spirit possesses. Little if any confidence or courage come to modern man from his wider, cosmic environment where, as we have seen, all is blind, relative, and transient. In this sense, he is truly "on his own," an alien set within a context that is indifferent and so irrelevant to his own deepest purposes, and whatever hope and meaning he may have must come to him from himself.

The fourth category of modern secularity is, therefore, the autonomy and freedom of man, his inalienable birthright and, fortunately, his innate capacity to know his own truth, to decide about his own existence, to create his own meaning, and to establish his own values. This view of man as a self-creative being first began to manifest itself, one might say, in the Renaissance and Reformation, but has become stronger, more precise and more inward since then. It increased in the Enlightenment drive for intellectual and political freedom,[25] and in the Romantic movement's emphasis on the uniqueness and inwardness of each individual man's experience and feeling;[26] and it has been made fully explicit in our day in existentialism, psychoanalysis, and democratic theories. This affirmation of freedom, or of self-determination by one's own mind and will, as the essential character of man and so as the necessary condition for human self-realization, is one of the strongest voices of modernity and possibly the most creative. It is, as we noted, a closely correlative concept to those of becoming, of change, of history, and so of the openness of the future to creative action by man's freedom. The sense of the contingency, the relativity, and the transience of all that is, effected, so to speak, the destruction of the "gods" who had determined man's life without his consent; and this relativization and secularization of the given structures of life opened the present and, through it, the future to man's creativity. And with this toppling of sacral orders inherited from the past, man was now free *in* history in a new way, on his own in a history to which he and he alone must give structure and meaning. The sense of the "historicity" of man, a typically modern concept, thus involves not only the imbeddedness of man within historical relativity, but paradoxically also his power through autonomous freedom to rise above that nexus and to create his own essence in an open future.

In any case, this emphasis on freedom and autonomy lies

[25] Cf., as three examples, John Locke, *Concerning Civil Government*, Chapters I and X; Immanuel Kant, "What Is Enlightenment?"; and John Stuart Mill, *On Liberty*.
[26] Cf., for example, F. Schleiermacher, *On Religion: Speeches to Its Cultured Despisers,* trans. John Oman (New York: Frederick Ungar, 1955), Speeches I and II.

behind those social ideals, essential to modern existence, of the unhampered freedom of scientific and of scholarly inquiry. It forms both the deepest basis and the acknowledged goal of our educational institutions, our creative political structures, our efforts at social reform, our burgeoning psychoanalysis and counseling, and even our endeavors to control our environment and ourselves through scientific knowledge and technology.[27] And it provides the deepest themes for our current literature, existentialist philosophy and theology. If it believes anything at all, the modern spirit holds that a man must, in some essential regard, live his life in autonomy if that life is to be creative and human, and insofar as it is optimistic in mood, this spirit believes that man can increasingly exercise his freedom over the blind forces of destiny and so "be master of his own fate." Thus the modern spirit, at least in the West, is dedicated to the proposition that any external social authority—whether of church, of state, of local community, or of family—will in the end only crush man's humanity if his own personal being does not participate fully and voluntarily in whatever help that authority represents and in whatever creative forms his life may take. And where that personal freedom is not so highly valued, as in the East, it is the freedom of socialist man as a communal being over the economic and political fates that is affirmed.

It is, perhaps, over an assessment of the possibilities of

[27] This assertion of freedom and autonomy is, of course, in real tension with that other aspect of the modern spirit which emphasizes that all events, including those which make up the human organism, have determining causes and are therefore amenable to scientific understanding. To unravel this paradox of freedom and determinism within modern scientific thought itself is too big a task for a footnote. Suffice it here to say that, when modern science reviews its *conclusions* about man as an *object* of its inquiry, it finds man almost totally determined. When, however, it considers science itself as a human enterprise carried on necessarily by free, inquiring scientists manipulating their environment and rationally arriving at their conclusions, that is, when scientific man is the *subject* and not the *object* of science, the scientific mentality is inclined to emphasize freedom and not determinism. That is to say, it emphasizes the necessity for science of a context of freedom, and the real possibilities of new freedom over human destiny which scientific knowledge and technology bring to man.

this freedom for creative action in history that the major trends of modern thought diverge. For the Marxists, freedom, once realized through the revolution and the establishment of the communist stage, can create a totally new day for man in history where external authority, alienation, injustice, and even selfishness will vanish; where, in Marx's words, "the free development of each is the condition for the free development of all."[28] The more naturalistic and pragmatic American tradition sees in a free, scientific intelligence and a democratic morality emancipated from past religious absolutes, the possibility of the creation of ever more meaningful structures in our natural and social relations.[29] The existentialists, typically European in tradition, take a dimmer view of these external and historical possibilities and see this freedom as only the inward capacity for personal autonomy and integrity in the face of a meaningless cosmos and an equally erratic history which we can neither affect nor control. However much they may diverge in their assessments of the potentialities of free action in relation to historical progress and the achievement of objective social values, each of these three potent contemporary alternatives regards the full usage of creative human freedom as the essential key to the realization of value. Modern man is not seeking for a lost "essence" or "order" which he may regain; he is seeking rather for the opportunity to exercise his own freedom in order to create value and so to refashion history according to his freely chosen images. For all forms of modern thought, salvation comes *through* the realization of freedom; it can never be a salvation *from* freedom, or even a transformation from beyond ourselves *of* our freedom. In this sense, autonomy is the key to the modern understanding of freedom and the corresponding key to most of our hopes.

Obviously, this assertion of autonomous freedom and self-direction as the key to human self-fulfilment is subversive

---

[28] Karl Marx and Friedrich Engels, *Manifesto of the Communist Party*.

[29] More than any other great contemporary figure, John Dewey represents this optimistic view of human autonomy when it is freed from dogma, guided by the scientific method and spirit, and applied morally to our social problems.

of many of the historic forms of religion, with their traditional authorities of various sorts stemming from the distant past, their requirements of faith, obedience, submission, and self-surrender, and their insistence that man is fulfilled when he patterns himself according to the divine image. Is not—so the modern spirit declares—revelation the denial of all autonomy in inquiry and rationality; is not a divine law the denial of personal autonomy in ethics; above all, is not God, if he be at all, the final challenge to my creativity as a man? Religion, said Ludwig Feuerbach, drains away all the vitality and interest man may summon for autonomous efforts; it smothers in passivity the infinite possibilities of control over his own destiny which man might exert; and it makes of him a submissive, weak, empty creature dependent on unreal forces beyond him.[30] And for much the same reason Nietzsche defiantly cried that, if there were a God, he would be the final challenge to his creativity as a man—to his ability, that is, to draw all of his values and meanings from out of his own self-creativity.[31] This sense of opposition between creative autonomy and religion has been one of the most recurrent themes of modern philosophy, psychology, literature, and even theology, and we must admit that the history of the resistance by religious authorities against the establishment of these freedoms hardly refutes this secular thesis.

In the above, we have tried to give a picture of the main elements of the secular spirit, those fundamental assumptions about reality, truth, and value which determine our period and in terms of which any creative cultural expression, literary, artistic, philosophical, or religious, must express itself if it is to be relevant and meaningful to us. The main picture we have gained from our description is that which shows man as set within a contingent, relative, and temporal context in which no ultimate order, coherence, or meaning—either in terms of an eternal rational structure or a sovereign divine will—appears, and so in which man is forced

[30] Cf. Ludwig Feuerbach, *The Essence of Christianity* (New York: Harper Torchbooks, 1957), especially Chapter I.

[31] Friedrich Nietzsche, *Thus Spake Zarathustra*, Section 24, "In the Happy Isles."

(or enabled) to create by his own powers whatever meaning his life on earth may achieve. What man can know and speak meaningfully about is only the changing natural and social world around him which he directly experiences, and possibly his own inner psyche; what he can do is confined to the worlds of engineering, economics, politics, and culture; what he values are his relations to nature, the products of his industry, the artistic works he can create or enjoy, the reforms in historical life he can institute, and the personal contacts with others he can have. Whatever reality, knowledge, or value there may be anywhere lies in the immediate, the here and now, in this world which we can sense and manipulate. And whatever language is intelligible and meaningful in such a world is monodimensional language, referent to the nexus of natural, historical, and psychological causes that surround and create us, but not referent to any dimension or factor beyond that realm of contingency, relativity, and transience. Such a mood knows or needs no other sacred world beyond this and agrees that language referent to another such world, in terms either of philosophical thought or of religious faith, seems unreal and meaningless.

At its worst, this secular spirit is explicitly materialistic, hedonistic, and driven toward worldly success and power. At its best, it has developed a healthy love of the joys of life and, in its developing humanitarianism, a compassionate concern for the neighbor's welfare, seeking to bring well-being into all of life, to increase freedom, to strengthen selfhood and dignity, and to spread the goods brought by technology and industry to all men alike. We should note that current discussions among Christians about ethical matters center around issues raised in connection with these two sets of *secular* values, that is, self-oriented material values as opposed to other-oriented humanitarian ones. Such traditionally "nonsecular" goals of Christian striving as a personal holiness required for heavenly salvation, asceticism, or a mystical contemplation directed to some transcendent goal are considered largely archaic and irrelevant by contemporary Christian ethicists.

As this last comment illustrates, churchmen, laity and theologians alike, are also secular. We not only accept, consciously and unconsciously, most of the attitudes we have here described; what is more, we rejoice in them and would defend them if challenged—possibly for theological reasons derived from the Bible! We use and enjoy the technology this spirit has produced; we approve its scientific methods and the knowledge derived therefrom; we seek to interpret and to validate our own religious faith as best we can with its categories and its criteria; and we understand whatever blessings religion gives to us largely in its valuational terms. We in the Church have, moreover, learned much from it. Mutual tolerance of differences of viewpoint and a humble spirit about the relative truths we continue to treasure have both come from this secular mood of relativity, historicity, and perpetual change. Above all, its humanitarian spirit has forced us to reaffirm that New Testament ideal of love for the neighbor that the churches had been wont to ignore. Secularism has been a more faithful and helpful critic of the churches than they have been of their society.

It is because of this developing vision that modern man's institutions, standards, and decisions have gradually become secular, based on his own powers of knowledge and of comprehension, and directed by his own pragmatic and immediate needs for this life, rather than on a sacred or ultimate ground given to us from beyond. Moreover, and this is a most relevant point for our purposes, each of these particular elements of this mood: its this-worldly character, its sense of contingency, relativism, temporality, and autonomy, and its confinement of thought and language to the sphere of the immediately given, have been in increasing tension if not in contradiction with traditional religious beliefs, ideas, and attitudes. It is in the light of this tension between the secular vision so understood and the characteristic emphases of Christian faith that the recent history of theology, and especially the present ferment, are to be understood. In order, however, to comprehend the movements in theology which have led up to this ferment, let us look for a moment at the historical development of this secular spirit—the successive stages in which it manifested itself. For it did not arrive in its present form, as described above, all at once or full-blown.

The development of this spirit or mood is, of course, practically coextensive with the history of Western culture since the Renaissance. We shall mention only the progress of that aspect of this mood which is central to theology, namely the loss of a sense of ultimate coherence or meaning in the cosmic environment of man and the gradual shifting of the locus of meaning and hope to the capacities of autonomous man. Perhaps the most significant factor for theology in the historical development of the secular spirit has been the vastly increasing radicality with which this denial of ultimate coherence has been expressed. When this spirit first appeared, some three hundred years ago, with the early Enlightenment criticism of a transrational revelation and a transcendent God beyond the reach of man's thinking, there was still retained, in Descartes, Leibniz, and Spinoza,[32] in the Deists, and even in the atheistic French physiocrats, a sense of an ultimate rational order in Nature which gave form and coherence to man's life.[33] Such a belief in an objective, rational order received, then, a further shock from the more radical criticism of British empiricism, culminating in Hume, and in the critical phase of Kant's writings.[34] In both, it became clear that thinking could neither assume nor establish through philosophical argument this environment of ultimate coherence, whether divine or otherwise, although to be sure other powers of man's spirit, related to other

[32] Cf. especially René Descartes, *Discourse on Method* and *Meditations;* Liebniz, *The Monadology* and *The Theodicy;* and Spinoza, *The Ethics*, especially the first part.

[33] The role of Nature as exemplifying a rational and moral order of coherence and thus as the foundation rather than the antithesis of human meanings and hope, is well illustrated by the following from Buffon: "Oh Nature, sovereign of all beings! And ye, her adorable daughters, Virtue, Reason, and Truth! remain forever our revered protectors! it is to you that belong the praises of the human race.... Show us then, O Nature! that which man ought to do. . . . unite, O assisting deities! . . . Banish error from our mind; wickedness from our hearts; confusion from our footsteps; cause knowledge to extend its salubrious reign; goodness to occupy our souls; serenity to occupy our bosoms." *Epoques de la Nature*, VII, quoted in J. H. Randall, Jr., *The Making of the Modern Mind* (Cambridge, Mass.: Houghton Mifflin Co., 1940), p. 279.

[34] Cf. especially David Hume's *Essay Concerning Human Understanding and Dialogues Concerning Natural Religion,* and Kant's *Critique of Pure Reason,* Book II, Chapters 2 and 3.

aspects of experience (in Kant's case, the moral nature of man[35]), might reach beyond this strict confinement of thinking to the manifold of sensible experience and arrive at noumenal reality and the divine. In the Romantic philosophies that were based on these other aspects of experience, the attack on a transcendent deity continued. In Hegel, Schelling, and Schleiermacher, the divine was brought down out of its changeless, self-sufficient, and separated heaven and related intrinsically to the finite realities that make up the concreteness of our experience. An Absolute remains in each of these great Romantic systems, but in each case it is as the Whole or Unity of the particulars immanent within the immediate and not separable from it, and to be described always in relation to our concrete feelings and thinking, never in abstraction or isolation from them "as it is in itself."[36] With the further development of evolutionistic and process forms of thought in the second half of the nineteenth century, these immanent rational and Romantic Absolutes themselves vanished. All now becomes in process, all changes and develops, and nothing original is ever the same at the end; we are in a world of continual flux, where forms themselves are fluid and only process is real. Nevertheless, the nineteenth-century vision of total becoming is by no means the end of the secular road. A permanent structure of coherence within this universal flux remained for most of the nineteenth century as a dominant factor guiding these processes of change. This coherence was most widely conceived of in Evolutionary terms as the universal Law of Progress, or as the developing Deity of Process,[37] which in each changing epoch integrates into an increasing harmony the finite, contingent, and transient realities of ordinary experience. Thus, to sum up, during the eighteenth and nineteenth centuries the concept of a transcendent, self-sufficient Absolute or deity gradually disap-

[35] Cf. Kant, *Critique of Practical Reason*, Book II, Chapter 2.

[36] Cf. Hegel, *Philosophy of History*, Introduction; and *The Phenomenology of Spirit;* and Friedrich Schleiermacher, *On Religion: Speeches to Its Cultured Despisers* and *The Christian Faith*.

[37] Cf. especially Samuel Alexander, *Space, Time, and Deity* (New York: The Humanities Press, 1950), and *Philosophical and Literary Pieces* (London: Macmillan & Company, 1939); and Whitehead, *Process and Reality,* Book 5.

pears; still there does remain for the secular minds of these times
a sense of an ultimate order, coherence, and purpose residing in
the temporal passage of things, directing it onward toward
higher value and thus giving it meaning. It is this assumption that
lies at the base of present process philosophy, perhaps the most
lively remaining form of speculative rationalism.

When, however, we move out of nineteenth-century
thinking into those forms of thought which we take to be more
typical of twentieth-century philosophy, even this sense of an
immanent teleology, of an abiding principle of coherence in the
environment as a whole, vanishes. The virtual death of speculative idealism among relevant philosophies is one major sign of
this increasingly radical assessment of the widest environment of
the "real"; no longer can man meaningfully conceive it as characterized by the meanings, purposes, experience, and thought he
finds in himself—as all idealism assumed.[38] Moreover, those philosophies which have replaced idealism—empiricism, relativism, modern naturalism, linguistic philosophy, and existentialism—however they may differ in other regards, unite in their
picture of man and the relation of his existence to the real environment that has produced him. In naturalism, that cosmos is
merely Nature, blind and purposeless, and so, while it supports
the existence and survival of man its child, his inwardness, his
search for meaning, for order, and for love find no reflection or
counterpart in the world around him. For naturalism there is no
"ultimate meaning" to the system of things, and man must be
content with the plural world of finite causes and contingent entities in which he finds himself and which his critical intelligence
may direct to his own purposes. Much the same fundamental
vision lies back of most linguistic philosophy, both positivistic
and analytic, although this vision is here expressed in linguistic
and not in ontological form. Man's reflective thought, says this

---

[38] Only Edmund Husserl, among influential modern philosophers, represents this idealistic heritage with his concept of the transcendental ego creative of its world; however, his radical adherence to
the *epoche*, to the bracketing of questions of reality and of being, indicates that with him, too, speculative idealism, an "overview" of all of
reality, has died. Edmund Husserl, *Ideas* (New York: Collier Books,
1962), on the ego, pp. 136ff., 142; and on bracketing, pp. 163ff., 206,
and 244.

whole movement, cannot by rational intuition or speculative generalization reach beyond the given, as known by science or common sense, to discover an ultimate order, purpose, or being.[39] Philosophical inquiry neither *knows* reality more deeply, nor can it know any other reality than is known in commonsense life or in science: we have given up, says John Wisdom, "the absurdity of exploring the universe in an armchair";[40] what philosophy can do is not to talk about the Real, but only to talk about talk alone.[41] All man can know, therefore, and thus guide his life by, are the factual situations that he can investigate by science, the psychological, historical, and social situations within which his emo-

[39] Cf. A. J. Ayer's well-known description of the futility of metaphysical inquiry: "We may accordingly define a metaphysical sentence as a sentence which purports to express a genuine proposition, but does, in fact, express neither a tautology nor an empirical hypothesis. And as tautologies and empirical hypotheses form the entire class of significant propositions, we are justified in concluding that all metaphysical assertions are nonsensible." A. J. Ayer, *Language, Truth, and Logic* (London: Victor Gollancz, Ltd., 1950), p. 41.

Two quotations from the later Wittgenstein illustrate this noncognitive role for language philosophy, i.e., that it is not a mode of *knowing* reality as in science, but only of analyzing the way we speak about things. Its object is not the "real," "concreteness," nor the actual entity, but the usages and rules of speech. "Philosophers constantly see the method of science before their eyes, and they are irresistibly tempted to ask and answer questions in the way science does. This tendency is the real source of metaphysics and leads the philosopher into complete darkness. I want to say here that it can never be our job to reduce anything to anything, or to explain anything. Philosophy really *is* 'purely description.'" Ludwig Wittgenstein, *The Blue and Brown Books* (New York: Harper & Brothers, 1960), p. 18.

"We must do away with all *explanation,* and description alone must take its place. And this description gets its light, that is to say, its purpose, from the philosophical problems. These are, of course, not empirical problems; they are solved, rather, by looking into the workings of our language, and that in such a way as to make us recognize these workings: *in despite of* an urge to misunderstand them . . . philosophy is a battle against the bewitchment of our intelligence by means of language." Wittgenstein, *Philosophical Investigations* (Oxford: Blackwell, 1963), p. 47e (no. 109).

[40] John Wisdom, "The Metamorphosis of Metaphysics," ed. J. M. Findlay, *Studies in Philosophy* (London: Oxford University Press, 1966), p. 218.

[41] A further clarification of the characteristic aims and limits of

tional, political, and moral senses arise, and the linguistic situations expressive of these other areas—and only expressive of them and not of any further order or realm. Here, too, since our knowledge is confined to the world of science and of our ordinary experience of things and persons, no wider or ultimate structure in which man's life is set is or can be known. Where, therefore, it is not infused by a specifically religious interest, linguistic philosophy, too, tends to reflect the naturalistic attitudes toward what is real in our world and so toward the limits of possible thinking.

In existentialism, this separation of man's inwardness and thought from the wider cosmic environment reaches its climax.[42] Not only, on this view, is the objective environment of

what is now called "ordinary language philosophy" is the following from the later, and much chastened, A. J. Ayer: "But however uncertain they may be about the details, there is a fair measure of agreement among philosophers that theirs is what is technically called a second-order subject. They do not set out to describe, or even to explain, the world, still less to change it. Their concern is only with the way in which we speak about the world. Philosophy is, it has been said, talk about talk." A. J. Ayer, *The Concept of a Person and Other Essays* (London: Macmillan & Company, 1963), p. 3.

[42] In a brilliant series of essays, Karl Löwith has phrased very powerfully this mood of alienation from the universe characteristic, as he sees it, of the modern spirit and exemplified primarily in existentialism: "It is against the background of nature as conceived by modern natural science that existentialism itself comes into existence, for its basic experience is not the historicity but the contingency of human existence within the whole of the natural world. . . . There is an intimate relation between the experience of a naked, factual, absurd existence, cast into the world, and the anonymity of the world itself in which we happen to exist. . . . And indeed, how can one feel at home in a universe which is conceived as the chance result of statistical probabilities and which is said to come into existence through an explosion? Such a universe cannot inspire confidence or sympathy, nor can it give orientation and meaning to man's existence in it. We are then indeed cast into this world, and have therefore to 'project' ourselves. . . . Perhaps one could say that modernity begins with the dissolution of a natural and social order in which man was supposed to have a definite nature and place, while modern man 'exists,' displaced and out of place, in extreme situations on the edge of chaos." Karl Löwith, *Nature, History, and Existentialism.*, pp. 24, 25, 28, and 32.

man's life blind, mechanical, and inexorable power—it is absurd; and it is absurd because it is totally antithetical to all the important aspects, characteristics, and tasks of man's own being.[43] Even knowledge of that universe is irrelevant to human beings, since for man to understand himself in any terms similar to his scientific understanding of the objective nature around him spells destruction for the unique being of man.[44] While the naturalist understands himself as merely a part of mechanical and blind nature and hopes to use technological intelligence to better his life, and the positivist tries his best not to think at all about these things, the existentialist deliberately cuts the cord between himself and his objective environment. An objective order in which man's life is set would, to him, crush man's freedom completely and shatter his chance of becoming, through his own decision and will, the kind of authentic being he is. Alone, anxious, driving toward death, founded upon an absurd Void, a Nothing that will in the end claim him, and yet personally responsible for himself, man in existentialism can only realize himself through his own inner resoluteness and creative freedom.

It is not rash to state that these forms of thought—naturalism, linguistic analysis, and existentialism—are typical of our time, for, except where specific religious interests maintain an older speculative metaphysical tradition, as in process philosophy, or else give wings to the reach of linguistic analysis, of existentialism, or of phenomenology, these three approaches remain dominant in the West. For all their manifest differences, in

[43] It is Albert Camus who expresses most powerfully this existential sense of the utter irrationality and absurdity (to man) of his world and so the most extreme alienation from the universe around us: "In this unintelligible and limited universe, man's fate henceforth assumes its meaning. A horde of irrationals has sprung up and surrounds him until his ultimate end. In his recovered and now studied lucidity, the feeling of the absurd becomes clear and definite. . . . This world in itself is not reasonable, that is all that can be said. But what is absurd is the confrontation of this irrational and the wild longing for clarity whose call echoes in the human heart." "The absurd is borne of this confrontation between the human need and the unreasonable silence of the world." Albert Camus, *The Myth of Sisyphus,* translated by Justin O'Brien (New York: Vintage Books, 1955), pp. 16 and 21.
[44] Cf. Martin Heidegger, *Being and time,* pp. 79–86.

each of them one sees a vivid expression of what we are calling the present-day "raw" or hard secularity, far different from the sense of a divine rationality of Nature in the eighteenth century or of Evolutionary Progress in the nineteenth. Whatever our culture's pious or traditional protestations, man clearly no longer feels himself to be set within any basic order or context in terms of which he understands himself, that is, from which he draws not only his being, but also the meanings, standards, and values of his life. He is here alone an alien in the flux of reality, quite autonomous with regard to meaning and value, and able to speak and think intelligibly only of the things and persons around him, or of the character and depth of his own existence.[45]

It is no accident that the phrase "God is dead" has been taken as the symbol of this present-day mood.[46] But since, for this spirit, objective reality is also humanly speaking blind, purposeless, the absurd, we should add that *all* the gods are dead— that is, all ultimate structures of coherence, order, and value in the wider environment of man's life have vanished; and, finally, that symbolic or religious speech, referent to a dimension of mystery beyond the evident and the sensible, is also dead.[47]

[45] Cf. the excellent descriptions of the secular spirit in G. Vahanian, *The Death of God* (New York: George Braziller, 1961), pp. 147 and 187; and Cox, *The Secular City,* pp. 60–61.

[46] We have elaborated our view of the "secular mood" in terms of contemporary forms of philosophy for various reasons, some good and some bad. A quite similar conclusion could, I believe, have been achieved by an analysis of the modern sensibility as reported in contemporary literature and drama, in which the same fundamental vision appears: in the works of Kafka, Sartre, Camus, and Beckett; in Hemingway, Faulkner, Steinbeck, Golding, and Bellow; in Williams, O'Neill, Miller, Pinter, Ionesco, Genet—all bespeak, in optimistic or pessimistic fashion (usually the latter), the sense of man's ultimate estrangement from his universe, the lack of a sense of final order, harmony, purpose, or goodness to the world in which he finds himself, and so his consequent utter dependence on his own courage, love, "faith," and creativity to forge what meaning he can find in the brief span given to him—whether it is the form of Moses Herzog or of Zorba. For a very perceptive study of this mood expressing a "vacuum of belief" in a culture with a "metaphysical void," see the writings of Nathan A. Scott, Jr., especially his recent *The Broken Center,* *op. cit.*

[47] Again Richard Rubenstein expresses well this "naturalistic"

Darwin and Nietzsche, Russell and Freud, not Marx and Kierkegaard, are the real fathers of the present *Geist*. And it is this
spirit that provides, on the one hand, the deepest background for
the theological ferment we are describing and, on the other, sets
for other forms of contemporary theology their most baffling
problems. How *does* one speak of God in such a cultural mood?

---

awareness and so the feeling of living in an age of "the death of all
gods": "When I say we live in the time of the death of God, I mean that
the thread uniting God and man, heaven and earth, has been broken. We
stand in a cold, silent, unfeeling cosmos, unaided by any purposeful power
beyond our own resources. After Auschwitz, what else can a Jew say
about God? . . . I see no other way [than the phrase "death of God"] of
expressing the Void that confronts man where once God stood." Rubenstein, *After Auschwitz* (Indianapolis: Bobbs-Merrill Company, 1966),
p. 49.

3 / The Theological Background of the Present Crisis

As CAN BE IMAGINED, the influence of the accelerating secularity we have just outlined on religion and on religious thought has been immense. Some forms of Christianity and Judaism have sought to ward off this influence and to preserve their traditional doctrines, standards, and modes of worship virtually unchanged. In Protestantism, this has been the aim of many conservative and almost all fundamentalist groups; in Roman Catholicism, Vatican I is the permanent symbol of this effort; and in Judaism, Orthodoxy has represented this tendency. To this writer the more creative reaction has been to seek to come to terms explicitly with the modern world, largely on the wise ground that, if we are modern men in the balance of our life, we must be no less modern in our religious faith if that faith is to have any meaning for us or vitality in us. In general, there have been, since about 1800, two predominant reactions of accommodation to modern secularity on the part of Protestant Christianity: the first one, which characterized the creative wing of nineteenth-century Protestantism, is called "liberalism"; and the second, which has dominated twentieth-century Protestantism, is generally called "neoorthodoxy." Specifically, it is the breakup of *both* of these forms of accommodation to the secular spirit that has set the context for the present ferment; so let us briefly describe what these two movements were, and why they have tended in the present decade to dissolve.

Liberal theology can, I believe, best be described as the

deliberate attempt of religious thinkers, who accepted the results
of modern physical science and modern historical study, to make
their faith intelligible to the increasingly secular mind of the
nineteenth and early twentieth centuries. They felt that this accommodation was forced upon them because both the *basis* of traditional doctrines and the *content* of these doctrines seemed incredible to the intelligentsia of that age. The basis of Christian
doctrines, or the ground for belief in them—for example, creation, the fall, the election of Israel, the Incarnation, eternal life,
and so on—had for most of Protestantism been the infallible inspiration of scripture. This basis, however, had dissipated due to
the developments of science which had demonstrated the error of
important aspects of the traditional forms of these doctrines (for
example, that the earth had been created in six days circa 4004
B.C.). And as Auguste Sabatier pointed out in the latter part of
the nineteenth century, if *part* of an absolute authority, for example, an important statement of scripture, is shown to be false, then
the scripture in and of itself ceases to be an authority; for even
if we still accept other aspects of its message, it is on other
grounds than simply their presence in scripture.[1] Liberal Christians, who accepted these results of science, were forced therefore
to find other, more immediate grounds for Christian certainties
than the traditional Biblical authority that had broken down.
Hegel, for example, sought to establish the certainties of religious
faith on the basis of rational philosophical inquiry. Friedrich
Schleiermacher, the greatest of the early liberals, founded Christian doctrines on Christian religious experience. Albrecht Ritschl
rejected both metaphysics and experience as bases for religion
and, following Kant, established religion on the basis of man's
moral nature and its fulfilment in the historical growth of the
kingdom of God; religion, said he, provides the fundamental attitude toward reality and values which makes the historical and
personal development of man as a moral being in history pos-

---

[1] As Sabatier argues, to question even *one* proposition in scripture is to divest scripture of its own absolute authority, and to remove
that authority into the critical, questioning, and judging mind of the
reader. Cf. Auguste Sabatier, *Religions of Authority and the Religion of
the Spirit* (London: Williams & Norgate, 1904), pp. 255–260.

sible.[2] The many liberal theologies that followed generally took one of these roads, or a combination of them. In each case, some present facet of contemporary experience—rational or scientific inquiry, religious experience, or moral experience—was accepted as the base for religion and religious discourse, and so, quite naturally, traditional doctrines that contradicted the shape of that contemporary experience—that were incredible to the nineteenth-century mind—tended to disappear from liberal theology.

For this reason, with regard also to its *content*, liberal theology reflected the guiding ideas of the nineteenth century. To that scientific, immanentist, optimistic, and progressivist age, such traditional concepts as the supernatural and the transcendent, and the orthodox beliefs in miraculous intervention, in the fall of man into depravity, in the inability of man to know or to do the good, and in an ultimate condemnation of most men for eternity, seemed barbaric in the extreme, a function of the priestly gloom of earlier times, and by no means acceptable to a modern man. In place of these notions of divine transcendence, human depravity, and miraculous revelation and salvation, liberalism used that cluster of ideas which, as we noted, characterized the dominant forms of secularity in the nineteenth century. Especially relevant was the notion of reality as an immanent, evolutionary process of development over time from relative chaos to higher forms of life and of culture. The divine force, said liberal theology, whose immanent work in the process has brought about such progress toward higher, more coherent, more adaptive, and more moral goals, is what men have called God;[3] the gradual purposive de-

[2] Cf. Albrecht Ritschl, *The Christian Doctrine of Justification and Reconciliation* [translation of Volume III of the original work] (Clifton, N.J.: Reference Book Publishers, 1966); "Instruction in the Christian Religion," in A. T. Swing, *The Theology of Albrecht Ritschl* (London: Longmans, Green, and Company, 1901). For an interesting and new interpretation of Ritschl and his influence, emphasizing his own concern for history as the locus of religion and of religious certainty, cf. Philip Hefner, *The Vitalities of History* (New York: Harper & Row, 1966).

[3] This description of the view of God in liberal theology cannot be established by documentation here. Suffice it to say that the writer is confident that these characteristic features of the liberal God apply, with

velopment of man in history, from the level of primitive bar-
barism to that of the love exemplified by Jesus and the moral
idealism evident in liberal civilization, represents in actuality what
men once called the history of revelation and the history of salvation; and the eschatological goal of the divine purpose is not the
heaven of orthodox doctrine but the achievement of a historical
kingdom of God, a society of love and justice among men here
on earth. Liberalism was able thus to reformulate Christian doctrine on the basis of contemporary experience because the spirit
of its age, while more secular by far than that of the sixteenth or
seventeenth centuries, in which orthodoxy had been fashioned,
nevertheless retained that faith in the ultimate progressive order
and harmony of things which made belief in "higher purposes"
still obvious to most nineteenth-century men, and so made language about God and his intentions intelligible to their minds.

    Liberalism was one of the most courageous and momen-
tous movements of theology in all of Christian history. First of all,
let us note that it was "secular" in two specific and important respects: (1) it accepted as normative criteria for theology the
dominant scientific, philosophical, historical, and moral ideas of
its culture; and (2) it regarded Christian faith as relevant and
important solely because of its creative potentialities for the transformation of the common, historical life of mankind, that is, of
the secular world of social history. Thus it prepared the way for
whatever is currently creative in either Catholic or Protestant
aggiornamento, since it was the pioneer in transforming Christian thought and life in order that it might enter into the life of
the modern world.

    Liberalism achieved this accommodation to the modern
world in four creative ways, none of which has been repudiated
in subsequent movements in theology. (1) Under the impact of
the growth of physical science, it changed the conception of
Christian truth from that of divinely given and so infallible
propositions about all manner of things in heaven, on earth, and

---

variations, of course, for all its varieties, from Hegel and the right-wing
Hegelians, through Schleiermacher, Ritschl, Sabatier, and Walter Rauschenbusch, to H. N. Wieman, A. N. Whitehead, and Charles Hartshorne.

in history (the age, geography, and early history of the universe, for example), into a system of human, and so relative, symbols which elucidate the depth and mystery of existence but do not compete directly with either scientific or historical knowledge. (2) With the development of the sense of historical relativity, it changed the understanding of Christian doctrine from that of eternal statements of unchanging and thus unalterable validity, to that of relative human statements of Christian truth for their time, statements that reflect their own cultural situation and needs.[4] (3) It changed the understanding of the Christian life from that of a life directed by divine rules of holiness toward the transcendent goal of heaven, to that of a life devoted in present human community to the worldly goods of more justice, more freedom, and more security for all men.[5] (4) Finally, it conceived of the Christian as primarily obligated to show love and tolerance to all, whether they agreed with him religiously or not, and whether they are in his eyes heretics or not. Love of the dissenting neighbor rather than defense of the doctrines of the faith became the main Christian obligation, and tolerance became widespread among the churches. Every creative form of modern Christian

[4] Perhaps the first expression of this new view of doctrine appears with Schleiermacher in 1823, who, as is well known, understood all Christian dogmas and doctrines as reflections on Christian piety "for its time"; cf. *The Christian Faith*, trans. H. R. Mackintosh and J. S. Stewart (Edinburgh: T. and T. Clark, 1928), paragraphs 19 and 154. It was, however, Adolph von Harnack and Ernst Troeltsch at the turn of the century who most clearly realized this new "historical" view of doctrinal developments. Among the many problems involved in absorbing the modern spirit which contemporary liberal Roman Catholic thought has had to face, the admission that doctrines and even creeds are historical in character, relative to their time in that sense, and so subject to later change, criticism, and even abandonment, has been one of the most difficult. Cf. on this issue the work of Karl Rahner, S.J., especially *Theological Investigations* (Baltimore: Helicon Press, 1961–1967); vol. I, chaps. 1 and 3; vol. II, chaps. 2, 4, and 5; vol. V, chaps. 1, 4, and especially 19.

[5] There are many great liberal names connected with the rise of a reformist social or political consciousness as an essential element in Christian piety, but surely the greatest is that of Walter Rauschenbusch; cf. his *A Theology for the Social Gospel* (New York: Macmillan Co., 1918) and *Christianizing the Social Order* (New York: Macmillan Co., 1912).

7878   78 8

life, Protestant or Catholic (expressed universally in the documents of Vatican II), assumes these basic liberal contributions, however much they may or may not agree with other aspects of liberal theology.

In the second and third decades of the twentieth century, however, liberal theology ran into serious difficulties, both philosophical and religious, and gradually dissolved. The philosophical difficulties are evident from our discussion of the development of the secular mood from the nineteenth into the twentieth centuries. On its philosophical side, liberal theology had been based on the cognitive capacity of speculative or metaphysical reason to discern and establish an order of ultimate coherence and value in process which might be called God or which might be a trustworthy indication of God. Correspondingly, as the possibility of such rational metaphysical speculation leading to deity receded —with the rise of empirical naturalism, of positivism, and of existentialism—liberal theological discourse about God, based on either idealistic, evolutionistic, or process metaphysics, tended to become philosophically questionable. What had seemed eminently reasonable to the confident thinkers at the end of the nineteenth century, became sheer myth, the meaningless confusion or bewitchment of language, or an exercise in futile speculation undertaken only by pious minds, to most of the radically empirical or linguistic philosophers of the twentieth century.

Probably more important in the breakdown of liberal theology, however, were what may be called the "religious" difficulties of liberalism. As we have said, along with its scientific and historical concerns, liberalism imbibed from the nineteenth century a great many of that century's fundamental convictions about the ultimate destiny of history and of mankind—convictions that can only be termed "religious" in character, but which seemed at the time to be among the conclusions of modern science.[6] Prominent among these were the cosmic principle of Evo-

---

[6] For a most perceptive discussion of these "religious myths" that have paraded as science, and their relation to scientific discourse, see Stephen Toulmin, "Contemporary Scientific Mythology," in *Metaphysical Beliefs* (London: SCM Press, 1957), pp. 13–81. Toulmin's analysis is a good example of the way in which modern language philosophy

lution and its two important implications, namely the notion of the rational and moral perfectability of man, and the theory of historical progress. It was, as we noted, in terms of these concepts that liberalism understood the providential and saving activity of God in the world. Some of the more perceptive thinkers of the nineteenth century had, to be sure, already questioned the historical optimism latent in these notions.[7] But it was only with the turbulences, cruelty, and tragic dilemmas of twentieth-century experience that moderns generally realized that, in its optimism about the goodness of man and the progress of history, nineteenth-century culture had simply been wrong; history seemed to the twentieth-century mind as full of depravity and meaninglessness as was any period in the past. The consequent disintegration of the theory of universal progress meant the loss of that last vestige of faith in a cosmic order and meaning inherited from the Hellenic and the Christian past, and so there resulted that "raw secularity" with its antimetaphysical mood expressed in naturalism, positivism, and the existentialist philosophies of estrangement, which we have described.

In relation to such a secular spirit, the theology of liberalism inevitably disintegrated. For it had, as we saw, been founded on the nineteenth-century belief that ordinary, secular experience revealed an evolutionary, purposive order in things, that the character of process and of history was in evident fact a developmental career toward increased value. When twentieth-century secular life, as expressed in its philosophy, religion, and literature, could no longer find on the surface of history traces of such

---

questions on purely philosophical grounds those elements of ultimate meaning and coherence that still permeated nineteenth-century scientific and philosophical thinking, especially in relation to the category of evolution. As Toulmin argues, this principle of ultimate coherence and development is, if it has any ground at all, a *religious* principle and has neither a scientific nor a philosophical basis to which to appeal.

[7] Cf. the view of Jacob Burckhardt in his *Force and Freedom* (Boston: Beacon Press, 1964), especially Introduction, Chapters 4 and 6. Karl Löwith has an interesting essay showing that a gloomy view of the prospects of history—or, as *we* would put it, a "realistic" view—long antedated in the nineteenth century the general collapse of optimism in Europe with World War I. See, Löwith, *Nature, History, and Existentialism* (Evanston, Ill.: Northwestern University Press, 1966), Chapter 1.

an objective law of progress, a theology based on secular wisdom had no longer any way of speaking about God.

Certainly the most crucial factor both in this change in
the secular mood and in the consequent shift in theology was the
vastly increased sense of human and historical evil that has dominated the consciousness of the twentieth century. This sense of
evil has in turn created an awareness of the very possible, not to
say inevitable, breakdown of those historic liberal institutions
and values on which the nineteenth-century confidence in progress had been built. The two world wars, the breakup not only
of traditional but even of democratic and liberal European society, the eruption of massive evil in Nazism, the potentiality of
atomic destruction, the further potentiality of the future domination of the world's life by a totalitarian culture, even by that of
our own nation—all of these have made the doctrine of historical
progress and the notion of the perfectability of man and of society
incredible notions to most twentieth-century minds—except for
some remaining pockets of optimism in Middlewestern and West
Coast academic and bourgeois American life. History, taken in
its own terms, seemed devoid of coherence or meaning; whatever
hope man may have, therefore, cannot come from any built-in
cosmic or historical law or other immanent divine source. It must,
that is, come either from autonomous man's use of his scientific
intelligence and his innate moral will—from some purely autonomous source—or from some transcendent source beyond tragedy,[8] beyond the evident ambiguities of nature and history. And
because during the first half of the century the faith in man's
autonomous intelligence and goodwill and so his ability creatively
to deal with his social problems had rough going, the existentialist mood of cosmic despair seemed to dominate the intellectual world.

It was, therefore, in this historical situation that neoorthodox theology was born. But this theology drew a different con-

[8] *Beyond Tragedy* (New York: Scribner's, 1937) was the title
of one of Reinhold Niebuhr's earlier books which began to introduce
these themes into American religious life. Other crucial books of his
which heralded the advent and the actual domination in America of "neoorthodoxy" were *Moral Man and Immoral Society* (New York: Scribner's, 1932); *Reflections on the End of an Era* (New York: Charles Scribner's Sons, 1936); and *An Interpretation of Christian Ethics* (New York:
Harper & Bros., 1935).

clusion than did the secular philosophies of despair from this collapse of the optimism of nineteenth-century culture.[9] If, said the theologians, despite the now evident evil and tragedy of history, man is still to believe in God, in the goodness of life, and in the meaningfulness of history—and all neoorthodoxy assumed this not only as a possibility but even more as a necessity for creative human life—he must do so on grounds quite other than, if not antithetical to, secular wisdom.[10] "The word of man" (as Barth put it) had been shown to be false and self-destructive: false when it proclaimed the optimism of the nineteenth century, and demonic when this optimism changed into the fanaticisms of

[9] This description of neoorthodoxy is inescapably brief, and so, like all generalizations, at many points inaccurate. It is necessary, however, to attempt in some way to characterize recent Protestant theology if we are to understand its present predicaments. Under the term "neoorthodoxy," we mean to include, of course, such obvious figures as Karl Barth and Emil Brunner, Gustav Aulen, Anders Nygren, and, with qualifications to be mentioned, Paul Tillich and Rudolph Bultmann—and all those innumerable Continental figures who have reflected the neo-Reformation position. We would also include those "milder" Anglo-Saxon forms of neoorthodoxy or neo-Biblical theology represented by C. H. Dodd, Alan Richardson, John Marsh, John Baillie of the 1930s and 1940s, Donald Baillie and, as Americans, Reinhold Niebuhr, H. Richard Niebuhr, and, with some modifications, Robert Calhoun, John Bennett, Paul Lehman, David Roberts, and their many followers. As the literature of liberalism composed most of the creative theology written from 1820 to 1920, so the literature of neoorthodoxy composed most of the leading Protestant theological productions (except in Chicago) in Europe, England, and America, from 1918 (in Europe) and 1935 (in America) until roughly 1960.

[10] A prominent example of neoorthodox apologetics is found in the writings of Reinhold Niebuhr: history on its own reveals no ultimate coherence or meaning; man must have a faith in meaning if he is to avoid despair and to be creative; therefore belief in God, who alone can give meaning to history, is a necessity for creative worldliness—see especially *Faith and History* (New York: Charles Scribner's Sons, 1949). This argument was very potent against the optimistic secular culture which also assumed that history must have meaning if despair is to be avoided, but which could no longer find "secular evidences" of that meaning in a turbulent history. It broke down, however, when the existentialists, especially Camus, appeared and said man can only be authentic man if he does *not* believe in historical meaning; to be over against the Absurd is not to despair but, on the contrary, to encounter precisely the sole possibility for authenticity.

the twentieth century. If man is to be related to any sort of healing truth about himself and his destiny, he must listen not to the
immanent voice of human reason but to the Word of God alone.
Thus it was the vivid experience of cultural and historical breakdown that turned Christian minds away from the liberal theologies that had accommodated themselves with the crumbling
culture and, as grounds for Christian faith and hope, toward the
transcultural sources of religious faith and religious truth: to revelation, to the Bible, and to the classical doctrines of Creation, Fall,
Incarnation, and Grace which were found in the indigenous traditions of the churches. Instead of a "secular theology" of the
liberal sort, there appeared, therefore, a theology that deliberately
eschewed secular wisdom and sought to be Biblical and orthodox
in the twentieth-century world. Since this theology was, needless
to say, exceedingly wary of finding its truth compromised either
by the excessive optimism or by the excessive despair to which
the cultural *Geist* now seemed to be prone, its fundamental intention was to be *autonomous* in relation to worldly truth in the
sense that its central religious affirmations were to be based on
its own religious resources in revelation and tradition and not on
the problematic wisdom of man.[11]

   This theology, however, was by no means a simple return
to an unworldly orthodoxy. On the contrary, despite its antipathy
to much of the humanism that characterized the modern mind, it
accepted a great deal of its own liberal inheritance and so many
of the basic assumptions of the modern world view. It was at
least half secular and naturalistic in its attitudes, and was thus

----

[11] See especially Emil Brunner, *The Theology of Crisis* (New
York: Charles Scribner's Sons, 1929), *The Philosophy of Religion* (New
York: Scribner's, 1937), *Revelation and Reason* (Philadelphia: West-
minster Press, 1946); Karl Barth, *The Epistle to the Romans* (London:
Oxford University Press, 1933), *The Word of God and the Word of
Man* (New York: Harper Torchbooks, 1957); Erich Frank, *Philosophical
Understanding and Religious Truth* (London: Oxford University Press,
1945); Rudolph Bultmann, *Essays*, trans. J. C. G. Grieg (London: SCM
Press, 1955), Chapter 1, "The Crisis in Belief," and Chapter 5, "The
Question of Natural Revelation." The classic locus of neoorthodox theory
with regard to revelation and its relation to reason is, of course, Karl
Barth, *Church Dogmatics* (Edinburgh: T. & T. Clark, 1930 and 1956),
vol. I, pt. 1 and 2, and vol. II, pt. 1.

genuinely *neo*orthodox.[12] First of all, it accepted for the purposes of rational understanding—if not for "faith"—the naturalistic account of all space-time events as being caused by other preceding finite factors (natural or human) and not by miraculous
divine interventions. It accepted, moreover, the concept of historical relativity, with regard even to its own scriptural writings
and doctrines. It agreed that, whatever revelation might mean, it
did *not* mean the communication of divine information about
space-time events, but that, on the contrary, we can know about
such matters as the early stages of the world, the size and regions
of the given universe, the early history of Israel, the actual historical happenings of New Testament times, and so on, only through
scientific and historical inquiry. Surprisingly, no neoorthodox
ever criticized either in principle or in practice the biological theory of evolution or the liberal practice of Biblical criticism, although theologically they tended to ignore both these products of
scientific inquiry on which, at least in part, liberal theology had
been founded. No more for them than for the liberals did the
Bible communicate information about "matters of fact"—as the
orthodox had surely thought, and as fundamentalists still believe.
Rather, for them scripture mediates its truth existentially to Christian faith and to its reflection solely in terms of myths and symbols. Biblical doctrines, then, are reflections on an existential encounter with God in his Word, as Emil Brunner insisted, and so
are to be taken "seriously but not literally," as Reinhold Niebuhr
put it.[13] They express in the form of narrative what faith believes about the relations of the transcendent God to the moving
world of history.[14] They are symbolic accounts of the way God

[12] For a longer discussion of this dual character of neoorthodoxy
as both "orthodox" and "neo-," see the writer's article on "Neo-orthodoxy," in *A Handbook of Christian Theology* (Cleveland: Living Age
Books, 1958).

[13] See Emil Brunner, *The Divine-Human Encounter* (Philadelphia: Westminster Press, 1943), and Reinhold Niebuhr, *Beyond Tragedy*, Chapter 1, "As Deceivers, Yet True."

[14] For an account of what the traditional doctrine of creation out
of nothing, taken in this sense as "religious myth," might mean in the
context of modern science and philosophy, and of how this form of theology understood its mythical and Biblical language, see the writer's

acts in history, creating it, judging it, and yet in his mercy acting
redemptively in it to bring it to repentance and faith and to saving
knowledge of his purposes and Lordship. Religious truth is not
information about either the world or God as he is in himself; it
is a symbolic expression of the existential and living relation of
man to God that is established by God's action in history. Christian doctrines are thus mythical reflections upon faith, and faith
itself is a response to the speaking of God to us through his Word
in historical events, especially that of Christ, a Word witnessed
to by the writings of scripture and the preaching of the Church.
Neoorthodoxy was, therefore, on two counts in tune with the contemporary "secular" mind: (1) it agreed that God was *not* revealed in ordinary secular life, and (2) it accepted the naturalistic
account of the system of space-time events. On the other hand, it
was "orthodox" in the sense that for it the *religious* meanings of
this naturalistically interpreted life, its "ultimate concerns" and
ultimate questions of faith, meaning, and hope, were not to be
resolved by man's wisdom alone on the level of either nature or
history, but to be resolved only by a faith attendant to the transcendent Word. It attempted to accept the secular world *secularly*,
but to retain the Biblical and orthodox worlds *religiously*. As we
shall see, this dual posture, while the source of its very considerable power, proved its undoing in the end.

On many issues, of course, the neoorthodox disagreed
among themselves, and often these arguments became fairly
fierce, as all family disputes are.[15] Among the subjects debated
were the sharpness of the separation of the Word of God from

Maker of Heaven and Earth (New York: Doubleday, 1959, and Doubleday Anchor, 1965).

[15] See, for example: (1) the sharp disagreement between Barth
and Brunner over the possibility of a "point of connection" between man
and God and so of the category of general revelation, *Natural Theology,*
ed. John Baillie (London: Centenary Press, 1946); (2) the strong disagreements between Paul Tillich and Reinhold Niebuhr, on the one hand,
and the Barthians, on the other, with regard to the necessity of conversation
with the world of philosophy, psychology, anthropology, and ethics; and
(3) the continuing disagreements between Barthians and Bultmannians
after 1945 with regard to the relevance of modern scientific viewpoints
for hermeneutics and so with regard to the necessity of "demythologizing"
in the modern Church.

that of man; the depth of the cleavage between ordinary secular experience and the reception in faith of the Word of God; the width of the gulf between categories applicable to nature and human life and the transcendent, "wholly other" God; the amount and depth of the Fall, and many others. Each side of these family quarrels, however, assumed the general neoorthodox stance with regard to the centrality of God for man, the lostness of man without God, the sinful and disrupted character of ordinary human existence, and the dependence of man on the revealed Word, and so on faith alone, for truth and goodness. On these points all neoorthodox agreed—and even such deviants as Paul Tillich and Rudolph Bultmann, in agreeing on *these* principles, found themselves among this general post-liberal, neo-Reformation cluster of theologians.

We are now, perhaps, in a better position to understand the general shape of neoorthodox theology against which the radical theologians of the present are in reaction, taking their own form from the rejection of this established form of doctrine— as neoorthodoxy itself had done in relation to liberalism. Generalizations are always at best precarious, but we can, I believe, comprehend the content we are calling the neoorthodox vision and most of its varieties in terms of six major assertions.

(1) The reality, the sovereignty, and the all-sufficiency of God for all of his creation, especially for mankind and his troubled history, and the consequent need on the part of man for God, if man is to find true self-understanding and a genuinely creative life in history. God is not only "the most real"; even more, he is most necessary if man is to be, and to be man. (2) The corresponding lostness, estrangement, helplessness, sinfulness, and error of man and his works, even his culturally and spiritually most creative works, when he is separated from God, i.e., when man is "secular man." Thus the "world" is here characterized negatively by sin and error fully as much as it is positively by creative possibilities, and consequently purely secular norms and concepts can play no finally determinative role in a valid ultimate commitment, in true worship, in creative ethical judgments, or, correspondingly, in any true theology.[16] (3) Consequently, man

---

[16] The classic neoorthodox treatment of the nature of man, as creative child of God and yet as sinner, as partially intelligible in terms

is absolutely dependent for both truth and grace on the only
places where God does meet him: in special revelation centering
in the divine activity in relation to the Hebrew people and especially through Jesus Christ. As a result, scripture and tradition,
through which our present faith is related to these events of
revelation in the past, are the normative sources for true Christian
theology and life, and function as objective data out of which
valid theological discourse can unfold. Thus from such objective
givens as "the kerygma proclaimed to faith," "the Biblical faith,"
or "the historic Christian viewpoint," theological statements could
be drawn, whether or not the theologian could establish them
personally in testable experience or by the criteria of philosophical
inquiry.[17] Thus theology is here defined as the "translation of
the Word of God communicated to faith through the scripture
into the thought patterns of our time," "the gospel *in* our situation"; it is "the bridge between the Word in scripture and the
Word in sermon."[18] It begins with divine revelation, received in

---

of secular life but only fully comprehended by Biblical faith, is Reinhold
Niebuhr's *The Nature and Destiny of Man,* Volumes I and II (New
York: Charles Scribner's Sons, 1941–43). For the application of this
view to the problems of the meaning of history, see his *Faith and History.*
For other neoorthodox treatments of some of these same themes, cf. Emil
Brunner, *Man in Revolt* (Philadelphia: Westminster Press, 1947),
Gustav Aulen, *The Faith of the Christian Church* (Philadelphia: Muh-
lenberg Press, 1948), Alexander Miller, *The Renewal of Man* (New
York: Doubleday, 1955), David Roberts, *The Grandeur and Misery of
Man* (New York: Oxford University Press, 1955), and *Existentialism
and Religious Belief* (New York: Oxford University Press, 1957).

[17] Cf. especially Karl Barth, *Church Dogmatics, op. cit.,* Volume I,
Parts 1 and 2; and Emil Brunner, *Revelation and Reason, op. cit.* For a
good expression of what the "Biblical view" of man, God, and history
was taken to be, see Walter Eichrodt, *Theology of the Old Testament,*
trans. J. A. Baker (Philadelphia: Westminster Press, 1961); G. E. Wright
and Reginald H. Fuller, *The Book of the Acts of God* (Garden City, N.Y.:
Doubleday, 1957); Alan Richardson, *Theological Word Book of the
Bible* (New York: Macmillan Co., 1950); the *locus classicus* for the
"Biblical view" of everything imaginable is Gerhard Kittel, *Theologisches
Wörterbuch zum Neuen Testament* (Stuttgart: Vereagoon W. Kohl-
hammer, 1933).

[18] Heinrich Ott, "What Is Systematic Theology?" in J. M. Robinson and J. B. Cobb, Jr., *The Later Heidegger and Theology* (New
York: Harper & Row, 1963), pp. 79–82. As this quotation from a con-

faith, as its source and material, and proceeds from there into our world as the intelligible explication of faith, the understanding in our time of the divine Word made known in the event of Christ. From all of this follow, of course, the familiar neoorthodox contrasts between unbelief in the world and faith in the Church, between the secularity of society and the covenant community of the Church, between reason and revelation, and between worldly idolatry and Christian commitment.

(4) As a further consequence, knowledge gained by the ordinary disciplines of science or of historiography can at best be only supplementary to Christian theology. Theology begins and ends with faith, which is a relation to the transcendent God as he manifests himself through historical events whose religious meaning is visible only to those with eyes to see, and theology concerns itself only with this revealing activity hidden to the secular or profane gaze. Thus the objects of religious concern and of theological discourse transcend the realm of empirical, rational, and so historical investigation. The "Mighty acts of God in history," the "Christ of faith" revealed in the New Testament documents and proclaimed to faith in the kerygma, the New Being within the man Jesus, and the presence of the "Risen Lord" to his faithful community, all of these remain quite hidden to the eyes of secularity—and, as we have noted, twentieth-century secularity thoroughly agreed about this hiddenness! By the same token, the historical Jesus—that figure which secular research might or might not discover through the documents—tended to disappear; the man Jesus visible on the plane of history was merely an "incognito," a mask or disguise for the real Christ, who was seen only by faith. Jesus Christ was, to be sure, the cen-

---

temporary Continental theologian indicates, this basic neoorthodox definition of the task of theology is still dominant on the Continent, however many changes from its Barthian form may have transpired. Wherever today theology is called "hermeneutical," this view is probably presupposed. Also it has reappeared in the writings of newer eschatological theologians, who are as critical of their neoorthodox predecessors with regard to content as are the radicals, but are completely in agreement with the former nevertheless that theology's task is simply to expound the meaning for today of the given divine Word enshrined in Holy Scripture. Cf. Jürgen Moltmann, *The Theology of Hope* (New York: Harper & Row, 1967), especially Chapters 1, 2, 3.

ter of all forms of neoorthodox theology, but it was solely the divine activity which faith might discern within the historical event of Jesus, not on Jesus himself as a human figure, that neoorthodox piety and theology were based. Faith encountered *God* in the gospel about Jesus, that is, in him it knew the divine election, agape, grace, and power as shown in the Incarnation, the Atonement, and the Resurrection; and none of this divine activity, nor any of its significant content for faith, could be known by the profane, historical inquirer.[19] (5) As a result, neoorthodoxy frequently seemed to be dealing with and talking about events, categories, forces, and factors which were invisible, inaudible, unknowable, and surely undemonstrable to anyone outside of the circle of faith, and so to have a structure of discourse relevant, meaningful, and valid *only* if faith is presupposed. Its language was thus radically unconnected with the ordinary structures and language of secular life. It had, perhaps rightly, fixed its hope on the transcendent God rather than on anything in his visible creation, and placed its trust in God's Word rather than in all the wayward opinions of his creatures. But it seemed to be forced thereby to inhabit its own separated, irrelevant, and so apparently illusory world.

(6) Finally, for this viewpoint faith (or the new being) was the necessary precondition for works of love, and so correspondingly, theological understanding was necessary as a prerequisite for ethics. No phrase was more beloved by the neoorthodox than Luther's phrase, "Faith is the doer, love the deed."[20] Since man is theonomous and not autonomous man, he is creative in his ontic behavior, especially in relation to others, only when he has a healthy relation to God. Thus when his rela-

---

[19] For a particularly sharp critique of this neoorthodox understanding of faith and its relation to the historical events on which it itself was grounded, cf. Van A. Harvey, *The Historian and the Believer* (New York: Macmillan Company, 1966). The significance of this criticism is not only that it comes from one who once accepted this general understanding of the relation of faith and history, but even more that Harvey's main point is that, if one accepts the criteria of the secular historian, as the neoorthodox desired to do, one cannot also accept the neoorthodox resolution of the problem so created.

[20] Martin Luther, *Treatise on Christian Liberty* and *Commentary on Galatians* (Gal. 5:6).

tion to God is restored (on the level of existence by faith, on that of thought by theology), then he can love in his existence and understand his duties and roles of life on the level of thought. Correspondingly, when there is no faith, there can be only idolatry and its ethical consequences. Since creative action in the world presupposes, therefore, a sense of repentance and of trust, which can be dealt with only "religiously" before God in faith, action in the world without faith thus in neoorthodoxy tended to be regarded as demonic. Where the problem of the vertical dimension (the religious dimension) has not yet been resolved, there can be no real hope on the horizontal dimension. Thus, all its language to the contrary, neoorthodoxy was a markedly "religious" view of man, seeing faith in God as the necessary prerequisite for love of the neighbor, and theological understanding as the necessary prerequisite for creative ethical and social theory. For these reasons, in its understanding of the Church this theology concentrated its primary attention on the Word and the sacraments through which faith was born and nourished in the community, and so, despite its undoubted concern for social justice, it placed the Church's "mission" and "works" in the world in a secondary and dependent position.

Here, then, was an impressive vision of man in his lostness, sin, and error, redeemed by God in his majesty, goodness, and love. This vision of God's glory and man's need reflected the vivid historical experience which the twentieth century had had of a break, fissure, a rent in the older order and meanings of man's ordinary life in the world, a distortion believed to be healed through God's grace received in faith. Consequently, there is no doubt that this vision of man's need and God's answer fitted the historical experience and the believed reality of those who formulated neoorthodoxy after World War I, and those who supported it during and after the second; it validated itself over and over for at least a pair of generations. But there is also no doubt that this scheme of thought did in time cease to be the symbolic vehicle of a new vision of the truth and became instead an established system to be learned and defended. It is, I suspect, at this latter point that the new generation has encountered it; that is, when it was a series of established and solidified theological expressions that only dubiously fitted the truth of recent postwar life, instead of a true vision of actual experience receiving exciting new embodiment.

When the deeper vision which a particular theological language expresses fades, then the power and invulnerability of its unique symbols weaken as well. Instead of symbols communicating a deeply felt truth about life, and so invulnerable to moral and intellectual criticism, these words then become empty dogmatic signs, aspects of a structure learned in study but not in life, imperfect, finite, contradicted by obvious facts, and probably immoral. When, for example, the deep, personal awareness of the distortion and sin of man's existence is dispelled, the theological symbols of sin, guilt, or existential anxiety cease to provide healing pointers to experienced truth, creating intelligibility out of a felt chaos. Instead, now, these symbols of disruption appear as weak dogmas, foisted unscrupulously on an innocent and inwardly untroubled secularity. It is, said Bonhoeffer, "an ignoble task" to use such doctrines to sniff out a man's "unreal" problems in order to convert him—clearly presupposing that man's life is naturally untroubled until the theologian appears with his gloomy line. When the sense of the healing power of the realm of grace has receded, symbols pointing to the transcendence of God, the coming in of his grace from beyond ourselves and our powers— symbols such as those of depth, judgment, repentance, revelation, assurance, unmerited grace, forgiveness, sovereignty, and so on —cease to be vehicles of a real experience of true healing, and instead become empty symbols referent to dubious nonentities, needing to be demonstrated despite their clear unreality, and probably only impediments to the real business of living. Thus can the symbolic power of a theological "gestalt" vanish when that gestalt becomes an entrenched system bypassed by its time's vision, leaving only a vulnerable shell, impotent, illogical, and unreal.

Moreover, as neoorthodoxy developed, its original powerful vision of the mystery of God's grace and of man's need hardened into supernatural doctrines which presented us often with a system of divine answers to problems and crises of which we were not aware, and resolved them with divine realities and events invisible to us. As Hamilton and van Buren remind us, this theology at the end claimed to know too much. A vision that had begun with a sense of the almost impenetrable mystery of life amidst loss and despair, ended as a system of dogmas asserted with apodictic certainty and vast overconfidence; like a good political administration that had been in power too long, it was ripe for a fall. Such apparently was neoorthodoxy to those who learned it in its triumphant glory, and then rejected it when they themselves came of age. Thus there is health in the negative reaction of our day, however disturbing it may be to many. To a slightly older generation, who experienced in the Depression, in Fascism, and in World War II, the truth of this vision before they learned its technical terms, neoorthodoxy, in one of its forms or another, will probably continue to provide much of the general shape of their own theology, however drastically the latter may have to be reformulated in the new situation.

In these two chapters we have discussed the two sources of the current theological situation: the developing secularity of the modern world and the traditions of liberal and of neoorthodox theology. Now let us put these two sources briefly together, for it is out of their confluence in the postwar world that the breakdown of neoorthodoxy has occurred and that the new theological ferment has arisen. We have said that in its last days neoorthodoxy seemed illogical and unreal—let us now explore the reasons for the internal difficulties that brought about its downfall.

Neoorthodoxy accepted, for the purposes of its own inquiries, the modern secular understanding of the spatiotemporal world process—the world of nature and of history. Onto that contemporary scientific understanding of observable events, they attempted to ingraft the more traditional Biblical understanding of God as transcendent creator and sovereign Lord, dynamically active in history in both judgment and redemption, and manifesting himself to men with faith in the events of the life of the Israelite people and especially in the event of Jesus Christ. This synthesis was at best only an uneasy dualism, with a naturalistically interpreted world and a Biblically understood God who by his activity in that world gives to it meaning and coherence. The union of these two world views, one modern and one ancient,

proved more difficult than at first it promised to be; the secular
elements warred against the Biblical ones, and the result was the
ultimate breakup on the intellectual level of neoorthodox theology.

In the first place, the acceptance of the causal order gov-
erning finite events meant that observable miracles and special
divine interventions were not a possible part of a neoorthodox
framework. Biblical theologians shuddered as much as did the
liberals or the secularists when Cecil B. DeMille's camera showed
the Israelites walking through the Red Sea between walls of
water and staring at the fish! No, said they, God acts in history,
but not *that* way! He is no miraculous cause on the surface of history where natural and historical causes are exclusively at work
as far as "explanations" are concerned. And as one prominent
Biblical theologian hazarded, probably what caused whatever
happened at the Red Sea was an unusually strong east wind![21] But
if events, viewed naturally, had an immanent explanation in
terms of natural and historical causes, what did it *mean* to say that
they were *God's* action? A miracle, in the sense of a divine intervention into the natural and historical orders, is, to be sure,
an "act of God," and we seem to know what we mean when we
speak of the divine activity in relation to such an event. But if,
even for faith, there *were* no such plagues in Egypt, no miraculous parting of the waters of the Red Sea, no strange pillar of
fire, no divinely inscribed stone tablets, and so on, what do we
mean by our verbs in the phrases, "God *rescued* Israel," "God
spoke to Moses," "God *established* the Covenant," "God *revealed* His Law?"[22] Do these verbs refer to any real actions, if
there are sufficient natural or historical causes; and if they do not,
is the God who acts there, and who is, moreover, to be understood
solely in and through these actions, real at all? Has not the disbe-

[21] Cf. especially Bernard W. Anderson, *Understanding the Old
Testament* (Englewood, N.J.: Prentice-Hall, 1957), pp. 47–49; G. E.
Wright and Reginald Fuller, *The Book of the Acts of God,* pp. 80–82.
[22] Cf. John Calvin, *Commentary on Exodus,* Chapter 3. Let us
note that Calvin, in commenting on the event of the Red Sea, hazards the
guess that were there *neither* miracles *nor* the divine voice accompanying
these events, the Israelites would have had no idea that Jahweh was at
work here, and would have thought precisely that it *was* the work of an
east wind (or maybe of a god of an east wind!).

lief in the miraculous in effect emptied all these words of any significant meaning, of any touch with our ordinary usage of them; can there be even any analogical meanings to the Biblical language of the divine "activity" in a naturalistically viewed world? Above all, when we come to the "mightiest" act of all, the Resurrection, if there were no miraculous removal of the body, no empty tomb, no later appearances in miraculous form— if in fact it was not an "event" in the ordinary sense of an observable occurrence in the space-time nexus—what do the words "event" or "act" mean here? How does God act in history in this "pseudo-event," and what on earth does it mean to say God *acted* here if nothing happened more than the appearance of faith among the disciples?[23] Language about God in Biblical theology had been based on a recital of the acts of God for man in history; but if there was no conceptual content or meaning that could be given to these acts or to this activity on the historical level, was this language of action in history meaningful at all?

As for "ordinary" events in the general course of nature or of ordinary history—diseases, floods, tragic accidents, depressions, and wars, as well as more creative happenings—again the neoorthodox as modern men hesitated to say God *caused* these occurrences. This not only would make him too finite and even "physical," one cause among others, and run directly counter to

[23] The literature on the meaning of the "event" of the Resurrection in neoorthodox theology is endless, since recent criticisms have been directed at the views of both the leading Continental theologians in the postwar world, Karl Barth and Rudolph Bultmann. For the former's difficult discussions, see *The Resurrection of the Dead* (New York: Fleming H. Revell, 1933), and *Church Dogmatics* (New York: Charles Scribner's Sons, 1936 ff.), vol. I, pt. 2; vol. III, pt. 2; vol. IV, pt. 2; for the latter's, see *Theology of the New Testament*, trans. Kendrick Grobel (London: SCM Press, 1952 and 1955), vol. I, II. The two best critical treatments of the leading neoorthodox views, written from quite different points of view, are Richard R. Niebuhr's *Resurrection and Historical Reason* (New York: Charles Scribner's Sons, 1957), and Van A. Harvey's recent *The Historian and the Believer*. The most recent critique, from a perspective which wishes to reestablish the historicity of the event, cf. Moltmann, *The Theology of Hope, op. cit.*, Chapter 3, and Wolfhart Panenberg, *Grundzüge der Christologie* (Gutersloh: G. Mohn, 1964). Carl Braaten has an excellent chapter in his *History and Hermeneutics* (Philadelphia: Westminster Press, 1966) on this critique of neoorthodoxy on the Continent (Chapter 4).

their allegiance to some form of the causal nexus; but it raised painful questions about his goodness. Consequently, the problem of the meaning of the language about God's sovereignty over the course of nature and of ordinary history arose with a new sharpness: what *was* meant when we said that God ruled in history? Was he there a factor like an ordinary cause whose presence could be experienced and so verified? And if not, as all agreed, then was the traditional language of God's universal creativity and providence merely pious language applied to events which had their own sufficient secular causes—or, almost as bad, "metaphysical language" which, though only understood by philosophers anyway, was now being violently repudiated by them? In what sense, then, was he the Lord over history which theology proclaimed, or in what sense did he reveal himself there by his activity, as this view insisted?[24]

Let us note in passing that the contemporary criticism, common among both language analysts and radical theologians, that God-language is "meaningless," arose sharply in relation to neoorthodox theology.[25] Although strictly speaking, of course, no verification or falsification, i.e., no establishment of the validity of their propositions, would have been possible for orthodox or liberal theologians, still both of them might have said with some precision and force what they thought they *meant* by the activity of God. The orthodox man frequently pointed to such observable effects as wars, floods, economic successes, health, and even boils, and witnessed forthrightly to his belief that God's will was their effective "cause." One might not have agreed with him, but what sort of claim one was disbelieving, the sorts of things he affirmed God caused, and what therefore the divine sovereignty

---

[24] For a more detailed discussion of the problems of the meaning of the "activity of God in history" in contemporary Biblical theology, see the writer's "Cosmology, Ontology, and the Travail of Biblical Language" and "The Concept of Providence in Contemporary Theology," *Journal of Religion,* July 1961 and July 1963.

[25] For the best and most influential statement of this criticism of "meaninglessness," cf. Antony Flew's essay in *New Essays in Philosophical Theology* (London: SCM Press, 1955) entitled "Theology and Falsification." For an earlier form of the same critique, see John Dewey, *Experience and Nature* (New York: W. W. Norton and Co., 1929), and *A Common Faith* (New Haven: Yale University Press, 1934).

he proclaimed might mean, were very plain. Correspondingly, the liberal could have pointed to many signs, evident to the eyes of his generation, of the divine activity: the growing coherence of the cosmos, the evolutionary rise of animal species to man's level, the steady progress in history and society of morals and of culture, the clear superiority of a Christian civilization over its more primitive competitors, and the beneficent influence of Christian morals and ideals on the world at large. God, as he was understood in liberal theology and philosophy of religion, was the ultimate cause of these "facts," facts accepted as self-evident by the liberal world and which could hardly have brought themselves about. God's action *meant* that universally recognized force for order and for value in the temporal development of the process— as H. N. Wieman defined it, "the creative event"—a force that was accepted as evident by everyone because its effects, to that age, were universally visible. All that was needed in order to show the intelligibility of our words about God was, therefore, a careful metaphysical explication of that commonly accepted vision.

Neoorthodoxy, on the other hand, when asked the same question, "What do you *mean* by the acts of God?" had no such accepted secular or ordinary evidences of God's actions to point to. His mighty acts are, said they, seen only by faith. But this was only a stalling measure: when asked the further question, "And what is it that you see by faith?" Biblical theology was even more embarrassed. For when Biblical scholars reconstructed historically "what must really have happened" in Old and New Testament times, their accounts sounded very much like those naturalistic explanations one gives to the origins of another religious movement. The "acts of God" appeared only when they reconstructed Hebrew and apostolic *faith*, not when they reconstructed their *history*. And yet Biblical *theology* required that these historical events be considered by faith to be the results of a transhistorical activity and thus unique—because there the God of all history was manifesting himself "in events" to men. The naturalistic historical assumptions of neoorthodox Biblical theology seemed to make meaningless if not impossible its theological affirmations about the activity of God in history.

The second intellectual or theoretical difficulty with neo-

orthodox theological language came with regard to the other
major category of the divine in this modern Biblical theology: not
God's acts but his Word. God had revealed his Word in the Covenant and in the Christ, and thus this Word was the center of
validity and of grace both in the life of the Church and of the
individual.[26] For it was in response to this appearance of the
Word that the faith which defined the Church and healed the
individual arose. Faith responding to the divine Word was (and
remains) the central epistemological category of all important
forms of contemporary Continental theology. For neoorthodox
theology, therefore, the Word, as the exclusive principle of divine
self-manifestation to men, is the sole aspect of divinity and so of
absoluteness with which man has contact. Logically it is, therefore, the sole source and object of faith and of theological reflection; and, moreover, it is the divine and thus absolute critic of
human wisdom and inquiry, not its relative result. But what was
this divine Word in a Bible studied like any other ancient document, and thus broken down over and over again into innumerable relative, even human, points of view, into a thousand vary-
ing and fallible "words"? Biblical theology seemed to require an
absolute and unified and authoritative Word in scripture, which
would judge, correct, and redeem the wayward mind of man and
give him grounds for saying things about God that his own mind
could neither discover nor test. Critical Biblical scholarship and
the new world views created by science, on the other hand, seemed
to lead in the opposite direction, namely to the necessity of judging, sifting, rejecting, and reinterpreting the very human document before them; and as a consequence it shattered that unified
and authoritative Biblical view into a mass of relative and unrelated bits and pieces. Ironically the only consistent threads in the
Bible as a whole that resulted from this study were neither God's
acts nor even a unified theological message, but, as in any study

[26] For an explication of this view of the Church as centered about
the Word, cf. Emil Brunner's *The Misunderstanding of the Church* (Philadelphia: Westminster Press, 1953); J. Robert Nelson, *The Realm of
Redemption* (Greenwich, Conn.: Seabury Press, 1951); James Gustaf-
son, *Treasure in Earthen Vessels* (New York: Harper & Row, 1961);
and the writer's *How the Church Can Minister to the World without
Losing Itself* (New York: Harper & Row, 1964).

of the history of the other religions, an account of the historic life and faith of the Judaic and the Christian communities. For this theological perspective, however, historic Judaism and early Christianity, even as they appear in the Bible, are necessarily the results in *religion* of revelation and not its revealed substance. For all of these reasons, any simple identification of the Word of God with scripture was for most of neoorthodoxy impossible. Again, the modern side of neoorthodoxy seemed to make impossible what its orthodox side required, namely a direct relation with an objective divine Word of revelation.

The result was that (with the exception of Karl Barth) neoorthodoxy more and more tended, almost against its will, to locate the "place" of the Word not so much objectively in scripture as subjectively in our own personal experience, in the encounter of faith with God through the scriptural Word, in the challenge of the kerygma (the gospel proclaimed) to our existential self-understanding and authenticity. The logical base for the neoorthodox claim that through these Biblical symbols we confront and meet *reality* and so *a fortiori* ultimate reality or God, lay not primarily in the fact that these symbols resided in scripture—for much else that was by no means regarded as divinely inspired was also found there—but that through them a real encounter of the soul with God took place when the scripture was read, proclaimed, and enacted sacramentally in the community of faith. Despite all its talk of "objective divine Acts in history" and "an objective Word in scripture," ironically most neoorthodox theologies seemed in the end logically to ground their language where their great liberal antagonist, Schleiermacher, had also placed it: in the personal "religious" experience of faith in relation to the Word of God, in which the human self of man encounters the Thou of God.[27]

[27] For examples of this "interiorization" from historical act to word of communication, see the following from Brunner: "As a matter of fact, it is precisely in God's giving himself to be known and in this knowledge of God that the essence of the relation between God and man lies. . . . The revelation of God to men is the decisive element in what God *does* for them [emphasis added]. For the Word is the way in which mind communicates to mind, subject with subject, will with will. . . . Since therefore the Word is the form and means which Person reveals and gives himself to person, through which, therefore, fellowship be-

The logical starting point, then, for neoorthodoxy was the reality of the divine-human encounter of faith through the Word of law and of gospel—and this remains the assumed basis for most current Continental theology. So long as that experience was felt to be *real* and *definite*, this theology appeared viable and strong. But even here, too, the acids of modernity were at work— for of all things difficult for a modern man, perhaps a direct experience of an I-Thou encounter with God the Lord through scripture, sermonic proclamation, or sacrament is almost the most difficult. Over and over, the divine Word in sermon was fragmented into the human opinions of the preacher; the divine presence of the sacrament dissipated in the barrenness of modern liturgical life; the divine judgment in the experience of guilt dissolved in the psychoanalytic session into various facets of neurosis; the divine norms of law muddied by the changing and relative requirements of the context; and every religiously serious twentieth-century man is tortured by the difficulty of finding God directly through private prayer and devotion. It was easy enough to *speak* theologically about an "existential" encounter with God through the Word in faith. But to *experience* this was hard and

---

tween Persons is created, it is through his Word that God realizes his Will in and for man." Emil Brunner, *The Divine-Human Encounter, op. cit.,* pp. 51 and 67.

From Bultmann: "When we speak of God as acting, we mean that we are confronted with God, addressed, asked, judged, or blessed by God." Rudolph Bultmann, *Jesus Christ and Mythology* (New York: Charles Scribner's Sons, 1958), p. 68.

From Ebeling: "For with God, Word and deed are one: his speaking is the way of his acting." Gerhard Ebeling, *The Nature of Faith* (Philadelphia: Muhlenberg Press, 1961), p. 90. The same appears in Heinrich Ott: "The first [subject matter of theology] is the Christ event, the reality of revelation and of believing. This is no 'fact' that can be 'stated' and communicated in plain words, but rather a reality that makes itself heard in poetic and thinking speech and thus becomes present." Ott, "What Is Systematic Theology?" pp. 86–87. This is the "self-manifestation" of God to the "interior" of man which Moltmann so vigorously and brilliantly criticizes, and for this internal dialogue has substituted (1) the verbal promises of God in scripture and (2) the objective eschatological arising of the "new" in future history. Cf. *The Theology of Hope, op. cit.,* especially Chapters 1, 2, and 4.

rare. Thus a theology that was existential in essence, and so totally predicated on the reality in our *actual existence* of this
experience was vulnerable in the end to the secularity of our life
—for which precisely this experience had at best only the most
elusive reality. Moreover, as we have seen, this experience of
faith in the Word was in neoorthodoxy the *sole* basis of religious
certainty. Neoorthodoxy, more in its Continental than in its
American forms, had deliberately separated its theological discourse from ordinary experience and centered its language exclusively on the reception of the Word and so on the traditional
Biblical forms. There was thus little way in which this Biblical
language could be related to secular experience and in which the
now shaky certainties of faith in our reception of the spoken divine Word could be "checked" or "buttressed" in terms of the
common experiences of ordinary life. In a time of experienced
chaos in secular life, this separation of faith and its language
from ordinary experience and its modes of speech had been an
aspect of strength. In the end it proved, I believe, fatal. When
the religious foundations of faith themselves began to waver, the
esoteric character of this language in relation to the real stuff of
ordinary life made it doubly vulnerable to the winds of doubt at
work in the world.[28]

The third problem, closely related to the other two, arose
with regard to the relation of the divine activity in the Word,
centering in the divine event of Christ, to the historical facts of
Jesus' life and death. Was our faith in this divine act and so our
understanding and certainty of the Word dependent on our *his-*

[28] It was, I believe, the realization of this danger of the separation of religious experience and language from the stuff of ordinary life
that, in the last decade of the neoorthodox period (1950–1960), brought
both Rudolph Bultmann and Paul Tillich to clear dominance of the
Protestant theological scene. For among all the great theologians of this
group, these two most arduously tried to build bridges to secular experience and to shape their understanding of Christian faith—based, to be
sure, on divine revelation—to fit the categories, standards, and attitudes
of contemporary man. In this sense, more than any other "neoorthodox,"
they have been mediating figures between that period and the present
secular, skeptical, and worldly period—and their influence continues to
permeate the theological scene.

torical certainties about the events of his life? If one said, "No,"
one had then to ask whether faith in God's action in the Word
could be thus separated from the facts of history and not thereby
be transformed into an un-Christian mysticism or philosophy of
religion. And if one said, "Yes," then how was an ultimate faith
to deal with the inevitable uncertainties that arise in relation to
any knowledge of historical facts in the distant past? Again, the
tension between the naturalistic assumptions (in this case the assumptions of historiography) and the Biblical faith of neoorthodoxy began to disintegrate the very center of the relation to God
as that theology viewed it. It seemed almost impossible even to
speak meaningfully about the relation of God's central acts of
revealing grace to the historical events and to the documents re-
porting them on which Christianity was founded and which in
neoorthodoxy provided the sole base for Christian language about
God.

At this point, a new interpretation of our relation to the
Word and the scriptures witnessing to it appeared and seemed to
provide an "out" from these difficulties. This was the existentialist mode of interpretation developed by Bultmann and his many
followers. What the theologian can find in the scriptures is not so
much objective language about either God or the world—most
of which is mythological and therefore relative to its time—as it
is the self-understanding of man presented in the New Testament. Hence, neither set Biblical doctrines about God nor historical facts about Jesus are important; let them be washed away in
the flood of critical study. What remains is the existential self-
understanding presented there, a self-understanding to which
the kerygmatic proclamation of the gospel leads each of us in
turn who hear it in faith. Biblical theology, therefore, elaborates
an anthropology, the Biblical self-understanding of man, and
does not construct objective doctrines about God, who as eternally
the *subject* of the encounter of faith, cannot in any case be a
direct object of theological discourse. God can be a part of the
language of kerygmatic preaching, to be sure; but theological
discourse must be directly about man and his self-understanding,
and only by a tenuous form of analogy about God.[29] Ironically, a

[29] For Bultmann's discussions of the problems of God-language,
see especially "What Sense Is There To Speak of God?" *Christian*

form of Christian faith that centered itself on the presence and the activity of God through his Word, found itself at the end almost unable to speak of God at all. And since a theological viewpoint based on divine revelation which is barely able to speak about God is hardly a viable form of theology, this remains one of the central difficulties of Bultmannianism and all its most recent offshoots.[30] The "God is dead" theology, therefore, has not been alone in raising the question of God-language; the internal difficulties of neoorthodoxy had raised this question long before this attack from outside appeared.

The deepest level of the problem, however, involves more than the separation of theological discourse from ordinary life and the consequent intellectual conflict of naturalistic and Biblical assumptions. It was rather the fact that the secular spirit itself— to which, as neoorthodoxy was well aware, "faith in the Word" seemed bizarre in the extreme—in fact permeated the existence,

---

Scholar, V: 43 (Fall 1960); and "The Meaning of God as Acting," in *Jesus Christ and Mythology;* see also the excellent commentaries of Ogden (*The Reality of God* [New York: Harper & Row, 1966], pp. 104, 118, 164–187, and *Christ Without Myth* [New York: Harper & Row, 1961]) and of H. W. Bartsch, in *Kerygma and Myth*, vol. II (London: SPCK, 1962), pp. 195–215.

[30] In a perceptive article on some of the above developments, Robert Funk, now at the University of Montana, puts this inability to speak of God in this way: "In view of the widespread dissemination of neoorthodoxy, it is surprising that the category of transcendence should be problematic. For many younger men, however, it is perhaps the most questionable category of all. . . . There is a general disinclination to regard conventional God-language as meaningful. This skepticism rests on two points: (1) language analysis has made it difficult to proceed unless one has first established that language about God can have other than purely emotive or connotative meaning; (2) neoorthodoxy taught that God is never object but subject, with the result that third-generation neoorthodox theologians have been forced to wrestle with the nonphenomenal character of God. They are unwilling to settle for God as noumenon . . . which means that for them God does not 'appear' at all. Consequently, there is a tendency to focus on 'the phenomena,' (e.g., Jesus, faith, language of faith, tradition) [one could also add 'man's self-understanding']." Robert Funk, "Colloquium on Hermeneutic," *Theology Today*, vol. 21, no. 3 (October 1964), p. 303.

attitudes, and mind of lay churchmen, seminarians, and theologians alike. The citadel of faith within the Church might, in other words, have been held had the city really been kept clear of the Church's walls. But this was impossible. Christians were modern men, living in the world, thinking its thoughts and absorbing those most fundamental attitudes we have sought to outline. Thus within the Church itself, with the preaching of every Biblical sermon, and within the mind of the preacher, too, the esoteric Biblical language of God, his acts, his speech to us, and of an encounter with him, seemed meaningless and confusing to the laity who listened, and more and more unreal to the clerical speaker. What declared itself in ecclesiology (the theological theory about the Church) to be "the language of the Church," turned out to be actually language almost as strange in church as in the country club, the marketplace, and the cocktail party.

One could sum up the problem thus: Neoorthodox theology presupposed a stark and real separation between the Church and the world, between belief and unbelief, between the Word of God and the secular. Its religious discourse proceeded on the assumption that its hearers *were* this Church, *had* this belief, and *heard* the Word. But the actual situation was by no means characterized by any such clear and distinct separation: the world was within the Church, belief was saturated by secular doubt, and no one, either in pew or in pulpit, was sure a divine Word had been heard at all or a divine presence manifested. In such a situation, the theology that was unable to relate itself to ordinary experience was bound to falter—and it did.

Younger clerics and theologians began to wonder if they were talking about anything they themselves knew about when they spoke about God, of his mighty acts in history, of an "encounter" with him, of the eschatological event, and of faith. Do these words, they asked, point to anything *real*, or are they just words, traditional symbols referring more to our hopes than to experienced realities? Because of this personal and vivid experience of the apparent unreality, or at least the elusiveness, of the divine—now not merely in secular culture but rather in relation to the very encounter of faith where alone God was to be met—these theologians began to listen again to almost forgotten naturalistic and positivistic accusations of the meaninglessness of religious discourse, and to the existentialists' proclamations of the death of God in our time. For many, therefore, it was but a small step, and one made with great inward relief, to relinquish this now arduous and unreal language of transcendence, and to become a "secular Christian" in terms of the discourse of our ordinary, day-to-day speech.

The greatest problem for the neoorthodox theologian, therefore, was the experience of a radical split between his own actual existence and his own theological thought—a split particularly embarrassing to an existential theology fed upon the biting sarcasm of Kierkegaard at just such a split within abstract philosophy. The men who sought to think through their theology in strictly Biblical terms found themselves *existing* secularly and so in an entirely different world, using different sorts of language, making quite different assumptions about reality, causality, truth, and even value than those which their Biblical theology entailed —in fact, just those assumptions we outlined in the last chapter. Try as they might, they could not seem to *exist* in that world of divine speech, of a radical sense of sin, of dialogic encounter, of mighty acts, and of eschatological events. The present unreality and so seeming impossibility of theological language about God stems fundamentally, we believe, from this split between our existence in the secular world which all Christians share, on the one hand, and a theological language, on the other, that has had no essential touch with that world.[31] And since this sense of the elusiveness of the divine remains the predominant reality of the present religious situation, these questions of the reality of God and the possibility of language about him are still our most press-

---

[31] Ebeling puts this "existential problem of faith" in the modern secular context as follows: "For faith and the understanding of reality are in danger of breaking apart, so that the Christian thinks and lives in two entirely different systems of thought, in the everyday world of work and play on the one hand, and on the other in the Sunday world of religious ideas." Gerhard Ebeling, *The Nature of Faith,* p. 118. As we shall argue, it is this "schizophrenia" of the modern theologian that requires a new form of theological inquiry, and that renders dubious the neoorthodox starting point, namely that of a coherent, certain, and cognitively effective "faith" with which, without further prolegomenon, theological thought can

ing current theological problems, prior to all other theological issues.

One final comment about the significance of this issue in the present situation is in order. Many loyal churchmen, both clerical and lay, have found themselves shocked at the radical questioning of the reality of God pointed to in these remarks and expressed openly in the radical theologies, and have intimated, or at least felt, that these doubts represent a quite atypical and probably overintellectualized segment in relation to the burgeoning church life in pious America. "God dead in our time? God absent or unreal in our experience? Look at our full churches! Atheism is no problem in American society, for 99 percent of the people declare that they believe in God!"

The fact of the matter is, however, that these doubts and the theologies that express them are anything but unexpressive of current American religion, however much the latter may protest. Our churches are, to be sure, full, respected, loved, and supported by staggering donations of human time, energy, and money. Their membership, their physical plant, and their activities increase yearly. As innumerable commentators have witnessed, however, ranging from worried laymen through perceptive clerics to professional secular social analysts, what is precisely absent in all this ecclesiastical bustle is any evidence of a vital, significant, or "real" experience of the presence of God: whether through private devotions, Bible reading, worship, sacrament, preaching, or any semblance of sacrifice in the life and work of the Church. Increasingly, even in the Church, it seems difficult to speak or think about God. The Bible is seldom read and its

---

begin, as for example when Ott says, "The subject matter of believing is an indivisible unity; it is a meaning-laden, significant unity, comprising an unmistakable meaning," and since "Theology is thinking in relation to believing, systematic theology reflects upon this subject matter with which the church has to do." Thus grounded in such a certain and richly filled "faith," theology neither needs nor can have any wider scope or other materials for its thought. Ott, "What is Systematic Theology?" pp. 99 and 90 respectively.

contents are virtually unknown—though it is in theory greatly revered. Theology and doctrines are little discussed and very rarely understood or even recognized; few laymen, however devoted or conservative, can express in their own words what they believe about religion or about God, or understand what the relation of their beliefs might be to their ordinary lives and behavior, or comprehend what is *meant* when they are told Christianity might involve some sacrifice of cherished attitudes and standards. Generally, when questioned about matters of faith or belief, they say, "Ask the preacher; he is 'religious' and knows about this sort of thing." All alike love the Church, but when they say why, their references are generally to its warm and needed fellowship, its moral influence on society and on their children, and its function as the stable bearer of values in our mobile and rootless communal life—each a fine element of the Church's total task, no doubt, but still a strictly "secular" concern.

All this may be true, it is said, of liberal, sophisticated churches; but how about conservative Protestantism? Is God elusive there, too, in our age? Revival meetings are held in most conservative churches; still, as everyone knows, but few will admit, no one gets "revived." Old members attend faithfully, but no great "experiences" appear; and if an old-time experience did in the ordinary middle-class church send some executive to his knees, or his wife to confessing, people would probably be more worried for the sanity or for the future social prospects of these two unfortunates than impressed and gladdened by the redemptive work of the Holy Spirit! Among our most conservative groups, this elusiveness of God expresses itself strangely but pervasively: in nostalgia for old-time religion, for the religion of father and even of grandfather. We call this nostalgia for another time rather than real religion because the suburban layman who wants this kind of religion has no intention of living in the *rest* of his existence in terms of this old-time faith, as his small-town forebears surely did. He maintains his big car, his modern house, his conventional habits, and his drinks on the back patio throughout the week—as his religious grandfather, who lived in this faith's terms, never would have. His religion is thus the one place where his life, his thinking, and his standards reflect this old small-town existence out of which he came. He actually exists, therefore, in another world, in the modern suburban, commercial world—and he has no intention of relinquishing *that* world! So he merely "hankers" after this religion his predecessors had possessed, and would not dream of living within its terms or within its set of meanings. The one thing he knows about religion is that this old-time religion was "real," and, sensing the implication that his own is not—but merely a matter of helping to increase the membership of the church, of helping to build its plant, to enlarge the Sunday School, or to make the men's club program a success—he grasps passionately but futilely after what he was sure was the religious reality of another day.

American Church life, liberal and conservative, is weakest, therefore, at the level of its religious content, at the point where the community acknowledges a Word addressed to it, is aware of, dependent on, and refreshed by the presence of the divine in its midst, and feels obligated to challenge and, with divine aid, to transform its patterns of life. The category of the holy seems as absent from our piety as it is from the theologies we have been elaborating. What has in current theology been *atypical* of our Church life has been the emphasis in neoorthodox Biblical theology on the reality, the sovereignty, the claim and so the Lordship of the Word of God over the Church—and this is probably why clerics and laymen alike found its language obscure, unreal, and strange in our secular world. Secularity has penetrated as deeply into our churches as it has into the minds of our theologians, and has made the problem of the reality of God even more of a basic issue for our parish life than it is for the experience of our younger teachers and seminarians.

4 / The Radical Theologies

THE FIRST STRIKING TRAIT of the present situation in theology is its sharp reversal of all that characterized the neoorthodox
period that preceded it. For the latter, as we have seen, religious
existence and so theological language were based solely on the
certainty of faith in the transcendent divine Word and were
separated as fully as possible from the ambiguities of secular experience in the world. In the present situation, on the other hand,
religious existence and theological discourse are in part immobil-
ized and in part energized by the secular in all of its aspects. On
the one hand, because of that secular spirit, a sense of doubt, of
emptiness, and at best of preliminary and tentative steps forward
pervades the theological enterprise. On the other hand, whatever
elements of creative life and power exist in our churches are to be
found precisely in the identity of Christian existence with the suffering, problems, and hopes of the world. Instead of blocking
out the world and centering itself on the relation to the transcendent, the contemporary religious and theological mood blocks out
the transcendent dimension of religion and concentrates its ener-
gies on being "secular" and "worldly" in both thought and practice, theology and behavior.

This movement toward the world characterizes every
aspect of the Church's present situation. As we shall see, it dominates all its most recent theologies; it has led within the last few
years to an almost total rethinking and potential restructuring of
the task of the Church in relation to the world and of the under-

standing of the ministry of the Church; and it has resulted both in a new awareness of the responsibility of the Christian to and for the world, and in a new view of the Christian style of life as one characterized by worldly action rather than by inward obedience and faith. Thus has the Urban Training Center for ministers in the midst of the city rightly become the symbol of present crea-tive movements within Christianity, as formerly the theological classrooms in the seminary, and the pulpit in the church, were the symbols of a theology based on the inward reception of the divine Word in faith. In the midst of such a sudden and sharp reversal as this—it manifested itself clearly only as recently as 1963—theological concepts as well as ecclesiastical forms are bound to be in ferment, with new methods of both theology and ministry being tried, old doctrines and attitudes torn down, re-jected, or radically reformulated, and a wide variety of untested positions and approaches appearing on the scene. Theoretically, practically, and institutionally, wherever one looks, in Protes-tantism, Catholicism, or Judaism, things are radically fluid, noth-ing is certain, and all oracles or prophecies are suspect.

It was Dietrich Bonhoeffer, martyred by the Nazis, who became the main instigator and so creator of this radical move-ment toward the world, and his influence has correspondingly been immense. Although this writer believes that Bonhoeffer himself probably retained the centrality of the vertical dimension of faith in relation to God—and therefore remained fundamen-tally neoorthodox—nevertheless, some of the things he *said* in his latest writings could be interpreted as a rejection of this whole religious or vertical dimension of Christianity in favor of action in and for the world.[1] Man has, he wrote, come of age; he no longer needs God to solve his problems, and the symbol God has long since become meaningless to the world's important ques-tions.[2] Thus real Christianity is "religionless."[3] It does not seek

[1] Dietrich Bonhoeffer, *Letters and Papers from Prison* (London: Fontana Books, 1963), especially pp. 88–125.

[2] "Man has learned to cope with all questions of importance without recourse to God as a working hypothesis. . . . It is becoming evi-dent that everything goes along without 'God' and just as well as before." *Ibid.*, pp. 106–107.

[3] The word "religionless" has, like many important theological words, a recently ambiguous history. The present author can think of

God to fulfill a need in us; it turns its face from the religious and so from God, and toward the world, which it serves in love and self-giving. A creative Christianity is not religious, dependent on God, but worldly, being in the world as Jesus had been.

When this religionless and worldly form of neoorthodox Lutheranism crossed both English Channel and Atlantic Ocean, and there met a form of theology and Church life much more closely related to the secular world than is any Continental religiosity, its radical implications were actualized. For as we have noted, the internal dissolution of neoorthodoxy had been proceeding apace in empiricist and secular America, its language had become arduous and unreal, and its experiences elusive—the whole superstructure of neoorthodoxy, with its transcendent realities, its unobservable events, and its esoteric forms of word and sacrament, had in the new, postwar world gradually become a burden rather than a refuge from chaos, as it had been before. In this American mood, Bonhoeffer exploded: his words functioned now in a context of secularity rather than in that of Lutheranism, and the "God is dead" theology appeared. The key to understanding the ferment, therefore, is to comprehend (1) the dissolution of neoorthodox theology, (2) the character, scope, and power of the secular spirit in the American cultural and so Church scene, and (3) to see the resulting radical theology as an effort to interpret Christianity, as Bonhoeffer said, in worldly terms, where "worldly" is defined and limited by the secular spirit as we have sought to describe it.

---

three quite distinct meanings or connotations theologically of the word: (1) that of Barth, where "religionless" means a faith founded on special revelation, and so solely on the initiative of God, rather than on "human religion," and thus on the initiative of man; (2) a form of Christian faith in God which realizes itself, not in "religious" action (worship, prayer, and so on) directed at God or the Church, but "secular action" in the world, suffering and serving there—this is, we take it, Bonhoeffer's meaning; (3) a form of "religionless faith" which is not only "worldly" in its arena of action, but unrelated to God at all and so related only to the human Jesus—which we take it is the understanding of "religionless" in the radical theologians, which understanding we will be discussing in this chapter. On the whole, this author thinks the whole category "religionless" applied to what is patently and in ordinary usage a form of religion, whether we speak of definitions (1), (2), or (3) above, creates more confusion than clarity in theology.

The radical or "God is dead" theology, which has captured so much of our attention in the last two or three years, is
therefore an attempt to understand Christianity from a secular
point of view, within terms of the world view of secular man. It
is, as we said in Chapter I, immensely important for two reasons:
(1) because it expresses the secular mind of modern religious
and Christian man, and thus is in much closer touch than was
neoorthodoxy with the actual spiritual situation of both clergy
and laity in the second half of the twentieth century; (2) because
radical theology forces theological attention on the primary rather
than the secondary theological problems of our age. By raising
radically the question of the reality of God, by asserting that
modern man has inwardly lost God, and by denying that Christian man has any need of God or that Christian faith has any essential relation to him, this theology has forced theological reflection
to deal directly, for the first time in this century, with the question of God. Is there anything beyond the secular to talk about;
is any sort of religious language meaningful; is there any Word
beyond human words, any reality beyond the contingent, relative
realities around us—or is the whole traditional transcendent
reference of Christian faith irrelevant, empty, or meaningless in
our age? These are the questions which express contemporary
Christian doubts—and such doubts are universally prevalent—
and therefore should exercise contemporary theological reflection.
To this writer, other current options in theology are to be understood and judged with regard to their relevance in the light of
this primary question of the reality of God and the meaningfulness of language about him in our secular age and for us secular
men—who aim to be Christians. Without some answer to this
question of God, all talk about Word and sacrament, about scripture and hermeneutic, about the covenant community of the
Church, about a Christ who is Lord of our life and of history, and
about an eschatological interpretation of history in God's action,
is vain and empty—for without God these do not exist as theological concerns. Let us, therefore, turn to the radical theologians and see the way in which they have raised these problems
with which all religious thought must now deal. We shall confine
ourselves to the movement as it has appeared in America, because
here it is, I believe, more radical than in England or on the

Continent, and thus focuses the central issues for theology more sharply.[4]

The central theme that unites the radical theologians is well expressed in the enigmatic slogan "God is dead."[5] Although each of them means by this phrase something slightly different, its general import for all is that, first, the God who has been the

---

[4] This is the reason, as we noted above, that we shall not discuss the most widely read of the general group of radical theologians, namely Bishop John Robinson. However, such writers as R. B. Braithwaite and John Wren-Lewis in England have, as lay theologians, represented positions similar to those discussed below. Generally speaking, however, the debate in England has not taken as radical a form as it has here.

We shall also not discuss various Continental representatives of the "absence of God" movement, such as Herbert Braun and Arnold Metzger. The reason is that, to this writer at least, while these men are very much aware of our present inability to speak of God or to experience him, they do not seem to conclude from this that God is *unreal* and that consequently we live in a naturalistic universe devoid of all deity. The problem for them is, therefore, to find some experienced aspect of life: the Word, the relations of men to men, our ordinary life of hope, and so on, in which the hiddenness of God may become presence, and so in which God and language about him may be found. It is not, therefore, the problem of constructing a form of Christianity which has within it no relation at all to deity. The ontological framework for the experience of the "absence of God" in Continental theology remains the reality of a God now hidden, veiled, or absent; the ontological framework for the experience of the "absence of God" in the American movement is a naturalistic universe, which makes it a much more radical movement. The Continentals agree that, in our *experienced world*, God is absent, but as children of the Word of God theology, this does not mean to them that God is unreal; the Americans, being more empirical and less "Word of God" in their theological approach, conclude from the absence of God in our experienced world that he is unreal, and that therefore the cosmos is merely "blind nature." The Continental position, that God is absent from secular experience, but still there in his Word, is in America best represented by Gabriel Vahanian in his many searching and yet lively books.

[5] Ironically, all the strange linguistic puzzles and weird entailments that arise when we speak of God's existence—e.g., how it can be that *he* exists, how *he*, being God, must exist *necessarily*, etc.—crop up again when we try to say that he is dead. For, we ask, how can *God* die? If he be God, surely he is eternal by definition and so cannot be contingent and mortal. Thus if he ever has been at all—and he must have been "alive" in order to be able to "die"—then how could *he* ever cease to be?

center of faith and theological reflection for the Judeo-Christian tradition is now seen to be nonexistent, unreal, and an illusion; and, secondly, that Christianity (or Judaism)[6] must henceforth understand itself without him. In slightly different ways, therefore, this group accepts as the truth the naturalistic viewpoint characteristic of the secular spirit as we have described it: we live in a cosmos without God, without an ultimate coherence or meaning on which we can depend and to which we should in faith, worship, and obedience relate ourselves. And as a consequence, what meaning we can find in life must come from our own autonomous human powers, and what religion we can affirm must be one structured alone on our own worldly obligations and possibilities.

For all of them, moreover, it is the *authentic* God of Christian (or Jewish) faith who is gone. They are *not* attacking an idol, a misunderstanding of God, a wrong sort of theological conception of God—perhaps philosophical or mythological. It is the God to which our symbols seek to point who is dead, not our own faulty interpretation of him. What they are saying is that there is no God anywhere; the cosmos is stripped bare of such a divine being, or of such a divine source of being. It is not that God is hiding, or beyond our experience; it is that the total universe is made up of rocks, stars, and beetles, and nothing at all like God is there or ever has been there. Thus for most of them the strange word "death" in the phrase "death of God," implying as it does that what is now said to be "dead" was once alive, refers only to a *cultural* event, the death of *belief* in God, which they accept as a fact of our time. In the same way one might speak meaningfully of the "death of the witches" in the eighteenth and nineteenth centuries, and not imply thereby that witches had been really existent in the seventeenth century, when they were believed in. Obviously this disbelief in the reality of God has for some time been characteristic of the atheist and humanist tradi-

---

[6] In these remarks, I refer to Judaism as well as to Christianity because (*a*) secularism has had many of the same effects on Judaism, and (*b*) one of the most powerful expressions of this movement has come from Rabbi Richard Rubenstein, whose thought we will summarize briefly below.

tions in Western culture. What is new in this movement is the
acceptance by a group of theologians of this secular spirit as true,
and the attempt to formulate an interpretation of Christianity or
of Judaism on its basis.

When we scrutinize in more detail the positive content
of radical theology, we find, I think, six guiding principles that
characterize most of its present forms. The way in which all
thought takes its shape in reaction to what preceded it is here
vividly illustrated: these six principles are almost the exact in-
verse of the corresponding principles of neoorthodoxy we have
noted. One qualification must be made: while, as we shall see,
Altizer shares the three most important of these principles, nevertheless his thought deviates importantly from the last three. Let
us now review these basic affirmations of radical theology, and
then show how each of the three men interprets them in his own
unique way.

(1) The unreality of God for our age; his absence from
our current experience; the irrelevance and meaninglessness of
all talk about him; the emptiness and actual harmfulness of any
so-called relation to him; the difficulty of understanding our
experience of evil if we try to believe in him. Above all, the
impossibility of being contemporary and secular, that is, of being
ourselves, if we as Christians try to believe and speak of God—
all of these leading to the one central assertion: God is dead in
our time. (2) The principle of the "coming of age of man," that
is, that man does not need God as the center of his existence. This
means, in terms of a doctrine of man, the denial of the *imago
dei*, or of any religious *a priori* or religious dimension as basic
to man. Here man is in his essential nature viewed as autonomous
and not theonomous; and as autonomous he is thoroughly capable through his own rational, moral, and social powers of "get -
ting along." There follows as a consequence the affirmation of
the world and so of secular culture, created by autonomous man,
as providing the sole relevant environment, spiritual as well as
physical, in which modern man and so the modern Christian can
live. Thus the standards that the world recognizes as normative
for inquiry are accepted as valid totally in theology; the attitudes
accepted in that world determine what Christians can believe;

and, presumably, the goals of the world's life are regarded as
normative for our moral life—though there appears to be real
ambiguity with regard to this latter point.

(3) With the loss of the divine, and so any possibility
of a category of revelation or of religious experience, there is in
Christian faith no longer any "religious mode of knowing" and
thus no possibility of a deposit of sacred truth, held in either
scripture or tradition and received by faith. The Divine Word
and faith, therefore, cease to be authorities for valid theological
statements. Consequently a new principle appears: the restriction
of theological statements to what I can actually believe and accept
myself, and so to what makes sense in my cultural context, whose
principles I share in my thinking. This may be called, as it was in
the Enlightenment, the principle of personal intellectual honesty,
a refusal to accept any statement as true on a merely authoritative
or traditional ground[7] (for example, because it is "the Biblical
view," or because "the Church has always said that . . ."). There
is here, then, no bias toward saving or even reinterpreting any
elements of Christian belief that are not immediately commen-
surate with the modern understanding. (4) The centrality of
the *historical* Jesus as our sole Lord, as he who ethically claims
and guides us into the new worldly life, and as the sole subject
of contemporary theological discourse. (5) The tendency to dispense with all mythological, suprahistorical, divine, eschatological, or otherwise nonvisible and merely "theological" entities or
categories because they are meaningless in a secular age; and the
consequent confining of attention to this world and to what is
directly visible, experienceable, and verifiable within it.

(6) Finally, this is an action-centered view of human
existence. It repudiates the neoorthodox view that one must have
one's faith and one's theology in hand before one enters the world
to act creatively—how many people in the civil rights or the

---

[7] John Locke stated this same principle in 1700: "I think there
is one unerring mark of it [a love of truth] viz. The not entertaining any
Proposition with greater assurance than the proofs it is built on will warrant. Whoever goes beyond this measure of Assent, 'tis plain receives not
Truth in the love of it; loves not Truth for Truth's sake, but for some
other bye end." "Of Enthusiasm," from *Essay Concerning Human Understanding.*

peace movements have read Barth, Niebuhr, or even Luther? Rather, if man does not "need" God to do good—and the evidence seems to indicate that he does not—then why waste time on the abstract theological matters of faith before one plunges into the busy life of the world? Is there any legitimate role that religion, understood as the relation to God of the individual soul, plays in being a Christian, which surely means simply and solely "standing by the neighbor in the world"? Has not this sort of "religion," this emphasis on an impractical faith and theology centered in the parish church, become merely a way of justifying the religious establishments of the middle class which shun creative worldliness in the cities? No, says the modern man, to be a Christian is to act, to become involved, to enter the worldly scene in love and service, and *there* to be like "Jesus to the world." In doing this, such theology as is relevant, that is, such experience of the divine as might help a real Christian faith, will be discovered and then fashioned. Theology does not precede and condition action in the world; insofar as it exists and is relevant at all, it follows it and formulates what is experienced of the divine there; and faith is merely one's inner response to what one discovers of God by being a good neighbor within the worldly scene, or perhaps by being involved in revolutionary action. As Aristotle might have said to Luther: "One becomes good, and so becomes a believer, by doing good actions—not by believing first and then acting afterwards."[8] Needless to say, in this way the radical theology challenged at its deepest level the predominance of faith and of theology as prerequisites to active life in the Church and tended to make life in the academic seminaries of our land even more frustrated than it was before!

William Hamilton was the earliest, and perhaps remains the most influential, of the radical theologians.[9] He found himself, he says, unable as a theologian to speak of God for two main reasons:

[8] Cf. Martin Luther, *The Treatise on Christian Liberty.*

[9] The best expression of the early stages of Hamilton's "radical" thought is found in his book *The New Essence of Christianity* (New York: Association Press, 1961); later developments of Hamilton's theology can be seen in his essays in the book, written with Thomas Altizer, *Radical Theology and the Death of God* (Indianapolis: Bobbs-Merrill, 1966).

(1) the evil of the world made it impossible for him honestly to believe in, or even to wish to believe in, a God who ruled over nature and history; (2) the absence of God in his own experience, his inability to encounter God through faith, Word, or prayer, meant that there was, when he was honest with himself, no basis for either believing in God or speaking about him any longer. As he put this, doubt had so permeated faith as to take away all of the latter's certainty and so its power to give us knowledge of God. "Perhaps we ought to conclude that the special Christian burden of our time is the situation of being without God. There is for some reason no possession of God for us, but only a hope, only a waiting. . . . To be a Christian today is to stand, somehow, as a man without God, but with hope."[10]

Thus any theological language which presupposes either the gift or the present possession of faith is, if we are honest, neither valid nor authoritative. We cannot easily say "faith declares," or "faith assures us," or "faith knows"[11] when we speak of God, for in fact our faith, being not a present possession but only a hope, has no cognitive powers and thus is not able to say any of these things, and so neither should we.[12] Theology can-

[10] Hamilton, *The New Essence,* pp. 63–64.

[11] See the following from H. Richard Niebuhr as a particularly clear and persuasive example of the way the older theology regarded (1) *faith* as a direct and relatively autonomous cognitive relation to God in which God is "known" as objective reality, and (2) *theology*, therefore, as the rational explication of what is known of God in "religious faith": "It [theos] is the name for that objective being, that other-than-the-self, which men have before them as they *believe* rather than as they see, hear, feel, or even as they reason. This objective reality—God or the gods—is acknowledged or known in faith we say. . . . Theology must attend to the God of faith if it is to understand faith no less than it must attend to faith in God if it would understand God. Faith is at least as much an unavoidable counterpart of the presence of God as sense experience is an unavoidable counterpart of the presence of natural entities or powers . . . but faith and God belong together somewhat as sense experience and physical reality do." H. Richard Niebuhr, *Radical Monotheism and Western Culture* (New York: Harper & Bros., 1943), pp. 12 and 13.

[12] "Those of us who are trying to make the Christian faith intelligible to ourselves and to others have probably spent too much time and too many words saying that we saw and believed what we did not truly see and believe, and we did not like the experience of having deceived

not, therefore, begin with faith as if it were a cognitively certain starting point. For we are personally not at all *at* that starting point, and in reality our faith is not at all certain that it knows God. Consequently, since Hamilton has neither interest nor confidence in natural theology or metaphysical analysis, he finds no grounds for saying anything whatsoever about God.

This weakening of the cognitive certainty of personal faith is, I think, the crucial element in the movement we have been tracing from neoorthodoxy to the radical theology, and Hamilton has been the most helpful in documenting it in his writings. In neoorthodoxy, as we saw, all knowledge of God and so all language about him developed from the faith encounter. The intelligibility and so certainty of its God-language were, therefore, directly dependent on the cognitive power, that is, the definiteness, the authenticity, and the certainty involved in the faith relationship to God. Outside of that relation to the "Wholly Other," experience in general was devoid of God, the world was secular, and no theological language was possible. When, therefore, that relation itself seemed to dissolve through the acids of secularity, the sole touch to God in neoorthodoxy vanished as well. It is, says Hamilton, "a short step, but a critical one, to move from the otherness of God to the absence of God."[13]

Since the publication of this earlier book, Hamilton's thought with regard to God has become a good deal more radical. He has dropped his earlier categories of "waiting" for God, and of "enjoying God" instead of "needing Him." Thus the absence or removal of God have been replaced by "the death of God," "My Protestant has no God, has no faith in God, and affirms

---

ourselves, even if we deceived no one else." Hamilton, *The New Essence,* pp. 28–29. Here is a clear expression not only of the paucity of present faith, but also of what we have called the "principle of radical personal honesty," and so the rejection of theological statements on the sole basis of either scripture or tradition. It is surely also significant of our wider spiritual situation that close on the heels of the linguistic philosophers' denial of the cognitive powers of speculative reason comes the radical theologians' equally vehement denial of the cognitive powers of religious faith. Perhaps the main question of this book is, when all such transimmediate cognitive powers are culturally denied, how *does* the Church know "God"?

[13] *Ibid.*, p. 55.

both the death of God and all forms of theism," and, now "the death of God radical theologians . . . are men without God who do not anticipate his return."[14]

This death, moreover, is not merely an individual matter, says Hamilton, but a fact for our whole culture, for everyone. It represents a historic, cultural event that signifies an irrevocable change in fundamental attitudes and so the virtual impossibility for men now to believe in God, if, of course, they are real participants in our contemporary cultural life. He and his group, he says, witness to this event [the death of the experience and so the symbol of God] as happening objectively in our time,[15] that is, as a cultural event of universal, contemporary scope. In speaking, then, of the death of God, Hamilton does not seem to envision any change in the ontological structure of the universe as does Altizer, but he does imply a change in the character of our cultural mood or spirit, a change so fundamental as to make belief in God impossible in our age.

How is it possible to be a Christian in this time of the death of God; can there be a religionless and godless Christian theology? Hamilton answers this question, and so distinguishes himself from atheistic humanism, in terms of a continuing and, to him, essential relationship to Jesus and to the community formed around and through him. Jesus retains, in his view, a central and necessary role in the Christian's life, even if God be gone. It is he who, in effect, gives us a model of who we are and what we should be and do, and so who shapes that style of life which characterizes Christian existence. He loved the world, served it, stood beside the neighbor in need, and finally suffered in its hands out of love; this pattern is our pattern, so we should "become like Jesus in and to the world."[16] Christian faith, then, is not a relation to God or a basis of knowing God, surrendering to him or serving him; it is, rather, "a place to be," namely being in the world alongside the neighbor in love. Thus human beings, in their acts of love through community, can do for one another all that "God" was once supposed to have done, and all the prob-

[14] Altizer and Hamilton, *Radical Theology,* pp. 37 and 6.
[15] Cf. *ibid.,* pp. 27–28 and 46–47.
[16] *Ibid.* p. 49.

lems that can be solved are removable by such loving communal action.[17]

As these last comments indicate, a second important shift in Hamilton's theology has been his gradually growing optimism about man and about the possibility of historical progress. This optimism, to be sure, has always been implicit: to relinquish God and to retain a pessimistic view of man's capabilities is to invite despair. Furthermore, one of Hamilton's main themes has been the affirmation of man's autonomy. By this he means that man does not need God at all; if man has problems, and of course he does, solutions to these problems must come from man himself: "There are thus no places in the self or the world . . . where problems emerge that only God can solve. There are problems and needs, to be sure, but the world itself is the source of the solutions, not God."[18] In such a situation, where there are no intractable human dilemmas but only "problems" solvable by man's capacities, religion, which proclaims man's religious dependence on God for the resolution of his basic difficulties, can

[17] *Ibid.,* p. 116, and especially "The New Optimism," pp. 157–169.

[18] *Ibid.,* p. 116. In these remarks, and in his acceptance of Bonhoeffer's description of God as a "problem-solver," Hamilton has indicated clearly from the beginning his fundamentally optimistic or autonomous view of man. For "problems" are by nature solvable by human brains and application: like mending a roof, solving an equation, or dealing with a recalcitrant germ, mountainside, or even neighbor. They are soluble, to be mastered by a better technique, a more considered approach, a more energetic and dedicated application of will, i.e., they are to be solved by human powers in human ways. Classically, theology has dealt not with such "problems" but with real "dilemmas," where human powers are not effective, where precisely man finds himself unable to cope, either by intelligence or by will, with what confronts him: namely sin, fate, and death. To call God a "problem solver" is, therefore, first of all to misinterpret the main thrust of the classical tradition *vis à vis* the *kind* of need fulfilled by God, but even more it is *ipso facto* to declare that such dilemmas do not in fact exist, and so that everything that confronts man is a problem which human will and intelligence can resolve. In other words, it is to enunciate a very optimistic view of the human condition as subject to neither sin nor fate, and so as capable, in concert if not individually, of solving all the problems of life that can in any way be resolved.

be only a useless and distracting "crutch."[19] By implication, then, even in his darker earlier writings, Hamilton implied that, if men were free of religion and committed with Jesus to serving the world, man's major problems might be solved.

Now, however, this optimism has become explicit: the world is no longer cruel, and our godlessness is no tragic fate. Rather, the world is a place of joy, of creative discovery, of developing reform, and of expanding values. If we Christians can catch this mood—from the social sciences, our developing technology, creative and innocent social protest, former President Johnson himself, contemporary poetry, song, the dance, and the Beatles —we can be relieved of our theological gloom and learn to play, to be vital, creative, and good. Secular progress on all fronts— especially in civil rights and the peace movement—in our democratic, pluralistic, and idealistic society assures us that man in community can make a better life for himself, and the Christian should join in—though what the Christian (or Jesus) adds to the game is not so easy any longer to discover. It seems unquestionable to this observer that more and more Hamilton's thought is taking on the lineaments of liberal humanistic faith in man at the very moment when, ironically, the most "with it" movements in secularism, the hippies, the New Left, and the black power movement have precisely lost this faith in the possibilities of our democratic society. Only the continuing centering of this ethical

---

[19] Clearly Hamilton more and more reflects the fundamental concepts of the great atheistic humanist, Ludwig Feuerbach: for Feuerbach, (1) belief in God is a diversion from man's real work for man, making him think that without his effort the good can be accomplished; religion provides, that is, an unreal and futile *deus ex machina* that keeps man from active service; (2) what people once thought that only God could do, the community can do: judging, forgiving, supporting in time of individual need, providing ethical ideals, and so on. As Feuerbach says, the worship and dependence given to God should be directed at the species; and the love man thinks he owes to God, he should owe to his neighbor. The only significant difference between Feuerbach's thought and Hamilton's present position is the centrality of Jesus in the theology of the latter. Whether Hamilton can accept so much of Feuerbach and not go all the way to humanism with him is a question we shall further discuss in Chapter 5. Cf. Ludwig Feuerbach, *The Essence of Christianity* (New York: Harper Torchbooks, 1957).

humanism on the figure of Jesus as inspiration and model and Hamilton's personal sense of identification with the Christian community keep this thought in touch with any elements of the classical Christian tradition.[20]

One of the continuing dilemmas of radical theology, well illustrated by Hamilton, is the problem of method, that is, of the sources, content, and criteria of theology as a form of thought. In line with the "secular spirit" in both its antimetaphysical and its antitheological aspects, radical theology has rejected both metaphysical speculation and special religious sources, such as revelation or religious experience, for theological reflection, and it has embraced the secular as providing the materials, insights, and criteria for its thinking. Thus theology has relinquished any "home ground," so to speak, for its thought, and must find its place among the specialized and unconnected disciplines of secular life. If, like van Buren, the theologian is also a philosopher by training, nature, and inclination, he can, of course, move onto the ground of linguistic philosophy and carry on in the general field of analytic philosophy of religion. But if he is not, he is driven to depend on various other secular disciplines to supplement his own personal experience of life. Thus, as in Hamilton's case, literature becomes one central source for reflective theological insight, and we find theological ideas being developed out of the analyses of such literary figures as Dostoevski and Shakespeare, and categories such as "a Hamlet theology" and "an Orestes theology" appearing prominently in his writings. A second source is provided by studies of culture by social scientists and other experts;[21] here, too, Hamilton finds ideas about man, his prospects, and his destiny which are useful to the new theology.

[20] See Altizer and Hamilton, *Radical Theology*, pp. 48–49. In this place, Hamilton denies that his position is "sheer atheistic humanism" on two grounds: (1) the category of "waiting" (i.e., agnosticism) and (2) the relation to Jesus as Lord. Since the first category has been removed in his later thought, our analysis seems fair: this is ontologically atheistic, but inwardly it is a "religion" in the sense of involving an ultimate commitment to follow Jesus.

[21] Cf. Hamilton, *ibid.*, "Banished from the Land of Unity," pp. 53–84, and for the other references, cf. "Thursday's Child" for a brief dis-

There are, however, several serious problems for theological method and so for the theologian as a craftsman involved in this inevitable shift to the secular. In the first place, the theologian has no special competence in literary criticism or in social science. As a theologian, he carries no authority in these fields, and thus the truth of what he says must depend entirely either on his own personal insight as an amateur critic or else on the competence of others who are specialists, which tends in the long run to weaken both the creativity and the persuasiveness of his thought. Secondly, what he draws from the other disciplines, say from the social sciences, are not those elements of their thought in which these scientists are most competent, for Hamilton is not writing social science. What he can use in his theological reflection are only their convictions, guesses, hopes, conclusions, and prophecies about the ultimate nature and destiny of man and of the human story; not the scientific content of the social sciences but what Stephen Toulmin would call their mythical or "religious" meanings are grist to his mill. But it is obvious that, on this level, social science, and literary or cultural criticism as well, are at their weakest. In speaking of man's nature and destiny, that is, in providing us with either an optimistic or a pessimistic view of man, they have moved out of their field of special competence, where they contribute to our knowledge, into the realms of philosophy, religion, and myth. Here, like all of us, they are amateurs, and as often as not, like many physical scientists on this level, they merely reflect the unexamined and quite often naïve faiths and myths of our wider cultural context. The radical theologian, in sum, has no *Fach* or profession of his own. He tends to be an amateur in cultural analysis, and what he can elicit from specialized studies is precisely what is least authoritative in these fields. One wonders how long theology itself can live after the death of its traditional object and the consequent loss of its own indigenous methods.

---

cussion of his sources, pp. 89–90; "The Death of God Theologies Today," pp. 42–46; and "The New Optimism—from Prufrock to Ringo," pp. 157–69.

Despite this criticism, what Hamilton is saying has important theological implications. These concern, I believe, the subtle and honest way in which he has explored the relation of doubt to personal faith in a secular time, and the very significant results that this has for Christian faith and theological method. First of all, he has asked us to examine honestly not the doubt that permeates the world outside, but that which is there in both our personal and our corporate Christian existence: is there here either in our individual experience or in the communal life of worship anything resembling a sure possessed faith, an actual experience of "encounter" with God that can be regarded as so certain and filled with cognitive content as to base thereon a *knowledge* of God sufficient for theological discourse? Is not faith *actually*, in ourselves and in our concrete communities, an unrealized hope rather than a realized possession; and therefore can we really say we "know God in faith," as neoorthodox and hermeneutical theological methods have assumed?

Secondly, he has, I think, called the bluff involved in our usual answer to the question of the relation of doubt to faith. Far too often we have, either on Biblical or existential grounds, accepted doubt as one of the "normal" elements of vital faith— which it probably is. Thus we have said in effect, "However much I doubt, this does not touch my faith, for does not (*a*) Biblical faith always include doubt, or (*b*) does not the existential passion of doubt imply the stronger possession of faith?" Hamilton points out quite realistically that there comes a point where doubt ceases to reassure faith of its Biblical and/or its existential authenticity; rather, at that point it simply demolishes faith. If I *really* doubt that God is there, or that I have heard or encountered his Word in faith, this does not buttress my faith in him or in his revelation. What it does, in fact, is to replace it. It may indicate the death of God rather than the elusive hiddenness of the real God. In one of his best passages, Hamilton says:

> Let us continue to say that doubt is a necessary way for many of us to faith; that faith never overcomes doubt finally and completely; that lively faith can bear a good deal of doubt around the edges. But the depth of doubt is not the depth of

faith; these are two places, not one, and a choice must finally
be made between them. We cannot evade such a problem by a
trick of redefinition.[22]

In an age where secular *existence* has cast deep doubt on
the possibility of an encounter in faith with God, and so on both
the meaning and the validity of theological language, this honest
appraisal of the relation of doubt to faith inside Christian experience itself has great significance for Christian existence and not
least for the viability of a "faith" starting point for theology.

Despite his very different bent of mind and quite different perspective, Paul van Buren, in his book *The Secular Meaning of the
Gospel*,[23] nevertheless presented much the same picture of a contemporary secular Christianity. He shares with Bonhoeffer and
Hamilton the acceptance of the world as the center and goal of
Christian life, the consequent repudiation of "religion" as a false,
individualistic withdrawal from real life and duty, and the assertion that a Christianity devoted to the life of the world is thus
both secular and Biblical. Instead, however, of beginning with a
personal and existential experience of doubt, van Buren found
himself questioning, on philosophical grounds, the meaningfulness of language about God, of any language about ultimate reality
and ultimate meaning. Although he had been a Barthian, finally he
had to admit to himself that he was too much a thoroughly secular
man to find meaning in this esoteric Biblical language, and thus
that any faith that was to be credible to him must accord with the
principles of his own secularity. This meant that any viable faith
must be empirical, for, said he, empiricism is the essence of our
modern spirit, and empirical means "verifiable or falsifiable,"
much as A. J. Ayer and Antony Flew had insisted.[24] But no

---

[22] Hamilton, *The New Essence, op. cit.*, p. 61.

[23] Paul van Buren, *The Secular Meaning of the Gospel* (New
York: Macmillan Company, 1963).

[24] For the former, see the important but now quite dated book,
A. J. Ayer, *Language, Truth, and Logic* (London: Victor Gollancz, Ltd.,
1946), pp. 35 and 41, and for the latter, Antony Flew, ed., *New
Essays in Philosophical Theology* (London: SCM Press, 1955), especially
Chapter 6, "Theology and Falsification." For Ayer's own repudiation of

statement about God fits this standard of meaningful discourse. It is, for example, impossible to specify the objective conditions which could either verify or falsify, establish or disprove, the proposition that God is love. Thus language about God is literally meaningless to the modern empirical mood, and the *word* "God" is dead in our age. As van Buren puts this strongly: "Today we cannot even understand the Nietzschian cry that 'God is dead!', for if it were so, how could we know? No, the problem now is that the *word* 'God' is dead."[25]

Like Hamilton, however, van Buren does not feel that Christianity has died with its God. The loss of words about God should, he says, be no more serious for theology than were similar losses of words about divine forces in the movement from astrology to astronomy or from alchemy to chemistry.[26] Christians still have the Jesus of history, a man remarkable in his freedom, in his love, and in the authenticity and creativity of his life. The "contagion" of his freedom uniquely affected his followers after Easter and continues to challenge, grasp, and even transform our own freedom into a similar form of authentic life.[27] Jesus thus

---

the stringent uses of this verification principle, and the admission of the meaningfulness of limited metaphysical investigation, cf. A. J. Ayer, *The Concept of a Person and Other Essays* (London: Macmillan & Company, 1963), especially the essay "Philosophy and Language."

[25] Van Buren, *The Secular Meaning of the Gospel*, p. 103.

[26] "Theology cannot escape this tendency [i.e., to reduce its language from a God-centered language to a secular language] if it is to be a serious mode of contemporary thought, and such a 'reduction' of content [i.e., eliminating God] need no more be regretted in theology than in astronomy, chemistry, or painting" (i.e., when, in the case of the first two, astrology was reduced to astronomy and alchemy to chemistry). Van Buren, *ibid.,* p. 198. One may note, however, that the move from alchemy to chemistry was not a move *within* a given science, but a move from one dubious discipline to another, quite different, "scientific" one, whereas van Buren envisages this as a continuous progression within theology.

[27] *Ibid.,* pp. 128, 132, 141, 155, 169. For example, ". . . on Easter they [the disciples] found that Jesus had a new power which he had not had, or had not exercised, before: the power to awaken freedom also in them," p. 132; and "The Christian has seen a man of remarkable and particular freedom, and this freedom has become contagious for him, as it was for the apostles at Easter," p. 155.

remains our Lord, and theological statements are statements about him, his effects on us, the character of his life, and the perspective on ourselves and our behavior which he gives to us. Van Buren unfortunately adds that this is what the New Testament "really" said, and what (even more strangely) the Council and the Creed of Chalcedon "really meant," showing that, while an Episcopalian can dispense with God, he has a harder time relieving himself of ecclesiastical tradition!

When, later, van Buren was pressed about the empirical verifiability and thus meaning of his crucial word "contagion" (that is, "How does Jesus' contagion *work?*" "How can such an influence, whatever it is, be verified?" "How does or could *Jesus* grasp us?" "What does contagion *mean* here?" and so on), he admitted the dubious meaningfulness of this seemingly unverifiable or unfalsifiable usage of words. There being no possible physical virus with which the long-deceased Jesus could infect us today, use of the word "contagion" clearly illustrated no ordinary, univocal medical usage. If this language is to have any analogical meaning at all, therefore, propositions containing the word "contagion" must point to some sort of transnatural divine power or virus which links us with Jesus and so, seemingly, to imply the traditional (and exceedingly nonverifiable) God-language of the concept of grace! Thus it soon appeared that the category of the "contagion of Jesus" which grasps and transforms us is supernatural in its reference, and so must vanish along with deity from the secular theology. But this relation between our freedom in the present and the dead Jesus in the distant past is precisely the gospel as van Buren pictures it: "The Christian gospel is the news of a free man who did not merely challenge men to become free; he set men free."[28] And with the inability to speak intelligibly of this influence of Jesus on us, this relation becomes a great deal more tenuous than van Buren had at first proposed. Clearly the "Jesus-centric" character of this theology and thus its dependence upon scripture, the last carryover from the historic Christian tradition, becomes percarious without some semblance of God-language—even when the Lordship of Christ

[28] *Ibid.*, p. 169; cf. also pp. 128, 141.

has been reduced to the "contagion" of the historical Jesus.[29]

In *The Secular Meaning of the Gospel,* van Buren had used a rather strict interpretation of the verification principle of meaning as the instrument with which he attacked God-language. As is well known, philosophical criticism of this principle by language analysts themselves has not only challenged such usage but has begun to admit the possibility of meaningful metaphysical discourse. Following this general trend in language philosophy, van Buren, too, has recently tended to focus his critical attention on our ordinary usage of words, reflecting as they do our ordinary experience of things, of people and their finite, relative, and contingent interrelationships. Thus his current philosophical viewpoint comes out to look very much like the naturalistic pluralism that preceded positivism in this country (and most probably always functioned as its "metaphysical presupposition"), especially that of John Dewey.[30] Man is here set within a shifting context of natural forces and of people in society with which he has innumerable transactions and which make up what he ordi-

[29] By far the best criticism of the philosophical foundations of this book to have appeared is that of Professor Harmon Holcomb in "Christology without God," *Foundations,* January 1965. For a poor second (if that), see the author's review in the *Journal of Religion,* July 1964, reprinted as "A New Linguistic Madness" in *New Theology II,* ed. Martin E. Marty and Dean G. Peerman (New York: Macmillan Company, 1965).

[30] In a paper delivered in the spring of 1964 at Drew University, and subsequently published in a new series of essays called *Theological Explorations* (New York: Macmillan Company, 1968), van Buren admitted some quite significant changes in his own position: (1) meaningful language is no longer defined by a verification principle but by usage; (2) that usage can vary widely in correlation with its emotional content and its communal and cultural context; (3) the way is open, therefore, for metaphysical language as giving proposals as to "how things are"—not as providing information but as a proposal regarding the structure or gestalt of things. Personally, he said, this must be "naturalistic" to be meaningful for him, but that this is a more open position *vis à vis* traditional theology he fully agreed. For some of the background of this general viewpoint *vis à vis* religious language, see John Dewey's *Experience and Nature* (Chicago: Open Court Press, 1925), *A Common Faith* (New Haven: Yale University Press, 1934).

narily calls "reality." Any attempt by thought to move beyond this reality to an absolute or to pull it all together into a rational, harmonious, unified system is unwarranted and slightly arrogant. Man can study it through science, and he can seek to control these factors through his projected ideals; but to confuse the realm of the real with that of the ideal, to identify the ideal which man envisions with the real which he seeks to shape, is a very serious error. The symbol "God" may be useful as a symbol of man's own ideals and dreams; but this symbol is only misleading and false if taken as a way of thinking about the contingent and blind reality of natural life with which man has ultimately to deal. This is, to be sure, an admission both that metaphysical propositions about the contingent realities of ordinary experience are now possible and that God-language may have some valid if strictly limited usage. Nevertheless, since van Buren envisions nothing remotely resembling either an "ultimate reality" or a permanent source of order in the plural and purposeless cosmos he believes to be the case, no substantial change with regard to the issue of the reality of God has occurred in this change of his own view.

Van Buren has been widely criticized for his "tardy" use of the verification principle after that principle had been somewhat thoroughly falsified in the course of philosophical discussion. For this reason, there has been a tendency among defenders of God-language to think that the problem of meaninglessness that he had raised by means of this principle has likewise been laid to rest—as if by showing positivism to be wrong, one had shown with relief that metaphysical and/or theological language was thereby meaningful to our age! As we have tried to argue, positivism is merely *one* expression, a particularly rough one to be sure, of the inability of our age to speak meaningfully about the wider environment of man's existence. The same hesitancy to embark on language about the ultimate nature of things appears in empirical naturalism, existentialism, and linguistic philosophy —and the same sense of the meaninglessness of religious discourse is all too evident in our Christian life, both individual and communal. This problem was not created by positivism's rigors, nor will it end with the death of the verification principle: it is *there* embedded deeply in the fundamental *Geist* of our age. Van Buren is important for having raised it so pointedly. In so doing, he has challenged the easy assumptions of *both* revelational and philosophical theology that their forms of language —the one Biblical and founded on faith, the other metaphysical and founded on speculative generalizations—were meaningful to their age. Further, he has cogently implied that, in carrying on these sorts of language, these two types of theology were in fact removing themselves into a world of unreal and empty symbols and using in that world a currency that was not negotiable in the life that men of the twentieth century—and therefore theologians, too—are really living.[31] What he has forced upon theology, therefore, is the important task of investigating how religious language (God-language)—whether in Biblical or metaphysical form—is possible, and what sorts of meanings it in fact possesses. If, in other words, Hamilton has asked us, "How can we speak of God if he eludes our personal experience and if our personal faith is submerged in doubt?" van Buren has asked us, "How can any talk of God be meaningful if we live in a culture that knows nothing transcendent or ultimate at all?" And just as it is no answer to the first to appeal to the authority of the Word, of faith, or of the Church, so it is no answer to the second to insist that, since positivism is dead, a translation from mythical to metaphysical categories answers the modern question of meaningful discourse.

[31] Schubert Ogden seems to recognize van Buren's fundamental point, as we have formulated it here, in his new book, *The Reality of God* (New York: Harper & Row, 1966). Although there he still maintains (officially, might one say?) that the question of the meaningfulness of theological categories is resolved in the translation of Biblical words into the concepts of neoclassical speculative metaphysics (Chapters 2, 3, and 6), nevertheless, when he really conducts an argument on his own to establish the possibility and even the necessity of God-language, it is not to the method of speculative metaphysics that he turns, but to a combination of linguistic and phenomenological analysis of man's existential and moral problems (see pp. 22ff., 110ff.). Apparently, just as fideistic theologians are less and less able merely to appeal to "the Word received in faith," to ground the meaning and validity of their discourse, so the metaphysical thinker, despite himself, turns away from these forms of abstraction to other, more concrete and immediate forms of argument.

In many ways the most intriguing and certainly the most original of the Christian radical theologians is Thomas J. J. Altizer. Initially he impresses the reader as the most unabashedly atheistic of the trio. The cry "God is dead" is here voiced with increased vehemence: "It is precisely the acceptance of Nietzsche's proclamation of the death of God that is the real test of a contemporary form of faith."[32] "Furthermore, we shall simply assume the truth of Nietzsche's proclamation of the death of God. . . . This means we shall understand the death of God as an historical event: God has died in *our* time, in *our* history, in *our* existence."[33] And as if this were not enough: "Nor will it suffice for theology merely to accept the death of God. If theology is truly to die, it must *will* the death of God, must *will* the death of Christendom, must freely choose the destiny before it, and therefore must cease to be itself. Everything that theology has thus far become must now be negated."[34] "Never before has faith been called upon to negate all *religious* meaning."[35]

When one reads these strident sentences, it seems at first that all touch with what has traditionally been called Christianity has been relinquished, and one wonders what sort of "Christian theology," which is what Altizer purports to be writing, is now possible. This is revolutionary fare, but still it claims to be Christian: "No, the radical Christian is a revolutionary, he is given to a total transformation of Christianity, a rebirth of the Christian Word in a new and final form."[36] But a further study of these oracular, often brilliant, and certainly original writings gradually unveils a quite new vision of Christianity which, while accepting most of the principles of radical theology, in the end differs almost as much from that of van Buren and Hamilton

[32] T. J. J. Altizer, "America and the Future of Theology," *Radical Theology, op. cit.*, p. 11. Cf. also the following: "A theology that chooses to meet our times, a theology that accepts the destiny of history, must first assess the theological significance of the death of God." *Ibid.*

[33] Altizer and Hamilton, *Radical Theology*, p. 95. For other writings of Altizer, cf. *Mircea Eliade and the Dialectic of the Sacred* (Philadelphia: Westminster Press, 1963) and *Oriental Mysticism and Biblical Eschatology* (Philadelphia: Westminster Press, 1961).

[34] Altizer and Hamilton, *Radical Theology*, p. 15.

[35] *Ibid.*, p. 13.

[36] *Ibid.*, p. 26.

as it does from traditional Christian theology. In fact, as we shall see, while the most vehement in proclaiming the death of God, Altizer is the one member of the trio who does not believe for a moment that the divine is unreal or nonexistent. By no means a naturalistic, humanistic theologian, Altizer is inspired by a mystical awareness of, dependence on, and waiting for the divine power that manifests itself in current life and in history.

In order to understand this paradoxical theology, we have to move back into the nineteenth century, especially to the thought of Hegel, Nietzsche, Blake, Melville, and Freud, and above all we must bring to mind the radical polemic in the early Hegel against any form of transcendence and any attempt to freeze or render static that which is real. Following this tradition, then, Altizer's is a process, immanentist theology with a vengeance, the divine is life, flesh and world; and it despises any God separated in transcendence from flesh, life, and history. It is, then, precisely that transcendent, separated God who has died for Altizer. But that every aspect of the divine "principle" of this theology is dead, or that Altizer's ecstatic theological style follows van Buren's cool advice to eschew all forms of religious, mystical, or metaphysical God-language (unverifiable and unempirical) would be a vast overstatement! This theology is saturated with a consciousness of the dynamic, redemptive power of the sacred; and in fact, the word "God" forms the active subject of most of the important theological statements in his most recent book. This is, then, a reformulation, not a denial of God-language in theology. Admittedly, God acts here in a very "queer" sort of way, but that the divine is for Altizer real, significant, and alive, there can be no doubt.[37]

[37] To take random samples of this affirmation of the reality and existence of God—at least as a very active subject of theological sentences: "God has negated and transcended himself in the incarnation, and thereby he has fully and finally ceased to exist in his original or primordial form. To know that God *is* Jesus is to know that God himself has become flesh; no longer does God exist as transcendent spirit or sovereign Lord, now God *is* love." *The Gospel of Christian Atheism* (Philadelphia: Westminster Press, 1966), p. 67. "The forward movement of the Incarnate Word is from God to Jesus, and the Word continues its kenotic movement and direction by moving from the historical Jesus to

How, then, are we to understand his proclamation of the
death of God side by side with his continual assertions of the divine activity? The key to Altizer's thought is his concept of the
living Christian Word. It is in the terms of this symbol that he
interprets the other Christian symbols which he finds helpful,
namely the Incarnation, eschatology, the Kingdom of God, and,
of course, the real nature of the divine or God. This Word is for
him, as for Hegel, now radically immanent, in process, forward
moving and dynamic; implicitly it is the source of life, of meaning, and so of all cultural creativity.

Apparently, however, this total immanence of the divine
was not always the case. God himself, for Altizer as for Hegel,
is in dynamic process, and this process consists in going out from
himself in negation into an Other (the finite, the fleshly, and the
historical), identifying himself dialectically with that Other, and
forming a new dialectical synthesis out of the prior thesis of the
transcendent, separate God, and the prior antithesis of the dynamic, finite, and contingent world. This dynamic process of self-
alienation, self-negation, and final synthesis is for Altizer *historical*, it happens in *temporal* stages (whereas, one suspects, it was
logical and ontological for Hegel). That is to say, the stages of

---

the universal body of humanity." *Ibid.*, p. 83. "Obviously the relation between man and God must undergo genuine transformations as this process
unfolds. Yet if this process is actual and real, that is to say, if it is a historical process occurring in the concrete contingencies of time and space,
then God himself must act and exist in such a manner as to negate his
primordial mode of Being," *Ibid.*, p. 87.

While these quotations surely prove that this is a theology with
a dynamic, immanentist deity, they certainly *also* establish that the divine
here is a real, active, significant factor in the objective process of things,
and that therefore this vision is anything but "naturalistic," "empirical,"
or even "humanistic" in the sense upheld by the theologies of Hamilton
and van Buren. For this reason, I do not agree with Rubenstein's esti-
mates of Altizer's thought as being radically humanistic and optimistic
(see Richard L. Rubenstein, Jr., *After Auschwitz* [Indianapolis: Bobbs-
Merrill, 1966], pp. 247ff.). It is the transcendent, separated deity that
Altizer rejects with such vehemence; however, an immanent deity or
principle of the sacred, incarnated in human flesh in the processes of history rather than the "autonomous" natural powers of human life, is for
him the source and ground of salvation.

this dialectic represent definite historical moments or periods within the development of process, and changes from stage to stage occurred as definite historical events. There was *once* the transcendent deity who was creator and lord of creation; but *then,* in the moment of historical time Christian faith calls the Incarnation, he negated himself, entered the Other in kenosis, and became radically immanent within that Other. The meaning of the symbols of the Incarnation and of the Atonement, therefore, is precisely that here in this total event the transcendent Lord came into the finite and identified himself totally with it. At the Incarnation, then, it was not only Christ the Son who entered flesh and died; rather the transcendent, separate God himself entered history and died as *transcendent,* through an act of self-negation.[38]

This is a new and quite unique meaning to the phrase "death of God," entirely different from anything Hamilton or van Buren had envisioned. It means, apparently, an ontological-historical event, not alone in man's culture but in the development of reality itself.[39] For Altizer, moreover, it is to this event

[38] Students of historical theology may possibly be able to place Altizer's thought by recalling the early Christian view (or heresy) called "modalism" or "patripassionism," a view associated with the name of Sabellius, and influential in Roman circles in the later second and early third centuries. There, too, a transcendent Lord changed his status, identified himself in kenotic self-giving in the Incarnation with the figure of Jesus, and so "died" on the cross, initiating thereby a third and final mode of his own existence, namely one of radical immanence in the Spirit. Strangely, Moltmann's view, as he admitted at a colloquium at Duke University, could *also* be described as a modern form of Sabellianism, except that there the roles of father, son, and spirit are reversed, and the father comes last, as the culminating eschatological event, not at creation!

[39] References affirming the ontological-cosmic character of the event of the "death of God" are legion in Altizer's later works. Here are two samples: "At no point in this process is God uniquely himself: each point or moment in the process embodies a metamorphosis of God, as God remains himself even while estranged from himself, for it is precisely God's self-estrangement or self-negation that actualizes his forward movement and process. . . . Yet the Christian confesses that it is God who has become Christ; and the God who became Christ was once manifest and real as Creator and Lord. . . . Therefore to speak of God as a dialectical process rather than as an existent Being is to speak of the God who

of the divine self-negation that an authentic Christianity witnesses. And it is this new, dynamic, divine-finite synthesis of God
and the historical to which Altizer refers when he speaks of "the
Christian Word." This is not a changeless Word spoken and
established by a God who otherwise still remains transcendent;
on the contrary, it is a dynamic Word established precisely by the
death or self-negation of the transcendent God.[40] It is this dynamic Word, passing from God to Jesus and thence in immanence
out into history and into humanity, that can renew life, mankind,
and all things. In this Word lies the principle of salvation, a
salvation of and by God, through Jesus and realized in history,
but pointing ever toward a future culmination, when "God will
be all in all."[41] This future epiphany is that to which the Kingdom of God and all the other crucial eschatological symbols of
the tradition refer. It is to this possibility, namely of a new age of
the spirit in which the dialectical oppositions of the sacred and
the profane, of the God who has died and thus entered life, are
known and proclaimed, that the living Christian faith witnesses—

---

has emptied himself of God in Christ." *The Gospel of Christian Atheism,*
p. 90. "The radical Christian proclaims that God has actually died in
Christ, that this death is both a historical and a cosmic event, and as such,
it is a final and irrevocable event, which cannot be reversed by a subsequent religious or cosmic movement." *Ibid.,* p. 103.

[40] "Before the Incarnation can be understood as a decisive and
real event, it must be known as effecting a real change or movement in
God himself: God becomes incarnate in the Word, and he becomes fully
incarnate, thereby ceasing to exist or to be present in his primordial form."
Ibid., p. 44. "As one who is called to witness to the dynamic presence and
the forward movement of the Word, the Christian must always be open
to the transfiguring power of the Incarnate Word, knowing that the
Word is in process of renewing all things, not by recalling them to their
pristine form in the Beginning, but rather by making them new so that
they can pass into the End." *Ibid.,* p. 18. "For the Christian *Word* is an
evolving Word, a forward moving Word, a Word that only exists and is
real only in the concrete life of history." *Ibid.,* p. 45.

[41] "The forward movement of the Incarnate Word is from God
to Jesus, and the Word continues its kenotic movement and direction by
moving from the historical Jesus to the universal body of humanity,
thereby undergoing an epiphany in every human hand and face." *Ibid.,*
p. 83.

not to a "religious" return to an original, transcendent being, separated from concrete existence, repressive of it, and finally now, in our time, dead from emptiness, exhaustion, and just sheer satanic evil!

In its strange way, this remarkable and highly original vision reflects many elements of the classical structure of Christian orthodox faith: dependence throughout on God's dynamic activity, the centrality of the Incarnation, a relation to salvation through the continuing activity of the Spirit, all moving forward into the future to an eschatological end. And, as we noted, the central Christian symbols of God, creation, fall, Incarnation, Word, Spirit, Kingdom of God, etc., form the symbolic foundation on which this thought is constructed. From this point of view, this theology is much more conservative than are those of Hamilton and van Buren. There is no hint of materialistic naturalism, of an optimistic dependence on human autonomy alone,[42] or of a drastic reduction in modes of theological language, and this viewpoint could hardly be called "atheistic," despite the title of Altizer's main work.

On the other hand, Altizer's theology is in other respects more radical than that of the others. The central principle of the dynamic, forward-moving, ever-changing Word gives to his thought an essentially revolutionary character that the thought of the other two, with their present concern for the historical Jesus, cannot have. For Altizer insists repeatedly that the forms of the Word have continually changed and will always do so, often actually "negating" former forms and even negating the original form of the Word in Jesus himself. Thus no traditional theological categories, whether those of the Bible generally, of the New Testament gospels, or of ecclesiastical history have any real authority at all for the present Christian.[43] The theologian must

[42] "Yet now the Christian God is dead! The transcendence of Being has been transformed into the radical immanence of Eternal Recurrence: to exist in our time is to exist in a chaos freed of every semblance of cosmological meaning or order." Altizer and Hamilton, *Radical Theology*, p. 102.

[43] As opposed to the other "radicals," Altizer rejects completely the authority for faith and life of the *historical* Jesus: "But by opening

speak of the living Word in the present, and the forms of his
thought are determined alone by that present and not by the dead
and heavy hand of the past.[44] The concept of the dynamic Word,
therefore, provides the theological basis for Altizer's insistence
that theology must be a *contemporary* witness to the cultural
mood of its present and must "accept the destiny of its time"—
and so, in our godless age, theology must affirm the death of God.
This is, then, a revolutionary theology of the Spirit, as Altizer
realizes, for the Word is not a Word of the past, nor even a Word
once and finally shaped by the authority of Jesus.[45] It is present,
alive, moving, changing—and so, presumably, is the theology
that speaks of it.

For Altizer, therefore, there are no recognizable criteria

---

ourselves to the immediate actuality of the moment before us, we can
know the Jesus who is present in the fullness of time itself, even if that
time should prove to be a negation or reversal of the past event of Jesus
of Nazareth." *The Gospel of Christian Atheism, op. cit.,* p. 61. For other
assertions of the irrelevance of the historical Jesus as a criterion of the
present Word—as well as the impossibility of establishing what he was
like—see *ibid.,* pp. 48–54 and *Radical Theology, op. cit.,* pp. 104 and
123–125.

[44] "Each historical expression of the Word will bear its own peculiar and distinct reality, and while no clear path may be seen to lie
between one and another, faith must ever seek that particular form of
the Word which acts in its own presence." *Gospel of Christian Atheism,
op. cit.,* p. 46. "A Word must be judged to be non-Christian if it cannot
appear and become real in a present and human act of faith, and it is
non-Christian to the extent it cannot become incarnate in the immediate
horizon of faith." *Radical Theology, op. cit.,* p. 122. See the remarkably
similar assertion from the nineteenth-century liberal Auguste Sabatier:
"Every divine revelation, every religious experience fit to nourish and
sustain your soul, must be able to repeat and continue itself as an actual
revelation and an individual experience in your own consciousness." *Outline of a Philosophy of Religion Based on Psychology and History* (London: Hodder & Stoughton, 1906), pp. 62–63.

[45] As he had disputed the authority of the *historical* Jesus, for
faith, so one of the traditional Christian themes most frequently rejected
by Altizer is the ultimacy, the *Einmaligkeit,* of the total Christ-event, so
central to all forms of neoorthodox theology as a final revelation of the
character of the Word of God: "At no point in this process does the incarnate Word or Spirit assume a final and definitive form." *Gospel of
Christian Atheism, op. cit.,* p. 104; cf. also *ibid.,* p. 58 and *Radical Theology, op. cit.,* pp. 18–19.

for what the Christian theologian should say, as there are in a Biblical theology, a confessional or a philosophical theology, or even as in theologies based, as were those of van Buren and Hamilton, on contemporary reflection on the life and death of Jesus. Having heard Altizer say on occasion that *everything* that theology has been must now be negated,[46] and that we have lost *all* our Christain images, the reader wonders to what criteria, besides the formulations made explicit in his own theology, Altizer could point if he wished to say of a given form of thought, "No, that is not Christian," or to claim for his own thought that it is. And then one wonders, too, what conceivable principles can allow Altizer to appeal, as he frequently does, to an "authentic Christian faith" or to "the fundamental if underlying meaning of the earliest expressions of the Christian faith,"[47] and use as authorities for his own theology such "authentic" symbols, as he calls them, from the past as the Incarnation, the Fall, and eschatology.

Perhaps, as these remarks hint, the main difficulty with this theology is the apparent impossibility of arguing with it; and the correlative difficulty for its proponent that it fails to convince. That is to say, it is hard to know, on the one hand, on what common ground we can disagree with Altizer and, on the other, what grounds *he* can appeal to to persuade us that what he says is true. The appeal to some agreed "authority" (whether of sense experience, scripture, "science," logic or custom) is, let us note, inescapable in the enterprise of rational discourse or argumentation. For such appeal is the basis both of disproof or rejection of ideas, on the one hand and, on the other hand, of persuasion, of eliciting from the hearer agreement and conviction of the truth of what is said because it agrees with this commonly accepted authority. In inquiry some mode of "authority" provides the ground, or is the ground, for the verification or falsification of any hypothesis, and so the question "What is the authority to which you appeal?" is in effect the question "On what basis do you claim your statements to be true?"

Now, the point is that this theology seems to have rejected at one time or another all the familar theological author-

[46] Altizer and Hamilton, *Radical Theology*, p. 15.
[47] Altizer, *The Gospel of Christian Atheism*, p. 105.

ities: the Biblical Word in any of its forms; the historical facts
of Jesus' life; classical, traditional, or modern Church doctrine;
the consensus of the Church in the present; an analysis of religious experience, Christian or universal; philosophical inquiry
into general experience, metaphysical, phenomenological, or linguistic; and certainly "science" in all its forms—all of these possible grounds for theological assertions are upset, overturned, or
rendered irrelevant by the principle of the fast-moving Word.
Even present culture in its specific philosophical forms is disre-
garded according to the dialectical principle that the "truth" of
the present always negates the "surface" of the present.[48] This
makes it impossible to argue with Altizer, for no common ground
with his reader is presented—except for the authority of such
figures as Hegel, Nietzsche, Blake, and Melville. And certainly
it is useless to argue whether or not this theology is "contemporary," perhaps the one available criterion Altizer seems to
recognize. For if there was ever a unique and "unsecular" form
of thought, "far out" in relation to the contemporary mood of
an empirical, scientific culture, it is this latter-day Hegelian, dialectical, and mystical vision of a dynamic, self-negating, divine
immanence.

Correspondingly, however, one also does not know how
one might be persuaded of its truth. Hegel argued laboriously by
means of philosophical, logical, and historical analyses for a ver-
sion of the same position; other theologians have argued for their
positions on the grounds of the authority of scripture, tradition,
"religious experience," or have carried on some sort of intelligible analysis of general human experience, individual and social. Altizer argues in none of these ways. He seems to appeal
only to the thematic characteristics of Christian faith to persuade
us: to the meanings implicit in such symbols as the Incarnation,
the Word, eschatology, saying, in effect, "If you take these symbols seriously, you must understand them in such and such a
way." This is not an impossible form of theological argument,
as the Swedish school of *Motiv-forschung* has shown; but the
theological force of their argument lay ultimately in the authority
of scripture and tradition where these themes were discovered,

[48] Altizer and Hamilton, *Radical Theology,* pp. 140–141.

and Altizer has already repudiated the validity of these two authorities. In the end, therefore, bereft of scripture, of tradition, of philosophical method, of an appeal to personal experience, or of social analysis, this theology presents us as its sole authority the brilliant but quite particular vision of the author and of the literary tradition he represents. Because he provides us with no "place," besides his own thought itself, where we can look for the validation of his thought, we close his book with a feeling that, while he can proclaim powerfully to us and interest us masterfully, in the end he cannot persuade us that what he says is true.

Besides its inherent interest and stimulating power, what does this unique vision of Christianity offer us? For this writer, the most valuable contribution of Altizer is that through him—and through no other theologian of whom I am aware—the powerful polemic of nineteenth-century Romanticism, especially that of Hegel, Nietzsche, and Freud, against the transcendent, separated deity of orthodoxy, has entered and challenged the theological consciousness. This is a tradition which exulted in life, in joy, in the strength and courage to bear pain, in freedom, in the spontaneous, in the creative—that found living being a veritable spring of the only real values that there are. It was a tradition, therefore, that saw plainly that the *transcendent* as well as the "idolatrous" could function in a demonic manner in human life; that, to use Tillich's terms, emphasized the creativity of *autonomy* because it saw so clearly the dangers of the heteronomous.[49] To be sure, elements of the neoorthodox movement felt

---

[49] By "heteronomy" is meant an external divine power, separated from the essential nature and so creativity of the creature, which by its power and authority crushes and ultimately destroys the freedom and the autonomous powers of the creature. The concept goes back to Hegel in his criticism of the transcendent principle of Judaism and of historical Christian theology. In Hegel's own view, the Absolute works in and through the creature and so does not destroy it. The same point was made by Tillich in his defense of a theonomous religious principle. For this whole tradition, therefore, the supernatural that is separated, "above" and "over against" the creature, is essentially destructive of the natural life and powers of the creature, once the latter has experienced the infinite power of its own rational and moral freedom—and thus can no transcendent principle be borne or tolerated by modern man.

traces of this inheritance of Romanticism—or discovered it on
the couch!—and so tried, not unsuccessfully, to establish these
values of *life* and the joyous living of it through its doctrines of
creation, Incarnation, and the reevaluation of most ethical problems. Having thus given a nod to this tradition of immanence,
it tended then, however, to talk for the next four hundred pages
about transcendence, judgment, external grace, and obedience.
With the exception of Paul Tillich, dialectical theology had, in
other words, far too little sense of the demonic possibilities of
transcendence as well as of immanence, possibly because (having
been reared by liberals and not by orthodox), its proponents
were conscious only of the dangers of immanence and conceived
of only the *prophetic* rather than the *repressive* possibilities of
transcendence. But historically, psychologically, and theoretically,
transcendence has often warred with joy in life, with human creativity, and with freedom—with the free exultant realization of
one's own potentialities as a finite being. It is no accident that the
symbol of transcendence and the symbol of the father figure have
always been historically identified. This proclamation of autonomy, and of its joys and its possibilities, free now from the transcendent that sets for it given rules, or carves out for it an *a priori*
niche, is one of the most creative elements of our modern secularity, and it is this that Altizer's thought has brought into theology. From now on, everyone will be more wary than before of
any categories of transcendence that theology might be able to
muster. Altizer argues that transcendence and life are essentially
irreconcilable. To counter this as erroneous, and to assert that the
creative joy in life is not only consistent with but ultimately dependent on a sense of the transcendent depths and inexhaustible
mystery of God, will be one of the main burdens of the second
part of this volume.

The most compelling of the radical theologians in our view is
Rabbi Richard L. Rubenstein, whose book *After Auschwitz*[50]
appeared late in 1966. To Rubenstein, the experience of the death
of six million Jews has made forever incredible the two cardinal

[50] For details of *After Auschwitz*, see note 37.

beliefs of historic Judaism: that there is a God who is Lord of history, and that this God has a special relation to the Jewish people. If these two assertions are true, says Rubenstein, then the murder of the Jews must have been a part of God's purposes, and "I would rather live in an absurd, indifferent cosmos than believe that." The cosmos, therefore, for Rubenstein, is blind, unfeeling, indifferent—unrelated to any human meanings and projects except that it has produced us and will claim us in the end, in death. Meanwhile, our task is to find, create, and enjoy what meanings there are and can be in this ultimately hopeless situation, and to be able to live the one life we have with as much creativity, joy, and shared community as is possible. Three quotations give the primary substance of his position:

> He [Camus in *The Plague*] would rather live in an absurd, indifferent cosmos in which men suffer and die meaninglessly but still retain a measure of tragic integrity than see every last human event encased in a pitiless framework of meaning which deprives man of even the consolation that suffering, though inevitable, is not entirely merited or earned. . . . We concur with this choice of an absurd and ultimately tragic cosmos. We do so because we share with Camus a greater feeling for human solidarity than the prophetic-Deuteronomic view of God and of history can possibly allow. . . . We have turned away from the God of history to share the tragic fatalities of the God of nature. . . . After the experiences of our time, we can neither affirm the myth of the omnipotent God of History nor can we maintain its corrolary, the election of Israel. . . . Jews do not need these doctrines to remain a religious community.[51]

> If there is a God of history, he is the ultimate author of Auschwitz. I am willing to believe in God, the holy nothingness who is our source and our final destiny, but never again in a God of history. . . . What the existentialists do mean is that there is no *ultimate* meaning to existence. They call upon men to create with lucidity their own private meanings and purposes in the knowledge that no power in the cosmos will ultimately sustain or validate them. . . . What the death of God theologians depict is an undoubted *cultural fact* in our

[51] *Ibid.*, pp. 67–69.

time: God is totally unavailable as a source of meaning or value. There is no vertical transcendence. Our problem is not how we shall think of God in a secular way. It is how men can best share the decisive crises of life, given the cold, unfeeling, indifferent cosmos that surrounds us and given the fact that God, the Holy Nothingness, offers us only disillusion and death as the way out of earthly existence. It is in this situation that the traditional church and synagogue are most meaningful.[52]

There is only one Messiah who redeems us from the irony, the travail and the limitations of human existence. Surely he will come. He is the Angel of Death. Death is the true Messiah and the land of the dead the place of God's true kingdom. Only in death are we redeemed from the vicissitudes of human existence. We enter God's kingdom only when we enter His holy Nothingness.[53]

We are called, then, to create with our own human powers and projects a creative life in the midst of this nothingness. Such a creative human life is for Rubenstein, therefore, no easy task: technology, "goods," "progress," and even better political, social, and economic structures make little real difference to the character of human existence. Man's life is difficult and tragic in every age, and his fundamental problems of loving and being loved, of loneliness, guilt, aging, and death are much the same from generation to generation. What is necessary in order to bear these tragic aspects of life and so to become a "decent human animal," is that we are aware of and know who we are, what our stage of life is, how our acts are suffused with guilt, how lonely and isolated we often feel, and how death is to be borne. To know this in a community that shares with us in lucidity and honesty this awareness of fragmentariness and mortality is essential. For this, a religious community is necessary, and especially one structured by traditional rituals which allow us communally to express and so to relieve these recurrent, cyclical crises of human existence. "In a world without God religion is more necessary than ever," a religion that is man-made, priestly in form, ritualistic in practice,

[52] *Ibid.*, pp. 204–205.
[53] *Ibid.*, p. 198.

communal—and of psychological validity only.[54] As Rubenstein puts this, we must relinquish the God of history and return to the gods of nature—of life, birth, family, passage, and death—a pagan form of Judaism is the only viable form of modern Jewish existence.[55] In Rubenstein, the sense of the death of God in a tragic and meaningless world has led to possibly the most violent upheaval of established theological concepts of all. For a rabbi to defend the pagan gods against the Lord of history is in truth something new under the sun!

One must, however, posit a fundamental question about this interpretation, profound as it is. First, can ritual ever be separated as fully as Rubenstein wishes, from its accompanying myth, without losing the strength and meaningfulness of the ritual acts themselves? Rubenstein is right that consciously held doctrines and consciously determined deeds are not the substance of religion and do not touch the subconscious depths of personality where both destruction and health originate. But surely it is obvious that ritual without *any* accompanying conscious elements, in this case some deeply affirmed religious myth or doctrine, is equally vapid and meaningless, done by rote for traditional reasons and so incapable of generating precisely the psychological forces of release, self-acceptance, and identity that Rubenstein feels we need so desperately. Ritual alone, the sacrament without the Word, the Jewish liturgy without any inward belief at all in the divine relation to history, is as barren as is the Word alone. Rubenstein has dispensed with the traditional "myths" of Judaism in which this ritualistic scheme of atonement, sacrifice, membership in the community, and death has found its meaning for

---

[54] An ironical aspect for Christian theology of Rubenstein's thought is that this "psychological, man-made, ritualistic" *religion*, unrelated to any divine activity or revelation at all, is precisely the picture of "religion" that neoorthodoxy found so appalling. That Rubenstein should find this "demonic" (to neoorthodoxy) human creation the sole form of "faith" possible to modern man shows the vast shift of theological temper that has taken place. We should also note that it marks a turn away even from Bonhoeffer, who wished to "speak about God without religion," whereas Rubenstein seeks to speak of religion without God.

[55] *Ibid.*, pp. 93–111, p. 240.

conscious awareness; he cannot hope to reinstate these ritual forms today in terms of whatever pagan mythos preceded Sinai. One wonders, therefore, how stable is this complex ritualistic edifice in the naturalistic-existential universe Rubenstein affirms, and so whether, with the demise of the Lord of history, his gods of nature and of earth will not also weaken and die. Especially is this the case, an outsider feels, in Judaism, where the very depth of the understanding through its ritual of the anxieties of finitude and guilt, as well as the strength of its communal sense, both of which Rubenstein extols, depend on the very concepts of the Lord of history and of the covenant people which he has rejected. One suspects that *real* paganism, untouched by the covenant and by prophetic insight, would not help Rubenstein with his life's problems much more than would the busy optimism of our current secular world. It was, after all, the Teutonic, pagan gods of earth, place, and of race and blood, resurrected in the new technological world, that played at least a partial role in the events he deplores. Perhaps the same Canaanite deities in sunny Israel will prove more benevolent, though that itself is possibly dubious. But in the one case as in the other, some prophetic transcendence over the meanings and loyalties generated by community and racial ties seems necessary if the quietly creative humanity for which Rubenstein yearns is to be preserved—and not least when these religious communities reach political autonomy, as in Israel.

Among the many powerful themes in Rubenstein's thought, the one that carries the most force in his denial of God is surely his dealing with the problem of evil. The reality of tragedy in history has, as we noted in an earlier chapter, been a strong ally of recent neoorthodox apologetics in an age where secular humanism was "optimistic" and theology "realistic." Thus theologians could argue effectively, "*If* life is to have meaning as its necessary presupposition, that meaning must be affirmed by faith, and God must be affirmed as its sole source." A good many people in the twentieth century have believed in God *because* history was tragic, and they knew no other way to understand that tragedy creatively. Now Rubenstein—with the help of Camus, to be sure—has uncovered some of the deep problems of this ground for faith if it be the sole ground. Evil in history can reveal itself as so great that there is more existential meaning to life without belief in God than there is with it. As he argues, at a certain level of tragedy, it is surely easier to understand and to bear evil in a meaningless world than in one in which God rules. This potent argument poses a challenge very near to the heart of Biblical faith, which has always offered itself as the fullest answer in any existential situation to the problems of fate, sin, and death, and it represents the profoundest aspect of the mood of secular rebellion against the ancient sense of an ultimate order and goodness in the structure of being. Any theological answer to this revolt against God must incorporate this modern sensitivity to evil at its deepest point and never relinquish it—rather than simply using evil to lead thought to the God who can resolve it away.

In the radical theologians, therefore, we have protest against God-language on four related but significantly different grounds: the weakness of faith and the experience of the absence of God; the meaninglessness of all speech about reality as such, whether that speech be based on revelation or on metaphysical inquiry; the demonic character of the transcendent as a challenge to the joy and creativity of life; and, finally, the impossibility, nay the destructive immorality, of understanding historical evil on any other but naturalistic, radically secular terms. These protests are not by any means new to secular thought, but their appearance together as determinants of theological reflection create the new situation theologically.

5 / Critique: The Necessity of God-Language for Christian Discourse

I

F IN THE PRECEDING CHAPTER we have reviewed the character of the radical theology, it is now time to look at some of those not inconsiderable inconsistencies and problems which, we feel, prevent it from providing a creative theological answer to the problems of a secular age. Hamilton's description of theology is a classic.[1] It is, he says, like having six storm windows to cover eight dilapidated windows—wherever you put the six, leaks will appear behind you. Thus the theologian rushes continually about trying to plug up the openings that old formulations have created, only to find new leaks appearing at his rear. The radicals have ably spotted the gaps in neoorthodoxy, classical liberalism, and philosophical theology; let us return the compliment with the admonition that the leaks are considerably greater if God-language is omitted than if it is not.

In what follows, we shall not try to prove that these theologians are "un-Christian." In the first place, it is difficult to see to whom one could appeal to define authentic Christianity since for somebody somewhere *all* of us have left out something essential and are thus "heretics." Besides, it is futile to appeal to the standard authorities of scripture and tradition. They *are* authorities for theological thought only because revelation in some form is assumed to be mediated to us through them, and this assumption, or the presupposition of God on which it is

[1] William Hamilton, *The New Essence of Christianity* (New York: Association Press, 1961), pp. 43–44.

founded, is precisely what these men are involved in questioning.

What form, then, can a critique of radical theology take? First of all, such a critique can question the consistency of the theological structure here presented to us: Can its essential parts be held together intelligibly, or must they break apart because, some essential element being omitted, they are in their present form in contradiction to one another? To show this will be the enterprise of the present chapter. We shall argue that, without God-language, this theology cannot consistently hold onto the category of the Lordship of Jesus and that, without that category, it relinquishes its sole touch with the Christian tradition and so its claim, made clearly at present, that it presents itself to us as a Christian theology. Somewhat arbitrarily, we will address the balance of these critical remarks to what we take to be the dominant and most influential form of radical theology, namely that which centers its faith and its theological reflection around Jesus as Lord. Secondly, we can, I believe, show that the view which radical theology as a whole presents of contemporary human existence—as religionless, come of age, and self-sufficient in a Godless world—is neither a true nor an illuminating picture of our secular life as it actually is. This will be at least one aspect of the effort of the second part of this volume.

The central theological problem of the radical theology we are discussing—exemplified best in the thought of Hamilton and van Buren—is the inconsistency or contradiction between the two lordships that are there asserted: that of "the world" or of secularity, on the one hand, and that of Jesus, on the other. On the one hand, it is asserted that man has come of age, that he is now autonomous and so needs no divine problem-solver; he is on his own and can, individually or socially, deal with all his major problems—at least those which can in any manner, human or divine, be resolved. Correspondingly, the secular culture he has created out of his intelligence and will is held to be rightfully expressive of man's best hopes for truth and for goodness, and so with regard to valid propositions and valid goals, secular existence provides us with our normative criteria.

It is, let us note, because radical theology, in this context at least, unequivocally asserts this principle of human autonomy and self-sufficiency that these theologies also assert that God is dead. A deity, say they, is not needed by autonomous man; any such discourse is not meaningful to a secular and autonomous age; and any such relation to transcendence is destructive rather than creative for man, who must live wholly within the secular world. Hence God is dead for our age. So far as the personal experience of the absence of God is assumed to be *more* than a report of a mere personal experience, that is, insofar as it is taken as an indication of what is representative of the universal cultural *Geist*, and *a fortiori* what the real ontological situation is—and all radical theologians so take it—it is the assertion of the autonomy of modern man with regard to issues of truth and value that provides the foundation on which this negative side of radical theology rests.

Let us reiterate this point. To say, "I have not found God" is, of course, to appeal to direct experience, and certainly not yet to invoke the norms characteristic of contemporary autonomy and of secularity. But such a statement is merely a datum for theological reflection, an item in an autobiography; it is not yet a theological statement. To expand this beyond the level of personal autobiography into that of theological reflection is to move beyond the report of a personal experience into assertions about the contemporary human situation in general and on from there into the cosmic situation. "God is dead for me" is one sort of statement, important and devastating to be sure—but it is a quite different sort from the assertion "God is dead for our age" or "There is no God at all." In the latter case, the norm of current secular experience as godless or positivistic, a norm implying the meaninglessness of God-language, has necessarily been invoked in order to make legitimate the movement from a personal, autobiographical report to general, normative, theological assertions, such as "God is dead," "The symbol God is meaningless," "We must theologize now without God," or "We take this as a fact not about our psyches, but about the world." However much rooted in personal experience rather than in a survey of current opinion radical theology may be, in order to be *theology* it must make general assertions about reality, and thus it must ap-

peal to certain norms with which it interprets the relative validity
of personal experience. Secular norms thus function in this theology as providing the basis for the necessary translation of the
personal experience of loss into theological statements about the
death of God and about the corresponding autonomous situation
of man "on his own." So much, then, for the first "Lord," the
secular spirit dominant in our time which requires that Christian faith and theology be done without reference to God.

On the other hand, it is asserted with equal force by radical theology that Jesus is the rightful Lord of man's existence. It
is he who gives to us our "stance in life," who provides the model
for a really human style of life, who not only communicates to us
a picture of authentic existence, but seems as well to communicate
to us the power or the possibility of that authentic existence—
through the "contagion" of his freedom. Thus is he Lord, God
for us, the center of our ethical ultimate concern, he around
whom we build our humanity and so our active existence in the
world. In the view of this theology, we are, seemingly, and at
one and the same time, autonomous, mature men, self-directed
by our own norms of life and criteria of knowledge, and so reflecting a radically modern secularity—and thus without God
in the world. On the other hand, we are *also* dependent, in some
strange fashion, on this dim figure from a different cultural context in the distant past for our self-realization as humans and so
for authenticity. My present argument is that these two Lords, the
one of secular autonomy and the other of Jesus, cannot be united
together consistently in the terms given us by radical theology—
and, only by implication here, that they cannot be brought together unless God-language be retained.

1. The first important problem for a theology based on
the Lordship of the human Jesus in a world without God involves the difficulty of what we can know about the historical
Jesus. Clearly our relations to Jesus in a naturalistically interpreted world can only be historical in form, that is, only such as
we can have to any other human figure in the past. We can relate
to him and so know of him only through historical inquiry into

the documents and traditions communicated to us by human historical communities; there can here be no "existential" confrontation with him directly in the present through the Word speaking to our faith, such as one finds in a neoorthodox, a Bultmannian, or even a New Hermeneutic context—for these categories of present confrontation with the Word ingredient in passing history, with what Søren Kierkegaard called the "contemporary Christ" and recent theology has called the "risen Christ present in his Church," all appertain to deity and to revelation, to something that transcends natural and historical passage. Such categories are presumably not characteristic of our relation to other historical religious figures such as Zoroaster or Confucius—else we are in a strange world indeed and all sorts of other problems of other lords arise to plague us. If he be *merely* a man—and in the radical theologies, he must be—what we know of him is only through historical inquiry and historical influence.

This raises two difficulties for radical theology. First of all, if anything has come out of recent New Testament studies, it is that an authentic picture of this man by historical canons alone is extremely elusive, almost as elusive to the secular historian as God is to the secular man. Any model of human excellence or ethical perspective a historical picture of him might give us, is, therefore, too fluctuating, insecure, and subjective to function in the role of *Lord*, and so a theology built *exhaustively* on a *historical* picture of his authentic freedom for others provides no firm ground for theological discourse about ourselves. Our generation, too, peers down the well of history when it looks for him, and the reflection of an "authentic man for others" that now stares back at us, while not, to be sure, a nineteenth-century liberal face, may only be the visage of the twentieth-century existentialist personality. Correspondingly, a modern Feuerbachian humanist might with some validity say that this Lord represents merely our own present projection onto the dim past, not unlike an older and larger "religious" projection of human ideals onto the infinite. Such a projection is, therefore, not only unrelated to the actual, and to us very strange, figure of Nazareth, but also confusing to and destructive of our own relevant humanist images of authenticity. Can a merely historical Jesus *be* our Lord in the twentieth-century naturalistic world, where only the shifting results of historical inquiry relate us to him, and where there is nothing in our relation to him that transcends the eroding relativism of cultural epochs?[2]

The other difficulty with our knowledge of the historical Jesus is that the picture, such as it is, which historical scholarship gives us of him and of his teachings refuses to fit the requirements of a godless, religionless Christianity. Even if the apocalyptic proclaimer of Schweitzer's studies has itself faded from view, nevertheless recent scholarship has been able in no way to erase the centrality of God and his activities, of faith in God, and of the consequent imitation of God in the believer's life from the center of Jesus' teachings. As Norman Perrin has shown, three aspects of the gospel traditions that seem authentically to stem from Jesus himself are the parables, the teachings about the Kingdom of God, and the Lord's Prayer;[3] and in each of these, unquestionably the reality and activity of God take the central role.[4] Moreover, outside of this context of the divine rule and activity, there is no "ethic" of Jesus that can be legitimately derived. He does not present himself to us as merely a good or even an authentic man whose style of life can be simply followed by us: he proclaims the presence, the work, and the future of God, and on *that* basis alone reveals the possibilities of human existence and behavior.[5] Apparently if the secular world be in truth "godless," as the radicals insist, the authentic Jesus has as little place in a secular Christianity as the most medieval of theolo-

[2] It is significant that, as we noted, the third radical theologian, Thomas Altizer, recognizes completely the unavailability of the historical Jesus to be the center of a contemporary faith; in fact, he says more, namely that this figure, insofar as we can know him, is quite irrelevant to us. Cf. *Radical Theology and the Death of God* (Indianapolis: Bobbs-Merrill, 1966), p. 104, pp. 124–125; and *The Gospel of Christian Atheism* (Philadelphia: Westminster Press, 1966), p. 61.

[3] Norman Perrin, *Rediscovering the Teaching of Jesus* (New York: Harper & Row, 1967), p. 47.

[4] *Ibid.*, pp. 55ff., 145ff., 205.

[5] *Ibid.*, pp. 202ff.

gians, and his style of life—insofar as it was one of a trust centered on God—has as little meaning for really secular men as might that of a contemplative.

2. The second major problem of the two lordships, the one of Jesus and the other of secularity, has to do with the *content* of these two authorities, for in certain significant respects these two lords turn out to be opposed to one another. We are, we are told, to be secular men, to be worldly. If we ask of the radical theologian what this means, he answers that it involves two requirements which he regards apparently as harmonious: (1) to accept "secular" and so current norms for truth and value; and (2) to affirm the world, to live within it, to love it, especially the neighbor who suffers in the world—and this, it is claimed, is to "become like Jesus." Certainly we will agree that, in some sense, the picture we know of the human Jesus did affirm the world in freedom, in love, and in service, as well as the sovereignty and activity of God. "Worldliness" in *this* sense (sense 2) has an authentic New Testament ring to it. But to "accept secular norms of truth and value," to be secular, worldly, and contemporary in *that* sense (sense 1), is surely unlike Jesus either in relation both to his own surrounding culture and to our own.

Here a real paradox begins to appear: the value system of the secular world is *not* one which affirms the world in love, service, and self-giving. Rather, the world's ways tend to affirm the self and its interests, modulated, to be sure, by the requirements of justice and coercive order; but by no means, either as a standard or as a practice, does the world claim from us or encourage in us the kind of self-giving love that the Lordship of Jesus implies. Empirically considered, and it is hard to see how these theologies can define such symbols as "world" and "worldly" in any other way, the standards of the world represent in various forms the ideals of a prudent self-concern, self-advancement, and self-defense, and at the very best the ideal of an even-handed or reciprocal justice to the neighbor. The world's standards are those of the marketplace, the public forum, and the household budget, where the self is loved above all and so where in consequence one struggles as much against as for

the neighbor. As a result, the secular mind in fact finds such totally idealistic and selfless behavior as Jesus represented vastly
impractical and so precisely "unworldly." To be secular in the
mode of affirming the world in love *is* Christ-like; to be secular
in the mode of following the world's standards and ways is just
the opposite—and the Cross is the evidence of this opposition,
unless the world's character has most radically changed.

Thus if Jesus is to be ethically our Lord in any significant
sense, some strict limit must be placed to the Lordship of the
secular over our minds and hearts—for the two are surely not
one in their picture of what authentic humanity is and means for
one's style of life. If such a radical limitation on the authority of
the secular, and so on the autonomy of modern man to determine his own stance in life, appears, then one may well ask if
this is still a "secular" theology in any deeper sense than is any
other relevant theology, i.e., one which meets the secular in certain areas and deviates sharply from it in others? Why does this
strong limitation on the authority of the secular appear with
regard to issues of "works," i.e., in ethics, and not with regard
to issues of "faith," i.e., with regard to the question of the existence and the reality of God? And if we need Jesus to give us a
picture of authenticity in contradistinction to the world's picture,
and so to that created by autonomous man, what has happened to
the principle of the autonomy of modern man and so to the basis
for our dismissal of God? It looks as if radical theology is not
really as secular as it at first seemed, and that actually it has
hedged in its assertion of autonomy, at least at those points in
ethical theory where experience has revealed to these theologians
the limits and contradictions of autonomous secular existence.
But it is surely strange that the twentieth century needs help from
the first century in ethics but none in ontology; that the first
century is timeless in its ethical perspective although not in its
Weltanschauung. And one cannot but wonder what has happened to secular man as a competent problem-solver if he needs
extrasecular help from the first century in the crucial realm of
determining his style of life. Would a group of typically secular
men, say among the Jaycees, *really* find talk about God more incredible than serious talk about "becoming like Jesus" in their
actual day-to-day lives in the business and suburban worlds?

It seems, in other words, that a theology built around the ethical requirements or stance of Jesus is as radically unsecular and even heteronomous on the existential level as is any theology built around the transcendence of God and of revelation— and yet no justification appears in radical theology for this very unsecular ethical base. Is there an aura here of a now-defunct category of revelation that provides emotional if not theological ground for the *ethical* authority this man of the first century has over our quite different age and over its quite different standards? In any case, it is clear that, with regard to the *content* of ethical obligation, the Lordship of Jesus and that of autonomous, secular man are as opposed as they ever were, and that no principle of mediation appears in this theology to help us to comprehend or deal with this opposition.

3. It is, however, when we explore more fully the meaning of the concept of autonomy that this contradiction between the two Lords is most clearly revealed. In the secular tradition, developing with power since the Enlightenment, autonomy and coming of age have meant that man is free of all secular Lords. He is, of course, as the nineteenth century realized, never free of dependence upon his human fellows in society, but within that social context, nothing, says this tradition, should be *Lord* over his existence. That is to say, no power outside of himself is authoritatively and finally to determine for him his thoughts, his standards, his decisions, or to create his meaning. He and his fellows are together "on their own," and they must be creative of their own life through their own inherent powers of mind and will. Autonomy and coming of age in a secular context, therefore, mean moving from the tutelage of the external authority of some "other," some authority or Lord, to self-direction, and such self-direction is regarded as the sole level of creative humanity.[6] Whether it be a royal sovereign, an authoritative state, a traditional and sacrosanct law or code, an ecclesiastical magis-

[6] "Enlightenment [one could well substitute the current word "maturity"] is man's exodus from self-incurred tutelage. Tutelage is the inability to use one's understanding without the guidance of another person." Immanuel Kant, "Beantwortung der Frage: Was Ist Aufklärung?" quoted in E. Cassirer, *The Philosophy of the Enlightenment* (Boston: Beacon Press, 1951), p. 163.

terium, God, *or* a human savior, any such external, superior authority or Lord over life has seemed to modern secular views of autonomy to represent a relapse into immaturity and a loss of autonomy. Radical theologians recalled all this very vividly *vis à vis* God; but it seemed to have slipped their minds when they came to Jesus. For as the Enlightenment realized full well with regard to kings and priests (however noble they might be), and as real humanists know as well, a human "lord" challenges as much if not more than does deity the very autonomy which the secular spirit wishes to preserve and foster. If radical theology asserts the autonomy of men so strongly *vis à vis* God as to dispose of the latter, as Nietzsche and others have done, why on earth retract it all over again with affirmations that Jesus is our rightful Lord?[7]

Can there, moreover, consistently be a theology of Lordship if that theology is also one of unqualified autonomy? If Jesus presents to us our picture of authenticity and of autonomous manhood, as he seems to do here, then what he can give me is only *his own* mode of authentic and so autonomous existence. Otherwise, we are on different levels, he essentially autonomous and I essentially receptive and dependent, in which case the crucial category of autonomy for *us* and so for man as a whole has clearly disappeared. In a philosophy of autonomy, *his* autonomy as Lord must, unless we be unlike, become *mine* as well; as he has no Lord beyond himself, so must I have none beyond myself. Paradoxically, in becoming my Lord in the context of a philosophy of total autonomy, Jesus thus disposes of the cate-

---

[7] In this discussion of the categories of Lord and of Lordship, we are not concerned with either their etymological or their traditional meanings, both of which are clearly irrelevant to this argument with radical theology. We deal with these precisely because they have used them as pivotal to their claim to be proposing Christian theology. What in this usage is essential to these categories, therefore, is that they express an essential and necessary relation to Jesus which is the ground and source of whatever authentic life we now experience—hence, the radicals say, are we Christians at all, and thus we call him Lord. So all that we are concerned with here is *this* content to the notion of Lord, namely a human figure to whom I have an essential and necessary relation in that around him I build the authenticity of my life.

gory of Lordship. He becomes, therefore, not a Lord but only a preliminary example of my own possible self-realization, an embodiment of the potentialities latent in all men and so in me, who must become their own Lords if they are to be men, as both Socrates and Kierkegaard realized.[8] That is, Jesus cannot be essential to my authenticity, for then my authenticity, if it be defined in terms of radical autonomy, disappears. But, if he be nonessential, he is merely one among the many examples in history of merely the potentialities latent in me. This is how humanism sees him, and for the modern humanist, Jesus is and can be no Lord, even in the sense that these men used this term. For those who believe in autonomy, he and any other "hero" can bring me nothing I cannot in principle bring to myself, and thus he carries no unique or real authority over me. Such a view is, therefore, clearly moving logically toward a humanism which presents to us a multitude of historical examples of achieved humanity and no Lord but the self-directing self which chooses some model for itself among them. In a philosophy of autonomy, the concept of Lordship becomes meaningless, confusing, and destructive. Whatever Jesus is, I can and should be also, and so I have no need of him as Lord—unless we be on different levels, but then autonomy has been relinquished.

It is, in other words, impossible to understand this relation of Lordship if autonomy is asserted, and if autonomy is not asserted, then the whole structure of radical theology collapses. Why should we *need* the Lord at all, if we are really autonomous? If we do not need him in some essential way, then why speak of him as Lord and what does that category mean; or, more fundamentally, why (if we do not need him essentially) give him a central role in the fulfilment of my life, a role that apparently no other man does or can perform? For surely a "Lord" does something important for us, both which we need and which we cannot ourselves do. And if we do need him for this central and unique role, then what is it for? To give us an authentic picture of ourselves; or to communicate to us the possibility of embody-

[8] The reference in Søren Kierkegaard is to *Philosophical Fragments* (Princeton, N.J.: Princeton University Press, 1946), Chapter 1, pp. 6–9; to Socrates, among other places, *Theaetetus*, paragraph 150.

ing that picture even if we have it; or both? But if either of these two are the "needs" he fills, then it is difficult to see what autonomy, coming of age, and so on now mean. For now secular man cannot without this figure from the past and so in autonomy seem to understand himself authentically at all or to realize that self-understanding—and such is surely a most essential "need" of man. And so it is surely strange that "need" was a "bad" category, threatening to our sacred autonomy *vis à vis* God, but now it is a "good" category in relation to Jesus. Is he then also a "problem-solver," a *deus ex machina*, only now in the personal —and surely "religious"—problems of self-understanding, of the achievement of authenticity, and of finding a correct style of life? Apparently a religious *a priori* of some sort, a religious need, an "empty space to be filled by something from beyond ourselves," has appeared in relation to Jesus as possibly a lingering memory of the traditional one in relation to God.

If we say "No" to these questions about our essential need for Jesus on this view (that is, that we do *not* need him, that he does *nothing* essential for us, that we *can* do it all ourselves, and so on), then it seems plain that no meaning can be given to his role as Lord. If we say "Yes" to them, then our autonomy is certainly vigorously challenged, we seem to have important and serious religious needs; and his status as an ordinary man among needy men is surely compromised. How can he have what we do not have, and yet merely be one of us? And if he does not have some such transcending grace that gives him some unique status, how can he be my Lord? Only, I submit, if we understand ourselves in some such terms as the classical categories of creation and sin provide, and Jesus in some such terms as the category of incarnation supplies, can we make sense of those very theological categories the radical theology does wish to assert: namely the ambiguities of our real but needy humanity, the uniqueness of his real but authentic humanity, and the validity of his Lordship over our autonomous freedom.

To adopt the humanist hypothesis about the autonomous goodness and capacities of man to fulfill himself, and so his need of no Lord beyond himself, clarifies, therefore, one side of the contradiction in radical theology but makes quite unintelligible the other. For with this hypothesis of the autonomous capabilities of man, we can understand what we mean by the "coming of age of modern man," by "living without God in the world," by the adequacy of secular values and standards, and by the assertion that man has no longer any basic needs which his worldly existence cannot fulfill. But, as we have seen, this new clarity with regard to man's autonomous powers makes it now impossible for us to speak of the other major category, the centrality and the Lordship of Jesus. And if the category of his Lordship is relinquished, as the humanist must do and as the logic of this theology implies, then radical theology expires as a theology expressive of the Christian position and becomes instead a variant of the humanism we have described, an interesting, consistent, but not immediately relevant mode of thought to the theological enterprise.[9] For with the loss of this essential touch with Jesus, radical theology must give up its claim to be expressing norma-

---

[9] We should distinguish our present argument from that which Ogden and Harvey have leveled at Bultmann. They have maintained, much as we have, that if man is capable of authentic existence, as Bultmann seems to admit, then there is no place for the centrality of Jesus. Thus far our arguments are parallel. They go on, however, to propose that theology relinquish the centrality or Lordship of Jesus and regard authentic existence as a universal possibility for man as man. Granting for the present the validity and helpfulness of their proposal in the context of their theology, it might be asked, "Why cannot radical theology agree with them, and say, 'Authentic existence is a universal possibility for man, and thus Jesus is only a paradigm or example of excellence and not necessary or essential to our achievement of it'?" The answer is that Ogden and Harvey assume that this possibility is achieved in relation to the continual and universal activity of God on man. Thus, while they are willing to surrender the ultimacy or the *Einmaligkeit* of the event of Christ, they are *not* abandoning the necessity of the redemptive work of God. Whether or not any theology can be called "Christian" without asserting the centrality of the event of Christ is, of course, an interesting and extremely debatable issue, but one with which we are not here concerned. Surely, however, a theology that abandons *both* the redemptive role of God *and* the redemptive role of Jesus—as radical theology would do were it to agree with Ogden and Harvey on this point—could hardly retain any ties at all with the Christian position. Cf. Schubert M. Ogden, *Christ Without Myth* (New York: Harper & Row, 1961), and Van A. Harvey, *The Historian and the Believer* (New York: Macmillan Co., 1966).

tive Christianity, a claim it surely makes at the present time. It seems, in other words, unavoidable that, if this theology is to remain Christian (that is, expressive at the least of some essential relation to Jesus of Nazareth), it must reject the humanist hypothesis of man's self-sufficiency and assert the incapacity of man without Jesus to achieve authentic existence and freedom.[10]

4. In radical theology, as we have noted, the man Jesus can relate to us only as another man long past in the stream of history can relate to us. Such a relation is totally dependent on our own powers of memory and the influence which our own interest in him creates in us. We are here active, he passive; for he is dead and has insofar ceased to exist—except in our memories and through the exercise of our wills. What he can do for us, therefore, is only to present to our minds and to our interests a model or picture of authentic existence. He cannot, as now nonexistent, *effect* that picture in us by any mysterious principle of contagion or of grace. No dead man contains such powers over us, and in any case, no other *man* can or should change our capacities; he can only, at best, influence the way *we* develop and use those capacities. No mysterious power can still come to us from his person, now gone, transforming us in a way we cannot change ourselves—unless we are willing to use God-language and the language of grace. A living and transforming effect of

[10] At one point in conversation, Hamilton expressed his view of the Lordship of Jesus to this writer in somewhat the following fashion: "Our present secular difficulties with belief have, so to speak, removed for most of us the 'pie' of Christian doctrine: God, sin, revelation, and the divine nature and work of Christ have gone. We are left, therefore, with only one piece of the pie, namely the centrality of Jesus the man in our lives; this is all we have and are able to have in this day. What is wrong with that?" In the terms of his colorful illustration, the problem is whether the pie can be so easily divided as that so that parts of it can remain over at all, whether, that is, one *has* a piece left when all the rest is gone. Our argument in effect is that Christian theology and the faith it expresses represent more of a unity than this illustration might indicate, and that *if* one merely "has" the man Jesus in this sort of central role in our existence, in fact we must "have" some of the rest as well, else we are in self-contradiction, and ultimately he, too, disappears from our grasp.

Jesus over us, enabling our freedom to become itself, presupposes the category of deity and so transcends the present forms of radical theology.

Thus, in this theological context, he can present to our minds and wills only a picture or model for their enactment. He cannot give us the power to enact the picture. He is a Lord, in other words, of the law, not a Lord of grace. Here we shall not run through all the familiar problems that may beset religions of the law—pride, despair, bondage, and so on—for these have been clearly spelled out in Paul, Augustine, Luther, Kierkegaard, and a host of others. Let us merely suggest that all these problems reappear in this theology. For here is the same unbelievably high picture of human excellence, presented to us as an authoritative model of our own authenticity and so as the center around which our existence and our behavior are to revolve. On "becoming like him" depends, therefore, any fulfilment, self-realization, and self-acceptance our lives may achieve —else we surely should not call him Lord. And we are left quite alone, without any possible help—or mode of forgiveness and self-reconciliation—in achieving this model, in becoming like him in and to the world. How are we to relate to ourselves when we fail—as we surely will; how are we to accept ourselves when in the end we are *not* like him? Can we really, through willing, become this magnificently free and loving person? It seems that any notion of the problems to which the category of the bondage of our wills has traditionally referred has quite vanished from this thought, and the problem of subsequent experiences of guilt is not taken at all seriously. But surely such problems are still with us all—and especially if the self is to judge itself by a standard so high in relation to our own natural and normal tendencies. Above all, if the self judges itself by a standard so totally external to the natural capacities of the self as is that of Jesus, will it not encounter there new difficulties of despair and remorse? And if this standard is *not* in some sense external to these natural capacities, why need he rather than we ourselves present it to us, why need he be our Lord?

In maintaining the rigor of the Christian ethic without the resources of Christian grace, this theology—based on "be-

coming like Jesus to the world"—threatens to develop into a
new form of heteronomous moralism, a new and yet impotent
religion of the law in which a standard transcendent to man's
natural capacities crushes him without relief. In *this* situation,
it is surely healthier from a secular or human viewpoint to move
all the way into humanism. In humanism, contemporary man
is *in toto* his own Lord, both in setting his own standards according to his own capacities and enacting them by his own
powers, rather than, in this case, receiving these transcendent
and ultimate standards from outside—but finding from outside
no help to enact them. Psychologically speaking, man will surely
be less frustrated, more serene, less hostile and repressed if he
is autonomous with regard to his picture of authentic existence
and does not seek to find his picture of excellence in this external source unrelated to modern problems and modern goals.
The Jesus here presented can become a veritable superego, and
the picture he presents to us a law that kills us if he merely calls
us to become like him and leaves us, as here he must, to achieve
that on our own. A transcendent model for our ethical endeavor
is as crushing to the autonomy and health of man as is a transcendent deity—and for much the same reasons. It seems that,
even with regard to the ethical vision of authentic humanity,
humanism makes a better case than does this, its halfhearted
half-brother. For humanism finds its model in my own potentialities and my own autonomous standards, rather than in those
of another man whose ways are hardly my own.

Thus once again, and now on the deepest level of all,
human autonomy is at war with the category of Lordship. It
looks as if, to the secular psychologist as to the secular political
scientist, a man as Lord is in fact more destructive than God
as Lord—which is what Biblical religion had said all along.
And yet the Lordship of the human Jesus over my autonomy is
just the structure which this theology offers to us in the name
of secularity! Concluding this section, we may say that, if we
assert the principle of human autonomy strongly enough to
dispense with religious needs of all sorts and so with the category of God, then the Lordship of Jesus goes, too, for that
Lordship depends on these needs, and itself threatens even more

than does that of God the autonomy and the free self-realization of man as man. If, on the other hand, man's autonomy and
self-sufficiency are limited enough to allow the category of the
Lordship of Jesus to be relevant and meaningful—and only if
he be thus central can this theology without God retain any
touch with Christianity—man *ipso facto* has deep religious needs
he cannot himself fulfill; the secular world is not the mature
paradise these men have pictured; the bases for the rejection of
God disappear; and in fact God-language must return in order
to understand and explicate the authoritative role which Jesus
plays as our Lord. And no wonder, because a Jesus who is Lord
is in fact functioning as God and so, as we have sought to show,
is inconceivable, inconsistent, and even dangerous without the
divine background.

5. The radical theologies, like all Christian theologies,
speak about some kind of fulfilment, what they tend to call
"authentic existence." It is, therefore, relevant to a study of their
consistency to ask, "From whence does this authenticity, this
authentic existence, come?" Is it, on the one hand, derived
from man's autonomous development and use of his own
powers, as in humanism? Then, clearly, we run into the problem outlined above, namely that there seems here to be no
essential role for Jesus, and this view slips into humanism.

Does this authentic existence, on the other hand, come
from Jesus, and is this intelligible in this system? Let us now
explore this possibility of a source in Jesus for the authentic
existence which is here promised. Certainly we agree, it must
thus originate with him if he is to have the central role which
they give to him as Lord. For unless this capacity for freedom
comes from him in some sense, why should we look at all
beyond our own powers and potentials—why have a Lord at
all? And unless it comes *only* from him and from no others in
history, why is he alone our Lord, and not innumerable other
inspiring men? Thus the possibility of authentic existence within
this theology (as well as the category of Lordship) presupposes
the power of Jesus to act on us as other men do not, to act on us
now and to set us free from ourselves as he was free himself.

Only thus can he be Lord, only thus can the salvation here prof-
fered be possible, and only thus can this theology make a legitimate claim to be called "Christian."

   When, however, we survey the general structure of the
radical theology, we see that this saving role for Jesus is quite
unintelligible. That authentic existence is not in us we have
established—else he be no Lord—so apparently we are separated from authentic existence and unable to will it. But equally
clearly, it cannot come to us from the Jesus here pictured. For
there is, let us recall, no God, no category of divinity, no
divine ground of life and so no conquest of anyone's death, and
no divine power which can work in each passing creature and
so whose healing influence may reach every moment of history.[11]
In the "God is dead" theology, Jesus is himself a quite dead
martyr, and so his influence on us is solely that of any other historical figure, namely what our own historical memory and our
own wills choose to make of him. If in this sense we choose him
and thus give to him the prominence of some supreme example
or model for our lives, then in effect we save ourselves and do
not really need him. If in some sense he *gives* us authentic existence, so that he is central to us—as these theologies clearly
imply—then an active power emanates from him as it does
from no one else, a power that grasps and transforms us. But a
long-dead historical figure is quite incapable of such a uniquely
active, transforming power over us. In the cosmos they present
to us, there is beyond him nothing that can perform this task for
him, for there are present to us only whirling stars and circling
atoms, and other men as lost as ourselves. In none of this is
there the power to remake us implied in their category of the
present Lordship of Jesus over us, not to mention van Buren's
category of "contagion."

   [11] The presence of precisely these categories, powerfully operative in his theology, makes Altizer's "God-centered" thought vastly different on all these matters from the more naturalistic theologies of van
Buren and Hamilton. For this reason, these particular criticisms are not
relevant to Altizer's theology—and also for this reason, he can (like
Ogden and Harvey) question the ultimacy of the event of Jesus of Nazareth and avoid thereby moving directly into humanism.

If, then, we are in theology to speak of the promise of authentic existence through the Lordship of Jesus, and if we are thus to recognize that this salvation comes not entirely from ourselves but in some significant sense from him, then we must, to be consistent, introduce into our speech some category of the transcendent. For Jesus to have the role which these theologies give to him, there must be some reality beyond the immediate which bears the transforming power that was in him and presents it to us in our present experience. For the active, effective, and transforming immediacy of the man Jesus has long since departed, and so for a historical figure of the past to transform and rescue us, to provide us with what we cannot provide ourselves, requires a *present* power on and over our minds and wills which no man from past history can muster. Consequently, some reality that does not pass away must bear the power that was in Jesus after his own passage out of life and, being present with us now, mediate this creative power to our current needs. Moreover, only that which, in thus transcending our alienated and passing being, holds us to itself even when we are separated from it, and in love brings us in the end back to itself—only God, our creator, sustainer, and redeemer—can relate us, who are now inauthentic, in transforming power to a present, living Lord, Jesus Christ, and thus make us authentic. This divine reality, whose being transcends passage and whose love will not let us go, is the clear implication and requirement of that very essential relation to a past Jesus and of our certainty that through him alone has this salvation or freedom come to us which these theologies propose. An experience of what we must call "God" (or, more specifically, the "Holy Spirit") is, in other words, mediated inevitably through any such experience of the "benefits of Jesus" which the word and function "Lord" implies. And correspondingly, we cannot talk consistently of Jesus, of our need for him and of how he transforms our lives, without also talking of deity—a requirement as old as the first creedal statements that he is or somehow mediates God for us.

This is not to argue that all aspects of traditional God-language are implied in the twofold assertion of our need and of the Lordship of Jesus. It is to say, however, that, if we are to use problem-language about ourselves seriously, and to use Jesus-language or Lordship-language about our hopes for ourselves, then we must connect these two statements in some consistent way, and the connection can only be expressed in some form of God-language. Since these men continue to speak of Jesus as Lord and thus by implication require problem-language about ourselves as well, we can only declare that their rejection of God-language is contradictory to what they themselves want to say and that their thought will only become self-consistent when they reintroduce into it some language expressive of the transcendent. If they fail to do this, then they must either adopt the humanist alternative and reject the Lordship of Jesus, or they must adopt the posture of despair and abjure the promise of authentic existence. What we have tried to show in this part, then, is that, if intelligible Christian language is to be used at all, God-language is necessary.[12]

To these five criticisms of the inconsistencies of radical theology, most of its supporters will reply: But this is not primarily a *theology*. It is a style of life, a way of being in the world. Have

---

[12] To set the contours and limits of Christian language is, of course, a very difficult and risky task. But I suspect that most people would agree that a view of life that seeks to speak of man's deepest problems, that expresses a sense or at least a hope of their resolution, that centers that hope in the figure of Jesus, and that offers a picture of authentic human life in his terms, would meet many of the minimum requirements of a Christian view, at least descriptively speaking. Many would say that, without some form of the symbol God, no thought can be Christian, if for no other reason than that the symbol God seems to be important both to Jesus and to the scriptures as a whole; but since we are discussing theologies which seek to be Christian without God, it is useless to make this a criterion. One can safely say, perhaps, that, if the type of thought omits both God and the above elements centered around Jesus, and the hope of a new life, it has little claim to be called Christian—and probably little desire to be so labeled. In any case, the views we have here discussed are clearly "Christian," if the first criterion above is accepted—despite their manifest self-contradiction in saying all this without God-language. But, as we argued, if they seek to avoid this self-contradiction by taking either the humanist or the despairing alternatives, then they can no longer qualify descriptively as Christian.

you not yet realized that faith has collapsed into love, and theology into action for the modern secular Christian community? To be a Christian is to be in the world in joyous and perhaps suffering protest along with a neighbor who is in need. Why not just talk of selfless love, Jesus, and the world's many causes? Why is not action enough, and the reflection that grows out of action? Why must theology in some sense precede and condition action?[13]

As might be guessed by these questions, radical theology has been very much influenced by concern with and participation in the social struggles of our time. There is no question that active work in the civil-rights movement, in the sudden "plunge" into the urban and poverty problems, and in the peace movements has had an invigorating effect on this theology, providing most of the concrete content to such phrases as "being with the neighbor in the world" and "affirming the world." Correspondingly, there is even less doubt that this nontraditional, action-centered, humanly concerned, and theologically unencumbered viewpoint has provided many younger clergy and seminarians, intent on acting creatively in the problem areas of our society, with a very potent theological base with which to enter actively into our urban, racial, and international problems.

Now, civil rights is a movement in relation to which positive Christian commitment has been, for this writer, both obligatory and creative, whose moral issues have been clear and unambiguous, and where the action of dedicated, active groups has begun to have an observable and obviously healthy result. Consequently, much of recent radical theology, informed by Christian participation in the freedom movement, has appropriated its religion in terms of love and service, of commitment and self-giving, and of creative and hopeful action in the world. Since these motives of idealistic service do, fortunately, spring up in liberal breasts, both Christian and non-Christian, the theological reflection that is apt to eventuate from them tends to be humanistic and optimistic in form: where is the need for God

---

[13] See, for example, Hamilton, *The New Essence*, pp. 36–37.

or religion if men can, by dedicated activity in the secular realm, solve their own problems? Why do we need talk of sin, guilt, forgiveness, and the question of "meaning," if direct moral action for and in the world so clearly serves our brother and fulfils our own existence?[14]

Why, indeed? The reason is, I believe, that our action in the world cannot be either creative or really Christian if it is comprehended, as this theology seeks to do, solely under the general rubric of "becoming like Jesus in the world." And the reason is that the same disjunction, now on an ethical level, appears between the figure of Jesus and the realities of the world's actual life, forcing us to comprehend our Christian role therein in a wider and deeper framework than that provided by a simple moral idealism, however noble in intent. The discordant factors causing this disjunction between passive love and worldly action are the uncomfortable but ineradicable factors of power in the life of the real world and of consequent moral ambiguity in the course of the world's history.

For the secular world's actual life, whether we wish to recognize it or not, is centered on the struggle for, or the defense of, power: political power, economic power, social power, power to gain and preserve a group's security, power to achieve and maintain a group's goals in the welter of the forces that make up social existence. Accordingly, secular action in the world is action in pursuit of power; such pursuit may be, and often is, moral or just in the sense that the action promotes the power of per-

[14] Hamilton refers specifically to participation (by himself and by others) in the civil-rights movement as the formative influence on the optimism and so the shape of his theology: "That there is a gaiety, an absence of alienation, of vigorous and contagious hope at the center of this movement is obvious, and this optimism is the main source of its hold on the conscience of America, particularly younger America. . . . The sixties may well be a time for play, celebration, delight, and for hope." *Ibid.*, p. 164. And again: "It is not yet clear how the civil-rights movement is going to take on its theological significance, but it has begun, as the radical, Southern Negro comes out of the movement to seminary. He brings a passionate interest in the New Testament doctrines of discipleship and following Jesus, and very little interest in the doctrine of sin." *Ibid.*, p. 48.

sons or groups which heretofore have suffered from a total loss of power and thus have been oppressed, or in the sense that its exercise defends the legitimate power of persons or groups whose security is threatened and who thus face the peril of being themselves in turn oppressed. But in either case the goal of worldly or political action is power, and so any mode of action that takes no account of power is by no means "worldly," but precisely "unworldly."

Now, the reason that power complicates the ethical structure of worldly action is that the possession and exercise of power always brings corruption, or at best ambiguity, in its train. When a group has no power, it possesses a genuine measure of what may be called "outward innocence." Whatever hostilities it feels, it dares not yet express, and whatever dominating self-interest is there remains implicit and so cannot yet threaten others. In *this* situation, action by or with this group is outwardly innocent, uncorrupted, and so creative as innocent, for the only useful mode of action is that of protest or possibly passive suffering—as when civil-rights "action" was exclusively in the forms of nonviolent marches, picketing, rallies, and the like. In that brief social moment, being passively, powerlessly and so unambiguously with a neighbor in the world is creative in a "worldly" way, that is *politically* creative—and by taking that temporary situation as a model or norm of being in the world, one might conclude that worldly action and innocent, idealistic, Christian passivity fit together in a simple harmony. But as we noted, such a passive role is not the *aim* of worldly action; it is at best only one momentary state or step to a further aim. The final aim is the acquisition and exercise of political, economic and social power, and when that aim becomes explicit, it effects a total change in the ethical situation.

For power does corrupt, and the exercise of power is always ethically ambiguous. Power corrupts for a variety of reasons: the latent hatreds and hostilities, bred by oppression, now can express themselves freely; latent desires for prominence, security, even dominance over others, characteristic of every human group under the sun, now are able to appear. Above all, the acquisition of power breeds insecurity and resentment in

other groups, who react accordingly. Thus the new group, innocent at first, finds itself, now that it has a measure of power, in
a situation of implicit or overt conflict with all the ambiguities
that such a situation inevitably breeds. This movement from
innocence to ambiguity, and the sudden and disheartening appearance of all the familiar sins of humanity, are manifest in
every transformation of a nation from colonial status to independence, and appear in every revolutionary group known in
recent history when that group gains power—from the French
Revolution through Russia, China, Algeria, Cuba, and thence
to Ghana—and probably will become characteristic of our own
domestic crisis.

In any case, the appearance of the debate over Black
Power and the sudden appearance of uncontrolled and destructive violence in our riot-torn cities illustrate the point. The slogan "Black Power" surely declares explicitly for the first time
the legitimate goal of every social group, namely to acquire the
social power to redress its grievances and to preserve its legitimate rights. This goal is becoming explicit at this juncture partly
because it is now a possible goal, and partly because white in-
transigence has finally revealed the limits of passive protest.
With this change, therefore, this movement has entered into a
new "worldly stage," where power tends to replace love as a
means, where coercion—perhaps by economic and political
power, perhaps by the threat or even the use of violence—replaces passive protest, and where the explicit aim is the achievement of power over against the other side, rather than an ideal
harmony with that side in mutual love. As its new leaders have
realized, this is the way of the world, and to make one's way
in the real world, passive suffering is no substitute for active
and freely held power. Ironically, therefore, with this new
declaration of aim have appeared all the ambiguities and the potential corruptions of every movement in history that seeks or has
achieved power, ambiguities more than abetted by the frantic
reaction of the frightened white majority. Insofar, moreover, as
Black Power represents *more* than the claim to the legitimate
rights of any group to hold power, to advance its interests, to
redress its grievances, and to preserve its rights in the larger

society—insofar as it represents a vindictive threat to the rights, dignity and life of white people or a desire for total separation because the latter are evil or unworthy—it is, however understandable it may be, even less "innocent." In fact, in that case it sadly reflects the fact—long evident in the identical actions and attitudes of whites to blacks—that every group has its quota of inordinate love of self and detestation and fear of the other, which theology has called "sin"; and therefore, in that case, the religious problem of reconciliation and love for the "other" who is our neighbor is ultimately a black as well as a white problem.

Now, the point of this description of the development of the mounting crisis in civil rights is that it casts doubt on both the effectiveness and the appropriateness—even more the secularity—of the ethical perspective proposed to us here. We are, it is said, to "become like Jesus" and to "suffer with the neighbor at the hands of the godless world," and *this* is said to be "worldly." As we have indicated, this passive, powerless role of suffering was in truth relevant to the social world at a certain stage of the rights struggle. As its new leaders rightly insist, however, the point of the freedom movement is not this suffering, especially by white allies; this is a "religious" interpretation of the aim of the movement which they reject. The point—secular though it may be—is to gain power, political, economic, and social power, and so to end the suffering; and it is their right to wield this power in proportion to their numbers, as it is the right of any group in society. But this was an aim explicitly rejected by Jesus, insofar as we know anything of him at all; and the acquisition and wielding of power is by no means "passive" and is always far from innocent. To gain power from a group that does not wish to lose it requires the active use of some forms of coercion, economic, political, or whatever, and not merely the passivity of suffering. And power once gained reflects the interests of the group that holds it; its use, then, is always ambiguous, detrimental to the interests of others, and, because of the inevitable accompaniment of hatred and the desire for more power than is deserved, it is always in the end unjust and possibly cruel and violent.

As history reveals, therefore, the innocent, passive sufferer is always forced by the logic of social power to the edge of the real world of secularity and ultimately out of that world. He must leave a political and social movement the moment it seeks either to achieve or succeeds in reaching its real aim of ambiguous power. And this is even more true when, as in South America or possibly in our present ghettos, the only hope for those eager for sudden change may lie in some new form of revolutionary consciousness; to them, worldly action must be active, concerned with a direct acquisition of power, and thus precisely the opposite of a passive suffering at the hands of the world. Thus, passive suffering is not worldly enough for a real affirmation of the world's aims, and the struggle for sheer power is too partial and corrupt for this sort of pietistic idealism to contemplate. A Christian "being with the neighbor in the world" is, as the great Dr. Martin Luther King alone realized, a puzzling combination of the search for prudent and often ruthless economic and political power to move a recalcitrant foe, a sense of one's own guilt in the process, and a determination to be reconciled within and beyond the real struggle—and such a stance transcends the innocent, idealistic optimism with which this theology is imbued.

The role of the innocent, optimistic, and voluntary sufferer as the clue to Christian worldliness is thus not at all worldly. It is typically religious, typically naïve and typically upper class, reflecting a participation in a political movement for other purposes than those practical political and economic goals of the movement itself. Its real goals are for spiritual refreshment, a sense of inner integrity, and so the possibility of self-acceptance and self-affirmation. This voluntary participation by those not involved personally in the struggle, creative and surely admirable in the early stages, now in the new situation, where power has become the explicit rather than the implicit aim, finds itself unwanted and often irrelevant. And for good reason. The goals of all of us who did this were too purely "religious" or "spiritual" in character really to accord with the present very worldly, potentially very ambiguous and even dangerous, but, if controlled, perfectly legitimate aspirations of the movement.

As Dr. King well knew, moreover, it is in this situation of great ambiguity, where power is involved, simply not creative for those in the movement to say, "We have no sense of sin in this movement, and why should we?" In *any* potentially overt conflict, such claims to virtue from either group are clearly unfortunate and represent anything but a Christian perspective on one's own group and its behavior in a very worldly struggle. Innocent, voluntary suffering is thus no paradigm for the exercise of Christian responsibility in the real affairs of the world. For that, those more traditional theological categories which balance responsibility to my neighbor, joyous confidence, and a willingness to suffer, on the one hand, with a sense of the tragic, of judgment on ourselves, and of our own guilt, and of eschatological hope for the future, on the other, are far more congruent with the actual world of affairs.

Finally, the other great crisis of our worldly life tells much the same story. American action in Vietnam, in which our churches will, one trusts, become more and more involved in the days ahead, reveals the tragic and sinful dimensions of all worldly activity, even that with the best intentions. In such a situation, an innocent, well-intentioned "standing by the weak neighbor in need," or an "affirmation of the world to save the world" on the part of American power is *not* to follow the pattern of Jesus at all, but rather to follow the familiar, and very dangerous, patterns of American national messianism. Such simple, self-confident idealism can be very dangerous, leading a great power to self-delusion about what it is actually doing and why, and encouraging it to fanatical cruelty and belligerence without any possibility of any sense of the ambiguity of its course of action. This sense of their own innocence is, unfortunately, true of both sides in the present conflict. Both have deep motivations of self-interest, fear, and hostility which their simple idealism obscures; and both are, because they are so sure of their own virtue, unaware of the cruel carnage they are perpetuating on innocent victims and quite incomprehending of why the rest of the world is criticizing them.

Theological reflection on this crisis, where worldly action is taken not by the recently oppressed but by those who have held power, and in our case by those who are mighty, will also find relevant and even essential some of the old theological categories that point to a transcendent dimension in existence, a dimension that judges our sin and then redeems us despite our good intentions. For speaking in the most worldly terms, what is most needed now among us as a nation is a sense of our own potential and even actual guilt, that we are not so good as we claim, that self-interest and cruelty are part of our national makeup as well; a sense that even we may need forgiveness, chastisement in our pride of power and of virtue, and a realization that the pursuit of our own national security is no innocent search blessed by an admiring world, but that it can easily be selfish, arrogant and cruel, and can lead to the demonic destruction of the world. Thus what we need is repentance and the knowledge that we are obligated far beyond our own wishes to search for reconciliation even with those whom we consider evil.

Such an awareness of ourselves will never come if our theology merely speaks of the call to be good and to serve the world in the world—for this is precisely what we assume we are now doing. Above all, we need a confidence or hope, grounded only in a transcendent eschatology, in the meaningfulness of continuing participation in the world's life even when we finally behold the ambiguity and the evil consequences of all that we ourselves have done. For it is neither Christian nor worldly, then, to withdraw from participation in the world full of shame at what we have done and with disgust at the world —as some of the most significant "secular" movements are now inclined to do. Such an eschatological perspective on the ultimate movements of history is not readily gained in the world of naturalistic humanism—even with the paradigm of Jesus added to the picture. It is gained when there is an apprehension of God, who is the Father of us all, who calls us to responsible action, to be sure, but who also judges all our actions and who gives ultimate eschatological as well as historical meaning even to the tragic results of what we humans do. A creative worldliness neither can be merely optimistic, idealistic, and innocent; nor can it be guilt-ridden and in despair and withdrawing—the two temptations of liberal humanism. It must have elements of

both these extremes, and this balance comes only when there is
a transcendent dimension of judgment and eschatology to which
our life with all its moral obligation and yet its fateful ambiguity is related.[15]

To our criticism that the central role of Jesus in this theology
has not, in fact cannot, be made intelligible or convincing without God-language, the radical theologians have in general answered: "Yes, this is *not* explicable. This is a *Blik*, a perspective
I find meaningful; this is where I find myself as a Christian,
with Jesus as Lord and without God in a world come of age. It
may not seem logical to insist that, if man does not need God,
we must still place Jesus in this role; and it may seem arbitrary
to pick him rather than many another great and good man. But
I find I in fact do both these things, and because of my history
in fact must, and this is all I can say about your question and
about my position."

This answer is surely acceptable as an honest statement
of personal history and so of personal faith. But a statement
about one's own history and faith is still not theology, which, in
intention at least, is disciplined and consistent thought about

[15] It is significant that those theologies on the European continent which, in reaction to the tradition of neoorthodoxy and existentialism, are trying most deliberately to be "worldly" and are in consequence the most lively forms of thought to emanate from there, are now
eschatological in character. That is, they express an orientation *outward*
into the political, public world of social history, and *forward* to the
future and so unknown dimension of history. In this way, they are
both political and eschatological in character, and seek through this
combination to be both secular and Christian. Since it is clear that any
authentic eschatological dimension in theology depends ultimately on
the reality of that which transcends the natural and the historical dimensions, namely on God, these worldly and political theologies are,
for the reasons we have just noted, far different from our own radical
theologies. And as we have indicated earlier, since they depend episte-
mologically on the Word of God in scripture, they seem to this writer to
beg as well the questions of meaning and of authority in religious language which we are raising in this book. I refer here especially to the
work of Wolfhart Pannenberg, Jürgen Moltmann, and the Jesuit
Johannes B. Metz.

one's "perspective" or one's *Blik*. And this difference is crucial, especially since these men are proposing for us a *theology* appropriate to a modern man's faith. Now it is unarguable that there is a theological circle, that is, that the ultimate grounds for one's faith cannot be "proved" or even defended by objective criteria separated from the faith itself. In this sense, theology represents a rational explication of what is essentially prerational or believed. The irreduceability of one's ultimate stand in terms of rational elaboration, however, is not the same thing as a fundamental contradiction or an ultimate irrationality within the circle of ideas involved in that stance. If an ultimate act of belief is a prerational act, nevertheless *what* is believed, its contents and its elements, cannot be in contradiction to themselves. And it is *this* problem to which we have had reference here; not why do you believe in Jesus, but how does *this* belief square with the human autonomy you also proclaim, and how is what you say about him possible unless some form of deity be also involved in your faith? If such a contradiction among the elements of a faith really exists, one is led to suspect either that the theological elaboration has overlooked certain necessary aspects of the underlying prerational faith, or else that the stance itself represents a precarious marriage of two different prerational commitments.

But, it may be countered, "paradox" is a historically honored word in theology, and is not therefore the assertion of both the Lordship of Jesus and the autonomy of man simply another example of theological paradox, and thus strictly "kosher" with our neoorthodox critics? Perhaps so. But paradox is legitimate, if at all, as a mode of discourse about God, and possibly about the mysteries of the inner life of man. As a meaningful form of discourse in religion, it presupposes that the object of discourse has a mystery and a depth which our ordinary words and propositions cannot totally explicate, and that therefore we speak about that mystery in paradoxical terms to indicate facets of it that we do understand, but which we cannot put into a comprehended rational unity. In a theology for which God is dead, however, and so which recognizes no factors beyond the finite and contingent realities which we know in ordinary daily experience, such a level of mystery is scarcely credible. If Jesus has a relation to us in such a theology, it cannot be a "divine" relation or a mysterious one; it cannot possess any more mystery than that of my relation to any other man. Hence ordinary historical language is quite appropriate here, but not the quite unusual "paradoxical" language designed for theological usage about the transcendent.

Finally, perhaps the deepest problem about the "irrationality," the *Blik* character, of the relation to Jesus in a naturalistic theology is that this theology gives no grounds for why others might wish to share the faith it is seeking to explicate, and so it provides no basis for the perpetuation of the faith it represents. To say, "This is where I find myself" *and nothing more,* is to say in effect, "The commitment I find I now have makes no real sense in terms of my other present beliefs; in fact it once made sense—when I believed in God—but it does no longer. Thus I call it a '*Blik*'; its *reasons* have been lost with the loss of the faith in God. It is 'only where I find myself'— that is, as a secular man but one who was once a Christian and so who still has a commitment to Jesus."

What this theological structure explicates, therefore, in the terms of "doctrine," is actually only the story of a personal history, and its coherence is *historical* rather than theological. That is to say, it represents a personal movement from a Christian faith in Jesus because God was "in him," to a stance in which one is no longer able to believe in God, but continues to wish to remain a Christian and so to believe at least in Jesus. The theological contradiction we have pointed to, therefore, is the theoretical reflection of the existential contradiction of a newly emergent disbelief in God and an established and so continuing loyalty to Jesus. This position thus presupposes for its possibility this whole personal history, especially one's prior commitment to classical Christianity and thence to Jesus. But since its *reasons* for the relation to Jesus are only those coming out of a personal past history of Christian commitment—a commitment founded on grounds that are now lost—it contains within its own circle of thought no grounds for why anyone who does not share this personal history, and so this prior com-

mitment to Jesus' Lordship, should be at all interested in him.
In effect, it says, "If you are not there," that is, "If you do not
have this personal history, then I have no real word for you."
A theology, even if not apologetic in form, should give reasons
why what it holds is significant for man, and so why this faith
is important to life. If it proclaims Jesus as Lord, then, it has a
responsibility to those who listen to that proclamation for saying why we think he should be or rightfully is Lord of man. Not
to do so is to admit not only that we hold it "because we were
already Christians," i.e., for an essentially traditional reason
dating back to another context; but it is also to consign this modern faith to its own death as soon as those who became Christian
on other, more explicable grounds have passed from the scene.
A *Blik* that remains merely a *Blik,* that can give no reasons
for being held as true, cannot be communicated to others in any
other personal situation. And without God or the Holy Spirit, a
faith that cannot be communicated by the speech of men, faces
almost as early a death as the God whom, to its impoverishment,
it has already lost.

6 / Implications
for Theological Method
of the Present Situation

ORIGINAL AND INTERESTING as the radical theologies are, their significance for the current situation in theology does not lie in the concrete formulations of Christian faith which they propose, for these are, as we have just seen, extremely vulnerable to criticism. Rather, their significance resides in the fact that they express within the citadels of Christian discourse itself one or another facet of the dominant secular mood of our time, and consequently that the problems they raise are crucial for current theological method. Since this is the mood within which, whether we like it or not, present theology must do its work, the radical movement has at last made explicit the basic issues of twentieth-century theology—and for this we should be grateful. Their particular formulations may come and go, and the wide attention they have attracted may well fade. But the questions they have raised will not disappear, and this is their importance for us.

We noted in an earlier chapter that the most radical expression of the problem raised for theology by the "death of God" theologies, and through them by the secular mood of our times, could be expressed in terms of the problem of the meaningfulness of God-language. This issue was, of course, raised most pointedly by van Buren, although it also includes the main thrust of Hamilton's writings. Now, because the particular philosophical instrument van Buren used to pose the issue, namely the verification principle and the positivism founded upon it,

have themselves been discarded by philosophers generally, a
good many theologians have somewhat thankfully concluded
that this problem has itself gone away and that radical theology
is scarcely still relevant to the problems of theological method.
This we believe to be a delusion, and we sought to show this by
exhibiting the broad spectrum of contemporary philosophical
viewpoints which agreed with positivism on this issue, and the
serious problems which the secular mood as a whole poses for
the religious life of the Church as well as for theological language. Positivism was an extreme form of "secularity" as we
have defined that term; but the demise of the former is no
symptom of the unhealth of the latter as we all experience it in
ourselves. The issue of the meaningfulness of language about
the transcendent, about the ultimate reality or structure of
things, and about the sacral source, ground, and aim of all, remains as difficult and as significant for the religious and so the
Church life of our age as ever—for it is the secular spirit in us
all, and not a particular philosophical expression of it, which
generates this problem for the Church and for theology.

Assuming, therefore, that the issues they pose are real
and important issues and that it is useful to center them about
the question of the meaningfulness of religious discourse, let
us summarize briefly in terms of three cardinal points the problems that they and the mood they represent have raised so that
we can see their impact on the issue of contemporary theological
method:

1. Language referent to any transcendent, sacred, ultimate, or essential dimension of reality or of process is, in both
its metaphysical and its revelational forms, meaningless for any
modern men who share the secular experience of our age. Implied in this statement is (a) that there is no referent for such
a language, since the world is made up entirely of contingent,
blind, relative, and transient factors and that the mind cannot
move beyond the immediate, i.e., that God is dead; (b) that
nowhere in ordinary, or even in special, experience is there any
trace of a relation to such referents, and so neither any use for
this language game in our ordinary discourse nor any mode for

its validation. Ordinary experience is devoid of traces of the sacred or the ultimate, and the religious experience of the presence of God or knowledge of him through faith is more of a hope than of a reality for most of us in our age. Our secular experience is here regarded as strictly "secular," and thus it is not possible for us to think that the imaginary worlds referred to by religious discourse are actual in our real world; we can "think of" them, but we cannot think them in relation to the world we know to be real. Thus is "the Word of God dead" and the language game in which it functions speakable but meaningless. Let us note that none of the above requires the positivist position, and all of it is meant when it is said that religious language is meaningless in our age. Finally, let us recall that, when the reality of God is so radically questioned that all theological discourse seems in this sense meaningless and empty, no further *theological* problems exist, whether they be those of scripture, hermeneutic, Christology, ecclesiology, or eschatology. Each of them presupposes the reality of God and, as examples of theological discourse, the meaningfulness of that kind of language referent to the divine, namely religious discourse. The first order of business, then, for contemporary theological reflection is, we feel, to deal with the problem of the meaning of religious language and through that avenue to approach the deeper issue of the reality of God.

2. They have vividly illustrated the fact that the secular mood of our time, which has raised this question of the reality of God and the meaningfulness of religious discourse, is *in* the Church and so characterizes the mind-set, attitude, and spirit of layman, cleric, seminary student, and theologian alike. An immediate theological consequence of this important sociohistorical fact is that the problem of theological language is *not* that of finding words or categories with which the Church can communicate a possessed message to the "unbelievers" or to a secular world outside itself. The problem of theological language is the meaninglessness and unreality of that language for ourselves as churchmen and theologians. Our difficulties are then misunderstood if we think of them as involving the problems

of "communication" in a secular age: such a posing of the problem assumes we in the Church *have* the faith, that we have heard the Word, know what it is, and know that it is true, and then seek to communicate it to others. Rather, it is precisely our own certainty and so the meaning of this Word to ourselves that are problematic, and so it is about theological language in relation to ourselves as Christians that we must reflect theologically. And the reason is that the secular spirit permeates the churches and those who minister in them almost as fully as it does the world outside.

A further implication of this point is that the traditional distinction, accepted by most Protestant and Catholic theology alike, between a kerygmatic theology addressed to the Church and an apologetic theology addressed to the unbelieving world needs radically to be rethought. In neoorthodoxy, it was debated whether an apologetic theology was possible, faithful, or safe; but because it was assumed that the Church could be defined as the community that "had faith," it was never debated whether a kerygmatic theology addressed to believers was possible or meaningful. But, as is surely true, the believers are also in part "unbelievers," their faith is permeated with doubt and a sense of unreality, and the spirit of the Church is in part at least secular. From this fact radical theology has drawn the conclusion of the impossibility of any meaningful theological talk about God, even to believers in the Church, i.e., that kerygmatic theology itself should be secular. If we do not share this radical conclusion with them, at least it must be admitted that kerygmatic theology, the theology addressed by the Church to the "believing" Church, must be also apologetical theology, a theology addressed to the "doubting" world—for the Church *is* the world in so much of its spirit.

Now, to establish such a sense of the meaning of theological language to and for a situation of even partial unbelief, requires, as all apologetical theology illustrates, the discovery of a common ground with secular experience, either in the form of a natural theology or of a prolegomenon of some sort. If, then, the theology of the Church and addressed to the Church—and to the theologian himself—must be apologetic as well as kerygmatic if it is to have any meaning inside the Church and for the theologian, this means that some form of natural theology or prolegomenon is now an essential element of any creative *church*, dogmatic or kerygmatic theology in a secular age—not to mention a theology that can speak to those who do not believe at all. This insistence that *Church* theology be *apologetic* theology, even when addressed to itself, is perhaps the most revolutionary implication of the new situation for all those forms of current theology that follow the traditional, and neo-orthodox, pattern of speaking theologically solely from the position of faith receptive of the Word, and solely to those who it is assumed have a similar faith, a similar certainty, and a similar grasp of the meaningfulness of Biblical language.

3. A third implication of the secular mood for theological method cuts even deeper. Although the presence of this mood in the churches seems to call for a natural theology as a preliminary but essential aspect even of Church theology, nevertheless the *character* of that mood seems to make such a natural theology impossible. For as we have seen, perhaps the main shape of this mood is the loss of a sense of the ultimate coherence of things which reason might delineate—the loss, one might say, of any confidence in an ultimate logos in existence generally—and the consequent confinement of thought to the immediate. For this mood, metaphysical language about "the transcendent," "the ultimate," "the real," "the actual"—about, that is, the ultimate nature and system of things—tends to be as unreal and empty, as much a product of fantasy and bewilderment rather than of knowing, as is language based on revelation or the Word. Consequently, reason in the speculative sense of the word seems in as difficult a position as faith to establish either the meaningfulness or validity of theological discourse. Ironically, we need a basis for theology that is grounded on the powers of reason to explore secular experience, to find its universal structures, and thus to establish a rational and so common foundation for the utterances of faith; but this basis itself, presupposing as it does the confidence in the universal cognitive powers of reason, appears to be in as much difficulty as that

which it is called upon to support. The rest of this chapter will explore further these three interlocking problems raised by the secular mood in relation to the dominant theological options or trends in our own day.

One common interpretation of the significance of the present situation in theology is that the current breakdown of neoorthodoxy represents a vindication of the general mood and theological principles of liberal theology. Neoorthodox theology, it is said, had removed God from historical, cultural, and ordinary experience into sheer transcendence; it eschewed philosophical or empirical analysis and confined itself to the "mythological" language of the Bible; and it established our relation to this God on grace and faith in the Word alone. Current developments have shown that this supernaturalism does not work, that under these conditions God disappears and, like all missing persons after a time, is finally declared to be dead. Did not the great liberals long ago say precisely this about the transcendent mythical God of orthodoxy, and did they not then locate God in the ordinary experience of men and seek to understand him in the intelligible terms of modern thought? The best answer to the challenge of radical theology, then, is to return to liberal principles, to find God in the course of history, or in general secular experience by historical or metaphysical analysis, and to establish the possibility and intelligibility of God-language in tune with modern philosophy in that way.

While there is a good deal of truth in this general position, as we shall see, nevertheless in certain respects it is, it seems to me, in error. The present situation in theology does not represent a return to classical liberalism, nor do the theological methods of the great liberals provide any easy answer to the problems we actually face. While there are parallels between the challenge that liberalism faced and that with which we must deal, the cultural context within which we must now theologize is as different from that of the pre-World War I world in which liberalism was formed as it is from that of the neoorthodox environment of World War II; correspondingly, a parallel response would be fatally irrelevant to our present situation.

To be sure, when one scans the basic assertions of radical theology—the denial of the transcendent, absolute God, the acceptance of the authority of secular thought and norms, the principle of personal and intellectual honesty as against all appeals to authority, the emphasis on the historical Jesus, the rejection of all supernatural entities, and the emphasis on creative action rather than correct belief—one is inclined to say, "This is liberalism all over again, and so the best answer to it is a better, more profoundly philosophical or ethical liberal theology." And in a strange way, these *are* the formative principles of nineteenth- and early twentieth-century liberalism, as most of the radical movement seemingly fails to realize. Nevertheless, in its basic spirit, the second half of the twentieth century represents a very different context for theology than did that of late nineteenth-century culture. The ground for the distinction comes, I believe, from the different evaluation of the role of the divine and so of religion in life generally, and thus from the very different understanding of the meaning of secularity characteristic of classical liberalism and of the present secular mood. This new view of what secularity means runs through our whole culture and, correspondingly, through all of the affirmations of radical theology; it almost represents the guiding principle of the movement, separating it sharply from the liberalism it seems to resemble.

For the liberal theology of the nineteenth century, the divine was immanent in all of developing reality and so all creative experience, and so the divine principle and human existence in all of its aspects were believed to be in creative continuity. Consequently, on the one hand, God and human religion were virtually identified, or at least felt to be in the closest relationship; and, on the other, both the divine and the human religious response were regarded as continuous with general secular experience. Thus the divine power of coherence and goodness, manifesting itself in the cosmic and the historical processes of life, and inwardly in the religious, moral, and

aesthetic consciousness of man, was believed to provide the basis
for all creative evolutionary or cultural advance. A religion,
therefore, that was creative was "secularly oriented"—for that
was where the divine was clearly at work—and in turn any
secularity that was vital was at bottom religious. Liberalism
affirmed a triadic continuity among the divine, the religious,
and the developing secular order. Consequently, the God known
in specifically religious experience could also be found—by philosophical, social, historical, moral, or scientific analyses—as
the source of creativity in the general experience of men. On
the basis of this principle of the continuity of the divine with
the progressing secular order, then, liberalism could embrace
both religion and culture, accept cultural values and norms so
wholeheartedly, dispense with most categories of transcendence,
and make a valiant attempt to follow the religious and moral
example of Jesus within the world's busy life. Secular culture
was thus affirmed or accepted in liberalism *not* because it was
"merely secular" or "religionless" (such a culture was to it inconceivable). On the contrary, secular culture was embraced for
precisely the opposite reason, namely because it was within a
developing secularity that the divine power known in religious
experience increasingly manifested itself. And, as the point
where this creative divine élan or spiritual force within all culture becomes self-conscious, religion was for liberalism not the
antithesis of culture but the center and source of all of its dynamic life.[1]

[1] For a more complete description of the liberal belief in the
continuity of the divine with culture, see Kenneth Cauthen, *The Impact
of American Theological Liberalism* (New York: Harper & Row, 1962).
Cf. also William Pauck's analysis and definition of liberalism in his
book *The Heritage of the Reformation* (Boston: Beacon Press, 1950),
Chapter 17. The description in the text, we believe, holds for all the
great figures and "schools" of liberal theology: Hegelian, Kantian,
Schleiermachian, Ritschlian, Whiteheadian—and for such present-day
important liberal philosophers of religion as Wieman, Meland, and
Hartshorne. It is at *this* point, of course, that Paul Tillich is genuinely
liberal; and, correspondingly, it was his emphasis on transcendence,
estrangement, and so on revelation and on the uniqueness of the New
Being that separated him from this liberal tradition and placed him
among the "neoorthodox."

Liberalism was, therefore, founded on a belief in the universality of a relation to God, a relation that could in principle appear everywhere and that filled with increasing value every form of human life. Man here felt himself at home in the developing cosmic order, an order that was increasingly creative of all that he valued and so was sacral or religious in import. And further, on the same principles, liberalism had no great difficulty with God-language. Because of the continuity of universal moral, aesthetic, cognitive, and religious experience with the creative divine ground of all things, theological doctrines could be founded either on the results of scientific investigation (F. R. Tennant and today Teilhard de Chardin); on a metaphysical analysis of universal process (Hegel, Whitehead, and Hartshorne); on an analysis of moral or religious experience (Kant, Schleiermacher, and Ritschl); or an analysis of man's historical experience of creative goodness (H. N. Wieman). And God might be spoken of in terms of any of these basic forms of human experience. Although liberalism, therefore, believed firmly in human autonomy over against tradition, and in the secular as opposed to the ecclesiastical orders, nevertheless it understood the creativity of that autonomy and secularity in terms of man's relation to an immanent cosmic force which it called God. Man's being in the world was thus understood here, not in terms of his alienation from the universe, but precisely in terms of his deep and intimate relation to it. Its coherence reflected his intelligence, and its progressive drive toward value matched his own deepest purposes. Liberalism expressed therefore a sense of continuity and harmony of man with his cosmic setting, which was vividly different from our contemporary secular spirit, from most contemporary forms of philosophical thought, and certainly from all forms of radical theology.

As we have noted, the appearance of the "raw secularity" of the twentieth century, together with the new emphases of neoorthodoxy on the lostness of man and the transcendence of God, broke this liberal identity or continuity between secularity and deity, and tended to insist on a separation of the saving and creative relation to God from ordinary cultural experience. At this point, then, neoorthodoxy is more in agreement with the current secular mood, and so with the radical theologians, than is liberalism in any of its forms. Where neoorthodoxy broke with twentieth-century secularity was not in its negative assessments about the absence of God from ordinary life and so his transcendent mystery—for which liberalism criticizes it—but that it still retained any belief in God and his works at all, which belief it held in common with liberalism. To return to the simple "essentialism" of liberalism, where for metaphysical or historical inquiry the divine order is evident to secular searching, is to run counter not so much to neoorthodoxy as to the modern secular mood itself. As our analysis shows, such an essentialist faith in the continuity of the divine and human experience, God and the world order, or God and developing process, is as little available to contemporary secular man as is the Biblical faith it is to replace.

The heart of modern secularity is that human experience, secular or religious, is devoid of relation beyond itself to any ground or order, and that there is no form of human thought that can by speculation come to know of such a ground or order. Consequently, for this mood, philosophical analyses of the ontological structures of reality as in Whitehead, or of general religious experience as in Otto, of even moral experience as in the Kantian tradition, or of value experience as in Wieman, are themselves infinitely suspect and so contain no immediate bases for theological discourse. Clearly, for such a view, the philosophical sources of liberal religion, be they moral or religious experience, metaphysical speculation, or an analysis of either cosmic or human history, are as moribund as is the revelation which was the basis of Christianity's older dogmatic formulations. Thus to seek to build thereon a natural theology for the contemporary world is futile, since that which is to be a bridge to the modern man—the natural theological effort of liberalism —itself defies every basic tenet of modern spirituality. And this is why, when the neoorthodox revelationist and the liberal ontologist each declares that it is only the God of the other that is deceased in the new secular mood, the onlooker can only feel that each has quite missed the point of the present theological crisis.

The relations of the new situation in theology to both liberalism and neoorthodoxy are, therefore, dialectical in form, and thus the radical theologians' expressions of that situation agree and disagree at the same time with each of their predecessors. They support against neoorthodoxy the liberal principle that theology must be secular, based on man's general experience of nature and of history; and therefore as, for example, Ogden sees clearly, radical theology agrees with liberalism that categories of special revelation and radical transcendence are irrelevant and obscurantist. On the other hand, what the contemporary liberals do not see, is that radical theology and the secular spirit it expresses support against liberalism the neoorthodox principle that the secular spirit understands its own existence as devoid of the divine, and therefore that a religion based on secularity is one which affirms the death of God. For the most significant character of the contemporary mood for theology is its vision of the *total* secularity of all of existence. Hence a contemporary secular theology is not one of divine immanence at all, but a humanist one. Most important of all, modern secularity and thus radical theology are in disagreement with both liberalism and neoorthodoxy when radical theology asserts that a relation to a divine ground is impossible, irrelevant, and destructive to the life of modern man, whether that relation be found immanently in general religious experience or transcendently by revelation. Man is autonomous, on his own in a cosmos whose character is unrelated to his spiritual and moral life; hence religion of whatever sort is illusory, distracting man from life in the world and repressive of his most creative values. Religion as a relation to God is, for this mood, the antithesis rather than the basis of creative culture and of inner health. Neither liberalism nor neoorthodoxy, despite all their internal disagreements, ever saw Christian faith in these terms; for both understood man's fulfilment in terms of his relation to those aspects of his total environment, be they natural or supernatural, to which they applied the symbol God. Thus, because the modern mood expresses apparently a terminal stage in the process of secularization, in which the divine has finally absconded from immanence as well as from transcendence, the problem of a secular Christianity is a much deeper and more difficult one now than for the liberal nineteenth century, and it is understandable that the form of such a Christianity should be infinitely radical in comparison with the classical forms of liberalism.

Finally, it is evident that a mere change of method will not resolve the problem of religious discourse in our age. Certainly our difficulties are partly methodological in character, and this we shall discuss in detail. However, a method in theology is not a neutral tool for theological discovery such that its loss alone spells theological frustration, and its reappearance, whatever the context, augurs success. Rather, a method is itself a part of that wider whole which is expressed in an entire philosophical or theological system, and ultimately, as we have argued, a method is an expression, and only a partial one, of that deeper vision of things which dominates a whole era of cultural experience and thought. Thus methods "fit" the systems which they explain, and make little sense outside them; and a methodology which at one time seems to provide the answer to all outstanding puzzles, always seems to have little relevance to or effectiveness in the crises of a later time. No one would think now that the rationalistic, deductive method in the Cartesian period will resolve our present intellectual problems; for the wider historical vision in terms of which seventeenth-century man structured his *Lebenswelt*, his world of experience, has vastly shifted, and "clear and distinct ideas" alone are to us as little able to unlock the mystery of things as are the oracles of Delphi. Thus to argue that we should return to the methods of liberalism—or of neo-orthodoxy, for that matter—is futile for present theology. For, as we have argued at length, there is a vast difference between their *Lebenswelt*, characterized by progressive order and cumulative value, and ours. Philosophical and theological methods, as does all human thinking, exist in the *historical* dimension and so are relative to the *Geist* of their age; and like the habits of vernacular speech or the mores of local communities, they cannot be translated into another cultural epoch and be of very much value.

If we look at the main currents of contemporary theology in the light of the three problems or issues raised by radical the-

ology, we can see why present theology finds itself in such a
deep quandary. Gradually theologians are realizing that a new
and deeper issue confronts them than the one they have been
debating for the past thirty years: how do we speak of God, by
reason or by revelation; how is the Word to be interpreted today; how is the Christ-event related to the Jesus of history? And
so on. All of these theological questions presuppose a meaningful question which is now up for debate: the question whether
there is a God to speak of and whether, therefore, we can use
this sort of language at all. It is, therefore, to these prior questions that theological reflection must now address itself. But,
ironically, the very secular spirit that has made this the central
question has seemingly snatched from the hands of the theologians the familiar tools which in recent tradition they had become accustomed to and so with which they might tackle the
problem of God. To explicate this irony, let us now look at the
major forms or schools of contemporary theology.

Certainly the major recent tradition in Protestant theology is what we may call the "hermeneutical tradition."[2] Cen-

[2] Like most words when they have become central in theology,
"hermeneutical" is now very difficult to define. Originally it meant the
"principles for interpreting a historical text or document," hence in
theology the principles by which scripture is to be interpreted. As Ebeling argues, therefore, in Reformation-type theologies and so in neoorthodoxy, theology *is* hermeneutics. With Bultmann, these principles
of interpretation were expanded from a set of objective rules to encompass (1) the enterprise of demythologization so as to free the gospel
from false objectification, and to make possible a religious understanding of scripture today, and (2) the mode of existentialist interpretation
(*à la* the early Heidegger) of the real message of scripture, which was
the self-understanding communicated therein (see Rudolph Bultmann,
"The Problem of Hermeneutics," in *Essays* [New York: Macmillan and
Company, 1955]). In more recent theological developments, the hermeneutical task is not understood as one intent on discovering a self-
understanding behind the archaic words of scripture, but to find what
"linguistic-" or "Word-event" transpires in and through the text, what
"comes to expression there." In dependence on the later Heidegger,
Word-events, as seen by Fuchs and Ebeling, are the way Being (or God)
speaks to us through language; thus knowing Being or knowing God
is a hermeneutical task, a discovery of what is said in and through a
Word-event. Finally, in the current lingo of phenomenological philosophy, again *à la* Heidegger, hermeneutics is taken to refer to the phe-

tered largely in Germany, it represents, in our view, the present
complexion of the fairly continual stream of post-Reformation
Continental theology which, in the neoorthodox period, was re-
vitalized by Barth, set into a more liberal form by Bultmann,
and now continues in several post-Bultmannian forms.[3] The
main characteristic of this form of theology for our purposes is
that it defines theology as the explication of the Word of God, a
Word that is found in the scriptural witness to the event of

---

nomenological investigation of the *Lebenswelt*, the lived experience of
being in the world, which seeks to uncover the latent and obscure structures and characteristics of man's being (cf. Herbert Spiegelberg, *The
Phenomenological Movement* [The Hague: Martinus Nijhoff, 1965],
Volume I, pp. 318ff. and 349ff., Volume II, pp. 694ff.). It is *this* meaning of the word "hermeneutic" to which we shall later appeal in Part II,
Chapters II–IV. Frederick Herzog's book *Understanding God* accepts both
these two latter meanings of the word "hermeneutic," i.e., a study of scripture to see what "Word-events" transpired there, and a general but nonscientific form of human knowing of man's condition in the world: cf.
Understanding God (New York: Charles Scribner's Sons, 1966), pp. 13–
15. Even here, however, in its theological usage and certainly in Ebeling,
Fuchs, and Ott, theology as hermeneutic understands reality from the
point of view of the community of faith which receives the Word through
scripture and preaching, and not from the point of view of a general
examination (philosophical, existential, phenomenological, or what have
you) of general experience. Thus even in this modern theological usage,
hermeneutic, though to be sure an understanding of *all* of reality (Herzog, *op. cit.*, p. 91), remains related, or better restricted, to the understanding of the texts of scripture. Modern hermeneutical theology is thus
a part of the long tradition of Word-of-God theologies of European
Protestant thought, albeit "translated" now into the terms of the later
Heidegger and through that of phenomenology. The best description of
the tradition we are discussing, the character of its theology, and the
changing meanings of the central label, "hermeneutics," appears in the
two books edited by James M. Robinson and John B. Cobb, Jr., *New
Frontiers in Theology*, Volume I: *The Later Heidegger and Theology*, and
Volume II: *The New Hermeneutic* (New York: Harper & Row, 1963
and 1964). The most complete discussion of the new hermeneutic recently to appear is Robert Funk's *Language, Hermeneutic, and the Word
of God* (New York: Harper & Row, 1966).

[3] In these remarks, we will refer especially to the new hermeneutic theology of Ernst Fuchs, Gerhard Ebeling, and the different but nevertheless basically related hermeneutical theology of Heinrich Ott.

Christ, proclaimed as kerygma in the sermon, and received by faith by the covenant community of the Church. The task of theology is thus a hermeneutical one: the interpretation and understanding of the scriptures, or the translation of that Word into language appropriate and intelligible today.[4] The question we have to ask now is, how well is this tradition able to deal with the problems raised so forcefully by the secular spirit in

[4] Cf. Heinrich Ott, "The nature of theology as a whole is hermeneutical. . . . It is a matter of understanding Biblical texts, of understanding the subject matter that comes to expression in them, and ultimately of the understandability of the witness to the subject matter in each present situation. . . . A single arch stretches from the Biblical text to the contemporary preaching of the Church. It is the arch of the kerygma and of the understanding of the kerygma. It is a matter of the same kerygma becoming audible today as then, that of the witness being translated to our side of the shore. . . . Systematic theology finds its position, as it were, in the middle of the arch extending from the text to contemporary preaching." Heinrich Ott, "What Is Systematic Theology?" in Robinson and Cobb, *The Later Heidegger*, pp. 78–81.

And from Ebeling: "The question of hermeneutics forms the focal point of the theological problems today. . . . The difficult problem of theology's systematic method can be properly solved only when it is likewise set in the light of the question of hermeneutics. For resting on the exposition of scripture and the history of theology, dogmatics has the task of bringing the Church's teaching into contact and discussion with contemporary principles of thought, there to submit it to critical sifting and present it in its full inner coherence." Gerhard Ebeling, *Word and Faith* (Philadelphia: Fortress Press, 1963), p. 27. And that theology thus understood necessarily *presupposes* revelation, divine events, God, and so God-language, is clear from the following: "That is, the historical origin of Christianity is assigned the character of revelation. It is thereby withdrawn from the relativity and transience of all historical events. It forms a realm which is once and for all defined, distinct from all the other phenomena of history—a judgment which finds expression in the fixing of the canon of holy scripture." *Ibid.*, p. 29. As Ebeling makes clear, these are the central theological principles of both the Reformation and of neo-orthodoxy (pp. 17–18), however much the more liberal Ebeling may now emphasize the word "translation," and the necessity of using categories and forms of modern thought for effecting that translation into modern terms. Theology remains still bound exclusively to the Word and its sole task is that of setting that Word into contemporary understanding and terms; it is through and through hermeneutical, an interpretation and translation of a given sacred text.

which all of us, European and American, churched and un-
churched, now dwell?

With regard to its understanding of God-language, of
theological discourse about God, the hermeneutic theology and
its neoorthodox predecessors made three primary assumptions
which make it difficult if not impossible for this form of theology, even in its present "liberal" forms, to deal with the present
situation as we have characterized it. It is, we believe, for these
reasons that most current Continental theology exudes, on the
one hand, a sense of frustration and, on the other, an aura of
unreality, of really not being in the world with which it seeks to
cope. The central thrust of this tradition, as we saw, was the
view that man in the world is out of cognitive relation to God,
and that he is only in a cognitive relation to God through the
Word where God comes to man and allows himself to be
known. This form of theology, therefore, took secularity as a
total loss of God very seriously; what it failed to see was the
secularity in the church people and theologians themselves, in
their fundamental attitudes, values, and intellectual standards.
This secularity within has both undermined the presuppositions
on which this theology was built and correspondingly raised
problems with which this sort of theology cannot deal. The presuppositions of hermeneutical theology which secularity has undermined and to which we have referred are as follows:

1. The Continental tradition in theology has pictured
two worlds, interpenetrating in space but separated in spirit—
surely a questionable hope, in the long run! There is, on the one
hand, the world of the covenant community, of faith and the
divine Word, where that Word is heard in proclamation and enacted in sacrament. In this world of the Church, consequently,
the reality and the nature of God are manifested to men and
known by them; they hear, believe, and understand what they
believe. Here, therefore, meaningful religious and theological
language is used and understood; here this language game communicates, makes sense, and here its symbols have the feel of
reality. On the other hand, there is the world of unbelief, where
the Word is not heard and so where meaningful religious lan-

guage is not possible or present—the world of the secular. The Church is thus here defined as distinctively "over against" the world, as the community characterized essentially by this Word, this faith, this hearing, and this intelligibility. Strangely, most theologians of this tradition seem to feel that this is a "factual" description of the churches, rather than a doctrine of faith about them, or possibly an eschatological hope.

For example, Heinrich Ott says, "The Church of Jesus Christ is a brotherhood sharing in a common fate, a common destiny, a common experience, namely, the revelation of the living God. Because of this destiny all who belong to the Church stand in a common situation, without regard to all the differences of individuality and of time and place. It is in this factual [*sic*] situation of the *communio sanctorum* that the Gospel, the subject matter of believing and preaching, must in certain respects be clarified, preached, explained, explicated"[5]—which is the task of theology. Theology here understands itself in terms of the presuppositions of this community of hearing, belief, and experience of the Word of God—for only on that presupposition, as we shall see, can this restricted task of theology as solely involved in explicating the Word of God be intelligible.

Unfortunately, of course, these words describe the Church of dogmatic theology, the invisible Church in which, as Luther realistically said, we believe since it is a church which we do not see.[6] They are not descriptive of the visible or actual churches, nor of the situation and experience of the actual people in the Church to which, one hopes, theology will address itself. For these people are bothered with doubts, find these words frequently meaningless, and at best covet in hope or experience in fragmentary prospect—but surely not in unambiguous actuality —this "shared experience of the revelation of the living God." The actual Church is one of doubt and secularity as well as of halting faith. No wonder a theology which assumes that all of its hearers have experienced the reality of God through the hearing of the Word, and goes on from there, seems often unreal.

[5] Ott, "Systematic Theology," p. 101.
[6] Martin Luther, *The Papacy at Rome,* in *The Works of Martin Luther* (Philadelphia: Muhlenberg Press, 1943), Volume I, p. 361.

This assumption begs precisely the question most Christians are asking. The theological error involved here—and this is true of most Continental theology—is the effort to base an *actual* theology on the *invisible* Church, to found theological language not on what is actual about people and their experience, but on what is itself an article of belief. For the experience, the actuality with which this theology begins and must presuppose—what Ott calls strangely "the factual situation"—is a "fact" that is itself a *believed part* of the theology it purports to found. It is an article of faith, not of sight; hoped for, not experienced; often doubted and so not certain; it is certainly not where the people in the churches, in Europe or America, exist. Thus the whole system of language derived from this starting point revolves in a circular fashion far above the ground and touches nowhere in the world of contemporary experience. Because that section of earth, the "community of covenant people, faithful, obedient, and hearing the Word," with which it pretends to start, is itself in heaven.[7] Clearly a theology that assumes that people already have faith and so fails to explore the bases of faith in ordinary experience, compounds rather than solves the question raised by secularity about the possibility and meaningfulness of faith in our age.

2. A second presupposition of this theology follows from this initial assumption of the actual Church as defined by faithful hearing and acknowledgment of the divine Word: God *need* not be spoken of outside that context, and so theological reflection can be confined to the limits of the relation of Word, faith, and sermon. If such faith is there as so described, then all those agonizing questions about the reality and the nature of God sharply forced upon us today are already assumed to be satisfactorily answered by our definition of faith, since the faith knows God as real and language about him as intelligible. The task of theology is to explicate in contemporary thought forms this latent

[7] For a further discussion of these abstract and unreal—though theologically important—definitions of the Church, see this writer's *How the Church Can Minister to the World Without Losing Itself* (New York: Harper & Row, 1966), Chapter 6, "Language and the Church."

certainty and intelligibility of faith, to translate the gospel of God into modern speech, and to do no more than that.

In this task of translation, hermeneutical theology may make some limited use of philosophy, and thus it may seem to have related itself more closely with the experience and thought forms of the "world." It may, for example, seek to understand the experience of faith in the I-Thou categories of existentialism and of Martin Buber, as Brunner did, or to use the philosophy of the early Heidegger, as Bultmann did, or that of the later Heidegger, as both Ebeling and Ott now seek to do. Since, however, here the *reality* of God is already known by faith, and the *meaningfulness* of language about him already latent in the certainties of faith, neither this use of philosophy in hermeneutic nor the theology that results from this use of philosophy is devised to deal with our doubts about the reality of God or our questions about the use and meaning of language about him.[8] The use of Heideggerian philosophy, for example, to show that "existence is linguistic" is not designed as a prolegomenon to faith, that is, to assure us either of the intelligibility of what is here called a Word-event of revelation, or of the reality of God and his Word.

[8] These theological questions about the *presuppositions* behind faith are in this tradition not matters for theological reflection. Barthian neoorthodoxy has made this abundantly clear in its repudiation of both natural and apologetical theology; apparently the same assumption that neither of these are of use or necessary to faith is held by the proponents of the "new hermeneutic." Cf. this from Ebeling: "We here set aside questions that probe behind that [the concept of the Word as happening]— why the holy scripture that presses for proclamation or the proclamation that takes its stand on holy scripture should be marked out in particular above other scripture as Word of God; or what form of the Word of God to some extent precedes scripture; and whether the Word of God is not found also outside the relation of text and sermon. For according to Christian conviction the answers to all these questions can be truly known only in connection with that movement from the text to the sermon." Ebeling, *Word and Faith*, p. 311. All questions dealing with the presuppositions of the Word and so with the problem of the certainty and intelligibility of faith in that Word, are resolved *in* the hearing of the Word, and in no other context. This works if and only if such faith can be presupposed, if the actual Church is the invisible Church of faith.

It does not begin with the "secular" experience of "word-events" (in conversation, politics, and so on) and move from there into the realm of Christian discourse, i.e., to the Word-events of revelation, showing how existence generally really *is* linguistic and then by means of a delineation of the similarities and differences between "ordinary" and "revelational" Word-events, what a revelational Word-event might mean in that wider context of general experience. The Continent is still aghast at the thought of such a natural theology or of such a "secular" prolegomenon to the language of faith. Faith and the Word are presupposed as starting points even for this use of philosophy, setting the limits of all theological reflection. Philosophy helps us *within* that circle of faith by making comprehensible what has happened to us in the hearing of the Word; but the assumption that we *have* heard the Word is made before theological reflection begins. Theology and its use of philosophy in the new hermeneutic thus presuppose our "credo"; their job is to add intelligibility to this assumed faith that is given as already present and active in the life of the Church community. Neither philosophical nor theological reflection seeks to provide a defense of the meaningfulness in secular terms of the language game within which theological discourse functions, or to help us to locate the sense of the reality of God in other, more ordinary forms of experience than that of being in a pew and there hearing the Word.

The problem, obviously, is that this presupposition of faith and its hearing of the Word is as unreal as the first. To say this is not at all to assert that proclamation in Church is not and cannot be a place where faith is born and where God is known both as real and as intelligible through his Word. It is merely to say that this *assumption* that this has happened cannot be safely made by a theology that is to be relevant to the actual Church's present life. The faith of the actual Church, and much of it is there, is also saturated with doubt, and the language of theology is all too often meaningless and unreal both to those who listen and to those who speak. And this doubt questions primarily what is here assumed, namely that my faith is such that I *know* God to be real, and that language about him which is intelligible and meaningful to me is automatically latent in that faith when I hear the Word spoken from the pulpit. If I really wonder whether in proclamation or in the scriptures I am confronted by a divine Word, then merely hearing that same Word proclaimed again or even hearing it explained in the latest philosophers' terms, may not answer this question I have: Do I here in these words and these ritual acts have to do with a real God, or is this an empty fantasy? Not to tackle this question is to shirk the main theological burden of our time, and to refuse to do so on theological grounds makes one surmise that more anxiety than piety is here at work. This task can be undertaken only by seeking to relate the theological discourse of the sermon to other areas of felt experience, namely to the stuff of ordinary secular life where our deepest sense of reality and of intelligibility originates and lies. Our faith and its language will, I hazard, only bear a sense of validity and of meaningfulness if they are in some sense secular, if they are related to actual living, to the secular stuff of experience—if these religious symbols move out of the chapel on the hill into the city where we all live.[9]

[9] These comments on German hermeneutical theology, and its American offshoots, can be best expressed perhaps in an image. The image is of a *Festung* or castle belonging to the reigning bishop (one recalls Salzburg) high on a rock above a town now governed by other forces and other interests and so essentially unrelated to this ecclesiastical eminence—except for the important tourist trade, postcards, photographs, and so on. The theological questions of German theology, the hermeneutical question of understanding the Biblical Word of God in our age, are questions *within* this special covenant place, presupposing that we have left the secular world below and have been raised by grace and faith to membership in the sacral community, the covenant community. We question, however, whether there are any who really *exist* in our age in that castle—certainly neither the hopeful tourists nor the learned guides appropriate to tourists who are to be seen in the old castle. Such a community that is constituted solely by faith is, on the level of existence, as deserted as is the *Festung* of Salzburg. For both the bishops and their government have long since descended to live below in the town. The most relevant theological question is, therefore, not what do we say in the *Festung* (how do we move from Word of God to sermon?), presupposing we are already there? Rather it is, how can theological reflection, if it can, move intelligibly, honestly, and with regularity from our life in the town to an existence, insofar as such is possible, on these heights, and how does the Word of God heard there have credibility and usability in the life of the

3. The third and most serious implication of this form of a theology of the Word is that, for this view, God, faith, and the possibility of theological language *cannot* be spoken of at all outside of the situation of faith hearing the Word. In consequence, theology cannot deal with the ordinary, secular stuff of life at all —for it explicates only the Word in scripture, it moves from the Word proclaimed toward faith, it stays within the *Sitz im Leben* of life in church. We have seen the roots in neoorthodoxy of this separation of theological language from ordinary life, many of which were valid: for example, the sense of the absence of God in secular experience and the danger of idolatry in culture religions. We shall attempt to incorporate much of this view in our own positive formulation of theological method in the second part of this volume.

At the moment, however, we wish to stress the confining character in our situation of this view of theology as declarative *only* of what "comes to expression" in a Word-event to faith. It means that theological reflection cannot make contact with ordinary secular experience—and thus, as we have seen, that the meanings of its symbols suffer disjunction from the felt meanings of life, and hence become more and more unreal and empty. Theology here consists of a coherent system of concepts or words which are defined only in terms of other similar words and ultimately only in terms of tradition and scripture; but none of which—except those referent to the concrete religious experience of faith in relation to the Word—touch the contours, words, usages, and symbols, or the experiences and felt meanings of ordi-

---

town? Any other theology is a "tourist" theology, not existing where *we* exist and not dealing with the real problems that plague the townsfolk— and the theologians. If theological reflection cannot deal with the movement from the town to the *Festung*, from secular existence to existence within the convenant community, if it must always assume that all who write and all who read theology already have the precious gift of faith, how is it to speak to a secular age—and how is it to speak in the name of an honest theologian and his church? One wishes that the scholarly and brilliant German theologians were more aware of the depths of these problems for modern theology. For surely their towns—and their churches —are also filled with people living far below the ancient ecclesiastical *Festung*.

nary life.[10] It may be, as we hold, that God must finally be spoken of only in relation to revelation and to a faith that accepts and understands revelation. But for the language with which that God is symbolically described to be meaningful to us, the symbols of theology must also be related thematically to the felt meanings and experiences of actual life. For its symbols so to have meaning, theological reflection must somehow extend beyond the narrow religious range of the experience of faith and of the positive, doctrinal statements relative to hearing the Word in church. It must be able to deal systematically and effectively with the character of ordinary life and develop a set of symbols which refer *both* to these felt meanings in secular experience *and* to the positive content of tradition and revelation. Meaningful symbols must be symbols of life, and so a meaningful system of theological symbols must continually be related beyond its own formal range to the stuff of life to which they bring illumination. What is said about God on the basis of faith must be related to what is felt and experienced by man in the ordinary stuff of his life—and that means a theological method far wider than that provided by the older Word of God or the newer hermeneutic theologies of the continent of Europe.[11]

Our criticism of the relevance of hermeneutical theology

[10] In his recent book on ordinary language and religious discourse, Dallas High makes the important point that no "language game" is completely separate and autonomous from all the various usages of language that appear in the general and so ordinary context of life in the world. The frequent effort in linguistic theology to regard theology as a separate, clearly demarked language game has, he avers, represented a misunderstanding of Wittgenstein's analogy of "games," and such separation threatens to empty religious discourse of its use and so its meaning. This is precisely the point at issue, we believe, with the Word of God theologies that regard theological language as separable from ordinary language and ordinary experience. Cf. Dallas High, *Language, Persons, and Belief* (New York: Oxford, 1967), Chapter 3, "Language Games."

[11] So far as I know, the only hermeneutical theologian to attempt to deal with this problem of the reality of God and with the presuppositions of revelation is Frederick Herzog. The ambiguity as well as admiration this writer feels about his book *Understanding God* stems from the problem of attempting to use a "hermeneutical method" to tackle these wider theological problems. In his recent book, he asks, as a modern hermeneutical theologian concerned with how faith comes to expression in

in the contemporary situation is not so much that it is based on the Word as that it is a form of theological reflection confined to the relation of Word to faith and to what is implicit within the single experience of the Word-event of faith. It thus assumes answers to and so cannot deal with what are actually the central theological problems of our time, namely the questions of the reality of God, the presence of the Word, and the meaningfulness of the whole system of Biblical language. It is in this way confined, we have argued, because it does not, or possibly dare not, question that the Church is a community of certain faith, that in its sermonic life it simply "hears" the Word, and that in that hearing the reality of God and the intelligibility of theological language are *given* to Christian people. Consequently, this type of theology need not and in fact cannot move outside this purely religious situation or experience into our significant experiences within the secular order. This cluster of assumptions is, however, false. The ques-

---

language events, "How does the Christian come to an understanding of the reality of God?" "What is the process by which, for the Christian, this comes to conceptual consciousness?" Thus he is in part dealing precisely with the question we feel should be dealt with. But the problem is that he tries to do this task solely within the hermeneutical circle of the relation of faith to scripture, and thus in the end is unable to carry it out clearly and fully. As a hermeneutical theologian, he must begin with the assumption that the Church in a faithful response to the Word does assert the reality of God, and so it is not his task to unpack the grounds for that assertion or to explore its validity and meaning in relation to ordinary experience. Rather, as a hermeneutical theologian, he seeks solely to derive the knowledge of the reality of God from the experience of the Word in scripture, an experience which already presupposes that reality. His thought moves from the experience of faith to its intellectual self-consciousness—but it is precisely that experience as an experience of *God* that is problematical and must be made an object of theological reflection. For as we have seen, it is dubious that a meaningful understanding of God can be derived from so narrow a base. The strength of the book lies in the fact that this experience of God's reality in faith is in fact related by Herzog to man's ordinary, secular experience of being and of history, where man, says Herzog, senses an ultimacy with which he has to do, but can in fact come to no clarity about it or in relation to it. With all of this we are in enthusiastic agreement. It is only unfortunate that, as a hermeneutical theologian tied to the explication of the Word, he cannot examine, analyze, or make constructive use of these "secular aporias" and thus, to me, his method frustrates his own very great insights.

tions which are here assumed to be answered in faith and so are subsequently ignored, are pressing on us all because in church as well as out of it the sense of the unreality of God and the emptiness of theological discourse is omnipresent. A theology that does not or cannot heed these problems has not yet understood its own world, and is not in fact effecting that "meaningful translation" of the kerygma into our own age which is its own stated goal. The first significance of the present situation for theology is that it is now evident to us that these assumptions of neoorthodoxy and of the new hermeneutical theology are defective. Thus are all of us who stand in this tradition forced to undertake the task of seeking to widen the areas of theological discourse in a secular direction.

The other major tradition in recent theology has been that which has based the validity and the intelligibility of theological or religious discourse on speculative metaphysics. There have been two quite dissimilar wings to this tradition of philosophical theology, both of which have, however, understood the task of theology as that of translating the language of faith into metaphysical categories. The first, Catholic, wing, has continued the tradition of Thomism, comprehending its theological affirmations in the terms of a contemporary understanding of Aristotelian philosophy. In Roman circles, such names as Newman, Maritain, Gilson, Garrigou-Lagrange, and Pryzwara come to mind; in Anglo-Catholic thought, the leaders have undoubtedly been E. L. Mascall, Austin Farrer and Eugene Fairweather.[12] The other wing is

[12] E. L. Mascall, *He Who Is* (London: Longmans, Green, 1943) and *Existence and Analogy* (London: Longmans, Green, 1949). Austin Farrer should perhaps not be put within this general "Aristotelian" group, since, while he does seek to base theological language on metaphysics, he has attempted to create a form of metaphysics of the will which is not so much a modernizing of traditional Aristotelian categories as it is a radical reconstruction of the notion of substance. Thus while, as in more liberal Roman Catholic theology, some of the structural form of Thomism remains, the Aristotelian content seems to have been replaced by more modern and dynamic categories of activity and operation. Cf. Austin Farrer, *Finite and Infinite* (London: Westminster, 1943); *Glass of Vision* (Westminster, London: Dacre Press, 1948); and *The Freedom of the Will* (London: A & C Black, 1959). An excellent critical summary of Farrer's philosophical theology is John Glasse's "Doing Theology

that represented by process philosophy, beginning, of course, with
the magnificent speculative system of A. N. Whitehead, and
continuing, in forms more closely related to the concerns of religion, in the thought of Charles Hartshorne, probably the most
distinguished contemporary American philosopher of religion.
Present-day representatives of this school are Bernard Meland,
Daniel Day Williams, Bernard Loomer, Schubert M. Ogden, and
John B. Cobb, Jr.

In general, the Thomists seek to translate Christian discourse into the older Aristotelian metaphysical categories of being, essence, and existence, and to explicate through these categories a notion of a transcendent, absolute, and self-sufficient
deity. In contrast to this, the process thinkers use the modern
categories of activity and becoming; they subscribe to a universal
doctrine of internal relations and relativity; and thus they conceive of deity in terms of its relatedness to and dependence on
the world, its becomingness and its conditionedness. The *contents,*
therefore, of these two philosophical traditions in theology differ
radically, and consequently each is inclined to view the other as
the real menace in the present situation.[13] In this debate, the
process thinkers certainly have the best of it, since it is difficult
to see how a theology formed on the conceptual patterns of Hellenic metaphysics can be intelligible to the modern mind. However, in their common insistence that religious discourse must be
translated into metaphysical language to achieve both intelligibility and validity, they are at one. One may say perhaps that, while
Thomism faces problems *vis à vis* secularity both with regard to
its metaphysical content and its metaphysical form, process the-

---

Metaphysically: Austin Farrer," *Harvard Theological Review,* LIX, No. 4
(October 1966).

[13] Cf. the very negative Thomist reaction to the essentially "process" philosophical theology of Leslie Dewart's *The Future of Belief* (New
York: Herder and Herder, 1966) and the continual appraisal by process
thinkers such as, say, Ogden that it is the classical Aristotelian God of
Thomism that has alienated modern man from belief in God and from an
understanding of the validity of theological language. Cf. Ogden, *The
Reality of God* (New York: Harper & Row, 1966), pp. 16ff. and 48ff.
For another, quite extreme example from process thinkers of "blaming"
radical theology on the Thomist tradition, cf. Ralph E. James, *The
Concrete God* (Indianapolis: Bobbs-Merrill, 1967), Introduction.

ology has difficulty only in the latter area. Because, then, we are here concerned with the methodological question of whether metaphysics offers a helpful way out of our present dilemmas, we shall tackle this issue in relation to process thought, since, in relation to a modern metaphysics, no confusing issues are raised by the anachronistic character of the set of metaphysical categories involved.

The question we wish to pose is the following: Can a metaphysical analysis in our day be the basis for an assurance of the reality of God and of the meaningfulness of our language about him? Can it provide the prolegomenon to theological discourse which we have argued is needed? Clearly this is the question of the possibility in a secular age of a natural theology, taking the latter to include some form of what has traditionally been called a "philosophical" proof of God. By such a proof of God, we mean the establishment, through some sort of philosophical inquiry based upon ordinary secular experience, of the reality of that to which the symbol of God can legitimately refer, and the consequent elucidation of intelligible forms of language about him. The issue whether religious faith does or does not accompany, guide, or even direct such an enterprise is irrelevant at the moment; all we are concerned with is the question whether philosophical reason can, according to its own canons, alone establish by implication the reality of God and the intelligibility of language about him.[14] It is clear that, if such an enterprise were

[14] The relations of natural theology to faith have varied in the history of this tradition. Whatever the positions of Anselm and Thomas were on this issue, the Enlightenment clearly wished to exclude faith from natural theology, as an unwarranted irrational element in a purely rational endeavor. Since Schleiermacher, however, and especially since the appearance of the historicist and existentialist notions of a fundamental perspective underlying all philosophies, most philosophical theologians have recognized that, as the underlying possibility of any natural theology, there is always some sort of "religious feeling," religious insight, stance, or perspective. The writings of Newman, Gilson, Maritain, as well as those of Whitehead, Ogden, and Cobb illustrate this common development amply. In process theology, the role of faith as an underlying lure of philosophical theology has, I believe, increased, probably under existentialist and neoorthodox influence. Relatively speaking, it is only tangentially there in Whitehead, Wieman, and Hartshorne, and has become much more prominent in Meland, Williams,

possible, the problems raised by radical theology would be answered since the metaphysical discourse on which the proof is
founded is, in principle at least, a form of discourse applicable
to the whole range of ordinary and so secular experience. Therefore, the reality of God could be assured if not demonstrated in
a secular age, and language about him that has a demonstrably
meaningful connection with the language of our ordinary life
would be guaranteed. It is because metaphysics seems to promise
this sense of meaningfulness and validity that many contemporary
metaphysical theologians have regarded the God who is dead as
the God only of revelation and of Biblical mythical language.
Such mythical language, they recognize, is unintelligible to modern man and unrelated to his ordinary secular experience; and
the answer they propose is to translate this ancient Biblical language into the language of a compatible modern metaphysical
system which will both accord with the secular spirit and relate
religious discourse to the stuff of ordinary life.[15]

   The issue of the possibility and utility of philosophical

Ogden, and Cobb. With the latter group, one feels that the role of philosophy is almost that of making intelligible the credo of faith, which
is surely a different role for faith than in Whitehead or Hartshorne, for
whom metaphysical reason, while guided by the intuitions and concerns
of religion, can proceed much more on its own "secular" basis. Despite
these important differences, however, for all of this tradition the enterprise of establishing the reality of God and the intelligibility of language about him is a philosophical or metaphysical enterprise, dependent
on philosophical criteria alone, and to be defended solely by metaphysical
argument. It is this proposal that we wish here to examine.

   [15] Cf. the following clear statement from Ogden: "The point is
that the claim of a mythical utterance to be true is simply unsupportable
unless one has some conceptuality in which its meaning can be literally
and properly [sic] stated. It is all well and good to insist that there is a
truth in myths and that they therefore must always be taken seriously.
. . . If one is actually to take responsibility for such assertions, he must
be able to make use of terms and categories in which, unlike those of
myth itself, our understanding of ourselves and our faith may be appropriately represented. Thus to make good the claim that myth can be
true requires a prodigious philosophical undertaking. One must provide
nothing less than the 'right' philosophy which is the essential prerequisite of any adequate theological construction." Ogden, *Reality of God*,
pp. 118–119.

proofs of God is one of the most complex in philosophical theology. There are in general three kinds of question that can be asked about a proof of God or a natural theology:

1. There is the question of its *logical* meaning, so to speak, the purely philosophical possibility and competence of a proof of God. In any given proof, of the ontological, the cosmological, or the teleological form, one can ask: Are the premises of the proof coherent or self-contradictory; and do these premises really entail the conclusions derived from them, or is there a logical error or leap in the movement of the argument? Do they, in other words, logically demonstrate what they claim to establish, or is there something logically incompetent, some linguistic "cheating" going on here? Such discussions have been an important element of the history of philosophy of religion, beginning with Gaunilo's and Thomas's criticism of Anselm, continuing with Hume and Kant's criticism of all proofs on purely philosophical grounds, and culminating today in current positivistic and naturalistic critiques. Correspondingly, philosophical defenses of the possibility of proofs of God have appeared in the writings of Descartes, Spinoza, Hegel, Whitehead, Hartshorne, and Malcomb, not to mention Mascall and Farrer.[16] In such debates, it is, I think, fair to say that the proof is looked at as one might consider an unusual mathematical proof, merely with regard to its internal logical coherence alone. The question whether or not the God proved (or not proved) becomes through the proof a meaningful part of my real world, or true for me, that

[16] A surprisingly intense discussion of the logical possibility of a proof of God has arisen quite recently over the ontological argument, largely through the work of Norman Malcomb, William Alston, J. H. Findlay, and now Alvin Plantinga, and supplemented by the long-term reflection of Charles Hartshorne. Cf. the excellent summary of this discussion in Plantinga's *The Ontological Argument* (New York: Doubleday Anchor, 1965). Although many of the participants in this discussion may have personal religious interests in its outcome, the discussion itself has proceeded as a purely objective philosophical matter, and no particular existential or religious concerns have entered relevantly into the debate. And for a complete logical analysis in this vein of almost every possible proof of God, cf. Plantinga's most recent book, *God and Other Minds* (Ithaca, N.Y.: Cornell University Press, 1967).

is, religiously relevant, is not raised in these discussions; for the concern is with the proof as a logical abstraction, with, that is, its truth in terms of the logical interrelation of its concepts, not with the relations of the symbols with which it concludes to our felt experience of our own being in the world. While such a discussion, confined to the logical validity of a proof, is, to be sure, relevant to our present concern with the experienced meaning of theological discourse, it is clearly not central to it. Even a proof that is internally valid with regard to logic may yet hang there as an abstraction whose symbols remain unrelated to life and so of no more help to the theological enterprise than might be the internally consistent systems of revelational theology.

2. An entirely different sort of question with regard to natural theology can be raised about the *religious* meanings of the proof, the relation of the proof to the requirements of religious faith. Such a question asks not so much, "Is it logically valid?" as "Is it religiously fruitful or dangerous?" Does it establish or violate the interests and concerns of faith? Is its proved God really God, or are the two, the proof and God himself, the actual God, incompatible with one another—even if the first were logically possible and valid? This theme of the religious relevance of a proof of God we shall raise again in the following chapters. Much more than the critique from the point of view of logic, in which neoorthodoxy was only tangentially interested, it has provided the base for the neoorthodox criticism of natural theology, on the ground that any proved God is a manmade idol, and veils or replaces the real God of revelation and faith, and so threatens a valid religious relation with God.[17] Im-

---

[17] Several times the radical theologians have made the mistake of appealing to this neoorthodox criticism of natural theology in supporting their claim that natural theology is impossible. This appeal is for them illegitimate because this criticism of natural theology presupposes for its force that there *is* a God of revelation who is "veiled" or "replaced" by the idol of philosophy. If there be no God at all and so no possibly meaningful language about him, then a natural theology, while, to be sure, possibly illogical and so philosophically meaningless, can in no sense be blasphemous or idolatrous, since there is no God to be distorted by man's false understanding. Such a natural theology is for this view, therefore, merely harmless, vacuous, and foolish. Thus, for exam-

portant as this question may ultimately be for systematic theology, the relation of a proof to the God of faith is irrelevant to our present purposes. Even to pose this question presupposes faith and *its* knowledge of God, and we have agreed that, with regard to the issues that here concern us, the dual assumption of revelation and of the faith that knows God through it cannot usefully be made.

3. We can, finally, ask whether a proof of God can relate this concept to our own felt, actual world of experience and to the ordinary usages of language in that world, and so aid us in establishing both a sense of the reality of God and of the meaningfulness for us of the symbolic language of religious discourse. There are two wings, so to speak, to this question: (*a*) Can a metaphysical analysis give philosophical intelligibility—which is, after all, its purpose—in the contemporary philosophical situation to our religious concerns? For if it is a futile bridge to philosophy, philosophical speculation has surely lost some of its luster. (*b*) Is it a useful bridge to our more existential meanings, that is, can it help us all to gain a sense of reality and intelligibility for our religious language? There are, as our discussion will increasingly reveal, many meanings to the word "meaning": the relevant one here, we are suggesting, is that which points to the relation of symbolic forms to our apprehension of the *Lebenswelt*, to the way we apprehend the total range of felt experience, to our actual lived experience of being in the world. If the symbolic forms do not thematize some element within or some dimension of that felt or experienced totality, then, whatever logical validity they may or may not have, or however they may relate to a system of theological language, these forms will not *mean* anything to me as assertions about what is real. For explicitly abstract or analytical concepts which purport to make no reference to the world,

---

ple, van Buren is himself illogical when he says that he rejects natural theology not "because it is logically puzzling, but because of certain theological commitments," for, "that road has been clearly charted and finally marked with a dead end sign by the work of Karl Barth, and we see no reason to ignore the warning." Paul van Buren, *The Secular Meaning of the Gospel* (New York: Macmillan Company, 1963), p. 98.

this lack is not important—but for theological language, as our whole discussion has implied, it is devastating. If they are unrelated to lived experience, theological categories will not communicate a sense of the reality of that to which they seek to refer, and they will seem empty and vacuous, unrelated and irrelevant as a system of language. The question, then, the present theological situation as we have delineated it poses for a natural theology, or for a system of religious discourse founded on a metaphysical analysis, is "Does a natural theology based on metaphysics establish the meaningfulness in this sense of religious language to the secular mind of today, or is that mind such that the whole enterprise is itself unintelligible and its own referents unreal?"[18] Is metaphysics in our day a useful avenue either on a philosophical or an existential basis to reality and intelligibility? This is the question which we shall now explore.

What assumptions are necessary in order to establish philosophically the reality of God and the intelligibility of language about him? We shall suggest in the following that an examination of the form and structure of any proof reveals two fundamental and unavoidable assumptions:

    1. That the mind has the power to know reality as it is, to delineate its real and not merely apparent structures in a total system of metaphysical categories. This involves the power of the mind to move by rational implication alone beyond the immediate, given character of experience, beyond the data, and to construct a conceptual picture of (a) the real, the actual, the concrete (to use Whitehead's phrase) substances or entities that make up the process, and (b) to construct a conceptual picture of the struc-

18 That the question of the possibility of metaphysics for the modern secular spirit is a fair and relevant question to pose for the process philosophers is shown by the fact that they pose the identical question to the revelationist theologians, namely "How well does your mythological language fit the modern sensibility?" Cf. the following from Ogden: "The first principle of such a solution is that the demand for demythologization that arises with necessity from the situation of modern man must be accepted without condition." Ogden, *Christ Without Myth* (New York: Harper & Bros., 1961), p. 127.

ture of their interrelations as a whole system. We must know what reality is really like, both in its parts and as a whole, if we are to demonstrate that there is a God included therein. A proof of God's reality requires, in other words, the assumption that speculative reason is especially potent and supremely dependable as a mode of *knowing*, that assertions about the real world can originate from philosophical inquiry and be tested by philosophical criteria, that philosophy functions cognitively as does science only on a higher level, since it deals with "actuality," "concreteness," what is "really the case."

2. The second, closely related, assumption necessary for a proof of God, or a natural theology, is that there obtains in some form or another an ultimate identity or correlation between reality and the structures, requirements, and criteria of thought. This must be said carefully, for it seems to imply that all proofs of God depend upon an explicitly idealistic ontology, which is manifestly untrue. Although idealism is an extreme case of this identity between thought and reality, we intend the larger meaning to include the Aristotelian and Stoic ontologies, that of Descartes or Leibniz, and in our own day those of Whitehead or Hartshorne, none of which can be called idealistic in the usual sense. In all, however, there was the innate assumption or presupposition that reality exhibits a coherent order in correlation with the requirements of thought. In Aristotle's view, the law of sufficient reason held for what is real, in Descartes, clear and distinct ideas were true, and in Whitehead's vision, process is a system whose interrelations are not arbitrary but harmonious and rational, and whose main factors relate to one another in a coherence of mutual implication.[19]

[19] The following from Whitehead expresses very well this fundamental faith in cosmic coherence on which the enterprise of philosophy —and, so he believes, of civilization as well—rests. That the world may not in fact illustrate such an innate and all-inclusive coherence, seems literally never to have occurred to him, or to most of his generation. "Philosophers are rationalists. They are seeking to go behind stubborn and irreducible facts; they wish to explain in the light of universal principles the mutual reference between the various details entering into the flux of things. Also, they seek such principles as will eliminate mere arbi-

There are two reasons why this last assumption of a "logos" in objective reality is necessary for a proof of God. (1) Only if reality is thus coherent and follows the patterns of thought itself, can the implications and requirements of thought be assumed to be likely requirements for what is the case; that is, can the mind move confidently by implication alone to gain a *cognitive* relation to a level of actuality beyond what is given to immediate experience or developed in the special sciences. Every proof, as we shall see, calls for just this confidence in the cognitive relevance of the processes of rational implication. (2) Only if one assumes that reality is in fact a coherent system does it make sense to conclude that it cannot be incoherent, that an ultimate arbitrariness, irrationality, or "gap" in explanatory coherence is insupportable. And as we shall see, one can only conclude that God is *if* it be agreed that it is insupportable for a given significant aspect of known reality to lack an explanation. The assumption, therefore, of an objective logos as characteristic of existence generally, correlated to the logos or power of reason

---

trariness; so that, whatever portion of fact is assumed or given, the existence of the remainder of things shall satisfy some demand of rationality. They demand meaning." *Science and the Modern World* (New York: Macmillan Company, 1925), pp. 203–204. "That we fail to find in experience any elements intrinsically incapable of exhibition as examples of general theory is the hope of rationalism. This hope is not a metaphysical premise. It is the faith which forms the motive for the pursuit of all sciences alike, including metaphysics." *Process and Reality* (New York: The Macmillan Company, 1929), p. 67. "Faith in reason is the trust that the ultimate natures of things lie together in a harmony which excludes mere arbitrariness. It is the faith that at the base of things we shall not find mere arbitrary mystery. . . . This faith cannot be justified by any inductive generalization. It springs from direct inspection of the nature of things as disclosed to our own immediate present experience." *Science and the Modern World*, p. 27.

How far all of this is from the mood of the new theology, which we have called that of "hard secularity," can be seen if we recall Altizer's statement "To exist in our time is to exist in a chaos freed of every semblance of cosmological meaning or order" (*Radical Theology and the Death of God* [Indianapolis: Bobbs-Merrill, 1966], p. 102), or if we peruse Camus' *Myth of Sisyphus* (New York: Vintage Books, 1955), the plays of Samuel Beckett, or the novels of William Golding.

within man's mind, is necessary if a natural theology is to be possible. In this sense, any philosophical theology which seeks to found the existence of the divine and the intelligibility of language about it on philosophical speculation is incurably rationalist in temper.[20]

That these two interrelated assumptions—of the power of thought to know reality and the objective correlation of reality to the requirements of thought—are necessary for the ontological proof hardly needs elaboration. The essence of that proof has been that out of the logical necessities of the concept of God the existence or reality of God could validly be derived. As Malcomb

---

[20] Aristotelian and Whiteheadian philosophers of religion may feel that, in emphasizing the rationalistic side of their masters, this description hardly does justice to their empirical side. Aristotle and Whitehead were certainly both empirical in the sense that both insisted that no thought that was relevant could fail to start with experience; but this empirical base to their metaphysics does not mitigate the fact that they were also rationalistic philosophers. That is to say, they both assumed that, because reality was coherent and because the mind could know that coherent structure, speculation on the basis of experience could move beyond the immediate deliverances of experience. Thus the mind can move out from experience by recognized metaphysical principles to picture conceptually the "real," "substance," or "concrete actual entity," and can tell us the ultimate intelligible structure of all events everywhere, including that factor called "God." Both men affirm this rationalism unequivocally and are thus radically different from another empirical tradition which restricts thought to immediate experience and so to the special sciences. For an example of this empirical view of "empirical rationalism," see Hume's criticisms of Aristotle's proofs of God in the *Dialogues Concerning Natural Religion*, and A. E. Murphy's criticism of Whitehead's rationalism in Schilpp's *The Philosophy of Alfred North Whitehead* (Evanston, Ill.: Northwestern University Press, 1941). One problem for present-day "empirical theology," is that the word "empirical" functions here meaningfully in the *theological* context to distinguish this form of theology from revelational theology, since it is based on general experience and not on special revelation. In this title—valid for the theological context—this word is apt to veil the very considerable rationalistic assumptions which this form of theology requires. In a *philosophical* context, therefore, this form of theology, like the philosophies of Whitehead and Hartshorne themselves, appears at the far rationalistic end of the contemporary spectrum.

has pointed out, there are two forms of this proof in Anselm: (1) That an idea is greater if it contains the predicate existence, and thus God, as "that than which nothing greater can be conceived," must exist. This form has, of course, been subject to the criticism of Kant and many moderns that existence is not a legitimate predicate. (2) That a thing is greater if it exists necessarily than if it exists contingently, and thus God, as "the greatest possible concept," exists necessarily.[21] In both cases, it is clear that implications about reality are drawn from necessities inherent in concepts alone, existence from the content of essence, and thus that an identity of the closest sort between thought and reality is presupposed. The modern sentiment that, since existence is *in all cases* contingent, assertions about existence must be logically contingent and so must be discovered empirically, thus indicates a sense of separation of thought from what is, of essence from existence, that runs directly counter to the assumptions of the ontological proof.

Although less evident in other forms of natural theology which are based on analyses of experience rather than of concepts, nevertheless these two assumptions—of the objective and the subjective logos—are just as prerequisite in the cosmological and teleological proofs. To see this point, we must ask what the "anatomy" or logical structure of a proof of God from experience is, what presuppositions are entailed in each of its important moves.

   1. First of all, such a proof, while beginning with immediate experience, cannot be confined to the limits of immediacy, but rather requires the possibility of a full-blown metaphysical analysis of reality as a whole if it is to function at all. There are three reasons for this requirement of an implicit metaphysical system lying behind each empirical proof.

   a. The immediately evident data of experience are, from almost any metaphysical perspective, not direct copies of what is "there," and so what they represent is hardly fully "actual" or concrete. Rather, are they abstractions made by sense, symbols

[21] Plantinga, *The Ontological Argument*, pp. 136–147.

in part created by our own organs of experiencing.[22] Correspondingly the sciences, based on sense and verified there, deal with relative abstractions, symbolic accounts that represent at best only a partial and not a total view of the actuality of things.[23] As a consequence, what is really there as the actually functioning part of the system of things, what has been called "substance" or "actuality," lies, as Aristotle realized, beyond the inquiries of physics in those of metaphysics. Furthermore, immediate experience does not reveal to our awareness the universal structures of things, but only their significant differences. It requires, therefore, an act of metaphysical reflection to uncover those structures present to every sort of occasion.[24] It is metaphysics that studies what it is

[22] See these entrancing passages from George Santayana: "Sense is a faculty of calling names under provocation: all perception and thought are cries and comments elicited from the heart of some living creature. They are original, though not novel, like the feelings of lovers; normal phases of animation in animals, whose life carries this inner flux of pictures and currents in the fancy, mixed with little and great emotions and dull bodily feelings: nothing in all this discourse being a passive copy of existences elsewhere." "We read nature as the English used to read Latin, pronouncing it like English, but understanding it very well. . . . So each tribe of animals, each sense, each stage of experience and science, reads the book of nature according to a phonetic system of its own, with no possibility of exchanging it for the native sounds; but this situation, though hopeless in one sense, is not unsatisfactory practically, and is innocently humorous." George Santayana, *Skepticism and Animal Faith* (New York: Charles Scribner's Sons, 1929), pp. 86–89. For Whitehead's similar doctrine of the symbolic character of sense perception and so the abstractive character of science, see *Symbolism, Its Meaning and Effect* (New York: Macmillan Co., 1927).

[23] "It [philosophy] seeks those generalities that characterize the complete reality of fact, and apart from which any fact must sink into an abstraction. But science makes the abstraction, and is content to understand the complete fact in respect to only some of its essential aspects. . . . A philosophical system should present an elucidation of concrete facts from which the sciences abstract." A. N. Whitehead, *Adventures of Ideas* (New York: The Macmillan Company, 1933), p. 187. Cf. also *Science and the Modern World*, pp. 72, 82, and 122.

[24] "We habitually observe by the method of difference. Sometimes we see an elephant and sometimes we do not. . . . The metaphysical first principles cannot fail of exemplification. We can never catch the actual world taking a holiday from their sway. Thus, for the discovery

for a thing to be and to function, what categories must be present for it to exist at all,[25] and only on this level of universal categorization can we begin to talk of the actuality of God and of his role in the system of things. A "real" God can be inferred only from the characteristics of the actual world, not from a world of our subjective creation; and if he is to be *God*, he must be a universal or metaphysical factor in existence, required by the universal structures of things, unearthed by metaphysical reflection.[26]

[*sic*] of metaphysics, the method of pinning down thought to the systematization of detailed discrimination breaks down. . . . When the method of difference fails, factors which are constantly present may yet be observed under the influence of imaginative thought." A. N. Whitehead, *Process and Reality*, pp. 6–7. In this quotation, we see perhaps the heart of the argument between metaphysical speculation and most ordinary language philosophy. For the metaphysician, thought must leap *over* the "method of difference," those ordinary distinctions of ordinary language which give usual meanings to our words, in order to find the universal structures of things that are thus distinguished from nothing else. For the ordinary language philosopher, on the other hand, our words, based on the realm of ordinary experience where elements are there or are not there and are thus distinguishable from one another, such flights of imagination beyond ordinary experience and so beyond the usage of ordinary language are meaningless. Cf., for example, J. L. Austin's brilliant criticism of the use of such words as "real" (or "actual"), "good," and "exist," outside of the definite context of real ducks or actual ducks. As he makes clear, for language philosophy the classical "transcendentals" (real, actual, etc.) pointing to the universal structures of being or of becoming have become mere adjectives pointing only to the characteristics of singular objects. Cf. J. L. Austin, *Sense and Sensibilia* (New York: Oxford University Press, 1964), p. 68ff.

[25] "By 'metaphysics' I mean the science which seeks to discover the general ideas which are indispensably relevant to the analysis of everything that happens." A. N. Whitehead, *Religion in the Making* (Cambridge, Mass.: Harvard University Press, 1926), p. 84*n*. "Therefore that which is primarily, that is, not in any qualified sense but without qualification, must be substance." Aristotle, *Metaphysics*, 1028a, 28–30.

[26] "It may be doubted whether any properly general metaphysics can ever, without the illicit introduction of other considerations, get much further than Aristotle [i.e., with regard to the nature of God]. But his conclusion does represent a first step without which no evidence on a narrower experiential basis can be of much avail in shaping the conception. For nothing, within any limited type of ex-

Thus an empirical proof must be able by thought to reach the level of the universal structures of finite reality if it is to have a launching pad, so to speak, for the ascent to the reality of God. Ironically, an empirical theology—if by that phrase one means a theology based on metaphysical analysis—assumes the possibility of a rationalist metaphysics.

b. Further, even these contingent actual entities or finite substances uncovered by metaphysical analysis are not yet God, however we may define him. Thus in any proof of God thought must ascend beyond the level of "real creatures" or "actual entities" to what in some sense transcends them in some sort of unique function—for example, gives to them existence or form, provides them or the whole of which they are a part with order and value, imparts direction and purpose to their passage, and so on. However "immanent" the God proved may be and however univocally he may be conceived, he is still transcendent in some crucial mode to the relative and finite things of experienced passage, since by definition he performs some unique function which no "ordinary" creature might do. Otherwise, we could never prove *his* existence. A metaphysical analysis of the necessary structures of things can never establish the existence of any particular example of those structures, unless that "example" has a unique function necessary in the known character of the whole. Thus any proof requires not only that the mind be able to know the real and universal in experience; it also requires that it be able to move by implication beyond that level to uncover, amidst all the factors in the metaphysical situation, the unique functioning of that factor it is to call God.

c. Direct experience can, to be sure, manifest to profound intuition traces or effects of such a factor transcendent to ordinary, relative entities. For example, such traces or effects of God in past proofs have been the existence of things, their order, their value, the progress of their changes, aspects of permanence within

---

perience, can give intelligence to shape our ideas of any entity at the base of all actual things, unless the general character of things requires that there be such an entity." Whitehead, *Science and the Modern World*, pp. 249–250.

change, and so on. But with these traces we have not yet arrived at God, for other metaphysical explanations which do not include a factor God are readily conceivable for each of these characteristics of things—for example, those explanations offered by empirical naturalism. Thus God must be shown to be implied *necessarily* by these characteristics if we are to establish his reality. And God can be shown to be necessarily implied by them only by some form of speculative argument that demonstrates that he alone can adequately explain them, that is, that the real character of things is of such a sort that, without the factor God, all is incoherent, irrational, and so unexplained.

In fact, the fundamental anatomy of a proof is quite simply the metaphysical argument that finitude understood in its "real" character and taken as a whole is of such a sort as necessarily to require a factor God if that whole is to retain its coherence and its intelligibility. A proof, therefore, assumes the possibility of a completely articulated ontological analysis of the entire system of things, an analysis such that it can be shown that reality is incoherent if God be not posited. A proof thus never starts *de novo;* nor can it proceed on the basis solely of raw experience. It moves within the framework of a given metaphysical system showing that, if we view finitude as exhibiting such and such a structure, then God must be granted to complete the coherence of the whole. One of the essential presuppositions of such an intellectual enterprise is, therefore, the confidence that the mind can know what is real beyond immediate experience, and thence by speculative generalization move to know the coherent system of the whole, drawing therefrom legitimate inferences about what is or what is not required to maintain that universal coherence.

2. Granting, then, that a metaphysical understanding of the entire system of finite things forms the general framework for any proof of God, how then are the moves within that system from immediacy to God achieved, and what is required for them?

An empirical proof, we have seen, proceeds by locating and describing through metaphysical inquiry some unquestioned aspect of the real world of things—for example, their contingency, their motion, their order or harmony, their value, their

purposiveness, etc. Secondly, it argues that this admitted characteristic cannot be understood or explained, i.e., is not intelligible
to the mind, unless some further nonimmediate factor is posited
as its real and effective cause or ground. The reason this further
factor (i.e., God) is regarded as real is not because it is directly
confronted in experience—which would make this an experiential or confessional but not a natural theology—but because it is
the sole intelligible cause or ground of this universally present
aspect of things. And the intelligibility of our language about
this God is derived not from the characteristics of a direct, religious experience of him, but from the intelligibility of the system
of metaphysical discourse through which it is exhibited that he is
required for the coherence of the whole. Thus the movement
from the reality and intelligibility of things encountered in experience to the reality and intelligibility of God is solely dependent upon the strength of the process of rational implication
within the system of metaphysical coherence previously established.

That the crucial movement of any empirical proof is from
an experienced or assumed aspect of things, established and clarified by metaphysical analysis, to God as the sole explanation of
that aspect, can be seen from a few illustrations. In Thomas's
time, the universality of the motion and contingency of things
was obvious in all experience and was clarified and made intelligible, and set in a definite mold, by the recently accepted Aristotelian analysis of nature. What Thomas's proofs achieved was
to establish by metaphysical analysis that God was the sole cause
of the motion and contingency of things so interpreted, that is,
the only cause that could account intelligibly for them. The harmony of things has also been an obvious trait of existence and
was confirmed for most Enlightenment minds by early modern
science. What the natural theology of many of these scientists, in
a long line from Galileo, Bacon, Ray through Paley—and ending
with a thump with Darwin—achieved was to show by an analysis of this harmony that it could be explained rationally only if
an Original Planner were posited. The movement of the actual
passage of things toward value seemed obvious to all nineteenth-
century men after Kant, Herder, Hegel, and Darwin; and so what

Tennant and Whitehead, among others, achieved in establishing in a secular way the reality and nature of God was to show that the presence of a definite order within novelty required the existence of the Primordial Nature of God. The essential anatomy of every empirical natural theology represents a movement by metaphysical thought from some universally experienced aspect of things to God as the sole intelligible cause or ground of that assumed aspect.

This logical move from some characteristic of things to God has, in turn, two interrelated but distinguishable prerequisites, which clarify the concluding claim that God is real as the sole intelligible cause of that characteristic. In the first place, it must be clearly shown why no completely immanent explanation of this characteristic of things is acceptable; for if such were intelligible, then there would be no rational ground for moving beyond ordinary actual entities to God. An intelligible explanation would be ready at hand in terms of "creatures," and God would no longer be philosophically needed to exhibit the coherence of things. Newton and Darwin, one might say, torpedoed the proofs respectively from motion (as ordinarily understood) and from design, by unveiling precisely such satisfactory immanent or "natural" explanations of physical motion and of adaptation. Thus, in any successful natural theology, actual entities must be described in the original metaphysical analysis in such a way that an explanation of this aspect of their nature is *not* derivable from them alone—and so a further factor, God, is required. Finitude must be exhibited as essentially pointing beyond itself for an explanation of its motion, being, order, value, and so on. Let us note that such a metaphysical delineation of the insufficiency of the finite to explain itself must be a *total* delineation, lest it be claimed by some disgruntled naturalist that an immanent explanation still lurked somewhere in a dark corner that had been overlooked. As Hume reminded us with regard to the proof of a miracle, to establish that there has been here effective a transcendent cause, one must prove not simply that we do not *know* of a finite cause of such and such, but that there *cannot be* a merely finite cause. Again, for this crucial move, a complete metaphysical understanding of the totality of finitude, showing all of its relevant contours, and yet also showing that something about the system of finite things remains yet unexplained, is necessary.

The essential movement of an empirical proof is from the assertion, now established, (*a*) that the finite universe (as existing, good, orderly, etc.) as so far delineated is still unintelligible, to the second stage, namely the conclusion (*b*) that the required explanation is thereby known to exist. Unless one assumes that an explanatory cause that is required by thought is also existent in reality, there is no ground for positing God, for he "enters the metaphysical situation" (to use Whitehead's phrase) solely to provide an explanation for that which cannot otherwise be explained. Or, to put this another way, God appears metaphysically to "save the coherence" of things, for we know by philosophical reason that he is there only because we have shown that the actual world as we view it is incoherent, i.e., unexplained, without him. The procession of the proof from (*a*) to (*b*) requires, then, as a second prerequisite (the first was that an intelligible explanation was not available amidst the finite) that the universe as a whole is known with certainty to exhibit rational coherence. Coherence in this sense means that, when our minds require explanations, it can likewise be assumed that reality as well requires an explanatory cause; and correspondingly, when our minds are satisfied, then we assume that this satisfaction in us is a sign reflecting the real coherence of objective things. This parallelism or correlation of the order of thought and the order of reality is a prerequisite for all empirical proofs.

Another way to put this assumption is to say that, for it, arbitrariness or fundamental incoherence within reality is impossible, or could not be actual. For it is on the ground of the unreality—i.e., the ontological impossibility—of incoherence that it can be asserted that a God required for an intelligible explanation of something real is a God who is thereby also real. This becomes clear when one says, for example, with Camus, "Thought, to be sure, may require that there be explanations, that the universe be coherent to our thought and responsive to our search for intelligibility. But in fact the universe is not at all thus intelligible —it is absurd in the precise sense that what our spirits require of

it is exactly what it fails to manifest. The order that thought requires is merely a human cry flung out at a dark, unfeeling, irrational mystery which neither knows nor heeds such requirements."[27] If one says *that*, then the movement from the apparent
unintelligibility of things without God to the positing of God
"to save the coherence" has no ground or legitimacy. One may
say, therefore, that all empirical proofs of God presuppose that
the law of sufficient reason characterizes the universe as a whole.
Without that assumption of the coherence or logos of the entire
system of things, our minds cannot legitimately move from an
unexplained world to God, which move, as we have seen, forms
the crucial axis of all natural theologies.

This analysis illumines, we believe, the immense difficulties of natural theology in our age. It is not so much that these
arguments to God are logically invalid, nor even that they are
"idolatrous," though both might well in fact be true. It is that the
rationalistic assumptions on which natural theology is predicated,
and without which it cannot legitimately proceed, are not assumptions which the secular mind finds it either easy or natural
to make. The logos in the universe generally and known exclusively by the power of speculative intelligence seems as anachronistic an assumption to our age as is the affirmation that the logos
has been made flesh and is known by Biblical faith. And thus
metaphysical proofs and the theological language derived from
them have almost the same feeling of unreality and irrelevance
as does the theological discourse dependent on faith.[28] As we

[27] Cf. Camus, *The Rebel* (New York: Vintage Books, 1958),
especially Chapter 2, and *The Myth of Sisyphus* (New York: Vintage
Books, 1955).

[28] See van Buren's comment, "For him [the modern empirical
man] oblique language about God is no more useful than 'objectifying' language about God. The problem lies in the word God itself, and
in any other word supposedly referring to the transcendent." *Secular
Meaning*, p. 68. "Linguistic analysis challenges the qualified theism of
Bultmann and Ogden as much as that of more conservative theologians.
Whether objectifying or nonobjectifying, language about 'God who acts'
must be interpreted in some other way." *Ibid.*, p. 100. This challenge to
metaphysical language of the speculative sort as a base for God-talk is
not answered by showing the errors of positivism, since modern language philosophy, as well as existentialism and naturalism, agree on
this point with positivism.

have shown in our earlier chapters, neither one of these two major rationalistic assumptions is representative of the secular mind of our time.

As we have seen, one of the main ingredients of the present secular mood can be called its "posture of metaphysical modesty" or possibly the "inferiority complex of speculative reason." This posture represents a rejection of philosophy as a form of genuine knowing that can proceed by implication alone far beyond immediate experience not only to talk of the real but the real as a coherent whole. As we have seen, this posture in our present culture appears in a wide variety of philosophical guises. In the existentialism of Sartre and Camus, it is the claim that objective existence as we know it is "absurd" and cannot therefore be characterized by any rational objective meaning or coherence; in the positivism of the Vienna Circle and the earlier Ayer, it asserts that statements beyond the range of empirical verifiability, i.e., statements about reality itself or about process itself, are empty and meaningless. In the empirical naturalism of Dewey, Santayana, and other naturalists, it holds that all we can know are the contingent factors with which we have direct experience, and that we have no warrant for drawing metaphysical implications beyond that knowledge about concrete reality or process as a whole. It now appears in the assertion of all forms of linguistic philosophy that philosophy is a second-order enterprise, capable of uncovering cognitively no level of reality beyond that known in common sense and in science but able only to analyze the meaning structures of our ordinary discourse, and that such metaphysical questions as are necessary to the establishment of a proof of God are in fact unreal questions resulting only from a bewitchment of our minds through grammar. Finally, it is manifest in that earlier, more rigorous aspect of phenomenology which defined philosophy "as a science" on condition that it use the *epoché*, the transcendental reduction or bracketing of all mention of "reality," of the system of "real" things as a whole, and of God.[29] Almost the only issue on which these widely divergent strands of contemporary philosophy agree is with regard to their common denial of the possibility of speculative metaphysics and

[29] Edmund Husserl, *Ideas* (New York: Collier, 1967), pp. 157, 163, 206, 244.

their consequent universal rejection of those rationalistic assumptions on which a natural theology is necessarily based.

Two significant conclusions for the methodology of philosophical theology follow from this: (1) Since almost all present philosophy denies the rationalistic assumptions necessary for natural theology, it cannot be said that theology is rendered *philosophically* valid and intelligible by being translated into metaphysical categories, but only intelligible and clear to those who— on what we suspect are largely "religious grounds"—still hold the rationalistic assumptions necessary for a natural theology to be true. (2) Insofar as contemporary philosophy is a fair and accurate index of the secular mood—and we believe it is—the wellnigh universal rejection by that philosophy of these rationalistic assumptions shows that to that mind metaphysical discourse, and so *a fortiori* theological language predicated on it—is itself unintelligible to modern man. On both counts one wonders what is gained by this translation from one apparently anachronistic language game into another. Thus is this method of religious discourse, insofar as its claims rest on its philosophical clarity and validity, forced, like the theologies of the Word, fundamentally to reexamine its own presuppositions and its modes of procedure, and thus to widen its scope.

All this does not, let us note, mean that these rationalistic assumptions are untrue, or that in another age they may not again inaugurate philosophical inquiry. It merely means that they are almost as alien to the secular mood as is the assumption of the divine Word received in religious faith, and that the lack of religious faith in the logos made flesh is balanced in our time by the lack of philosophical faith in the universal logos in reality. And the important consequence is that, since in effect both are suffering from the same illness, the one cannot without further ado provide the basis for the intelligibility and validity of the other. To us, both of these are in their own way aspects of the manifestation of the divine to us, and so it is not at all strange that, if in our time it be true that "God" is dead, so is the faith in an ultimate rational coherence; nor is it a surprise that the philosophical assumption of the universal logos should appear almost exclusively among philosophical theologians rather than among "pure" philosophers. Speculative metaphysics seems indirectly religious as revelational theology is directly so, both being based on deep intuitions of the sacred ground in which all things are. In this sense, from our view, a proof of God is itself dependent on a deep prior awareness of the divine reality as logos, and through that awareness of the ultimate rationality and coherence of all things. A proof, therefore, does not so much establish the divine, as it explicitly seeks to do; rather, by its own inner development and anatomy, it can only witness to the divine ultimacy in the form of coherence—which coherence it has itself presupposed. And since the intelligibility and possibility of any metaphysical proof as an intellectual enterprise is dependent on that ultimate religious awareness of divine coherence, it is hard to see how it can itself effect the intellectual rescue of its own religious grounds.

In any case, the problems the modern spirit has set for natural theology are neither merely (*a*) that a brutal positivism momentarily captured philosophical attention, nor (*b*) that natural theology is tarred with the brush of an old, static, supernaturalistic metaphysics. It is rather that the rationalistic assumptions, essential to *all* forms of speculative metaphysics relevant to natural theology, are as strange in our age as are the assumptions of revelational faith.

Nor do these remarks entail that a philosophical theology based upon a metaphysical analysis is in the end impossible in our age. The hard secularity of the present is not an ultimate authority to which all our thinking must bow, and any theology— even radical theology, as we have shown—must part ways with it at some point or another. Undoubtedly, in this age of immediacy and so of indrawn analytical philosophy, speculative philosophy of some sort is both a courageous and a much needed enterprise, and, if successful, will be very fruitful for whole ranges of thought, including the theological. What it does mean, however, is that a new set of questions faces those philosophers of religion who wish to establish the possibility of God-language on a metaphysical basis. These questions revolve around the validity of assumptions fundamental to the metaphysical enterprise itself: How can it be established, in the face of the naturalist, the language philosopher, or the existentialist, that existence as a whole is coherent enough so that speculative thought about its ultimate structures is possible? How can we show that there are legitimate uses of cognitive thinking found in ordinary experience which by their character carry our cognitive thought beyond immediate experience?[30] How is it possible to demonstrate that all the aspects of culture—science, art, politics, law, and morals—presuppose a unity or coherence in experience that we can appeal to as a foundation for the unity and coherence normative for speculative thought? Above all, how is an ontological language about objects or categories, which are not directly experienced, but are known only by speculative generalizations, to achieve any reality in relation to the lived character of ordinary experience? Metaphysical language and Biblical language face very much the same problems—despite their manifest scorn of one another. Fundamentally, this is the problem of their disrelation in a secular age to immediate experience, its sense of direct validity and its modes of testing. Both have, to be sure, a sort of "ersatz" meaning to their adherents in the terms of the structural systems in which they participate: the Word can be defined in other theological terms, or, to take another example, "actual entities" can be described in terms of prehensions, eternal objects, subjective aims, and so on. But both types of language—on which theology has heretofore been almost entirely dependent—are vulnerable to the searching question: What do all these words mean, where do these mutually defining symbols touch and clarify direct and immediate experience, and how can I recapture any sense of their validity?

These questions, and their answers, concern the *founda-*

[30] For this writer, the most impressive example of a quite modern philosophy of religion, beginning with the secular experience of knowing, and trying thereby to recreate a basis for a cognitive metaphysical natural theology, is found in the work of The Rev. B. J. F. Lonergan, S. J., especially his massive and remarkable study of human knowing, *Insight* (London: Longmans, 1958). Cf. the remarkable exploration of this mode of thought in Michael Novak's graceful and honest book, *Belief and Unbelief* (New York: Macmillan Co., 1965). Other creative efforts at such theological "prolegomena" are Karl Rahner's *Hörer des Wortes* (Munchen: Kosel–Verlag, 1963), *Spirit in the World* (New York: Herder and Herder, 1968), and Leslie Dewart's, *Future of Belief.*

tions of metaphysical inquiry, and they require more than merely further elaboration of the religious relevance of a given speculative system. To tackle them, and to show that even in a secular age those assumptions on which metaphysical thinking is built are present in all ordinary discourse, though unrealized and often denied, and that therefore metaphysical language has both meaning and validity, is the task of this sort of current philosophy of religion. Merely to repeat in our day systems formed in another day, when, as in Whitehead's time, the unity and coherence of all existence and the power of thought to unveil its mysteries could be assumed, is, like the repetition of traditional revelationist theological language, not to speak to the really crucial philosophical or theological problems of our time. What is needed for this sort of philosophical theology is, in other words, a prolegomenon to metaphysical discourse, showing its possibility and meaningfulness, if metaphysics is to offer itself as a support for Biblical and Christian language.

In one sense or another, therefore, all of us in the contemporary situation find ourselves in a new theological "place," one in which the older theological methodologies—be they those of Thomas, Whitehead, and Hartshorne, or Brunner, Barth, Bultmann and the new hermeneuticists—are no longer directly helpful to us.[31] For as they did in their time, so we must, if we are to talk of God at all, construct a theology that can move beyond the immediate. Unlike them, however, we can presuppose without careful argument neither the ultimate rationality of general experience nor the intelligibility and certainty to ourselves of the special faith encounter as the basis for that movement—neither the logos nor the logos made flesh. All of us must, therefore, ask new questions. The Whiteheadian must ask himself why he believes, in the first place, in the objective rationality and coherence of process, and the power of speculative thought to reach beyond

---

[31] The careful reader will have noted an important omission in this discussion of viable options among recent theological and philosophical theological methods, namely that of language philosophy. Since this is, we feel, such an important and relevant option, we shall discuss its possibilities in the next chapter.

immediate experience, and how he might defend those beliefs intelligibly to the modern philosophical mind that finds both almost incredible. The Thomist must ask himself on what grounds meaningful to any modern man he can speak of a universal law of sufficient reason, of the supernatural, of the relation of nature to a realm of grace above it, of a changeless God beyond the world. And the revelationist must ask himself what elements of general experience point to, give meaning to, and help to validate what he wishes to say about man or God on the basis of his own admittedly precarious experience of revelation through the proclaimed Word.

In each case, we are examining on a deeper level than before what we had actually but unwittingly assumed, those unexamined presuppositions of recent theological debate that are now so dubious. If for nothing else, we should be grateful to the radical theologians for "smoking us out" of the positions and arguments framed by an older generation for past situations, and onto new ground, where in fact we may find ourselves closer together than we once thought and where we are certainly dealing with the real theological and religious problems of our present world. One can only find this new situation exhilarating, and the necessity to abandon old labels and schools and to strike out on our own exciting. And one can only hope that the theological thought of the next years will address itself to these central issues of our time and, in so doing, reflect this same excitement, this independence on the part of a new generation from its great predecessors, however wise they may have been, and thus provide a relevant, new answer to the problem of talking about God now in the present post-Christian world.

Part II

The Renewal of God-Language

1 / Negative Thoughts on Methodology

IF OUR EFFORTS so far have been successful, we have shown that the secular spirit which permeates our time makes God-language intensely difficult, if not impossible; that nevertheless the efforts of the radical theologians to construct an interpretation of Christianity without God-language have foundered in inconsistency; and finally that both the recognized methods of theological construction—that in terms of revelation and faith, and that in terms of metaphysical speculation—by which the reality of God and the intelligibility of language about him might be established, beg the question of God-language in a secular age. They do this because they presuppose precisely those affirmations which that age finds it impossible to grant and which are thus themselves the subject of theological and philosophical debate. We are left, then, with the most important question of all: If God-language is necessary for any Christian theology that is self-consistent, is God-language, and so Christian theology of any sort, possible and meaningful in a secular time? Is the general language game of religious discourse, of which Christian God-language is a particular example, applicable in secular existence; does it have any use there; do its symbols relevantly fit and so thematize our ordinary secular life? Or is the effort to understand our existence in terms of these sorts of symbols essentially meaningless, irrelevant, and opaque to those of us who share, whether we will or no, the cultural mood that we have described? Is humanism of some sort the only viable alternative of our time?

These questions require a very different set of answers than does the question whether Christian theology requires God-language. They require just the sort of prolegomenon for their answer that we have called for: i.e., a discussion of the possibility of God-language in a secular time through a demonstration of its usefulness or meaningfulness, in fact, its necessity for the ordinary life of man, and an elucidation of the conditions of its validity. Here we are no longer concerned with the internal consistency of Christian language, but with the viability of the whole structure of religious discourse for men who are secular and so who tend to wonder whether this language game has any meaning or use. And that is a much more complex enterprise than to show that, given any mode of recognizably Christian language, God-language is required. As we have seen, there are for us no well-laid-down paths by which we may proceed, nor surely is there any one theologically valid way out of these difficulties. Each of us must begin almost before the beginning in the task of uncovering the foundations for an intelligible theological language. The following chapters represent one such tentative effort among many to show the meaningfulness of religious discourse in its widest sense, and so to lay the foundation for the establishment of a valid and intelligible Christian theological language.

In embarking upon this prolegomenon to theological discourse, we are shifting to a much wider context than that which has occupied us previously. Deliberately we are seeking to move outside the walls of the Church into the broad arena of the world, where our own deepest attitudes about what is real and true are formed. We are thus not going to presuppose either the existential reality of faith in ourselves or the intelligibility to us of the language of faith, i.e., of Christian theological discourse, Biblical, traditional, or contemporary. We are going to inquire whether this mode or type of discourse has any relevance to and reality for secular life, whether in the secular context it has any viable or appropriate use or application. More specifically, the following questions are involved: Do we in fact use this sort of language in secular existence, and why; if we do, in what sorts of situations and with regard to what sorts of problems, issues, or questions is it appropriately used; and finally, what sorts of traits or rules of its usage appear in secular life? If we can give intelligible answers to these questions, we can, I believe, show that this sort of language is meaningful and even essential to secular existence, and that very possibly therefore its specifically Christian form can become intelligible again to our age and to ourselves—can experience, in fact, a renewal. Since in the process of this prolegomenon to the theological language of the Church we shall try to assume only the character of secular life as we find it, making no Christian presuppositions such as the possession of faith, the acknowledgment of revelation in the Word, or the assurance of the reality of God, it is best to speak henceforth of "religious discourse" in referring to this language game, rather than to use the more specifically Christian label, God-language.

When we say that this is a "secular" inquiry, we must be careful about what it is we are claiming and what not. We are not claiming that the mind that conducts the inquiry is thoroughly secular or even neutral. As we shall make clear, we do not believe that such a mind, neutral to all significant philosophical or religious issues, is a human possibility. Like all others, our thoughts are inescapably guided by the ultimate assumptions and attitudes of the person who thinks them, and in interpreting such a varied and rich "object" as secular experience with regard to such imprecise though important characteristics as its "meaning" and "character," such initial assumptions inevitably play a very heavy role in what is found there, in our thought as in all others of the same sort. It is a *theologian* who is writing here, and the way this fact will weight the inquiry from the start is freely admitted. What, then, is secular about all this? What is secular is that the materials investigated, described, and interpreted are parts of secular experience, available to any person immersed in cultural life and aware of that immersion. What can be asked of the inquirer is *not* that he dispense with his own assumptions—for then he could not inquire—but that he use them to discriminate elements in common experience, to give those elements conceptual or symbolic shape so that they are "disclosed" or "let be manifest," and then through his conclusions to point the eyes of his readers to those elements so discriminated and symbolized. He can only describe and point. That description is formed by his thinking as well as by the object he thinks about—but what in this case he points *to* is secular experience, the experience common to all of us, not religious experience or special experience of any sort. This is not so much a secular inquiry as an inquiry into the character of secular experience, and this is all that we claim. If it is to be judged invalid, it is to be so judged not because it inquires from a certain fundamental point of view, but because its descriptions are not an accurate account of what secular experience is really like.

Our task, then, is to investigate in the broad range of secular experience what function and use, and therefore what meaningfulness and intelligibility, the realm of discourse called "religious language" may have. We are trying to conduct a *hermeneutic of secular experience* to see what religious dimensions there may be there, and so what usage and meaningfulness religious discourse has in ordinary life.[1] It is *this* meaningfulness which provides a large part of the answer to the question, "What do your Christian theological symbols *mean*?" Clearly, to do this we must use some sort of philosophical mode of analysis, since we are seeking not to begin our inquiry with faith but to make the faith presuppositions necessary for theology in its classical form intelligible to our own secularity. We are embarked, therefore, on some form of philosophy of religion as a logical, if not existential, base for Christian theology. Obviously, moreover, another implication of our remarks to date has been that such a philosophical defense of the intelligibility of religious discourse cannot be accomplished in terms of the methods of metaphysical speculation. As we noted, since the presupposition of the logos on which that sort of philosophy of religion depended turned out to be as "unsecular," and its language as unreal to our age, as was

---

[1] We use the word "hermeneutic" here in the sense Heidegger has made common in phenomenological analysis, namely a study of lived experience which will uncover what is normally hidden and forgotten; in our case, this is the religious dimension within which man lives in the world. Cf. Heidegger, *Being and Time* (New York: Harper & Bros., 1962), pp. 49–63, and Spiegelberg, *The Phenomenological Movement* (The Hague: Martinus Nijhoff, 1965), Volume I, 318ff., Volume II, 694ff.

the language of faith, metaphysical discourse itself requires a prolegomenon and so cannot function as the basis of this one.

How, then, are we to proceed? The obvious way to establish the meaningfulness, i.e., the legitimacy or communicative use of religious language, is, as Wittgenstein said, "to look and see":[2] How is such language in fact used among us, what are its "stock forms," as Ryle would say,[3] in what sorts of contexts or situations is it employed, and what are its rules? And we could begin by the familiar methods to investigate how people typically use religious language, what they "do" with these kinds of words and symbols, what its logic is, and so be able to draw conclusions about its legitimate or illegitimate uses, and so on.

In fact, one might well say that the most lively form of contemporary philosophical theology has been based not at all on speculative metaphysical systems, but on the methods and practices of ordinary language philosophy. Centered mainly in Great Britain, this school has a number of distinguished names, headed surely by Archbishop (of Durham) Ian Ramsey, and including John Hick, R. M. Hare, Basil Mitchel, Ninian Smart, I. A. Crombie, Alistair MacIntyre, and, on the left, Anthony Flew, Ronald Hepburn, and R. B. Braithwaite; on this side Frederick Ferré, Donald Evans, and Dallas High have published recently in this vein. In various ways, and with a variety of results, these men have sought to apply the methods of linguistic analysis to religious discourse, to discover, if they can, "what it has to say" through an examination of its uses and its grammar or logic. Clearly there is no special vocabulary or "language" in religion; what, then, are the peculiar usages and rules of application that make ordinary words and propositions in this language game "religious" in character? This application of linguistic techniques to theological discourse has been tremendously clarifying for such questions as: What sort of usage of language constitutes religious discourse; is such usage cognitive, is it moral, merely emo-

[2] Ludwig Wittgenstein, *Philosophical Investigations*, trans., G. E. M. Anscombe (New York: Macmillan Company, 1953), para. 66.

[3] Gilbert Ryle, "Ordinary Language," in *Philosophy and Ordinary Language*, edited by C. E. Catan (Urbana, Ill.: University of Illinois Press, 1963), pp. 109–112.

tive, or what? How do myths *mean* or say whatever they may mean; to what do doctrines refer; how does analogy work; what are the differences and the similarities between ordinary empirical speech, scientific discourse, moral language, speculative language, and religious doctrines and assertions;[4] and, finally, how are religious assertions verified or tested, if at all? A great deal of the fuzziness of theological language has been cleared away, or at least challenged and made uncomfortable, by these men. For four reasons, however, we are convinced that such an approach is not all that the present situation requires; let us briefly see what these reasons are.

1. First of all, it is not the usual aim, at least of ordinary language philosophy, to try to establish or demonstrate the meaningfulness of a language game. Logical positivism certainly saw this as its goal through the application of the verification principle by which the meaningfulness, or the reverse, of a type of language might be established; and as we know, metaphysical or theological language, and certainly religious language as we shall define it, was declared to be meaningless. Ordinary language philosophy is explicitly different at this point: it sets out merely to see what kinds of meaning, or usages, as it prefers to call them, types of language in fact have. It deliberately does not bring to its investigation any prior criteria of meaning or of usage. Conversely, without prior criteria of meaningful language, it is not easy for analysis to demonstrate that a given form of language has meaning. It can, as Wittgenstein said, only "look and see" what usages language does in fact have. It follows, then, that, although ordinary language philosophy does not assume any single criterion of language, it does and must make one important assumption in order to carry on its inquiry, namely, that a particu-

---

[4] Dallas High has been especially helpful in pointing out two elements of Wittgenstein's analysis of language that are usually overlooked: (1) A language game does *not* mean a different set of words, but a different *usage* of ordinary words; and (2) the differences between language games are fully balanced by their similarities and the great overlapping between different modes of speech. Cf. High, *Language, Persons, and Belief* (New York: Oxford, 1967), pp. 72ff., and 86ff.

lar language game has in actual practice a "use," that it is "given" as a way people actually talk and communicate with one another.[5] It cannot say, "You *ought* to talk in this or that way," but only "Granting you *do* talk in this way, how does that talk function, what are its rules of usage, and, possibly, what are some further implications of this usage?" Now, the necessity of this assumption on the part of language analysis means that this form of philosophy has a strange, frustrating relation to our current theological dilemmas. For what we need is a prolegomenon to theological discourse to show its legitimate and essential usage in secular life, and yet, granted the necessity of this presupposition of actual usage, language philosophy cannot seem to do this; the next three points will spell out the anatomy of this difficulty.

2. If our description of the secular spirit has been correct, then it is precisely the sort of language we are calling "religious" which is *not* ordinarily used and which does *not* communicate in the secular context. What the historical process of secularization means linguistically is that religious discourse is no longer regarded by secular man as a discourse either essential for or even useful in the course of his daily life in the world (except perhaps when he is very upset!), in politics, economics, family affairs, personal mores, or cognitive inquiry. In the medieval world, moral, political, or economic language led inevitably to philosophical and religious language if they were to be inclusive of their own foundations. "Secularization" has meant that these foundations are now autonomous, and that therefore these ordinary forms of language do not in ordinary speech call for the usage of religious language if they are to be intelligible. Furthermore, if one translates all that we have said about the way secular man understands himself and his world, the way he views reality, truth, and value, and the sorts of things and issues that are meaningful to him, into the lingo of language analysis, what we have said—and what van Buren insisted upon

[5] Two quotations from Wittgenstein illustrate this requirement for language analysis: "Here the term 'language-*game*' is meant to bring into prominence the fact that the *speaking* of language is a part of an activity, or a form of life." Wittgenstein, *op. cit.*, para. 23. "What has to be accepted, the given, is—so one could say—*forms of life.*" *Ibid.*, p. 226.

—was that this language is meaningless or useless in the empirical, this-worldly world. And the clear implication of this corollary to secularization is that no *secular* analysis of the usages of religious modes of speech is possible, since there are "given" to us almost no such usages. The ordinary usage of a language game, which to ordinary language philosophy establishes its legitimacy or intelligibility through that usage, simply is not there in the case of religious discourse—and that is precisely the problem with which our prolegomenon is forced to deal.

3. The result of this correlation of secularity and the uselessness of religious language in the secular order, has been to drive this language into the churches and thence to the seminaries, where alone it is used and so where alone, presumably, it makes sense. This is, perhaps, the linguistic correlate of the development of neoorthodox or Biblical theology in which all relevant religious discourse was based on faith and explicative only of the divine Word, and it may explain why Biblical theology and language analysis have been such compatible partners. Hence most analyses of religious language have in fact been analyses of the language of the churches, their doctrines, their liturgy, their prayers, etc. The difficulties of this are, for our purposes twofold: (*a*) Such an analysis of Church language must, as we have seen, accept the language of the Church as "given" and therefore also its faith as "given." For both the faith of the Church and the main foundations or objects of that faith, namely God, his revelation in scripture, and his presence in the Holy Spirit through tradition, liturgy, sacrament, and preaching, are presupposed in the language of the Church; the one, faith, is "expressed" in this language, and the others, the objects of faith, are proclaimed, invoked, petitioned, etc. The religious language of the Church *is* the language of faith in relation to its object. In such a situation, an analysis of Church language can hardly tackle the question we feel needs theological discussion, namely whether or not the language of faith itself, the whole range of symbols used in religious discourse, has any meaning for ordinary life at all. (*b*) By its nature, linguistic analysis cannot move beyond this churchly scene to relate religious language to ordinary experience.

To take up (*a*) first, Church language, as language expressive of faith in relation to its object, presupposes and so is founded upon the truth and intelligibility of its language about God and his acts. It explicates that foundation as best it can, but in its liturgical, doctrinal, or kerygmatic uses, Church language hardly tries to make itself intelligible in terms external to that foundation, since the life of the Church traditionally has assumed faith on the part of its participants. Thus while to make the internal logic of Church language intelligible may relieve in many ways the minds of worried churchmen about the consistency and internal coherence of what they are saying in church, it cannot do more than that. It cannot, in an analysis of the system of Church language, show how that entire system of language is related beyond itself to life, how its symbolic forms make sense and communicate in important and essential ways in terms of the problems of daily living, in other words, why this whole structure of language is relevant to us as secular men at all. Thus, since it must presuppose the Church as a community of faith to which religious language is intelligible and valid, it cannot quell our questions whether or not the whole structure of Church discourse has any use and so meaning in life generally—and this, as we see it, is precisely the question for religious language that presses in upon theology at the present time. Like the theology confined to a hermeneutics of the Word, a language analysis confined to the religious discourse of faith will not be of service to us as a prolegomenon.

Furthermore (*b*), it cannot by its nature move beyond its churchly realm, where this language game is played, to explore the relations of this sort of discourse to the experiences of ordinary life. The reason for this is that perhaps the most fundamental tenet of language philosophy is, as we have seen, the view that philosophy is not a mode of examining experience at all, and so not a mode of *knowing*. Rather, it is a technique for analyzing language games, and the assertions contained within them but made on other grounds than philosophy itself, namely, for example, on the grounds of scientific inquiry, ordinary experience, moral commitments or attitudes, religious faith, etc. It is "talk about talk," talk about the various ways communities talk, and not talk about the world, about experience, about man, or about ultimate reality. As John Wisdom sardonically put it, the philosopher cannot dare "the absurdity of exploring the universe in an armchair." This means that, as a mode of analysis of religious discourse, such a form of philosophy cannot either initiate, test, or really defend religious assertions in relation to ordinary experience outside the Church. It can only analyze assertions, and so religious assertions, where they have already been made on other grounds. It must go to the place where people are already religious and are using religious language, and thus it must stay within the walls of the Church and analyze the forms of discourse found there.

4. The fourth problem of such an analysis is that, as we have noted, it is an optimist indeed who will state—except for the purposes of a theological analysis of this sort—that religious discourse, when used in the churches, communicates meaningfully to those who use and those who hear it. The usage of religious language in our churches is "queer" indeed, queerer than the language itself. In fact, the central theological problem of our time might be restated linguistically in the terms of the paradox that, while religious discourse is certainly used (officially) in the churches, it has not "meant" anything in that use; it has not, in other words, communicated within its own community. Rather, it has become unreal and empty, and even those who hear it and use it have begun to wonder deeply whether it has any relevance or value for their lives. Even if church members are able—though rarely—to talk *about* religious language, they are almost invariably unable to *use* that language themselves, and especially in application to actual life situations. In this sense, it is, as a language game, an *object* of Church discourse but not the language *used* by the Church to communicate important ideas, attitudes, and standards. In most churches, the language games that communicate, that are *used*, are those of moral and social discourse, "buildings and grounds" language, budget language, group-activities language, all of these intensely useful and important but nonetheless quite "secular" in character. To analyze the official religious language of the churches, therefore, is to analyze a ghostly language understood by very few, baffling to the vast majority, and almost not *used* at all. Thus it begs the very theological question we have posed, namely the question of the

meaningfulness to Christians in the churches of their own religious discourse, the question of the potentiality or possibility of its significant usage. For a prolegomenon to help us in this situation, it must help to *reestablish* religious discourse in the churches and not assume, as this form of analysis must, that it is already "given" there.[6] While for these reasons language analysis cannot directly provide for us a ready-made methodology by which to conduct our prolegomenon, nevertheless it does give us several most important hints or clues as to how we should proceed. The constructive use we can make of some of these themes of language philosophy will be a part of our methodological discussion in the next chapter.

Much like language philosophy, phenomenology, the other main philosophical movement of our day, plays both a negative and a positive, a frustrating and yet an alluring role in relation to our current problems in theological method. In the end, we believe, phenomenology will help us with our particular job more than will language analysis; but in this chapter let us say something of why it seems to us it, too, must be reconstructed for the theological task. It is far beyond our purpose or competence to give an exhaustive description of this elusive movement;[7] let us at this juncture only mention those aspects of phenomenology that prevent it from helping us "as is."

[6] That the analysis of Church discourse, the language of faith and so on, represents the only way of applying language analysis to theological questions is, of course, not so. Stephen Toulmin has shown briefly how the analysis of quite secular moral language—and other types as well—leads to religious discourse in the form of "limiting questions" to which "religious faith" of one sort or another and its appropriate language forms provide answers. This is, as will be seen, very close to what we are seeking to do, and is, as Ogden has repeatedly noted, very creative in the present situation. It also shows that our own turn away from language analysis per se is not the *only* path that can be taken at this juncture. Cf. Stephen Toulmin, *An Examination of the Place of Reason in Ethics* (New York: Cambridge University Press, 1964), Chapter 14.

[7] The best history of this movement is undoubtedly Spiegelberg's massive two-volume work, *The Phenomenological Movement, op. cit.;* other excellent statements are Pierre Thevanez, *What Is Phenomenology?* (Chicago: Quadrangle Books, 1962), and Merleau-Ponty, "Phenomenology and the Sciences of Man," in *The Primacy of Perception* (Evanston, Ill.: Northwestern University Press, 1964).

As is well known, phenomenology, as devised by Edmund Husserl, presented itself as an authoritative philosophical method which would, at one and the same time, (1) have the certainty and clarity of science;[8] (2) provide the missing foundations for scientific and commonsense judgments;[9] (3) achieve this by concentrating thought and understanding only on what actually appears to direct intuition (the phenomenological description of essence, *Wesenschau*), and thus on what is both certain and fundamental (hence the slogan, "To the things themselves");[10] and (4) enlarge the range of consciousness and thus knowing by bringing to light the neglected phenomena of experience, neglected because of inherited prejudices in the form of theories (especially naturalistic ones) which masked or dissolved actual elements or regions of experience.[11] Phenomenology was thus a careful, methodological study of immediate, direct experience, its characteristics and structures, abjuring all philosophies which might explain and so explain away aspects of experience,

[8] See the discussion of phenomenology, intuitional certainty, and science, a "science of pure essence," in Edmund Husserl, *Ideas* (New York: Collier Books, 1962), pp. 37, 56, 75, and 206; and Husserl, *Phenomenology and the Crisis of Philosophy* (New York: Harper Torchbooks, 1965), including "Philosophy as a Rigorous Science"; see pp. 142–144. See also Merleau-Ponty, "Phenomenology."

[9] Cf. *Ideas*, pp. 75, 83–84, 164–166. For an especially clear statement of this dependence of science on phenomenological inquiry, cf. Merleau-Ponty, *The Phenomenology of Perception*, translated by Colin Smith (London: Routledge and Kegan Paul, 1962), pp. viii–ix; and "Phenomenology and the Sciences of Man."

[10] A good example of Husserl's understanding of phenomenology as a science of description of immediate and so "pure" essences is the following: "If it figures as a science *within the limits of more immediate intuition*, a pure 'descriptive' science of Essential Being, the general nature of its procedure is given in advance. . . . It has to place before its own eyes as instances certain pure conscious events, to bring these to complete clearness, and within this zone of clearness to subject them to analysis and the apprehension of their essence." *Ideas*, p. 174; also pp. 40, 47, 49, 51, 105, 131, 161, etc. Cf. "Philosophy as a Rigorous Science," pp. 106–107.

[11] On this point, see especially Spiegelberg's excellent summary of phenomenology, making this perhaps its most important goal, *Phenomenological Movement*, vol. II, 656–658.

and based on the conviction that direct intuition is the one unquestionable basis of all certainty and so all authority in knowing.[12] These and other elements of its method as worked out later
in the tradition, we shall gratefully incorporate into our way of
proceeding. As it appeared initially, however, and insofar as it
remains either an "exact science" of description, or even a
method of precise, sharable, and testable description, it presents
difficulties for our project, and probably for any helpful theological usage. What are these?

Let us first summarize briefly and somewhat prematurely
our project in this prolegomenon. This is to investigate the *meaning* of religious symbols by an examination of our actual existence in the world, achieving our goal by uncovering a hidden
or forgotten dimension of ultimacy that, we believe, nevertheless
appears significantly in our experiences of our contingency, relativity, temporality, and autonomy. The relevance of aspects of
the phenomenological tradition to this enterprise are obvious;
however, two interrelated elements of "pure phenomenology"
make its application in our case difficult.

1. In order for phenomenological investigation to have
necessity, certainty, apodicity, and so authority, a major aim with
Husserl, it was, of course, necessary that it concern itself only
with the immediate, with what is indubitably given, with what
actually appears. All "hypotheses," whether scientific, metaphysical, or theological, about what lay behind, caused, or influenced
the phenomena, were rigidly rejected, bracketed out; these are
dubious and infinitely uncertain, only probable at best. What is
certain is the intuition of immediate appearance, the dator intuition of a given essence, and so correspondingly, its patient, me-
thodical, and so exact analysis and description. In this concentration on the immediately given, and in its refusal to construct

[12] Cf. the following from Husserl: "Genuine science, and the
genuine absence of bias which inwardly distinguishes it, demands as the
foundation of all proof judgments which as such are immediately valid,
drawing their validity directly from *primordial dator intuition*. . . . *Immediate 'seeing,'* not merely the sensory seeing of experience, but *seeing
in general as primordial dator consciousness of any kind whatsoever*, is
the ultimate justification of all rational statements." *Ideas, op. cit.*, pp.
75–76; cf. also p. 83.

hypotheses about reality or its character, early phenomenology illustrated perfectly the characteristic confinement of twentieth-century philosophy to the given, its rejection of the possibility of philosophical *knowledge* of transcendent reality, and its repudiation of ontological or metaphysical systems. Thus the *object* of phenomenological study was necessarily a particular phenomenon of perception, or an appearance in immediate perception of some discernible sort, albeit stripped now eidetically of its particular, historical context. Thus, because all methodological rigor in phenomenology comes from an analysis of an actual immediate datum, the sole objects to which this method apparently could be applied were essences *within* the stream of experience, i.e., directly apprehended in the experience of ourselves and of our given world.[13] Nothing outside the direct manifold of experience, no "transcendent" factors (except the absolute Ego itself) can be dealt with by phenomenology so defined. As Husserl agreed, "God" and every dimension of ultimacy or sacrality, not to mention "existing things," inevitably lay beyond its scope.[14] If it is to be methodologically certain, phenomenology can apparently only study immanent objects *in* experience, clear, particular, definite essences which result from particular experiences and are the objects of definite, unique, and clear intuitions. Needless to say, it is exceedingly difficult to conceive how, under these methodological requirements, our experience or awareness of a "sacred" or ultimate or unconditioned dimension might be described!

2. For many of the same reasons, the object of phenomenological analysis is not only a definite, particular essence; it is also, paradoxically, separated from its actual, existent character.

---

[13] Cf. *Ideas, op. cit.*, p. 161. Spiegelberg makes this point (that only particular, finite matters can be objects of phenomenological method) in his excellent description of the refined points of phenomenological intuition, analysis, and description, and the movement from particular essences in experience to general essences by eidetic analysis. *Phenomenological Movement*, Volume II, pp. 658–684.

[14] On this point, namely that no transcendent factor can be the object of phenomenological method, see one important implication of the vast series of "reductions" implicit in phenomenological analysis, namely of world, "things," God, etc. *Ideas, op. cit.*, 96ff., 154ff.

For Husserl, phenomenology dealt with no "facts"; the particular, contingent, historical, and unique character of the referent of experience, or of myself as a particular, contingent Ego, were all abstracted from and so left out of consideration. What is intuited, is the quality, the essence latent in the contingent experience or fact, and it is this eidetically distilled essence that is the object of phenomenological intuition, analysis, and description; correspondingly, the self that is thus implied is an absolute Ego, "pure consciousness," apparently unrelated (for analysis) to the actual, contingent self.[15] If, then, phenomenology can by its methods deal *neither* with that which transcends the realm of ordinary experience, nor with anything positive concerning real existence, how, we may ask, can it help us to find in our experience of our actual living in the world, a transcendent dimension? For surely one of the most universally recognized characteristics of the divine is that it does not "appear" as a direct object of experience and so of intuition—as might a bird, a color, a sound; rather, what is characteristic of religious experience is precisely that the divine manifests itself *through* a finite object, medium, or "symbol" which alone appears and so is alone immediately given. Also, it is generally agreed that, insofar as the divine is experienced at all, it is in direct relation to our existence as actual selves in the world. Phenomenology in its original form and theological inquiry seem, then, to be mutually exclusive.

One way out of this apparent impasse has been, of course, to examine phenomenologically the character of religious experience, to take this aspect or moment within the stream of experience, as Husserl put it, as an object of analysis and reflection. This was surely the method of the great Schleiermacher, who analyzed the structure of the "religious self-consciousness" and

---

[15] On this radical abstraction from particular facts into ideal (and so necessary) essences, cf. the following: "It follows essentially from all this that *the positing of the essence*, with the intuitive apprehension that immediately accompanies it, *does not* imply any positing of individual existence whatsoever. *Pure* essential truths do not make the slightest assertion *concerning facts*." *Ibid.*, p. 51. And with regard to the reduction away from all contingency, and so its exclusion as an object of phenomenological investigation, cf. pp. 131 and 206. See also "Philosophy as a Rigorous Science", *op. cit.*, pp. 112–113.

specially that of the Protestant religious self-consciousness, as a
new and secure base for Protestant theological doctrine. It was
also what Rudolf Otto did when he sought to describe the essential character of the "holy" through a phenomenological analysis
of the shape of religious experience.[16] Granting that direct statements about God can hardly be made through eidetic analysis of
what appears, is it not possible to apply phenomenology to religious experience however complex it may be? The evident difficulty here is analogous to the one we encountered *vis à vis* ordinary language philosophy. While in each case it is possible to
broaden the method of each to include the field of religion, in
the one case specifically religious language and in the other specifically religious experience, still both methods "as is" seem
unable to conduct an analysis relevant to religion but nonetheless
outside the strict area of religion. Language analysis seems able
only to analyze the religious language in the Church, phenomenology only explicitly religious experience. But it is precisely
both of these which are in our day problematic, wondered about
and so the object of questioning theological reflection. In neither
case does it seem possible to relate ordinary, secular life to religious symbols: to discover where in ordinary experience religious
apprehensions appear and so where religious words "fit"—and
that was the task of our prolegomenon. Somehow, both methods
must be stretched so that a religious analysis of secular experience
will be possible, if religious discourse is to find renewal in a
secular age. How these two philosophical methods may contribute to that form of analysis will be part of the subject of our next
chapter.

[16] Friedrich Schleiermacher, *The Christian Faith* (Edinburgh:
T. & T. Clark, 1928), para. 3, 4, 5, 10, 15, 32, etc.; and Rudolph Otto,
The Idea of the Holy, trans. John W. Harvey (London: Oxford Uni-
versity Press, 1923).

2/The Possibility
of Religious Discourse
in a Secular Age

After the last two chapters it seems as if our prolegomenon to theological discourse has run out of useful methodologies. We cannot make the assumptions necessary either for revelationist theology or for a metaphysical natural theology, since it is precisely these assumptions that our secular mood is questioning. And for many of the same reasons, we seem unable to embark helpfully on a linguistic analysis of ecclesiastical theological discourse, a phenomenological analysis of secular experience useful to religion, or even a phenomenological analysis of religious experience. But we must begin; and so in the balance of this chapter we shall attempt to sketch out the significant elements of one proposal for a prolegomenon, for a starting point for theological discourse. We shall then try to illustrate this method for a prolegomenon in the following two chapters, and finally, in the last, relate it to positive Christian theological affirmations. Any method in order to proceed must make certain assumptions both about the materials with which it will deal and about the ways in which it will handle these materials; and, we suspect, any theological method must make some use, implicit or explicit, of going philosophical modes of procedure. We can, as we have said, make no "nonsecular" assumptions, and we have found available philosophical methods initially unusable. What sorts of "secular" assumptions, then, are there which will, on the one hand, be useful to us in establishing the meaningfulness and importance of religious discourse in a secular age, and yet,

on the other, are not so hopelessly out of touch with ordinary
experience as to make our project useless; and what can we do
with current philosophical options to help us with our task? We
shall in the following list and defend five such assumptions concerning method and the possible use we can make of current
philosophy. In connection with each of them we shall begin to
delineate our own constructive view of man's being in the world
as requiring an intelligible religious self-understanding and so
the secular usage of religious symbols.

1. The first assumption of our methodological proposal
is that the fundamental self-understanding of modern man, expressed in what we have called the secular spirit, is separable
from and in visible tension with his actual existence. To us, secular man seems to understand himself and his relation to his
world in symbolic forms which do not "fit" either the felt tones
of his existence, or the modes of his behavior. The fundamental
Weltanschauung in terms of which he apprehends his world and
which his various philosophies express—the world of his self-
understanding which we have described as the secular spirit—
is in contrast to the character of his lived experience. It is into
this disjunction between the secular self-understanding and the
actual existence of secular man that our method will seek to
move in order to establish the secular relevance of religious
discourse.

Ironically, a similar disjunction of self-understanding
from existence, of symbolic forms from the lived experience they
were assumed to explicate, was, we found, the problem that beset modern theology. Modern Christians are in fact *more* secular
in their existence than their theological understanding symbolically presupposes. Now we are reversing this disjunction. Secular
man *exists* in significantly different terms than are indicated by
the secular symbols through which he understands his existence
symbolically. To show this disjunction will be the major effort of
the following chapters. Entailed in this disjunction is the thesis
that the developments of modern life have not made the radical
difference on the level of man's existence that the self-understanding of modern man presupposes, and that secular man on
the level of his existence is not as "unreligious" and so as free of

the need for mythical language in his self-understanding as he thinks. Thus many of the religious symbolic forms characteristic of former generations remain relevant to the way man actually lives.[1] If this is so, then religious discourse can be defended as meaningful by showing that it provides the only means through which we can thematize and symbolize the felt and lived character of our existence. In other words, while we are not now questioning that the secular spirit as we have delineated it is an accurate description of the way modern man understands himself and his world, that "secularism" defines the symbolic forms that he finds meaningful, we do question whether we exist or are able to exist in the terms of this framework. To us, the modality of our secular existence—in terms of both the positive and the negative character of the tone of our modern being in the world and so of our felt meanings and resultant behavior—is out of relation to the symbolic forms of its self-understanding.

A relevant prolegomenon, we have said, can make no nonsecular assumptions; it cannot import into its analysis anything that is not found or affirmed already to be there in concrete secular experience. This does not mean, however, that we need to accept all there is in the secular understanding or account of that existence, *if* that account does not accord with the lived character of secular life. In our prolegomenon, in other words, the secular spirit can be criticized only in terms of the essential characteristics of secular life itself. To do this, we shall consider each of the elements of the secular spirit which both defined its unique shape and also which made such difficulty for religious language:

[1] Along with Mircea Eliade, Paul Ricoeur has been perhaps the most powerful voice in contemporary philosophy stating that modernity has in fact *not* outgrown its need for religious symbolism if it is to understand itself: "Moreover this task [a philosophical meditation on religious symbols] has a precise meaning *now* . . . in connection with certain traits of our 'modernity.' The historical movement of the philosophy of symbols is that of forgetfulness and restoration. Forgetfulness of hierophanies, forgetfulness of the signs of the sacred, loss of man himself insofar as he belongs to the sacred. . . . It is in the age when our language has become more precise, more univocal, more technical in a word. . . . It is in this very age of discourse that we want to recharge our language, that we want to start again from the fullness of language." Paul Ricoeur, *The Symbolism of Evil,* translated by Emerson Buchanan (New York: Harper & Row, 1967), p. 349.

its sense of contingency, relativity, temporality, and its affirmation of autonomy. We shall ask now about the way these elements of secular life appear in felt experience, in the modes of our actual existence, both private and inward, on the one hand, and public, social, and historical, on the other. We shall suggest that, while the symbolic or conceptual effects of these elements of secular life have, as we noted earlier, been to lead to radical secularism, nevertheless on the level of felt existence they raise questions with which secular symbols cannot fruitfully deal, questions which only religious discourse and religious symbols or myths can thematize, and so questions to which specific religious answers are necessary if secular existence itself is to be intelligibly comprehended and creatively lived. We shall challenge the secular understanding of secular existence not on theological or metaphysical grounds, but on its failure to provide symbolic forms capable of thematizing the actual character of its own life. It is on this basis that we shall argue that religious discourse is meaningful in the midst of secular life. Our next question, then, concerns those aspects of the secular spirit that are valid and so essential for us to incorporate in our prolegomenon, and those aspects which reveal themselves as veiling rather than illuminating actual life, and so which we must challenge on the grounds of secular life itself if adequate symbolic self-understanding of our actual life is to be achieved.

Secularity, as we have described it, is fundamentally the affirmation of life in the world, of our ordinary daily existence among the things and people that make up our immediate environment. Here it is that reality, truth, and value are to be found. Man does not live in another realm than this, nor can he speak meaningfully about such a realm in itself; whatever language is therefore relevant and real to him must be derived from and related to this realm, and it must be intelligible in terms of the experiences he has here and now. If this, then, is the secular mood, it sets one unalterable requirement for any relevant theological language, namely that whatever religious faith or theological expression we advance must be related to this worldly life, evident within it, and creative for it. The symbols of a relevant theology must explicate and illumine our ordinary existence in the world, and conversely our experience of being in the world must give meaning and reality to our theological discourse. Here is where we all exist, and where meaning for us arises and is expressed. A creative theology cannot point our minds and spirits to another realm or use language intelligible only if we enter special religious situations and special religious places. However derived from special experiences the symbols of a relevant theology may ultimately be, still they must in our age be secular enough to function as the symbolic forms by means of which our ordinary life in the world is thematized and made intelligible; they must have a secular use and application, a secular meaning.

We have said, on the other hand, that a secular theology must at certain points dissent from some of the implications of the secular spirit in which it lives. This will occur wherever that spirit fails to provide symbolic forms that can thematize the stuff of actual existence. Where, then, does the secular spirit begin to lose touch with the character of lived experience, and so where must it, in order to thematize actual life, be transformed into religious or theological discourse?

Secularism has interpreted our existence within the world as if man's being were to be understood solely in terms of those finite forces with which he obviously interacts: the nature that has produced him, the social environment that shapes his capacities, and the latent powers that reside in him. It has emphasized, therefore, the contingency of man's existence and all that surrounds him, the relativity and transience of all that appears in history and so all that he can accomplish, and his autonomy and freedom in a world without ultimate coherence and so one in which he alone can be the creator of security and of meaning. And it has found intelligible only language referent to that realm of finite factors, and unintelligible all symbolic and mythical language referent to a region of sacrality, ultimacy, unconditionedness, and essential mystery. There are no longer any ultimates in either cosmos or history which support and guide man's life, and for the interpretation of which religious symbols are essential; man seems to be on his own, and to create out of the relativities of his experience of finite creatures whatever forms of discourse and practical guidelines may direct him.

Now, while a very great deal of this self-understanding of modern man—expressed in each of his most typical philosophies —is true, nevertheless this vision contains as well a good deal of error. We say error because this self-understanding does not accurately reflect our actual existence in the world, the way we *are* there as autonomous beings amidst contingency, relativity, and transience. It obscures, therefore, a great many undeniable and significant aspects of our ordinary, secular life, and is proved false by the test of secular existence itself. And what is much more important, it is not easy to live as a human in the world on this purely secular basis. Secular autonomy taken as a total view of ourselves is neither a true answer to our intellectual question —What is man like?—nor a helpful answer to the existential and personal question—How am I to live as a human being, in fullness and creativity? For that is what secularity, and all of us, wish to do; but it fails as an enterprise because it misunderstands us.

Let us, then, look briefly at those aspects of the secular self-understanding which, while containing a large measure of truth, can nevertheless lead to a misunderstanding of the felt character of our existence. The first of these is the modern sense of the total relativity of all things, the dissolution, as van Buren puts it, of all absolutes in our time. As we noted earlier, the sense of the relativity of everything historical—of every truth, of every creed, of each hypothesis, of all social systems, of each particular moral code—has been characteristic and creative in modern life. On it are based both the possibility of developing progress—in science, thought, social structures, and law—and the possibility of the tolerance that makes free dynamic community possible. Historical relativism has been immensely creative in culture and in religion, for it has freed man from the dominance of dogma and of tradition, and made it possible for him to take his life into his own hands and to create it anew. Modern man, therefore, knows nothing ultimate—neither in nature nor in cultural history does such a thing appear. Consequently, perhaps the dominant motif of secularity has been the assertion that flux is king and the absolute gods are all dead.

The actual experience man has in his day-to-day world,

however, is, we suggest, a more paradoxical one than this secular account implies. This human world is, to be sure, a world of relative, mutually dependent beings in common interaction with one another. Nevertheless, it is also a world where our own contingent existence must be affirmed; where knowledge and understanding of that network of interaction is possible; a world also characterized by the search for meanings and values in what we do there and in the history in which we participate; a world filled with the urge both for freedom and community, for selfhood and its integrity, and for love in its mutual dependence; and finally a world suffused with the shattering experience of radical temporality. In each of these areas of our ordinary experience, something strange enters, something not quite accounted for by the relativistic symbolic forms of the secular mood. A nonsecular dimension in our experience appears in the lived character of secular life, despite the fact that the forms of our modern self-understanding have no capacity for dealing with it. This strange interloper into our secularity appears not so much as a new reality or being, as rather the ultimate presupposition for dealing with the ordinary relative realities we meet; not so much a presence—though it may be—as a final limit and a demand; not so much an answer as an ultimate question. But what this presupposition entails, what the demand is about, and what the questions ask for is radically and qualitatively different from the rest. It has the character of ultimacy, of finality, of the unconditioned which transcends, undergirds, and even threatens our experience of the ordinary passage of things and our dealings with the entities in that passage. It is, therefore, sacred as well as ultimate, the region where value as well as existence is grounded. It is because of an awareness of this dimension of ultimacy that, on the positive side, we are able to be serenely the contingent and mortal beings we are, to know the relative truths we do, to embrace the relative and transient meanings we live by, and to evaluate and so choose by our relative standards. It is *also* because of an awareness of this dimension that our common life participates in such overwhelming negativities, that it can become demonic, filled with terrible conflict and cruelty, a life teetering always on the edge either of fanaticism or else of meaninglessness and of despair. Ultimacy is continually discovered in our secular life; if not in our thoughts *about* that life or our explicit self-understanding, nevertheless in the shape and tone *of* our existence, both private and public. For wherever fanaticism appears, there this category makes itself known; and whenever despair is felt, there an ultimate emptiness has manifested itself. We cannot, consequently, give appropriate symbolic form and so meaning to this actual lived existence unless our discourse is able to thematize this dimension of ultimacy that is inevitably there, unless, that is, we understand and use some form of religious symbolization.

It is, in fact, in relation to this dimension of his experience that man becomes man, that the uniquely human characteristics of our life appear. Built into his experience of himself and his world is a dimension that transcends both his selfhood and his environment, and that makes him human. To understand himself, therefore, man must understand himself in terms of this dimension, and so as a "religious" creature. This dimension in our world is not by any means simply or directly "God." Certainly it provides the region or the possibility of a relation to God, if there be one, and for many and varied important reasons, Christians *name* this dimension or region of ultimacy by the symbol of God and define it further in the terms of that symbol. But the presence universally in human experience of a dimension or region of ultimacy or sacrality does not demonstrate the validity of that Christian naming and the propositions connected with it. Here we are concerned only with the dimension as it is generally experienced, as it appears in and to our experience, not as Christians believe it to be and to be appropriately described. Ours is a phenomenology of the religious in secular experience, and it asks about neither the *reality* nor the ontological *nature* of that which lies behind or appears within the phenomena. As a dimension or region of our experience, however, the religious is an undeniable aspect of our being in the world, and so presumably of our nature, the most vital and even, paradoxically, secular aspect, since it is that in which our humanity appears, takes its characteristic forms, and is, if it is, fulfilled. From the viewpoint of our nature, then, this dimension or relatedness to ultimacy has been called the category of self-transcendence, of ultimate concern, the dimension of ultimacy—and secular existence in all its relativity could not do without it. Because of this presence of unconditionedness in our existence, there is the possibility of a meaningful religious language whose symbols illumine and conceptualize this dim horizon of all secular experience. The presence, then, of a dimension of ultimacy in all human being in the world—in secular existence of the most ordinary day-to-day sort—is the first point where the secular self-understanding misunderstands itself, and is therefore the first evidence of the disruption between that spirit and our actual life.

The confidence in the autonomy of modern man is the second aspect of our secular mood which contains truth and yet may imply a misunderstanding of ourselves. This theme is directly related to the loss of all historical ultimates. No longer does any divine ruler set man's laws; no divine book or absolute ecclesiastical authority any longer defines his truth; nor does any absolute moral authority or standard tell him what is right; his "father images" are all gone, and he must, whether he wish to or not, be adult. He lives within a pluralism of possible authorities, and thus essentially without any absolute authority except himself. Modern man is thus radically on his own, conscious that he and he alone must create his own social order, discover what truth he knows, and take responsibility for his own decisions. He is thrown into a historical involvement from which he cannot escape, with no ultimate authority to direct him. In this sense, we agree that in our time man has become autonomous and has truly come of age.

However, this truth about our present autonomy can be compounded with two errors. First of all, latent within the modern idea of autonomy is the notion that man, now freed from external authorities that formerly crushed, or at best educated, his rational creativity and often dominated his will, will exhibit such an objective mind and noble conscience that he can create a seamless society, a new history unruffled by conflict and tragedy. Man "come of age" is now taken to imply that man can at last become rational and moral, that, no longer under the control of alien or heteronomous absolutes, man now has control over himself, a conclusion hardly justified by logic and continually contra-

dicted by secular experience. It is mainly because of this optimistic self-understanding, reflected in humanism and much of the
radical theology, that the older religious symbols expressing dependence upon God, sin, and the need for repentence and grace
have seemed irrelevant in the new world.

Secondly, the notion of autonomy has frequently led to
the thought that man is now free of destiny or fate, of that aspect
of his historical existence which he can seemingly neither determine nor control. Are not his knowledge and his powers unlimited? Why, then, can he not take his destiny into his own hands
and create a new world? Not only does man conclude from his autonomy that he can now control himself; he concludes that he can
also control the stream of history in which he lives and moves.
Man was, to be sure, once determined by natural and historical
forces beyond his control; but now that he understands these
forces and can manipulate them, he can in turn control them
for his own ends, even his own evolution. The science which has,
more than anything else, taught man his contingency and relativity in his world has, ironically, led him to forget that contingency and relativity, and seriously to consider himself the potential master of his own fate.[2]

The essential error here on the part of much of our secular self-understanding is to have taken the main modern illustration of man's autonomy, namely his control through scientific
technology over natural forces, as the sole model with which
man understands his relation to the historical forces that shape

[2] For an extreme example of this confidence that scientific man,
because he now knows how to know, can thus determine his destiny, cf.
the following report of a speech in Washington by the scientist Dr.
Glenn Seaborg, as reported in *The New York Times* of January 17,
1963: "Dr. Seaborg expressed the faith that man could, if he tried, solve
all of today's agonizing problems—war, hunger, the population explosion, water shortages, pollution. 'Man may well have reached that point
in history, that stage in his development . . . when he has not only been
made master of his fate, but when his technology and his morality have
come face to face.' . . . Science has given mankind an opportunity 'to control and direct our future, our creative evolution. . . . I believe we can be
masters of our own fate.' " This confident prediction of "mastery," stated
of all places in Washington(!), illustrates vividly the vast gulf between
our present myth of autonomy and power and our historical actuality.

his destiny. Thus since, in the manipulation of nature through engineering, the main problem is man's ignorance and his lack of technical capacity, so by translation of this model to social existence, the main problems are seen to be a lack of scientific understanding of genetical, economic, and social forces. And just as a developed technology has led to an astounding control of the natural environment, so the growth of the biological and social sciences is taken to imply a like control over our human destiny. What is overlooked are two factors that make the engineering model of "problem-solving" particularly misleading when applied to social and historical issues: (1) the contexts within which knowledge is applied are here vastly different, and consequently (2) the application of knowledge in the new *social* context becomes a moral and political problem, not a problem in engineering. The past uses of political power in history provide a much more illuminating model of what "social control by scientific knowledge" might mean than scientific manipulation in the laboratory, and if the former is our model, we can see how much more ambiguous is human control over the destinies of other men than over inanimate nature. Above all, in history unintended but powerful historical forces shape the outcome of all our best intentions, creating results we did not intend and situations with which our best theories cannot cope—as the history of any revolution with the best intentions and any exercise politically of even the greatest power illustrate. Our control in history over both our own actions and the forces that determine us is real but exceedingly fragmentary. We move in a stream of history within which we have some limited freedom, to be sure, but whose basic course our own intentions and our power cannot control or direct, and in which the meanings we intend are at best only precariously achieved and secured.[3]

Despite the fact, therefore, that the forces that mold his-

[3] For a most authoritative and copiously illustrated presentation of the thesis that scientific rationality has led to man's total misunderstanding of the contingency of his role in history and so to an ignoring of the importance of politics in historical life, cf. Hans Morgenthau, *Scientific Man Versus Power Politics* (Chicago: University of Chicago Press, 1965).

tory have for us been stripped of their ultimacy, that by no means entails that they are under our rational or moral control. And further, as George Orwell and Aldous Huxley—as well as each most recent revolution—remind us, when men attempt too eagerly to control their destiny, more often than not a more terrible form of fate threatens the very freedom and autonomy they seek. Autonomous man has amassed unbelievable powers and knowledge, and yet destiny rides into history on these very powers, making the course of man's life as unpredictable and ambiguous as it has ever been. Whether it be the new weapons, automation, the new consciousness of freedom and of self-determination among formerly subject peoples, or new forms of social existence, each of these becomes a new form of "fate" recalling to us our own contingency, fragmentariness, and that of our values as well. Modern autonomy, then, does not mean the freedom from sin and the freedom from destiny of which modern secular thought has dreamed. If this be so, if the belief in the conquest of sin and fate has been in fact an invalid "myth," then there are perhaps ambiguities remaining in our experience of ourselves and of our history which secularism does not in fact understand, and so which call for religious symbolization, namely the mystery of our freedom, its proneness to waywardness, and its seeming bondage to "fault," and the mystery of our intentions and meanings in relation to the currents of destiny.

Autonomy has not conquered either the demons of sin or of fate, nor are we free from their corresponding effects of guilt, anxiety, and the threat of meaninglessness. Consequently, the ancient religious problems of confidence, repentance, reconciliation, and of hope are as much the deepest problems of a secular age, made up entirely of relative things and autonomous men, as they were in the life of primitive or ancient man, or in the holy world of the Church. And the classical religious and theological symbols of stain and sin, of faith and hope, of forgiveness and reconciliation, and of fate or providence are as relevant in our age as they ever were. Because of this continued relevance, modern man, too, lives by "myths" concerning the origin and eradication of his fault and expressing his faith about his destiny—and these forms of language operate as significantly in our modern private and public life as do any other, as any speech on science and man's future well illustrates.

We can now perhaps understand the dialectic of great hope and great despair to which a secular age is prone. When relativity has first dissolved the absolutes of history and freed man's powers for creative expansion, then man feels great confidence in himself and the meanings which he can create in history. So long as he maintains that self-confidence, his mood and the "secular" myths which reflect it will be optimistic in form, and classical religious problems will seem both unreal and old-fashioned—as they are to the present academic and scientific sides of our culture. But when a loss of confidence in his own rationality and goodness to control his historical destiny appears, as in fact it is bound to do, then this same relativism begins to haunt him. For now, seeing the relevance of these deeper religious issues of guilt, anxiety, and meaning, he can find no answers in the world of flux. He is plunged into the despair and the urge to "get out" of society of one who feels he has no intentional control over either his own selfhood or his fate—as our literary culture, on the one hand, and our youth movements of withdrawal, on the other, amply illustrate.

Both these secular alternatives of optimism and despair are, however, untrue to the experienced texture of our existence. Life seems in a baffling and mysterious way to share both creativity and sin, wonder and terror, joy and despair—and in the midst of its fateful tragedy to reveal facets of hope, renewal, and love. This strange characteristic of life, secularism seems not to comprehend—with its alternating optimism about man's rational and moral powers as a maker of history, and its despair at our loneliness in a cold, ruthless world. We are neither so good and so powerful as the optimistic secularist says, nor is life so empty and futile as the pessimistic secularist declares. And the problem of both answers is that they have cut man off from his roots, they have tried to understand him on his own terms alone, without the dimension of ultimacy and sacrality which makes him man, and so without comprehending either the creative resources or the demonic distortions which that dimension provides to his life.

A secular prolegomenon to theology, therefore, is one which begins in our ordinary experience of being in the world and elicits hermeneutically the meanings for religious language and its symbolic forms latent within that experience. What it seeks to uncover there are those aspects of daily experience which the secular mood has overlooked, and consequently has not thematized or made explicit in the symbolic forms of its self-understanding. For as we have argued, there are levels latent in secular life of which our age is undoubtedly aware but about which it is unable to speak or to think intelligibly. These elements are the dimension of ultimacy presupposed in all our interaction with the relative world, and the presence of ambiguity within our freedom and our creativity, of the demonic and the despairing in life as well as the joyful, with both of which secular experience is suffused. In these terms, the symbols of our theological tradition may come alive in a secular age, and the possibility of a meaningful discourse about God in our time be established.

2. The second methodological assertion or presupposition we shall suggest utilizes an important "clue" from language philosophy. It involves the distinction, so important for that form of philosophy, between the question of the meaningfulness or relevance of a system of language, or language game, and the question of the validity or truth of propositions within that system of discourse. That this distinction is important in our situation is clear from what has preceded about the present situation in theology. The precise problem which the secular spirit has raised for theological method is that the truth of religious assertions—for example, that God is, or that he is of such and such a nature—can be established only on the basis of certain assumptions which are radically nonsecular, either those of metaphysics concerning the ultimate coherence of existence to speculative thought, or those of faith and of revelation, of the logos in existence or the logos made flesh. Thus to begin a theology by talking positively and creatively about God from the point of view of either natural theology or revelation is to beg the theological questions that our secularity has raised for us about the possibility

of either speculative reason or faith, and their respective lan-
guages. We must, then, begin as best we can with the concrete
character of secular experience and defend religious discourse
only in terms of what we find there. But while, as we have just
shown, an analysis of secular experience as it is apprehended in
actual existence can perhaps discover the religious character of
man, his continual experience of a dimension of ultimacy—at
least in the form of a threat, a limit, and a question—it is obvious
that it does not uncover "God." For, in a secular age, God is precisely *not* found as *necessarily* implied by the character of our
ordinary life. Or, to put this another way, the essence of an honest secular apprehension of life is precisely that the divine or the
sacred is seemingly absent, not discoverable by merely looking
at life. Only the contingent, the relative and the transient can be
assumed or established by looking. And the overwhelming ambiguity of life, with regard to both freedom and destiny, makes
it impossible to discern easily whether the ultimate that does appear is negative or positive in character, a Void or God. If, then,
we agree to start *there*, with secular experience, the resulting analysis cannot provide, without "cheating" somewhere, a basis immediately for making valid theological assertions about God. A
genuinely secular starting point is not, in other words, a sufficient ground for positive theological affirmations, a first part of
a doctrinal system. Such an analysis can at best be only a prolegomenon to systematic theology as a whole, establishing the
meaningfulness of the general language game of theology, but
not a direct part of systematic theology; it is, if you will, anthropology and not yet theology.

Secondly, the problem of meaning is, paradoxically, both
a more radical and also a more common Church problem in our
day than is the problem of validity. As we argued in the first
chapter, to say, "I do not know even what this word 'God' might
mean," is to express a more radical rejection of the stance of
faith than it is to say, "I know what you mean by God, but I do
not believe that it is true that there is such a one." And this more
radical question of the meaning of religious language is, as we
noted, one of the most accurate ways in which to define the prob-

lem of secularism for theology. On the other hand, it is also strangely true that it is more the radical question of meaning that seems to bother Church people than it is the milder question of truth. Many are able to say that "they believe" religious doctrines; what is so hard for them is to go on and say what these doctrines might *mean* and to *use* them in understanding their ordinary life. It is, then, in the eradication of a sense of the meaningfulness of its language and so the loss of its real use that the secular spirit has permeated the churches—and thus this is the prior ecclesiastical issue, as well as the more radical theological one for us to tackle.

For these reasons, the distinction between the analysis of the meaning of a proposition and the establishment of its validity is of great aid to us in the construction of our prolegomenon. This significant distinction has been introduced by logical positivism and its contemporary derivatives into current philosophy. While large segments of language philosophy have insisted that the meaning of a proposition is intimately related to, if not identical with, the possibility of its verification, nevertheless all are clear that, in dealing with any form of discourse, the analysis of meaning, or later of usage, is a different enterprise than the establishment of validity. It is in fact this distinction that, for linguistic philosophy, marks off the task of philosophy from that of the scientist, the moralist, the citizen, or the theologian. Thus it is not on this view the function of the philosopher to test the truth of the propositions men use in their various forms of discourse. That is the role of the special sciences, which perform the verifying or falsifying experiments, and of social experience and common sense with regard to nonscientific modes of speech. For philosophy does not originate, nor does it establish, the truth of any statement. There is no "philosophical experience" out of which peculiarly philosophical assertions about reality might arise, and thus philosophy is not, say they, a form of *knowledge;* there are no philosophical assertions at all. Instead, it is the function of philosophical analysis to clarify the meanings and usages of our language (it is "talk about talk"), and it does this by showing the potential relation of our concepts and language games to the kinds of situations or experiences which can falsify or verify that language or in which it can be and is appropriately used.[4] The actual using, testing, or verifying of any given proposition within a language game is thus left to the special community which uses that form of discourse, which shares the experiences the language game expresses and which presumably validates it in its common life.

Even where language philosophy, under the tutelage of the later Wittgenstein, has turned from an analysis of meaning to an analysis of usage in order to clarify our language[5] this same important distinction remains. In ordinary language philosophy, the aim of philosophy is to show how we use a language game, in what situations it is appropriate, communicative, and makes sense. In discovering its proper usage, we discover what in "ordinary usage" the rest of us would say a word or a concept *means* or *is*. But such an exhibition of the proper usage and so

[4] For example, see these quotations from Schlick: "Stating the meaning of a sentence amounts to stating the rules according to which the sentence is to be used, and this is the same as stating the way in which it can be verified (or falsified). The meaning of a proposition is the method of its verification." "You cannot even start verifying before you know the meaning, i.e., before you have established the possibility of verification. . . . The empirical circumstances are all-important when you want to know if a proposition is *true* (which is the concern of the scientist), but they can have no influence on the *meaning* of the proposition (which is the concern of the philosopher)." M. Schlick, "Meaning and Verification," in *Readings in Philosophical Analysis*, edited by H. Feigl and W. Sellers (New York: Appleton-Century-Crofts, 1949), pp. 148 and 154 respectively.

[5] In his later thought, Wittgenstein has the following to say on the examination of meaning in relation to usage: "The meaning of a term is its use in the language." (43) "In such a difficulty, always ask yourself: How did we learn the meaning of this word (good, for instance)? From what sort of examples? In what language-games?" (77) "One cannot guess how a word functions. One has to *look at* its use and learn from that." (340) "To grasp the essence of a thing, one must always ask oneself: 'Is the word ever actually used in this way in the language-game which is its original home?'" (116) "Well, what does one include in 'thinking'? What has one learned to use this word for?" (328) Ludwig Wittgenstein, *Philosophical Investigations*, translated by G. E. M. Anscombe (New York: Macmillan Company, 1953). The number references are to the numbered paragraphs in this work.

meaning of a family of words is no guarantee of the validity
of propositions containing them, i.e., of the question of the truth
of the claims made in propositions in which these words are
used. As A. J. Ayer has pointed out, in the seventeenth century it
was not difficult to specify the proper usage of words about
demons and witches; one could, through paradigmatic examples,
indicate precisely in what sorts of situations these words made
sense, as apparently they did, to the people who commonly used
them.[6] But that analysis of proper usage in no way satisfies our

[6] A. J. Ayer, *The Concept of a Person and Other Essays* (London: Macmillan & Company, 1963), pp. 17–18. We should recognize,
of course, that according to positivism (to Schlick and to the early
Ayer), such common seventeenth-century usage *vis à vis* witches would
still not have been "meaningful" because this usage could not be verified
or falsified by sense experience. Thus, as Ayer sees and in part regrets,
the change from the canon of meaning as verification to that of ordinary
usage has meant almost a total loss of available criteria for intelligible
discourse. Almost the only thing ordinary language philosophy can say
about whether or not a language game has "meaningfulness" is that, if
the game is in use, it must have meaning, for use in a community equals
meaning. As we have argued, however, this change, however significant
in other respects, does not involve the distinction we are making between
the function of philosophical analysis as the analysis of meaning or usage,
and the establishment of validity, which is the prerogative of science and
of common sense.
   In fact, this distinction is reiterated by one of the leaders of the
newer trend, P. F. Strawson, in the following remarks: "Meaning (in at
least one important sense) is a function of the sentence or expression;
mentioning and referring, truth or falsity, are functions of the use of the
sentence or expression. To give the meaning of an expression . . . is to
give general *directions* for its use to refer to or mention particular objects
or persons; to give the meaning of a sentence is to give general *directions*
for its use in making true or false assertions. It is not talk about any
particular occasion of the use of the sentence or expression. . . . So the
question of whether a sentence or expression is *significant* or not has
nothing whatever to do with the question of whether the sentence, *ut-
tered on a particular occasion,* is on that occasion being used to make a
true or false assertion or not or of whether the expression is, on that
occasion, being used to refer to, or mention, anything at all." P. F. Strawson, "On Referring," in *Essays in Conceptual Analysis,* edited by A. Flew
(London: Macmillan & Company, 1956), pp. 30–31. And again, "In
knowing what it [a sentence] means, you are knowing how it could be

further questions about possible referents for this language game, or, more precisely, the validity of propositions that use this system of symbols, i.e., whether the claim that may have been made that there were in fact demons present in a certain situation is true or false. Language analysis can exhibit for us the intelligibility or meaningfulness (in a given culture) of a language system by showing its potential usage in certain specific situations and so the kinds of experiences to which its claims and assertions have reference. But this mode of analysis cannot provide for us— and does not seek to—any means for verifying or falsifying the truth of any of the propositions that use that system.

Although much of the earlier positivistic language philosophy was dubiously relevant to the theological enterprise, this distinction in analytic philosophy between a philosophical analysis of meaning and usage, on the one hand, and the process of verification and experience on the other, may have real usefulness, especially in relation to religious language. For it means that the theologian can mount a defense for the meaningfulness of religious discourse in general without, at least at the outset, raising the question of the validity of particular religious propositions and so of their truth for a given hearer. Thus discussion about religious discourse can be carried on without making the nonsecular assumptions either that we have had a religious experience or faith encounter with God, or that we agree to the rationalistic presuppositions necessary for a natural theology—obviously question-begging presuppositions. As we have noted, one of the weaknesses of revelationist theology in the contemporary situation was that such discussions with radical doubt, both inside or outside the circle of faith, were not possible, and thus that the radical and yet widespread problem of the meaning of religious discourse could not be reflected upon without assuming the absence of the very doubts which instigated the problem. In any case, with this distinction in mind, we can on secular terms

---

correctly used to talk about things: so knowing the meaning has nothing to do with knowing about any particular use of the sentence to talk about anything." *Ibid.*, p. 32.

attempt to exhibit the intelligibility and meaningfulness of the language game of religious discourse by showing its potential usage in certain specific sorts of situations, and so the relevance of its symbolic forms to ranges or areas of common human experience.

3. The third presupposition of our prolegomenon has to do with the way the meaningfulness of a language game is or can be established; here we begin to move from language analysis to phenomenology. The presupposition in question might be called the affirmation of the experiential meaning of meaning. How do we propose to show that religious discourse has meaning and even significance for secular man—especially since our precise problems are that he rarely if ever uses that sort of discourse and, when he does hear it used, that he wonders if it has any meaning? How is a discourse that is barely used, and when used seems empty, to be shown to be meaningful or significant? The answer of natural theology we have discussed; the question of the meaningfulness of the metaphysical language game is still with us at the close of any natural theology. The answer of positivism is equally unavailable. To seek to establish the meaningfulness of theological language in terms of its direct verifiability and falsifiability in immediate, sensory experience is, we believe, radically to misunderstand the nature of that form of discourse. For as the whole development of theology since the Enlightenment has gradually established, theological propositions do not directly make assertions about matters of fact, although, as we shall see, they may include and so presuppose certain factual statements. Rather, like metaphysical statements, statements about God concern that which grounds and structures all facts, and so is present in every fact, if it be there at all. Such statements of ontology or, in theology, about God's relation to the world thus cannot be falsified, since no account of experience will exhibit their absence. As Whitehead remarks, existence never takes a holiday from metaphysical structures; they are thus universal in scope and apply to every example of experience if they apply at all. To use, therefore, the criteria appropriate for hypotheses of limited scope on metaphysical and theological propositions is to misunderstand

the meaning of the latter—and, in the case of both, to reduce them to the level of meaningless pseudoscientific statements, which is, in itself, a major category mistake.[7] How, then, without begging our own question, or falling into various positivistic traps, can we begin to establish the meaningfulness or intelligibility of religious discourse, even in a secular age? Our suggestion at this point is that we borrow further clues from contemporary philosophy, an initial one from ordinary language philosophy, and then our major resource from phenomenology, and try to work out our problems in their light.

Let us look first to ordinary language philosophy and see what further help it can offer us. As we noted, language philosophy has relinquished the claim that it has criteria for "mean-

---

[7] The effort of John Hick to establish the meaningfulness of theological statements in terms of an "eschatological verification" is, it seems to me, misguided on three grounds: (1) in speaking of an *eschatological* verification, this argument, by using a theological term, thus presupposes what it wishes to establish, namely the meaningfulness of this sort of language. (2) Since it gives a theological, or "heavenly" rather than "earthly," definition of the words "verification" and "experience," it thus changes the meaning of the criteria in the middle of the argument. (3) As we noted in the text, in seeking to subsume religious assertions under the verification principle, however heavenly that principle may in this case be, it implies that the *meaning* of theological statements is contained in the factual assertions or information which they communicate to us, and this is seriously to misunderstand what theological affirmations have to say and so how, if they do, they "mean." For us, theological statements are, like metaphysical ones, assertions about "what is the case"; this does not mean, however, that they are "factual" assertions, statements informing us about the immediate and variable character of finite events and relations in the observable space-time nexus. Rather, they are assertions about the ultimate ground and the pervasive character or structure of that nexus. Thus they are not descriptions of certain sorts of facts but characterizations of those universal relations of every fact to its source and ground, characteristics therefore that apply to every fact and so cannot be "observed" or manifested, and in that way verified or falsified. To reduce them to the level of statements about finite interrelations that can be verified is thus to transform them from assertions about God and his pervasive relation to the world to assertions about "supernatural facts." Cf. John Hick, *Philosophy of Religion* (Englewood Cliffs, N. J.: Prentice-Hall, 1963), and "Theology and Verification," in John Hick, ed., *The Existence of God* (New York: Macmillan Company, 1964).

ing." It can, it maintains, only investigate usage on the assumption that a language is actually used, that it is "given" as an actual
mode of communication and so presumably intelligible and fruitful for some aspect of the life of a given community. Thus if,
according to this procedure, we wish to inquire what "freedom"
means, we inquire into the ways the word "freedom" and its
cognates are used in the ordinary speech of our culture, and by
there discovering paradigmatic uses, we discover whatever
"meanings" there may be in these words. The question of the
intelligibility of these "meanings" (our question, incidentally)
is quieted by the assumption that, granted the words are actually
used in this way, they thereby may be assumed to communicate
and to be intelligible. Usage, whenever it occurs, thus seems to
guarantee intelligibility. It appears that usage and meaning are
one and the same, though, as we have noted in the case of religious discourse, in certain cultural situations and with regard to
"official" forms of language, usage cannot be *identified* with
intelligibility.

Meaning is thus assuredly related to usage and a given
communal context. But what, we may ask, is really going on
when we inquire about usage? What are we doing when we describe a paradigmatic situation or context in which people appropriately use a word or a family of words? In answer we suggest
that in fact we are elucidating, appealing to, or evoking a memory of that region or area of our immediate or direct, and commonly shared, experience of things—for a "situation" is a region
or element of our experience of being in the world—in which
or to which the word is applicable.[8] And this applicability to or

---

[8] These two examples from J. L. Austin and A. J. Ayer respectively underline this intimate relation, in language analysis, between the
search for *usage* and the search for the *appropriate situation in common
experience*: "On the other hand, I might [to show the meaning of the
word 'racy'] do what we may call 'demonstrating the semantics' of the
word, by getting the questioner to *inquire* or even actually to *experience*
situations which we should describe correctly by means of sentences containing the words 'racy,' 'raciness,' etc., and again other situations where
we should *not* use these words." J. L. Austin, "The Meaning of a Word,"
in C. E. Caton, ed., *Philosophy in Ordinary Language* (Urbana: University of Illinois Press, 1963), p. 3.

"For the answer is that to specify the use of a sentence, in this in a given situation signifies that there the word serves an important function of clarifying and so, through the provision of thematic and symbolic forms, gives "meaning" to the felt character of that experience or situation which the community of usage shares amongst them. Words are symbols which thematize our felt and shared experiences; they are, to use the phrase of Paul Ricoeur, the light of the emotions, since they lift them out of their dimness into more precise and also sharable forms and so give to common experience "meanings."[9] Through these symbols related to our felt experience, the contradictions and turmoils of experience are rendered relatively coherent and orderly, and we can communicate to others and to ourselves what is going on in the various facets of our being in the common world. Meanings arise, to be sure, in a community of discourse. But at the most fundamental level they represent not only the lateral sharing of recognized usage, but also the interaction of symbols to our felt experience, the symbol providing thematic and so communicable form to the stream of experience, and *both* are essential if there is to be meaning at all.[10]

---

sense, is to describe the situations to which it is applied; in other words, to describe the situations, the states of affairs, by which the statement expressed would be verified. . . . The question is, given that we do make statements of such and such a sort, what are the circumstances that would make them true? In short, the emphasis is not on our verbal habits themselves, but on the situations to which they are adapted. . . . But when we examine how this process of looking into the workings of our language is actually conducted, we find once again that it is chiefly a matter of the meticulous inspection of a certain range of facts." Ayer, *Concept of a Person*, pp. 23–25.

[9] Ricoeur, *Symbolism*, p. 7. And in another, although applicable, context, "What is experienced as defilement, as sin, as guilt, requires the mediation of a specific language, the language of symbols. Without the help of that language, the experience would remain mute, obscure, and shut up in its implicit contradictions." *Ibid.*, p. 161.

[10] This entire discussion of meaning in terms of the relation of symbols to felt or lived experience is, of course, vastly indebted to current phenomenological literature, but we must acknowledge especially, along with the work of Professors Ricoeur and Eliade, the excellent book on this theme by Eugene T. Gendlin, *Experiencing and the Creation of Meaning* (Glencoe, Ill.: The Free Press, 1962). Professor Gendlin says: "Meaning is formed in the interaction of experiencing and something that functions symbolically. Feeling without symbolization is blind; symboli-

Symbols "mean" for us in part because they conceptualize
and so point to elements, aspects, ranges, and levels of common
experience, perhaps to objects in the foreground, to feelings inside, and even to the dim horizons which are also there to be
talked about. Thus are symbols the basis of all meaning, of our
communication with others about experience, and so the basis
of all of our own concepts and thoughts. But they communicate
meaning only because they thematize an experience shared by
those involved in the communication: in the first instance, symbols mean for us because of their relations to our felt meanings.[11]
Without the symbols the experienced world would be "meaningless" because blind and because communication would be impossible; without the common felt levels of experience, the symbols

zation without feeling is empty. . . . We cannot even know what a concept 'means' or use it meaningfully without the 'feel' of its meaning. No
amount of symbols, definitions, and the like can be used in the place of
the *felt* meaning. . . . Concepts are not meanings at all, except in relation
to experiencing," pp. 5–6. "A meaning is explicated in terms of symbols
whose meanings are felt or experienced. It is this feeling or experiencing
that constitutes the 'having' of an explicated meaning. . . . Our conclusion is that when we think a meaning, both symbols and felt meanings
are necessary," p. 67. "We do not usually explicate familiar symbols. We
say, *'they* mean' what they mean to us. However, *they mean*, in that *they
call forth* the felt meaning. We hear or see or think them, and in that act
feel their meaning. . . . *The symbols* there have 'meaning' in the sense
that they function to *call forth* in us the felt meaning," p. 101. "Meaning
depends on a relationship between experience and symbols," p. 125.

We should also add our indebtedness to the work of John Wild,
especially his *Existence and the World of Freedom* (Englewood, N. J.:
Prentice-Hall, 1965), especially chaps. 1–4. On this same theme of
the relation of phenomenological analysis to meaning and so to ordinary
language philosophy, see James M. Edie, ed., *An Invitation to Phenomenology* (Chicago: Quadrangle Books, 1965), especially the essays by Eugene Te Hennepe, Herbert Spiegelberg, and Eugene Gendlin.

[11] "It is the office of language to cause essence to exist in a state
of separation which is in fact merely apparent, since through language
they still rest upon the antepredicative life of consciousness. In the silence
of primary consciousness can be seen appearing not only what words
mean, but also what things mean: the core of primary meaning round
which the acts of naming and expression take shape." M. Merleau-Ponty,
Phenomenology of Perception (London: Routledge and Kegan Paul,
1962), p. xv.

would be meaningless because empty, rootless, and without intent. Meaning therefore involves both symbol and experience, in
creative interaction; it involves used symbols and shared experiences. Thus, to find what the "usage" of a language game is,
one inevitably asks for those aspects of experience, "the circumstances," which it thematizes. The examination of these paradigmatic "situations" in which a given language system is used is
in effect an examination of the areas of common experience of
being in the world which that language game successfully thematizes. And the analysis of the rules of application, the usages,
is an analysis of the commonly accepted ways we apply symbols
to these common situations in experience if we are to communicate to our fellows. Thus to ask, "Does it have a meaningful or
intelligible usage?" is to ask first of all, "Does this language
game thematize an area of shared, ordinary, day-to-day experience?" and only secondarily to ask about the rules of application of these common symbols.[12]

We are proposing, in other words, as essential for our
purposes, if not for others, a slightly variant and to us deeper
understanding of the word meaning than the linguistic criterion
of use and the discovery of usage. Among the many meanings
the word has in current philosophical usage, primary is the relation of linguistic symbols to felt experience. Our argument is that

[12] Interpreting Wittgenstein, Dallas High also lays stress on the
essential relation of usage (and so meaning) to the common life context of those who communicate meanings: "Mental processes are, in an
important sense, private and privileged. . . . 'Understanding,' 'meaning,'
and 'language using' are more or less public insofar as 'the *circumstances*' (or the common world of a language game) are shared by a
speaker and a hearer." *Language, Persons, and Belief* (New York: Oxford University Press, 1967), p. 45. "To appeal to the 'use' of language
for the understanding and recovery of the meaning of our language, is to
appeal to the ordinary linguistic activities of human life in their multiple
but mixed forms. What these activities are is shown by the way people
think and live as ways of being in the world. If there are many ways of
being in the world . . . aesthetic, ethical, and religious, it is absurd not to
say that there are at least aesthetic, ethical, and religious ways of saying
and meaning something (i.e., using language), which, however context-
ually distinguishable, may also be inexorably mixed in our form of culture or life." *Ibid.*, p. 69.

linguistic symbols, including those of religious language, cannot communicate, i.e., have meaning or use, if they do not function importantly to thematize some significant area of common, ordinary experience; and conversely if they *do* so function, then *ipso facto* they have, or can have, significant meanings in the life of even a secular age. The analysis of the meaning of ordinary language points, therefore, in three ways beyond the question of linguistic usage to the question of the relation of linguistic symbols to experience, and thus drives any analysis, especially of religious language, to this further "phenomenological" meaning of meaning.

(*a*) To analyze usage is in fact, as we suggested, to evoke or appeal to a situation in felt experience; to uncover use is to relate symbolic forms to their felt or experienced meanings. A word is used in ordinary language because it "means," and it means because it is an effective and usable symbol for some aspect of common, shared experiences of our human being in the world and among others.

(*b*) This relation of felt meanings to ranges or regions of lived experience is what is presupposed, but left unclarified, by the concepts "ordinary usage" or "currency in ordinary discourse," which, as we saw, were the bases in ordinary language philosophy for the assumption of the intelligibility or the legitimacy of the language games of speech. The *meaningfulness* assumed in the case of words with "ordinary" or stock usage, consists, we are suggesting, in the functioning of these symbols in thematizing the shared experiences of the community that uses them.

(*c*) "Meaning," as primarily consisting of the relation of symbol to experiencing, is further manifested by the particular problem currently facing religious or theological language. This language has in fact been used in church: in sermons, in liturgy, in official discourse of various sorts, and in theological discussion. As we have seen, however, the problem facing religious discourse is that, although used, this language has become "meaningless" or at least only barely meaningful to those laymen who wish to hear it used and those clerics who try to use it. Thus ours is one case where meaning and use (at least official use) are not to be identified, and so where the particular problem of meaning lies elsewhere than in the currency of a language game. We suggest that the problem of meaning in this case at least is that this language had no relation to the character of modern experiencing, it did not function to provide symbolic forms for ordinary and shared meanings, and thus, although theological discourse constituted a consistent and structured set of symbols (and may have had meaning in *that* sense), these symbols were empty and meaningless, they were symbols of no experience and so of nothing real or relevant.

Meaning is thus not only a logical matter of a definition, i.e., it is not exhausted by specifying its interrelations to the symbolic systems in which it functions; nor is it, in the reverse sense, only a matter of verification or falsification in terms of direct and particular sensory experiences. It is most fundamentally the product of a relation of a symbol to felt or immediate experiencing as a whole, to the *Lebenswelt* in which man finds himself existing. For no symbol or proposition can *mean* for us, and so communicate to us and be intelligible, unless it is a thematic expression of some lived experience. This is, to be sure, an "empirical" view of meaning. On this view, symbols cannot just be "revealed" and communicate anything to us. Unless they function purely abstractly, as in mathematics, they must be related to experience if they are to be used or even logically defined. On this view, then, the relation to the felt meanings of experiencing replaces the criteria of objective verification or falsification as the empirical anchor, so to speak, of the meaningfulness of symbolic forms that are in fact in ordinary usage. If language philosophy is not to be positivistic, it must, we feel, move toward a phenomenological hermeneutic of experience if it is really to explore the meaning of meaning.

In exploring, then, the meaningfulness of religious discourse, and in attempting to establish that it does have a meaning, we are interested in two questions: (*a*) in what sorts of situations is it used and useful; and (*b*) what is its relation to felt or lived experience in these situations? If, correspondingly, we can, on the one hand, find areas of ordinary, secular experience where religious symbolization is *used*, and, on the other, if we can lo-

cate areas where there are felt experiences that call for this sort
of symbolization, we have shown that this mode of discourse has
"meaning." One implication of our view is that, when in such
situations religious discourse is in fact not used or used only sur-
reptitiously, this is a function of the secular self-understanding
which blocks off a form of symbolization for which secular experience calls. Another implication is that it may well be that, if
religious symbols are empty when disrelated to secular experience, secular experience in turn may be blind and so again
meaningless—or at least impoverished—if there are significant
areas of its scope which it cannot symbolize in its own secular
terms.[13]

   To sum up this discussion of meaning in relation to words
and symbols, and so to kinds of symbolic systems or language
games, we can distinguish four kinds of questions involved in
the question "What do you mean by X?" or, to use a concrete
example, "What do you mean by God?" and we are asserting
here the logical primacy of the first and its overriding relevance
for our particular present contemporary theological dilemma.
(1) The meaning of a symbol (e.g., God), is to be discovered by
relating that symbol to those aspects of common experience
which it thematizes, conceptualizes, and so discloses to specific
awareness and communication. Here in method a phenomenological hermeneutic of experience is called for. (2) The meaning of a symbol is exhibited by showing how it is *used* in the
activities and speech of a community whose ordinary or current
(though possibly technical) speech includes that symbol, i.e.,
the rules and patterns of its use, etc. The question "What does
God mean?" here elicits the answer: "We use the word 'God' in
such and such situations, and this usage contains the following
logical forms, regular or queer, etc." Here clearly a linguistic
analysis of ordinary or "stock" usage is called for. (3) The meaning of a symbol is exhibited when its eidetic structure is related to
the other symbols together with which it forms a system of sym-

---

   [13] "What is myth if it is not gnosis? Once more we are brought
back to the function of the symbol. The symbol, we have said, opens up
and discloses a dimension of experience that, without it, would remain
closed and hidden." Ricoeur, *Symbolism*, p. 165.

bols. Here the essential structure or essence of a symbol is discovered, and, speaking methodologically, an eidetic analysis is called for. For example, the question "What do Christians *mean* by God?" could, in part, be answered by showing the interrelations of this symbol to other symbols in the same structural system, and thus uncovering its unique and essential character. The symbol "God" can here be understood in terms of its relations to Biblical symbols and to traditional "doctrinal" symbols such as creation, providence, man, sin, history, incarnation, atonement, church, and salvation. This sort of "meaning" has been the concern of most Biblical, historical, and systematic theology, but as our present dilemma shows, it is a necessary but not a sufficient condition for the symbol God to function meaningfully in Church discourse, since these systems of interrelation may be known and yet in our religious and church life there may remain a real question whether these symbols *mean* anything there. (4) A final aspect of the question of meaning, at least *vis à vis* a theological term, is its ontological or philosophical meaning. When we ask, "What do you mean by God?" we may be asking, "How do you conceive of God's relation to other things: to stars, atoms, ideas, gremlins, Middle Earth?" "What has knowing him to do with knowing other things?" and "What is his relation to and place and function within the system of things I call the world?" To make the idea of God intelligible, then, can also legitimately mean to relate it systematically to all that we know of other things. Speaking methodologically, this enterprise presupposes both epistemology and ontology, since, for various reasons, "God" does not as a symbol fit within the systems of scientific knowledge. Hence, as we have argued, this aspect of the question of meaning, although essential for theology, comes later on, when the possibility of ontology has been grounded on prior elements, and we have already established reasons for thinking we can talk about the ultimate structures of things. Hence our prolegomenon is an "ontic" rather than an "ontological" analysis, since the meaning for which it searches is of the first sort, namely the relation of words to lived experience, rather than the relation of symbols to the universal structures of being. As is obvious, a full theological account of meaning would require help from every branch of philosophical inquiry, linguistic, phenomenological, epistemological and ontological.

4. We have stated that, in order to show the meaningfulness of religious language, we must examine ordinary life to find there those ranges or regions of common experience for which religious discourse is appropriate; and we have provisionally delineated those regions relevant to religious language as those in which a dimension of ultimacy appears as the basis of our being and our power, and in which the ambiguity of our freedom manifests itself. But how, if we are not going to examine *language* directly, do we examine with any intellectual rigor or integrity "experience," and especially if what we are looking for there is not an easily identifiable object like "red," but a dimension of ultimacy and sacrality? Let us look now at those aspects of the phenomenological tradition that harmonize with our own goals and so may give us methodological clues as to how, with some rigor, discipline, and sense of direction, we might proceed.

First of all, it is generally agreed that a most significant goal of the phenomenological movement has been to provide a method that will (*a*) eradicate or set to one side our normal, cultural prejudices in order that (*b*) new or neglected phenomena, aspects of experience as it actually is, may be seen, appropriated, and comprehended. For this purpose among others, the bracketing moves, especially those of the transcendental or phenomenological reduction of all questions of reality, existence, or causality, were devised, and thus the main slogan of the movement was "to the things themselves."[14] As the effort, then, to look anew at

[14] See the excellent discussion of this purpose of phenomenology as a whole, and of the phenomenological reduction, in Speigelberg, *The Phenomenological Movement* (The Hague: Martinus Nijhoff, 1965), Part V: "The first objective of the phenomenological approach is the enlarging and deepening of the immediate range of experience: . . . Negatively, it expresses the revolt against an approach to philosophy that takes its point of departure from crystallized beliefs and theories handed down by a tradition which only too often perpetuates preconceptions and prejudgments," p. 656. It is interesting that the same refusal of philosophy to embark upon "explanations," and to confine itself to mere description, and so to dealing entirely with our given linguistic habits, is the heart of Wittgenstein, cf. *Philosophical Investigations*, para. 109.

experience as it manifests itself without the "blinders" of a cultural point of view, phenomenology encourages our enterprise, which was, as we have seen, an attempt to penetrate below our secular self-understanding, and below the categories and symbols with which we generally comprehend our world, to see if there are not in our actual experience significant elements which are important and yet which have been hidden by these secular categories.

Secondly, there is no question that phenomenological analysis has concentrated its efforts on the analysis of experience rather than of our linguistic expressions about experience.[15] This is not to denigrate or minimize the philosophical worth of the analysis of language. It is, however, to say that, for the resolution of *our* problem, the problem of the experiential meaning of religious language, it is essential to move below our customary expressions to the experiences or the phenomena to which they refer and which they make meaningful; and, secondly, that phenomenological analysis is based on the affirmation—over against linguistic philosophy[16]—that an analysis of prelinguistic experience by reflection is possible. Beginning with Husserl, the purpose of phenomenological analysis has been to uncover and thus to recover the character and structure of immediate experience through an analysis of the forms or essences that appear within

[15] Cf. the following from Spiegelberg: "By contrast [to linguistic philosophy], phenomenological analysis is not primarily concerned with linguistic expressions. . . . But this misinterpretation overlooks the fact that such analyses of terms were merely preparatory to the study of the referents, i.e., of the phenomena meant by the expressions. Phenomenological analysis, then, is analysis of the phenomena themselves, not of the expressions that refer to them." *The Phenomenological Movement* (The Hague: Martinus Nijhoff, 1965), vol. II, p. 669.

[16] Cf. the implication of Wittgenstein's famous "idling" analogy with regard to a description of thought or of thinking: To examine the "experience" of thinking is for him meaningless, for then the engine is idling and not "at work." To find the *meaning* of thinking, then, and so of thought, one should not look at the experience, but rather look at how one uses the words. Phenomenology at this point goes just the other way; in order to find the meaning of the word, it looks at the phenomena or the appearances—and their essential structures—to which the word or symbol has reference. For Wittgenstein, cf. *Philosophical Investigations*, pp. 51, 73ff., 104ff., 118, and 127.

it; and as all phenomenologists agree, the point of this analysis is to examine that prereflective or prethematized experience of which language represents the symbolic form.[17]

After Husserl, moreover, the emphasis on concrete, actual, rather than ideal, essential experience, encouraged by his later remarks on the *Lebenswelt*, grows. And in the recent forms of the movement, phenomenological reflection specifically sees as its task the examination of concrete experience as it is lived in the world and before it has received eidetic or essential form.[18] The way man *is* and apprehends himself *in* the world of objects, not the way appearances are to his consciousness, is thus the center; "being" or existing has replaced pure consciousness as the central ontological category.[19] Insofar as our goal, too, is that of

[17] That this possibility is envisioned by Husserl is clear from the following: "It is ideally possible for every experience not included in the glance to be 'brought under it'; a reflective act of the Ego is directed towards it, and it now becomes an object *for* the Ego." *Ideas* (New York: Collier Books, 1962), p. 197. "The whole stream of experience with its experiences lived after the *mode* of unreflecting *consciousness* can be made the subject of a scientific study of the nature of the essence." *Ibid.*, p. 199.

[18] Quoting Husserl, Merleau-Ponty says: " 'It is that as yet dumb experience. . .which we are concerned to lead to the pure expression of its own meaning.' [*Cartesian Meditations*, p. 33] Husserl's essences are destined to bring back all the living relationships of experience. . . . The separated essences are those of language. . . . Looking for the world's essence is not looking for what it is as an idea once it has been reduced to a theme of discourse: it is looking for what it is as a fact for us, before any thematization. . . . The eidetic reduction is, on the other hand, the determination to bring the world to light as it is before any falling back on ourselves has occurred, it is the ambition to make reflection emulate the unreflective life of consciousness." *Phenomenology*, pp. xv–xvi. An investigation of *how* such a reflective examination of prethematic experience is possible, is the main theme of Eugene Gendlin's excellent book, *op. cit.* Whether this emphasis of Heidegger, Sartre, and Merleau-Ponty on the examination of prethematic, actual, and so concrete experience of "being in the world" fits Husserl's ideal of a phenomenology as a rigorous and therefore ideal science is another question.

[19] Spiegelberg makes a good deal of this change in Heidegger, Sartre, and Merleau-Ponty from an idealism of pure consciousness to a concentration on being in the world, and thus on "real relations" as the basic given of human existence. *Phenomenological Movement*, vols. I, II, pp. 301, 488ff., 520ff., etc. The roots of this fundamental phenomenological

finding those regions of ordinary actual experience within which religious symbols are important, we need to devise a way of examining presymbolic or prereflective experience (experience unflattened by secular self-understanding) to uncover the dimensions of ultimacy and sacrality latent there. Whether what follows achieves phenomenological rigor is, we must admit, by no means apodictically certain! Difficulties remain in the application of the method, since ultimacy does not simply appear in experience, and so it manifests no easily discernible essence. Still, our enterprise is in accord with phenomenology in this effort to go beyond verbal symbols to that within experience which they "mean" or might mean, and to locate these regions of experience in our actual apprehension of ourselves as being in the world.[20]

The greater emphasis in phenomenology on the examination of our lived experience of the *Lebenswelt*, of our apprehension of our being in the world, has in turn led to a development away from the ideal of a rigorous method dealing with ideal essences and therefore capable of apodictic certainty in de-

---

doctrine of internal relations, that we are in the actual world and thus that thought begins with that essential interrelation, lie, however, in Husserl and the doctrine of intentionality. (For the definition of this, cf. *Ideas,* p. 108.) As Pierre Thevanez (*What is Phenomenology?* [Chicago: Quadrangle Books, 1962], p. 68) and Merleau-Ponty (*Phenomenology,* pp. xvii–lx) have pointed out, nevertheless there seems no question of the importance of this shift into the real world where an absolute consciousness is not "constitutive" of its object but where a contingent self discovers itself in interaction with real things around it.

[20] The same effort to get at concrete, actual experience—before it appears in "essential" form—is reflected in the movement of Paul Ricoeur's method from eidetics to a hermeneutics of religious symbols. An eidetic analysis of our experience of the will leaves us, he believes, with insight into its essential structures and so possibilities, but with no comprehension of its concrete actuality where actual evil occurs. Thus only the language of confession—the symbols of stain, sin, and guilt— and the myths narrative of the appearance of evil can manifest the concrete actuality of our human experience of will in its "fault" or its "transcendence." Cf. Paul Ricoeur, *Freedom and Nature* (Evanston, Ill.: Northwestern University Press, 1966); *Fallible Man* (Chicago: Henry Regnery Co., 1965); and *The Symbolism of Evil, op. cit.*; and "The Hermeneutics of Symbols and Philosophical Reflection," *International Philosophical Quarterly*, II, No. 2 (1913), 191–218.

lineating only what appears. What has replaced it has been the goal of a "hermeneutical" phenomenology, as Heidegger termed it, which would seek to elicit from the appearances the essential structures of our being in the world. Instead of analyzing with apodictic precision what appears in immediacy, this development of phenomenology now seeks to unveil or make manifest what had, on the level of "normal" immediacy, been hidden or forgotten; the given becomes a clue to what philosophical analysis seeks, not its sole object.[21] This hermeneutical phenomenology still exhibits the concern for new, unusual, and neglected aspects of immediate experience, especially those rendered "unreal" by reductionist categories or obscured by naturalistic explanations, for example, our experiences of freedom, anxiety, nothingness, and so on. This tendency of phenomenology has thus not so much uncovered, as Husserl did, the eternal, timeless, and necessary forms apparent to consciousness and the absolute Ego, as it seeks to bring to expression the characteristic structures (*existentials,* in Heidegger's language) of man's immediate awareness of himself as a concrete, contingent being in interaction with the world. Phenomenology of this sort is called "hermeneutical" because it seeks to interpret the latent *meanings,* i.e., unveil the implicit structures, of man's being in the world, structures not evident to our normal self-understanding.

The relevance of this sort of phenomenology to our enterprise is obvious. We wish to examine actual lived experience, and to uncover there, as we believe is possible, the latent but

21 The classic example of this phenomenological "making manifest" of the latent, but to normalcy, the hidden structures of man's being in the world is, of course, Martin Heidegger's *Being and Time* (New York: Harper and Row, 1962), as is Jean-Paul Sartre's *L'Être et le néant* (Paris: Gallimard, 1943). In both, the object of phenomenological analysis differs from that of Husserl's investigations in three ways: (1) Human being is substituted for pure consciousness and its structures. (2) It is the latent, hidden, and forgotten in experience that is sought for. (3) The goal of inquiry is an ontology. In other words, instead of a description of manifest essences or appearances, phenomenology appears as a method for discovering the hidden but universal structures of man's being; in this sense, it is a *hermeneutic* of experience. See Spiegelberg's somewhat dubious attitude toward this deviation from Husserl's phenomenology, *Phenomenological Movement,* vols. I, II, pp. 301ff., 481ff., and 491ff., and finally 691ff.

pervasive and immensely significant dimension of ultimacy and sacrality which forms the continual horizon of man's being in the world. Our purposes are, therefore, not immediately concerned with the ontological structures of man's being in the world; ours will not be an "ontological" analysis. We are concerned with our experiences of ultimacy as an aspect of our ordinary existence; we shall, therefore, conduct an "ontic" analysis, hoping to uncover the sacral dimension in man's secular life, the shape or character of the horizon of our existence as this is directly apprehended and experienced in our actual life.[22] Since such an "object" is and can never be directly "manifest" in an essence in the stream of experience, a *hermeneutical* process must be undertaken to uncover it. As we shall see, the essential character of the religious dimension is that it manifests itself in secular experience negatively and at best indirectly, *through* other things that appear directly.[23] We must, therefore, establish its

[22] The concept of a "fringe" or "horizon" to experience, that which lies behind, undergirds, and manifests itself through what appears directly, is common in phenomenological thought. "It can never," says Husserl, "be the direct object of intuition, but it can be brought into the light of intuition, and understanding of it and clarity about it can therefore grow." *Ideas*, p. 220. The same sense of an infinite horizon within which each experience subsists, which cannot itself become an object of eidetic study, but can be clarified by "an indefinite number of perspectival views," is expressed by Merleau-Ponty in "The Primacy of Perception," *Phenomenology*, p. 16. Our own effort is to bring to enough provisional clarity the character of that horizon or background of totality in order to establish that character as one of ultimacy and sacrality.

[23] As we shall see, the definition of religious language is that which is multivalent or symbolic in this special sense, namely a language that refers *both* to a finite entity, event, or person that does "appear," and the sacred that appears *through* it. Religious language is initially about things, but about them as manifesting a dimension of ultimacy beyond and in them. Thus, for phenomenological method, the uncovering of this dimension must be hermeneutical, i.e., a method that can move into and then through what directly appears to what appears *in* it, the sacred; hence its essentially negative and indirect character as a phenomenological inquiry. Needless to say, the use of the word "hermeneutic" to designate an examination of actual *experience* to find its latent sacred elements—and so the possible use of religious symbols—is almost the reverse of the usage of Paul Ricoeur. He uses the word "hermeneutic" to designate an analysis of religious *symbols* to see what they say to us about actual ex-

presence in terms of the *meanings* of our ontic feelings, the tones of our living, and our behavior patterns, i.e., by a hermeneutical process of investigation. Such a process has no element of exact science or of apodictic certainty about it; it is tentative and hypothetical at best, a proposal for an intuitive recognition that, in this specifically delineated way, the level of sacrality *does* appear in our ordinary existence. With the entire phenomenological tradition, though in a slightly different way, therefore, we assert the ultimate authority of intuition, or, in Whitehead's language, disclosure; as Husserl said: *"Immediate seeing [Sehen]*, not merely the sensory seeing of experience, but *seeing in general as primordial dator consciousness of any kind whatsoever,* is the ultimate source of justification for all rational statements."[24] In this case, our "establishment" of the presence of a dimension of ultimacy in ordinary experience by means of an analysis of our relevant experiences, moods, and behavior that make manifest this dimension, rests solely on our "seeing" for ourselves that we *do* experience this dimension, that it does in fact appear in its strange way in the experience of all of us. Analysis can disclose what is there and point to it; it cannot prove that it is there. Most philosophy has recognized this function of analysis and this limit to the possibilities of argument.

Finally, let us note that the phenomenological reduction, the *epoche* or bracket, so essential to phenomenological method, is very relevant to our needs. This reduction, as we recall, shut out questions of "explanation," of the reality and the ontological structure lying behind what appears. Though we *are* here concerned with our apprehension of the reality of our actual being in the world, and assume it, nevertheless as we made plain, we are not here interested in an ontology of the divine or of God, in fact in any sort of ontology. This is for two reasons. In the first place, we wish, with Husserl, to bracket out those naturalistic or

perience. Cf. *The Symbolism of Evil.* It also differs from the theological use of the term in Ebeling and in Fuchs, where it specifies (1) a hermeneutical analysis of the Word-event of faith and not of ordinary experience, and (2) where it emphasizes the (to me) strange ontology of the "linguisticality of reality" rather than the categories of existing or being, of process, of relatedness, and of experiencing, which to us lie ontologically behind and so make possible any "linguisticality."

[24] Cf. Husserl, *Ideas,* pp. 75–76.

secular assumptions about reality and truth that preclude our looking at the actual character of experience and finding there a dimension of ultimacy. And secondly, we do not wish in our prolegomenon to assume or to establish, in fact to treat directly at all, the question of the existence or actual character of the divine or of God, the question of the validity of particular religious propositions or claims. For reasons already explained and to be elaborated further, that is the task of systematic theology and not of prolegomenon. We wish only to show that a dimension of ultimacy does appear in our ordinary life and thus does give meaning to, and in fact provide the necessity for, religious symbols. The phenomenological *epoche* thus complements the linguistic distinctions between meaning and validity (1) by freeing us to look candidly at experience, (2) by defining the limits of our prolegomenon as concerned with appearances and their appropriate language and not with explanations, ontological, theological, or philosophical. In sum, by making the possibility of a relevant analysis of experience possible which will establish the meaningfulness of the symbolic discourse of religion, the *epoche* is fundamental to our prolegomenon and separates it definitively from the complementary but nevertheless quite different task of systematic theology.[25]

[25] The relevance of Husserl's phenomenological reduction to an investigation of religious language in its *meaningfulness*, if not its *validity*, is plain from the following: "Geometry and phenomenology, as sciences of pure essence, know nothing positive concerning pure existence. It hangs together with this, that clear fictions do not only serve these sciences for a foundation as well as do data of actual perception and experience, but to a certain extent even better. Now if phenomenology also has no existential judgments to make concerning experiences . . ." *Ideas*, p. 206. In such an investigation, all the religious symbols, positive and negative, plural and singular, ours and theirs, can be investigated with regard to the dimension of our experience to which these all refer, without raising the question whether this one or that, or any of them, is ontologically *true* or not. That question is not a question of prolegomenon, and thus our prolegomenon is *not* a natural theology. As we shall see in chapter V, the eidetic reduction in the phenomenological tradition we find more relevant as an aspect of the task of systematic theology, where the Biblical and traditional symbols must be examined for their "meanings" and related to the experiences of ordinary life structured by our present hermeneutical analysis.

Phenomenology, therefore, provides to us many and significant rules of the road for our enterprise. We shall attempt a hermeneutical analysis of our ordinary experience of our being in the world, seeking to make manifest what is frequently hidden in and to that experience, but manifest on the prereflective level of awareness, and so evident to intuition in the total and behavioral patterns of our life. We shall do this to see where and how an ultimate or sacral dimension appears in that experience, bracketing out the question of the reality of its referent or the character of its being, and seeking thereby only to establish the nature and the function of those symbols necessary for the thematization and so the comprehension of that level of our experience. Whether this is or not "phenomenology" we hardly dare to say; that we have been helped by this tradition, as by many of the aspects of language philosophy, will be evident at each step of the way.

5. The fifth introductory element of our methodological proposal concerns some further clarification of the sort of language we intend with the phrase "religious discourse." And by this we do not mean a separate system of words called "religious," but a religious *use* of language, and so an unusual usage of ordinary words and grammar in some special "situation" or region of experience. There is no religious language in the precise sense, but only a religious usage of ordinary language. We mean to go about this defining process in two interrelated ways, which together will provide a rough, preliminary definition of the sort of usage of words and symbols that constitutes religious language. We are going to ask (*a*) in what sorts of situations is this religious usage of language appropriate—when do we, if we do, use it, and why do we use it there? And (*b*) the correlated question: What elements of felt or lived experience do these symbols, so used, thematize, what ranges or regions of experience does this form of language symbolize and so make meaningful?[26]

[26] According to Urmson, J. L. Austin spoke of an "area of discourse," i.e., "terms are part of a single area of discourse if it is of interest to compare or contrast their employment, and if not, not." A list of such

The forms of religious discourse are, of course, almost infinite, and the essential character of their family resemblance is therefore extremely elusive. Not all concern God-figures, as Hinayana Buddhism demonstrates; not all concern something ultimate or even transcendent, as the political pragmatism of popular Chinese religion shows; nor are all primarily ethical or even existential in character, as Greek and Roman myths indicate. Thus any definition is at best an approximation, almost certainly contradicted by some legitimate form of religious language. Further, even within one religious tradition there are almost as many varieties and types of language as there are theologies; consider, for example, the vast difference in the use of the word "God" in literal fundamentalist speech from that of a modern philosophical theologian. A description of types of religious language, of the way religious symbols have functioned in thematizing man's understanding of himself, his world, and the gods would thus be endless, a task for the historian of religion and the historian of doctrine. Such a task, however, even if we could accomplish it, would not be completely relevant to our present purpose. That purpose is not to describe historical forms of religious discourse, but rather to show the relevance, meaning, and even necessity of this family of language to modern secular man, and specifically to the felt meanings his life enjoys. If this is *our* question with regard to the meaning of this language, then it needs only a brief and relevant definition so that we know in general the sort of usage of language we are dealing with and so where to look for the region or area of experience to which it might relate.

---

areas included discourse about responsibility, or perception, or meaning, and so on. J. O. Urmson's essay, "J. L. Austin," in R. M. Rorty, *The Linguistic Turn* (Chicago: University of Chicago Press, 1967), p. 233. In somewhat the same vein, Gustav Bergman refers to "areas of our experience": "The ideal language . . . must show, in principle, the structure or systematic arrangement of all the major areas of our experience." "Two Criteria for an Ideal Language," in Rorty, *ibid.*, p. 134. With much the same intention, we refer to "ranges or regions of experience," seeking, as these two philosophers have done, to delimit our scope to those "areas" in which religious discourse is appropriate and applicable, and yet not thereby to imply that it is a separate or isolated or unrelated region.

First, it is essential to note that an intelligible religious use of language is an unusual and strange use of words. That is to say, it is not like any of the other kinds of usage in ordinary discourse, and so cannot be fitted easily or simply into any of the other, more familiar categories: empirical or factual, abstractive, performative, moral, self-involving, or aesthetic. Unlike commonsense or scientific assertions, what is usually called "empirical" language, religious discourse is not directed primarily at informing us about or even explaining space-time events or matters of fact, or concerned with describing the character or delineating the order of interrelations within the space-time nexus —though on occasion, to its ultimate sorrow, it has sought to do just that. Its modes of meaning and its forms of validity are thus different from those of ordinary empirical assertions of what is the case in the world around us.[27]

Religious language, moreover, is not, like mathematical language, purely connotative or analytic in character, dealing only with abstract concepts and their meanings—though admittedly theological discourse, the reflective wing of religious language, often sounds that way. Nor is it purely imaginative, seeking only to spin out dreams and symbols as the artistic and literary fancy might dictate. The gods referred to by religious symbols are not regarded as universals, as intellectual or imaginative abstractions;

[27] This is where the frequent linguistic descriptions of religious language as "nonempirical" and therefore "nonassertive" or "noncognitive" are both right *and* wrong. They are right in that religious language is not essentially designed to provide a description of the observable world; it thus is not a part of the language game of ordinary empirical assertions of the type either of common sense or of science. And it is misunderstood if it is so interpreted; then, as positivism has shown, it *is* meaningless—i.e., a category mistake of the first order has been made. As we noted, this is the real problem with Hicks's attempt to understand religious language in terms of the empirical verification criterion. On the other hand, religious language *is* assertive, and thus, though it be (in the sense above) "nonempirical," is it *not* noncognitive; and it is misunderstood again if it is so labeled, as do Flew, Hare, Braithwaite, and van Buren. The question of the possibility or meaning of religious language is, of course, the question of the possibility of assertive statements that are in *this* sense "nonempirical," that do not inform us of "matters of fact" but only of the essential depth or ultimate structures of what is.

even in the most refined philosophical theologies, such as Thomism, this is denied.[28] On the contrary, religious language is necessarily assertive. It does not, while functioning *religiously*, concern merely pretty or salty stories, fables, or artistic or moral allegorical homilies—religious mythology becomes this only for later ages for whom the religious character of the myth has dissolved. Many propositions, though not all, in religious discourse claim to say something about the nature of the real, and thus they purport both to give expression to some form of cognition and to be classifiable according to the canons of truth and falsehood; and such a claim is not characteristic of the language of mathematics or of imaginative art. For many of the same reasons, religious language is not exclusively a pious form of moral discourse, though it is related to the latter; or even of "performatory," promissory, or self-involving discourse—forms of discourse which, respectively, assume an allegiance to a set of moral principles,[29] or which seek to evoke personal commitment.[30] Religious language, as we shall see, is intimately related both to moral attitudes and to self-involvement; but again it differs from each of these (as Ramsey and Evans know but apparently Braithwaite and van Buren do not) by the way this moral and existential commitment is related to the fundamental assertions about reality which religious language inevitably makes. The same can be said for aesthetic discourse: wonder and praise are each a part of religious language, but they are present there in a unique way, quite different from their appearance in response to a work of art. If we are, then, to be clear on what *differentiates* the use of words and symbols in religion from the empirical, mathematical, moral, existential, and aesthetic uses of them, the "language games" of ordinary experience, and what makes each of these usages slightly different when they appear within the context of

[28] Cf. St. Thomas, *Summa Theologica*, First Part, Q. 3, Art. 5 and 8, especially Objection 2.

[29] R. B. Braithwaite, *An Empiricist's View of Religious Belief* (New York: Cambridge University Press, 1955), p. 19; cf. also van Buren, *The Secular Meaning of the Gospel* (New York: Macmillan Company, 1963).

[30] Cf. Ian Ramsey, *Religious Language* (London: SCM Press, 1957), pp. 37 and 47; and, of course, Donald Evans' excellent *Logic of Self-Involvement* (London: SCM Press, 1963).

religious discourse, we must discover what areas of experience religious language as a whole intends to symbolize and thematize, or, in ordinary language, to what sorts of referents, supposed or real, its assertions aim to point. And secondly, we must discover how these characteristic assertions of religious language are related to these other ordinary forms of speech—for there is no other form of speech that purports to make just these sorts of assertions about what is real in the system of things.

While it is in its own way different from each of these types of ordinary discourse, religious language necessarily has relations to each of them. For it is less a unique type of its own than a way of speaking in each of these other modes: assertive, abstractive, moral, existential, and aesthetic. There is, first of all, no statement in religious discourse that is not in *some* way "empirical" or referential to some entity within space-time, or some aspect of entities there.[31] It always in some way talks about what "is the case in the world," about a bird, a mountain, a force or aspect of nature, the cosmos, an historical event, a people and their history, a man, an aspect of man (spirit), history itself, a book, an institution, wine, bread, etc. There is no "pure" speech about the divine, totally transcendent to nature, man, and history,

[31] More than any other scholar, Mircea Eliade has clarified for us the historical character of religious discourse as a language game made up fundamentally of *symbols*, i.e., of words (*a*) referent to finite actualities such as a stone, water, moon, birth, death, and so on; and yet (*b*) speaking of such activities in such a way as to refer to what transcends them and yet appears within and through them. In religion, finite things mediate a sacred and ultimate reality that manifests itself in and through them. Hence religious language refers both to the finite medium and the sacred that is manifested. "A thing becomes sacred insofar as it embodies (i.e., reveals) something other than itself." "In fact, this paradoxical coming together of sacred and profane, being and nonbeing, absolute and relative, the eternal and the becoming, is what every hierophany [manifestation of the sacred], even the most elementary, reveals." And, "Thus, firstly, symbolism carries further the dialectic of hierophanies by transforming things into *something other* than what they appear to profane experience to be: a stone becomes a symbol for the center of the world, and so on; and then, by becoming symbols, signs of a transcendent reality, those things abolish their natural limits and instead of being isolated fragments become parts of a whole system." Mircea Eliade, *Patterns in Comparative Religion* (New York: Meridian Books, 1963), pp. 13, 29, and 452 respectively.

for even the mystics who "know" God directly and so through no finite mediation, characteristically use negative language as they vanish and then become quite silent when their act of uniting or being absorbed has been completed.[32] But in religious discourse inclusive of the finite, we speak about the finite in a different way, with a different interest than in ordinary empirical language. Not, as we saw, to communicate empirical information about the finite entity, but as if we were talking about what is beyond and yet within it, a deeper dimension, a transcendent level to which in this case the finite gives access.[33] The finite here is included, but as itself a "symbol" of something beyond itself, and

[32] For example, Schleiermacher's insistence that the infinite is always experienced by us and so spoken about, in relation to some particular aspect of the finite in experience, *The Christian Faith* (Edinburgh: T. & T. Clark, 1928), para. 5; and similarly Tillich's discussion of the necessity of the *concrete* character of any embodiment of the divine, *Systematic Theology* (Chicago: University of Chicago Press, 1951), Volume I, 211ff., and 218ff. For this reason, "nonsymbolic language" about God, if it is ever to be found, is only possible at a point of *identity* between God and the finite, not at a point where the transcendent is mediated through the finite. Then, however, there is no longer analogical speech based on a hierophany in the finite; on the contrary, there would be no anchor to analogical speech but the total lack of speech, because all finitude, and so all discourse, have disappeared within the absolute. For the mystical silence when all such finite mediation and contact ceases, when all subjects and objects of ordinary experience are transcended, cf. Plotinus, *Ennead*, III, viii, x; and V, v, sections 4–8. The same emphasis upon the unnameability of the transcendent when all relations to finitude have vanished appears in the Upanishad, Brihad-Aranyaka Upanishad 2.4.14, 3.4.1, 3.8.2, 3.9.27, and 4.4.22. And finally, in F. H. Bradley the same point is made with regard to the unnameability and the unknowability of the Absolute, *Appearance and Reality* (Oxford: Clarendon Press, 1946), Chapters XXVI and XXVII.

[33] Eliade defines this "transcendence" which the finite symbol manifests as follows: "Nowhere in the history of religions do we find an adoration of any natural object in itself. A sacred thing, whatever its form and substance, is sacred because it reveals or shares in ultimate *reality*. Every religious object is always an 'incarnation' of something: of the *sacred*." *Patterns*, p. 158. And, "Under whatever form the divinity manifests itself, he or she is ultimate reality, absolute power, and this reality, this power, will not let itself be limited by any attributes whatsoever." *Ibid.*, p. 421.

it is talk about it in relation to the *beyond that appears within it* that constitutes religious discourse.[34] Religious language is thus first and foremost multivalent, or symbolic in a special sense; its symbols have a double intentionality.[35] A religious symbol points, on the one hand, to an ordinary object, event, or person and thus intends that "matter of fact": a storm, a birth, an historical event, a man, a scriptural document, an institution. But it is *religious* precisely because, in this case, this verbal sign for a finite referent also points beyond its finite object to the dimension of sacrality, of infinity, ultimacy, and unconditionedness, to a holy

[34] The author first apprehended this multivalent character of religious language as a climber of the sacred mountain of Japan, Fujiyama. As he then realized, the *religious* speech by a Shintoist about that mountain is not like the speech of a geologist, an engineer, a tourist, or even the "secular" mountain climber himself, admiring as the words of all of these might well be. And yet the former is certainly speech inclusive of the mountain itself and its natural characteristics. Nor does *religious* language about a "god," for example a wooden image of a seated Buddha, resemble the connoisseur's or the craftsman's language about the wooden figure in which the god resided, though all are in a way talking about the lovely entity before us. In a somewhat different way, Judeo-Christian language about God is about the finite in its relation to what transcends it: the created world, the event of Exodus, the history of Israel, the Incarnate One, and the Church—but not as the scientist, the historian, the archaeologist, or the sociologist would speak about them. It is speech about the presence and activity of *God* there, not about these finite entities in themselves: and thus appropriately its language is about these entities or facts, is "mythical," and then "doctrinal" language. Many of the difficulties of religious discourse center around the puzzling interrelations of these two forms of speech about the finite "media": ordinary scientific and historical speech about the entity or events (e.g., the historical events of Israel's life) and religious or theological speech about that entity or those events in relation to God (the "mighty acts of God" in Israel).

[35] Ricoeur, *Symbolism,* p. 11. As Ricoeur notes further, symbolic and mythical representation is necessary because the religious dimension, while manifested within ordinary experience, transcends the level of ordinary experience, thus it is the function of such representation to lift our awareness of the immediate beyond the "obvious" to the deeper meanings inherent in experience. "The experience [of fault] subsists only in connection with *symbols* that place fault in a totality which is not perceived, not experienced, but signified, aimed at, conjured up." *Ibid.,* pp. 170–171.

that is manifest in and through this finite medium. And all religious language has this multivalent character as symbolic of a sacrality within and yet beyond the observable world of things and people. It is, of course, for this reason that religious language is regarded as superstitious and nonsensical in a secular age that recognizes only monodimensional language as intelligible.

It follows from this multivalent, polysemic character of religious language that abstractive elements—the use of universals—are also a part of this language. Religious discourse cannot *just* point: its definitions are not and cannot be merely ostensive. As we have seen, the transcendent or sacred does not directly "appear" as an entity in experience, and what appears, the idol, the mountain, the historical event, is not in itself the concern of this language in the precise way it might be for the curio dealer, the geologist, or the historian. Thus we must point *and* speak about a finite medium, and the speech used must have double intentionality, i.e., it must carry the hearer's mind beyond the medium or deeper within it to what is sacred, peculiarly religious, and so not merely profane or creaturely there. The pairs: Word (or kerygma) and historical event; Word and scriptural book; Word and sacrament; myth and idol; myth and ritual—and the elaboration of the first of each of these pairs into theology as disciplined reflection—are natural and universal parts of religious discourse.[36] Furthermore, as we noted, this abstractive language, whether in narrative, mythical, or philosophical form, is never an end in itself, as in mathematics, fantasy, or art. Abstractive language here is a linguistic means by which that which resides in but also transcends the finite-medium or symbol is talked about: it is a vehicle of a language game of assertions about a removed, hidden, or different character of reality. This abstractive aspect of religious language is the tool with which religious discourse talks about the sacred which is in the finite, the transcendent that is there, noted, and worshipped, for it is only through

---

[36] It is because of this necessity of both act and speech, thing-symbol and Word, event and kerygma, ritual and theology that we suspect that Rubenstein's attempt to revitalize Jewish liturgy without either the God of the Jews or any comparable "mythos" is doomed to failure; cf. Part I, Chapter 4, above.

abstraction, and through the unveiling and the universalizing enterprise that abstractive language makes possible, that speech can reach toward the ultimate and the unconditioned. That ultimacy or unconditionedness, which manifests itself as the sacred within the finite, characterizes the final referents of all religious discourse.

Finally there are existential and moral usages of language here. As we shall see, the character of that which appears in the finite and is here talked about, or to, in wonder, praise, repentance, entreaty, and submission, or described to self and others in myth, saga, sermon, or teaching, is such that it involves us totally because on it we are totally dependent. Its power, goodness, and character are such that it is the foundation of all we are and value: perhaps of our food, protection, life, being, mores, or salvation. Thus, if we speak of it *religiously*, it is of ultimate concern to us as having to do with our very being and nonbeing, as Tillich insisted, and we are consequently totally involved with it so soon as its presence or relation to us is recognized. The ultimate here then becomes sacred, namely that on which our being and all our values depend, that which founds all that concerns, delights, helps, or saves us.[37] Consequently, discourse about it, religious discourse, involves within its scope the language of commitment, of self-involvement, existential language. But in religion the language of involvement and commitment functions always in relation to this transcending element of which we have spoken. As a consequence of this, finally, religious language is moral; such a fundamental relation of our being as this involves, implies new and ultimately significant standards, or put more concretely, models for our significant behavior. There norms appear in relation to all that is relevant to this divine power, and, if

[37] Again, Eliade makes clear that, for the primitive religious mind, the sacred in all its forms is the *foundation* for the profane in all its aspects, and thus for all that is of value in the normal life of man: his life, food, space, time, and so on. It is because of this absolute dependence on the sacred as the fount of all values that what man "ought" to do, i.e., his models or exemplars, is also patterned after the sacral structures in which things originate. Thus do his morals stem from the sacred as he apprehends it. See Eliade, *Patterns*, pp. 11–12, 31ff., and especially 410–431.

it be an *almighty* power, they necessarily cover every important facet of our life. Moreover, if the sacred be the foundation of all of our profane life, then our relation to the sacred will determine the patterns of our behavior in every secular realm. For this reason, every religious symbol or myth entails "models" for our existence, patterns of sacrality by means of which man comprehends the forms of his human excellence and so by which he patterns his life and that of his society. Religious discourse, therefore, does entail moral norms, models for man's cultural life, and consequently, it includes discourse related to personal moral stances and ethical perspectives. And insofar as no culture can exist without imagined forms of human excellence by which its life is guided, in just so far even a secular culture lives by its religious myths and images of man.

As this brief descriptive analysis of the discourse of man's religions has shown, while religious usages of language participate in and use almost all ordinary forms of speech, religion does something peculiar with each of these, and that peculiar twist has been given to it by the object or referent of that language, and the relation in life to that referent which the language presupposes and expresses. The essential core, insofar as we can find it, of this language thus lies here: in what it has sought to talk about. To put this point in the terms of our present discussion, the essential element of religious language is that peculiar region or range of experience to which it points and which it seeks to symbolize, a range of experience different from that with which other forms of discourse seek to deal, qualitatively different from the profane, as Eliade says, yet manifest in and through it.[38] That region of experience with which religious language deals is constituted by a level of ultimacy or of unconditionedness; it is concerned with that which transcends and so undergirds the ordinary sequences and relations of life, with, therefore, the holy and the sacred. This is, needless to say, precisely that system of language which has been effectively excluded from the realm of intelligible speech by the development of the secular spirit, and so which has been called "dead" by radical theology. And as their examples showed, without this element in its language,

[38] *Ibid.*, p. 30.

Christian theology ceased either to be consistent or to be Christian.

The character of this language as referent to the unconditioned, the transcendent, the ultimate—or whatever in a given
community's experience is taken to have these characteristics—
has differentiated it from other types of discourse. This separation from "secular" language has been recognized by many symbols or concepts descriptive of the linguistic forms of religious
speech and they are embedded within almost all forms of religious discourse itself. I refer to such categories as mystery, hiddenness, sacredness, holiness, transcendence, and silence; unveiling, revelation, paradox, analogy, orthodoxy, and heresy; and
there are many others. Whenever these symbols or concepts appear and are used with their essential meanings, there a form of
religious discourse has appeared.[39] The differences which are
here symbolized between this and other more ordinary types of
language do not mean, however, that this language game is either
totally separated from ordinary forms of speech, or that it lacks
meaning, for there are many different types of legitimate and
meaningful speech thematizing different regions of our expe-

[39] These concepts can, of course, be secularized and so lose their
characteristically differentiating function from other language games:
for example, "mystery" can become "what is not yet known," a problem
or a puzzle rather than what is essentially mystery because (1) it is transcendent to ordinary forms of knowing, and (2) it involves or grasps
us and therefore cannot be objectively investigated, manipulated, and conquered, as can other aspects of experience. For example, see the discussion of what is *essentially* mysterious in religious revelation in Tillich,
Systematic Theology, I, pp. 108–111; and the discussion of the same
subject in Emil Brunner, *Revelation and Reason* (Philadelphia: Westminster, 1946), Chapter I; and Gabriel Marcel's distinction between
a mystery and a puzzle in "The Ontological Mystery," *The Philosophy of
Existence* (London: Harvill Press, 1948).

Usually, therefore, where such symbols or concepts having to
do with "revelation," mentioned in the text, appear, there a religious dimension and so religious discourse has arrived. For example, the Marxist
internecine debates center about the issues of orthodoxy and heresy or
revisionism, and not about the issue of what is simply true or false, practical or impractical, prudent or foolish. Insofar as this issue comes to
the center, the dimension of ultimacy, of total involvement, of the sacred
(in scripture, tradition, church, or party) has manifested itself, and one
has a "religious" as well as a political, economic, and social form of discourse.

rience.[40] The meaningfulness of a mode of speech is established so long as we can exhibit by analysis the general rules and patterns of this usage, the ranges of experience which these symbols clarify, and some legitimate and useful means of validating what assertions are made therein, i.e., what one *does* with these words, how these symbolic forms thematize *ordinary* experience, and what *criteria* of truth and falsehood they offer.

To sum up, then, we may define religious language as fundamentally referent to the ultimate, the unconditioned, and the holy or sacred as these manifest themselves in human experience. Consequently all religious discourse has three characteristic features which tend to discriminate it from other types of language: (1) It is multivalent or doubly intentional, referring both to the finite world and to the sacred and the ultimate that is manifest in and through the finite. (2) It is concerned with existential or ultimate issues of life, the questions that involve us because they center around the security, meanings, frustrations, and hopes of our existence both individual and social. (3) It provides crucial models or norms by which life is directed and judged, and so by which culture as a whole is itself guided and assessed. Wherever these elements of speech appear, there is religious language. Insofar as these elements are humanly inescapable, such forms of discourse are also essential for all creative life, and insofar as a culture will not recognize these inescapable and foundational themes in its life, and has no symbolic forms with which to bring them to light, in just so far is that culture impoverished.

[40] This point is, of course, primarily the work of the later Wittgenstein: "But how many kinds of sentences are there? . . . There are *countless* kinds: countless different kinds of use of what we call 'symbols,' 'words,' 'sentences.' And this multiplicity is not something fixed, given once for all; but new types of language, new language-games, as we may say, come into existence, and others become obsolete and get forgotten." (23) "Philosophy may in no way interfere with the actual use of language; it can in the end only describe it. But it cannot give any foundation either. It leaves everything as it is." (124) "The paradox disappears only if we make a radical break with the idea that language always functions in one way, always serves the same purpose." (304) Wittgenstein, *Philosophical Investigations.* (Numbers in parentheses refer to paragraphs.)

If, then, historically the reference of religious language to the ultimate and the sacred has been its main characteristic, what relevance can this language have to ordinary secular life, when it is precisely the ultimate and the sacred that, according to secular self-understanding, are absent from modern experience? To what aspects of our secular experience can this language game now refer—for we agreed that this language game must relate to some felt aspect of our ordinary experience if these symbols were to mean anything to us? Do they appear in a laboratory, a travelog, in the stock market, the shopping center, or the family circle? On the contrary, have not all these gods of nature, community, agriculture, and the hearth, as well as the Lord of history and of covenant in whom our culture once believed, vanished from our midst? Does ultimacy appear to us in the twentieth century at all; is there any way in which the unconditioned, the transcendent, and the holy manifest themselves to secular men? This is the basic question of a prolegomenon to theology, for on it hangs the meaningfulness of religious discourse, its relevance to our ordinary experience, and so the life and not the death of the symbols of positive theological affirmation.

It is surely true that, for secular man, no ultimate confronts him either through an object in nature or even through an event or an institution in history; these have been relativized, pluralized, and thoroughly desacralized. Our suggestion is, however, that ultimacy has not thereby vanished—and could not vanish from modern experience. On the contrary, it is present, as it always has been in human life, as a base, ground, and limit of what we are, as a presupposition for ourselves, our thinking, our deciding, and our acting—all of which are, to be sure, relative. The ultimate or unconditioned element in experience is not so much the seen but the basis of seeing; not what is known as an object so much as the basis of knowing; not an object of value, but the ground of valuing; not the thing before us, but the source of things; not the particular meanings that generate our life in the world, but the ultimate context within which these meanings necessarily subsist. This range or region of experience is thus best indicated by four words—source, ground, horizon, and limit —that which is the presupposition and basis of all we are and do, of our experience of things, persons, and ourselves, and that which appears at the limits of our powers and capacities. Religious language is a way of talking of an area beyond and yet within the visible, sensible creaturely flux, where the ultimate origins and source of what we are is located, where the character of the existence in which we participate is ultimately determined, and so where our own role in existence as a whole is shaped. It points to and seeks symbolically to describe the contours of the ultimate horizon of our common being in the world.

The sacred, the ultimate, and the unconditioned, about which religious language seeks to speak, concern therefore the sources, the origins, the foundations, and the limits of our powers, capacities, and hopes. As we shall go on to suggest, there are in general four "situations" where this dimension of ultimacy appears in ordinary experience and so where this language is appropriately (and inescapably) used: (1) where the foundations of our being, of our meanings and our values, appear to us in the "given" which we do not create or control but which creates us and so represents the ground and limits of our powers; (2) when these foundational structures are threatened by Fate and we experience our absolute helplessness; (3) in the mystery of ambiguity as it appears within the midst of our own freedom and therefore quite beyond our own deliberate or rational control; and finally (4) this dimension appears in man's confidence and hopes despite these outer and inner threats to the security, meaning, and fulfilment of his life. Thus inevitably in any culture, secular or religious, religious discourse or myths appear in relation to the mysteries of our origins, our limits, our ambiguity and evil, and our hopes for the future. Correspondingly, these forms shape the basic joys, fears, values, and confidences of that culture, and in the end they dominate its practical decisions, its educational programs, its forms of human relation, and its interpretation of the mysteries of good and evil with which every society must in some manner cope.

In the Western tradition, of course, the symbol "God" has been the sole "name" by which this ultimate, transcendent, and sacral dimension has been thematized and comprehended, and so the sole religious form in terms of which the origins,

limits, and hopes of life have been comprehended. The linguistic meaning of theistic monotheism has been the reduction
of all alternative symbols of ultimacy to this one proper name.
We must recognize, however, that there have been many other
symbols that have been used to thematize this region of ultimacy
that penetrates all human experience. The gods, great and small,
of religions are examples of this: the Kami, Mana, Dionysius,
Zeus, Shiva, Vishnu, Kwanyin—and so on infinitely. Other
types of symbols express in different modes the same level of ultimacy, the origin and horizon of all experiencing: the One, Being,
Substance, the Whole, Process. All of these share the characteristics of ultimacy, transcendence, and sacrality—since it is from
them that all existence and values stem; and consequently each
functions in our discourse about our existence, its structures, and
its destiny, in much the same way. Such symbols may be partly
defined in precise or univocal language, but never fully; each
of these symbols preserves an essential area of mystery beyond
all symbolization that indicates the relation of this symbol to the
unconditioned to which it points. Positivism sought to eradicate
this whole range of discourse from philosophical language, and
failed. The metaphysical visions now being allowed back in
philosophical discussion must include some concept or symbol
expressive of this dimension, even if it be the mysterious "X"
which modern nonreductionist naturalism terms "Nature."

It is apparent that the depths of our experience to which
this language refers are not easy to scrutinize or to conceptualize.
There are, among others, two reasons for this opaque and mysterious character of all language about ultimacy: (1) As the
depth, ground, and limit of finite objects, this dimension cannot
be known in the same relatively precise manner as is the field of
objects itself. Direct sensory experience is not possible; defining and so limiting concepts are now not univocally applicable;
manipulation and testing are not available. Thus there is in this
area neither simple verification or falsification, nor precise definition. Above all, our symbols, directly applicable to the realm
of finitude, are only indirectly applicable to what is transcendent
to ordinary things and so to ordinary speech; to what is not an
object but the ultimate ground and limit of objects, the horizon

within which finite objects relate to us. Our speech here is un-avoidably evocative, diffracted, expressive, and often paradoxical —but by no means necessarily meaningless. If clarity and mean-ing in speaking of "what is" are not arbitrarily confined to speech about the plural things around us, but include as well their gen-eral ground or horizon, their source, limit, their ultimate order or structure, and their destiny, this inability of symbols to grapple *precisely* with this area is intelligible, and we can understand why, while the experience of the ultimate is "heavy" and of the utmost significance, it is by no means clear, definite, and easily discern-ible. (2) As the base and ground of *our* existing, knowing, valu-ing, doing, in fact of the being and meaning of our life, this region of experience involves *us* and so it involves and affects our thinking and speaking itself. Here resides that on which we ulti-mately and absolutely depend, since it provides the presupposi-tion for our powers and our values. Thus we are involved here— the question of the ultimate is a question about our own being; or, as Tillich said, in this region we do not *have* a question, we *are* the question. Thus again we cannot back off from this region and survey it, for both our powers of conceiving themselves and also the meaning and value of our life are at issue, since this is their source and ground.

To a culture that has assumed the "aseity" of human autonomy, that all our powers and choices are self-grounded in the contingent, that is ourselves, this region of ultimacy where these powers find their basis has seemed to be a land of unreal fantasy and irrelevance—as well as a threat to what such a culture meant by freedom. More knowable and practicable, and therefore more important, were the range and experience of empirical ob-jects which our intelligence and freedom can manipulate and comprehend. To us, this view of a world of objects without a horizon and of man as *"a se"* in himself and in his powers is against all the evidence. For there is no secular knowing or ma-nipulating, and no secular meaning to either activity, without this range of ultimacy which is the ground and context of all we know and do, all we fear and hope. This region is not properly *in* the world, but it is essential to the life of the world. It permeates all the world's comings and goings; it is the basis of all the world's

clarity and precision when it is about its important business; and
it certainly structures the world's goals. For this reason as the
foundation of our clarity and precision, and as that therefore in
which we are passionately involved because on which we are
ultimately dependent, this level of sacrality transcends the region
in which we can be clear and precise, in which our words have
clearly differentiated meanings and usages and recognizable public tests.[41] This is the region of the sacred, the holy, the ultimate,
the unconditioned with which religious discourse, in both its per-
sonalistic and its ontological, its religious and its philosophical
forms, deals.

Our experience, we believe, touches these depths, this region of ultimacy, at each crucial moment of our careers, and a
sense of their significance is always there, seen or felt, so to speak,
out of the corner of the eye. We hardly experience a significant
event, do an important action, or make a judgment that does not
make crucial and dependent reference to this area of ultimacy
that is the ground, horizon, and limit of our experience. Thus,
on our relations to and decisions concerning this realm, everything in our life that is of importance or value to us depends. For
this reason, this realm has not only the character of ultimacy, but
also of the sacred: It is the ground not only of being, but of
all value.

Correspondingly, a sense of loss here, of a void in which
no answers can be found at all, spells the loss of all sense of value

---

[41] This is, of course, precisely the point made by Stephen Toulmin in his important category of "limiting questions." When, he says, we
ask about the *foundations*, those presuppositions and assumptions that
ground our cultural activities such as morals, politics, or science, we have
moved to a type of question quite different from questions *within* the
patterns of reasoning, argument, testing, and demonstration of the activity itself. Here ordinary rational procedures and so ordinary linguistic
definitions are not possible—if they were, our question would not be a
"limiting" one concerned with the foundations of thinking, valuing, and
acting. Toulmin calls this a "religious" area of questioning, and so one in
which only faith can devise answers. Cf. Toulmin, *An Examination of
the Place of Reason in Ethics* (New York: Cambridge University Press,
1950), Chapter 14.

and meaning, and thus is the source of the deep undertone of anxiety in our life, and of its driving pressures on our nerves and capacities. On the other hand, it is from our experience of these depths that come whatever commitment, direction, potentiality and security our life may have. And surely it is plain that the evil man introduces into his world is generated here. What we do is evil because it harms life, especially human life. But the evil we do to one another has its peculiarly demonic, and therefore human, character precisely because, whether man wishes it or no, man injects this dimension of the ultimate into his actions within the common life. When we ask, then, *not*, "What do I see before me?" or "What use should I make of it?" but "Why am I?" "Who am I?" "What should I become and be?" "Why should I value truth and the good?" "What is the meaning and future destiny of my life and the history in which it participates?" "How can I be whole again?" and "What is the meaning of my death?" then we are exploring or encountering that region of experience where language about the ultimate, and so the language game that is called "religious discourse," becomes useful and intelligible.

In a secular prolegomenon, however, when we merely look into these depths, we find as yet nothing so definite as the God of Christian faith. At this point, the referent for this particular Christian symbol has not yet appeared. Rather, we are here only in the region of our experience where "God" *may* be known, and so where the meaningful usage of this particular symbol can be found, but also where, as we have noticed, not only may many other symbols be used to conceptualize our experience, but even more where the sacred may be experienced as totally silent or hidden. For there are many facets to this experience of ultimacy, as many as there are significant levels or aspects of our being in the world. And thus arise the multitude of religious symbols: of life, meaning, truth, value, commitment, judgment and mercy, death and eternity, each of them, in its wide variety of forms and connotations, pointing to some aspect of man's experience of this ultimate dimension. Also, our experience reveals as often as not the absence of God and so a sense of loss, of a Void where we are looking for something; but it is a special kind of a Void and a loss which, like our experience of sacrality, participates in the general character of this region of experience.[42] That character is best expressed, as we noted, by such words as "ultimate," "transcendent," and "unconditioned." For it is an unconditioned Void and loss, posing an ultimate threat to all we are and value, leaving us with nothing on which to stand, nowhere to turn and no way out, since the basis of our being and meaning has dissolved—a situation which modern literature and much existential philosophy, which have not at all discovered "God" anywhere, find not only meaningful but very real.

In an inquiry into the character of ordinary experience at this level, then, we uncover a point where human experience moves beyond the conditioned or creaturely to its ground, horizon, and limit, and so where we became aware that our finitude cannot provide the resolution we seek. Here we experience our own ultimate incapability; here we find we can only ask; we cannot ourselves answer. Thus there enters at this level the possibility of no answer at all, and so either the beginnings of despair or

[42] As we have noted, there are other contemporary symbols for this range of ultimacy in experience—for the source or ground or limit of our contingent and transient being—than God or its opposite, the Void. It could be said that, aside from such historically oriented symbols of ultimacy as Progress or the Material Dialectic, Nature is the other main contemporary secular symbol for this region. Both Nature (as understood in modern naturalism) and the Void (the common existentialist symbol) express the alienation of man from the cosmic source and ground of his existence, but they express this in different moods. Nature is, so to speak, the ultimate background of contingent, relative things taken intellectually (as science implies that background and source), and viewed contemplatively, serenely, and, as Santayana pleaded, "piously" as well. Since, however, Nature, so understood, is regarded as blind to our purposes and meanings, inexorable in its power, and utterly indifferent to our anxieties, ideals, and hopes, it still expresses in this contemplative mode the alienation of our humanity, if not of our bodies, from it. The Void is a symbol for the *same* horizon, only taken existentially, i.e., as to how that horizon *feels* in our actual self-awareness as existing beings, if not in all of our science and philosophy. When God is not known, then, History as development or dialectic, Nature, or the Void may be the central symbols by which man thematizes this range of experience.

of our own fanatical attempts to create an answer. Or, if some form of an answer appears to be given to us, it seems to come to us from beyond the creaturely and to participate in the transcendent character of this range of experience, to be, as we say, revealed or disclosed. To analyze these depths, then, is not necessarily to find "God"; a Void may be found there by our despair, or a demonic absolute may be found by our fanaticism. But what *will* be found is the category of the ultimate, the transcendence of the creaturely, negative and positive, and inextricably mixed with the finite as its ground, necessity, and limit. Such an analysis of secular experience is thus no demonstration of the reality of the Christian God. It is, however, a defense of the meaningfulness of the language game of religious discourse. For it is within this identifiable and familiar range of universal experience, in a region characterized by these contours known to every modern person and continually spoken of in the most secular human discourse, that religious symbols are intelligibly and meaningfully used.

Finally, let us be clear that, in seeking in this prolegomenon to relate religious symbols to cultural experience, we are not proposing what has often been called a "culture religion," i.e., a religion expressive simply of the symbolic forms of a particular culture and thus unable to judge or to transcend the life of that culture. What we are emphasizing is that, to be intelligible or meaningful, theological symbols must be related to ordinary and so to cultural experience. Now both men embedded within and so content with a particular culture and men in revolt against that culture participate in "historical" and so in "cultural" experience. The forms of their revolutionary or prophetic action, as well as of their thoughts about it, are as *cultural* and as *historical* as are those of their "conservative" neighbor. Part of the universal cultural and historical experience of man is precisely an experience of the injustice and the death of cultures, even of our own; and part of the history of culture is the history of criticism and of revolution. These experiences, relevant to the important religious symbols of judgment and eschatology, are surely as much "cultural" or "historical" as are the words and concepts with which we describe them. In fact it is, as we have said, precisely in an apprehension of its own limits, of the unconditioned threats to its being and meaning, and of its ultimate relation to value and so to a judgment from beyond itself, that culture becomes religious. For this reason, a prolegomenon relating religious language to cultural experience is as much a preparation for a "prophetic" as it is for a "cultural" religion.

3 / The Dimension of Ultimacy in Secular Experience: I

THE RANGE or aspect of common experience which we wish to uncover in this chapter is, we have said, not that in which finite objects appear to us in the web of relations that we have with them. For this reason, among others, the modern secular spirit has preferred to leave this region unthematized or forgotten as unreal because our ordinary language about things and relations did not seem to apply. The healthy secular concentration on being in the world has led to the limiting conclusion that the world of discrete, finite objects is all we have in important experience to talk about.

The result has been, as we shall endeavor to show, an impoverishment of the human spirit. For if we are right, secularism leaves significant and real areas of experience ignored. The deep sources of joy and serenity in life, the grounds on which we know both our place and ourselves, are unthematized and uncelebrated. Correspondingly, the ultimate sources of our most intense anxieties are unstructured for us, so that the whence of our deepest private and interior fears and the anatomy of our most frantic, foolish, and vicious public behavior remain in darkness, and we are left the vulnerable prey of demons we know not of. The virtual absence in modern secular life of fundamental symbols, myths, and rituals concerning our human origins, our identity, our values, and our destiny does not mean that anxiety about these matters is never present or questions about them raised. What it does mean is that pseudo-myths and futile an-

swers to these issues dominate our hopes and our fears. As current theology needs relevance to actual secular experience in
order that its often empty symbols attain vital and creative meaning, so secular experience, without consistent and profound religious symbolism, is blind. As a result, its joys are left uncelebrated and so unexperienced, and its terrors uncomprehended
and so unconquered.

It is our purpose in these next two chapters, then, to show
that, within ordinary secular experience, that deeper range, which
we have called that of ultimacy and which religious language
seeks to conceptualize, does appear; that in fact we are aware of
it; that many of our interior feelings and anxieties are concerned
with it; that our public or historical behavior is affected by it;
and that we do talk about it all the time, whatever our explicit
conceptualizations of experience may say or admit. If all this is
so, then religious symbolism of this range of experience is shown
to be both meaningful and necessary if life is to be human.

Let us first say something briefly about how we propose to
look, and then get down to it.

1. Clearly our search must be an "ontic" search, an examination of the shape of ordinary human experience in order to
find the dimension of ultimacy which we believe to be there.
Ontological analysis as a methodological possibility is, we have
said, itself dependent upon this dimension, since it proceeds only
on the basis of an ontic awareness of an ultimate coherence in
existence which is itself problematic today. Therefore we cannot begin with ontology.[1] We must start, then, with the concrete

---

[1] It will be noted by those familiar with existentialist philosophy
that our method involves an "ontic" rather than an "ontological" analysis,
that is, a description of the kinds of experiences human beings enjoy in
being in the world, rather than an analysis of the ontological structures of
either human being or Being generally. Clearly, an ontical analysis, if
valid, points beyond itself to an implied ontological view of both man
and Being generally; but this we are not explicating at this time. One of
the reasons is that, as mentioned in the text, the possibility of ontological
analysis is itself based on ontic experiences and decisions in the region of
ultimacy, namely the confidence in a universal logos in existence generally. Such a confidence cannot usefully be assumed in our day; prior to it,
the possibility of language about such an ultimate order must be shown,
and thereby the sources of such a confidence uncovered. Thus, logically

human experience of being in the world of nature and of society, and see if there, in that experience, this dimension appears.

2. Secondly, since ours *is* a secular culture, there are not present in our cultural life explicit and recognized media through which the sacred appears. Thus we can expect that this appearance will be covert rather than overt, appearing (*a*) as an *implication* of our feelings and our behavior patterns rather than a direct element within them, and (*b*) in turn these implications will appear largely in a negative rather than a positive form. Thus, as we have said, we need a hermeneutical analysis to uncover its presence. If, moreover, it be there but be not admitted or allowed in direct manifestation, which our remarks to date would lead us to suspect, the sacred will reveal itself mostly by its absence, and in traces within and effects upon our secular behavior. It is, therefore, for the traces and effects of this dimension in our ordinary feelings and behavior patterns, both in the private interior sphere and in our public historical life, that we will here search.

3. Thirdly, since our hypothesis is that a felt relation to the unconditioned horizon of experience is the ground or foundation of the *human* existence of all of us, it follows that such a relation accompanies our entire life and provides in each facet or level of our common life the basis for the peculiarly human tone to our existence. Thus, if we are right, we can find evidences of this dimension in each important aspect of human being: our existence, our search for meaning, our knowing, our valuing, and our search for identity, community, and hope. We shall, therefore, examine each of these fundamental areas in turn to see where and how, in both positive and negative guise, this dimension of ultimacy or sacrality appears in our experience of ourselves, our world, and our history.

4. Since this dimension is one of transcendence, appearing within the finite but manifesting something beyond the finite,

---

as well as prudentially, an ontic analysis must precede the ontological as the latter's possibility. It is this priority of the ontic over the ontological, providing the groundwork for theology, that distinguishes more than anything else (besides its relatively poor quality!) this analysis from that of Paul Tillich. For this distinction see Martin Heidegger, *Being and Time* (New York: Harper & Row, 1962), p. 31ff.

we see it, certainly, as the basis of our being in the world; nonetheless, we do not see it directly but continually only out of the
corner of our eye; it is there but at the depths of experience, at
its limits, on its edges. We confront this dimension explicitly
when our consciousness descends, so to speak, to explore the
foundations of our being in the world. And we do this whenever we ask, as we all must do in some mode or other, consciously
or unconsciously, those fundamental questions about the nature
and direction of our own being: who am I, what is it all about,
where am I going and why, and how can I become whole again?[2]
If it is in relation to this dimension of our existence that our creative powers emerge, that the meaning of our life is found, and

[2] The inescapability of these "ultimate questions" about our existence for modern secular as well as ancient religious man is well put
by Rubenstein in the following: "For every person who can look back on
his life and say, 'I'd do it the same way if I could do it over again,' there
are a hundred who have experienced a large measure of inner conflict,
turmoil, and defeat, no matter how outwardly successful they may appear. Few of them, few men of any condition can look with equanimity
on old age or death. It is not likely that any society will reduce the level
of realistic anxiety most men must endure. Men do wonder where they
come from, what is the meaning of life, and what shall be their ultimate
destiny." Rubenstein, *After Auschwitz* (Indianapolis: Bobbs-Merrill,
1966), p. 202.

    "Religious myth expresses many of the most abiding concerns
of human beings in every generation in a form that can be understood
by people of all levels of intellectual attainment. In all ages religion has
addressed itself through myth and ritual to such questions as 'What is my
origin? What is my destiny? How can I be cleansed of my guilt? What
is the meaning and purpose of life?' These are questions of ultimate
concern. The fact that myth and religious symbols no longer are regarded
as true at the manifest level is entirely irrelevant to their central function,
which is to give profound expression to our feelings at the decisive times
and crises of life." *Ibid.*, p. 233.

    John Wild puts the same point in terms of his phenomenological
existentialism: "To reflect upon these boundaries seriously is to raise the
ultimate questions of our existence. The way we face them reveals the
kind of being we are, for the way a finite being holds itself with respect
to its ultimate limits is the very core of that being. . . . But to be aware
belongs to the being of man. Hence, to become evasive or confused about
these limits is to confuse our existence at its very core." John Wild, *Existence and the World of Freedom* (Englewood Cliffs, N.J.: Prentice-
Hall, 1963), pp. 27–28.

that the fundamental tone of our life, be it one of joy and courage or one of despair, is determined, then we can expect the issues, crises, and feelings that give rise to these sorts of questions,
and the questions themselves, to emerge in all the significant
phases of our life—and this is what we shall seek to show.

One of the most striking things about our human existence in
this epoch is that we notice this relation to an unconditioned as
much by its absence as by its presence.[3] We become aware of the

[3] The revelation of being through negation, through an ontic
experience of its absence in anxiety, and then, in philosophy, through
asking the question of Being as opposed to nonbeing, saturates the
thought of Heidegger. Being, whether his own Dasein or the Being of
the beings, reveals itself to man through nullity and nonbeing. Cf. *Being
and Time*, chaps. 6 and 7, and *An Introduction to Metaphysics*, trans.
Ralph Manheim (New Haven: Yale University, 1959), chap. 1.

   Bultmann, in a neoorthodox context, makes the same point: "Is
he [man] acquainted with God because he has a *concept* of God? Not
in the least. *In it he has only reached the stage of an inquiry about God*;
and the knowledge contained in this inquiry is fundamentally none other
than *man's knowledge of himself*; a knowledge about what he has not
and is not, and yet of what he would like to have and to be; a knowledge
of the limitation and insignificance of man." Rudolph Bultmann, "The
Question of Natural Revelation," in *Essays* (New York: Macmillan
Company, 1955), p. 94.

   And Ebeling says much the same: "The question how God is
actually experienced, how it can become clear what God means in the context of the reality that encounters me, can be answered in the first instance
only by the pointer: God is experienced as a question. In the context
of the reality that encounters me, God encounters me as the question-
ableness of that encountering reality." Ebeling, *Word and Faith* (Philadelphia: Fortress Press, 1963), p. 347; see also *The Nature of Faith*
(Philadelphia: Muhlenberg Press, 1961), pp. 82–83. Tillich has powerfully put this point: "We are aware of the power of being through the
experience of the shock of non-being." *Systematic Theology* (Chicago:
University of Chicago Press, 1951), Volume I, pp. 110–115, 186–188.
Even the most positive apprehension of the divine comes to us from the
sense of negation, limit, or insufficiency on the level of the finite. This
aspect of the negation involved in the experience of the sacred—
as opposed to total absence—namely that the sacred appears when
the finite experiences its own limits and insufficiency, and thus knows
nonbeing, is probably the thread of continuity that runs through all
experiences of deity, primitive and modern, and which unites the modern consciousness of the absence of God with the primitive conscious-

problem of an ultimate source, an ultimate meaning or order in things, and so in the future, and an ultimate value to what we are and do—to what our tradition calls "the problem of God"— when we cannot seem to find them, when at our depths there seems to be only a painful Void. We are not sure what we expected to find there. If however, we find *nothing*, no foundational security or meaning in existence, then that nothing itself, as the now evident character of the horizon within which we exist, takes on an ultimate or an unconditioned quality. It ceases to be a "nothingness" temporarily resident within the secure whole of being; rather, it replaces Being and becomes the infinite Void threatening all we are and do. In relation, then, to such an experience of an infinity of nothingness, we feel a deep emptiness and anxiety, which may or may not be made explicit in despair. And this inner state of mind, of which we may only be aware in terms of the felt tone of anxiety, elicits from us the most strange sorts of behavioral reactions. When the coldness and infinity of the Void is felt, we look rather desperately for some means to fill up this infinite cavern or emptiness. It is in this situation that both the demonic and the meaningless, the fanatical and the despairing, appear as categories essential to any valid description of human existence. In these situations, we feel ourselves to be faced with a negative ultimate which threatens us, and our response to that apprehension is inevitably to search for some positive ultimate as an answer. And whether we create that ultimate in idolatry or lose it again in despair, we are searching for some aspect of ultimacy, for something unconditioned to give security, meaning, and direction to our lives. Our first certainty, then, of the reality of this dimension of experience comes from our sense of the terribleness of an ultimate emptiness, from the shattering effect of not finding anything sacred as the source and ground of our life. And much of what we do, like the debris on the surface of the ocean, reflects this cataclysm at the depths of our life.

Once, however, we have really begun to notice this dimension through an experience of its emptiness, then evidences

---

ness of the dialectic of the profane and the sacred. For the primitive apprehension of this dialectic, cf. Mircea Eliade, *Patterns in Comprehensive Religion* (New York: Meridian Books, 1963).

of a positive creative power resident in this dimension of ultimacy begin to appear in all facets of our life. We begin to notice,
to see, and to feel the immense creativity of the "given" in life,
those aspects of our being which neither we nor anyone else can
create and yet which are the foundation of all that we are and
love. It is this creativity of the given that other cultures have celebrated as the main positive or to-be-loved side of the ultimate or
the sacred. Common aspects of our experience: our deep joy in
living, a sense of the pulsating vitality and strength of life that
every creature knows; the awe at the common wonder and beauty
of life—perhaps in the creatures of nature or at the birth of a
child; the precious sense of meaning and of hope when we find
some purpose or activity that draws out our powers, and we know
who we are in history and why we are here at this time and place;
the wonder of community and of personal intercourse with another human being—these common experiences are given to us
and not created by us, but it is they which buoy us up, that make
us glad we are alive, that fill us with deep joy and refuel our
existence with a felt power—that are, in fact, the basis of all our
creativity. As gifts of existence, they reflect the power of life and
of meaning that come to us and in us from beyond ourselves,
from the ultimate source of power and meaning—though we
may never know that their source lay in this dimension of ultimacy. The dimension of ultimacy or of the sacred manifests itself,
we shall argue, both paradoxically in the negative terrors of the
Void without the sacred and so in the demonic sacralizing of the
profane, and in the positive creativity of the given on which
the values and capacities of our finite being and powers rest.[4]

Why do we call this range or level of experience—both
negative and positive—"religious," and why do we, in our tra-

[4] The relation of many classical symbols of deity or of the sacred
to this brief description of our common experience of it is obvious. Almost all of the great symbols of the divine have reflected this strong
negative-positive role, this weird combination of destruction and yet of
creation, of the power of life and the power of death—and yet of the
absolute dependence of all our values on this ultimacy that clearly transcends, often negates, and yet is the base of our values. The figures of
Shiva and of Dionysius, perhaps most profoundly of all, mirror this
dialectic; but, in a sense, every symbol of "God" has these same bewilder-
ing components.

dition, seem to imply that there is a relation of this ultimate source
and ground of our life to the symbol "God," and so to the language game of theological discourse? Why do we not just call
it the "natural world" or the "universe"? Are these not more
appropriate words for this horizon of our being from whence
both what we ultimately fear and what we are and enjoy finally
come? At this stage in our discussion, the reason is that, as we
shall subsequently try to show, the phenomenological character
of these experiences has a qualitatively different tone from our
experience of the system of finite things we investigate and call
the natural world or the universe. Inevitably, there appears in this
dimension a quality of the unconditioned, of the infinite, of
transcendence, of the ultimate, even of what we are calling the
"holy" or the "sacred," a quality which does not derive from
natural, finite things taken either separately or in systematic interrelations, and which in turn manifests itself as the basis or foundation of the being and the value of those things.[5]

We shall spell out more precisely in our discussion of
concrete experiences what the experiential or phenomenological
lineaments are to which these words "ultimacy" or "unconditionedness" point. Let us now merely summarize four elements
within its "appearance" that together characterize this range of

[5] Of course, any positive religion, and especially Christian faith,
goes much further in its descriptive discourse concerning the ultimate
than have these preliminary remarks. On the basis of its own special
forms of experience of this range of ultimacy (centering on the event of
Jesus Christ) Christian faith qualifies the character of the source of man's
existence and of his meaning with much more positive symbols, beginning with that of "God" and including such "personal" symbolic forms
as intentionality, purpose, love, knowledge, mercy, and so on. Such special language is not, I believe, derivable from our analysis so far; for
secular existence merely exhibits the dimension of ultimacy, and the
strangely negative-positive awareness of ultimate nonbeing and of ultimate Being, of the Void and of God. But that secular experience is suffused with this experience of ultimacy, and is shaped both negatively
and positively by it, of this we are sure; and thus is this language—the
kind of language we have called "God-language"—discourse appropriate to this dimension, and meaningful and intelligible even in a secular
age. One might, therefore, say that the symbols of Shiva and Dionysius
are in this sense more "secular" than is the classical Judeo-Christian symbol of "God."

experience and so serve to define those two words as we use them; we believe that each of these elements, when it appears, requires and so justifies the usage of such language. (1) Ultimacy appears in our experience, first of all, as the *source*, ground, or origin of what we are, and therefore of the finite and its characteristics. It has, therefore, neither the form nor the feel of an entity amidst the finite. Rather, in conditioning ourselves and other entities totally, it cannot be in turn conditioned by them—at least as another finite entity would be conditioned. More concretely, this experience of an unconditioned ground is manifested in the awareness that our being and its meanings are *given* to us; thus are we aware that they are not subject to the bidding, control, or direction of our intelligence or powers, but on the contrary are the foundation or presupposition of our possession and use of those powers. (2) Ultimacy also manifests itself in relation to an awareness of our *limits*, when we experience a fundamental or essential—not provisional or temporary—threat and helplessness. What is experienced here is again something we can neither create nor control; it is, rather, our limit, it is our horizon, our context, what controls us. On both counts, then, as ground and as limit, ultimacy appears as *transcendent* to our finite powers, and it is transcendent in both positive and negative roles, i.e., as paradoxically the source of all we are, as the ground or horizon of the given, and as an ultimate negation to all we are, as the limit and the threat of an infinite Void; and finally as the answer to that which thus threatens to engulf and overcome even our strongest powers and our most precious values. (3) In its positive role this principle of ultimacy is also the source and basis of our *values*; and consequently its loss spells the total eradication of all being and meaning, of all value whatever. Not only is it in relation to us transcendent and unconditioned, as the source of our being, and as a limit quite beyond our control; its value to us is also unconditioned since it manifests itself as the source of our values without which we are and have nothing. In this sense, it is appropriately called "sacred." (4) Because of these essential characteristics of source, limit, transcendence, and sacrality, and because of the strange dialectic of negation and affirmation involved in the experience of the ultimate, there is an element of *mystery* with regard to ultimacy, on the levels both of our experience of it and of our language about it. In terms of language, therefore, a need for a new mode of symbolization arises not evident in discourse about ordinary things over against us. Our relation to this dimension of ultimacy on which we depend, by which we are threatened, and through which we are rescued, is different from our relation to other things, and talk about it must likewise be different.

Precisely this union of categories pointing to ultimate reality, to ultimate value, and to ultimate mystery—as well as to an ultimate threat—has always indicated and so defined the sacred as experienced in specifically "religious" experiences. Our point in this discussion is that these *same* elements appear, albeit obliquely, in the center of secular experience as well, and they are manifest in relation to every important facet of our being. One consequence of this is that almost every philosophical expression of man's situation must use categories that illustrate most of these fundamental traits of the dim horizon of ultimacy within which man exists; even the naturalists capitalize the word "Nature" when they speak on this level, and pay homage to its essential mystery and creativity. This differentiating quality of unconditionedness, ultimacy, and sacrality appears wherever that which grounds and limits the finite and its values, and so threatens or rescues it at the deepest level, manifests itself in experience, and not unexpectedly this manifestation in ordinary life is continual and significant. It is this differentiating quality which, on the one hand, gives to this dimension in our experience its peculiar character, and which, on the other, causes the strange and unusual traits of the kind of language appropriate to this dimension, namely religious discourse.[6]

Now, however, our concern is briefly to describe some of those experiences in which the unconditioned depths of our existence, through an awareness both of its presence and its absence, reveals itself to us in our ordinary, day-to-day existence. To our secular age, this existence has seemed devoid of any relation to the ultimate; but in fact at every turn human experience mani-

---

[6] The anatomy of this peculiar characteristic of religious language is, we feel, perhaps best exhibited in the works of Ian Ramsey and then latterly in the work of Donald Evans.

fests itself as supported, qualified, and threatened because of this dimension. And it is precisely in relation to this level of ultimacy that the peculiar traits of the experience and behavior we call "human" appear. Every level of our life is so related to its ulti- mate ground; and so each level feels both the wonder, beauty, meaning, and joy of existence as it comes to us from transcen- dence, and the terror and emptiness of an ultimate Void. We shall try to point out as we go along how closely interrelated are these negative and positive aspects of this common experience of the unconditioned from which we come.[7]

We all love our own being, our existence, our life.[8] Humans are aware of many joys, of course, but underneath all of them there is the exultation in being alive, in feeling and using one's powers— of sensing, smelling, eating, loving, using one's body. Here we experience the sheer joy of being and of existing: here the reality and power of our *existence* are felt from the inside as joyful vitality.[9] And this inner and most vital joy is the center

[7] For reasons of space, we have omitted from these two chapters one significant aspect of our analysis, namely the effort to show the foundations of ultimacy in the activity of cognition or knowing. Since the capacity to know himself and his world is one of the central and unique powers of man, it is, we recognize, incumbent on us to show its essential relevance to ultimacy if we are to make our main point that man becomes man in this "religious" relation. We have made this at- tempt elsewhere, in the context of a discussion of the relations of reli- gion and science, a discussion that will soon be published under the title *Reflections on Myth, Science, and Theology* (New York: Harper & Row).

[8] Despite the ascetic themes that run throughout his thought, Augustine emphasizes in many places this innate, natural, and so uni- versal love of our being: "For we both are, and know that we are, and delight in our being, and our knowledge of it. Moreover, in these three things no true-seeming illusion disturbs us. . . . And truly the very fact of existing is by some natural spell so pleasant, that even the wretched are, for no other reason, unwilling to perish; and, when they feel that they are wretched, wish not that they themselves be annihilated, but that their misery be so." *The City of God*, Book XI, Chapters 26 and 27, in W. J. Oates, *Basic Writings of Augustine* (New York: Random House, 1948), pp. 168–169.

[9] Perhaps the first modern philosopher to express this apprehen- sion of and joy in *existing* as fundamental to all knowing and valuing was Spinoza in his notion of the *conatus* of every finite mode of reality. Cf. *Ethics*, Part III, Propositions 5–10.

and ground of all our valuing; it provides the most basic "reason" for existing, though it is much more a fundamental tone to our being in the world than it is a rational reason.[10] On the most direct level, when one asks what is it all about, this self-affirmation and self-love, this tone of underlying joy in being, provides a basic part of the answer, both secular and religious: To be and to love one's being.

To feel our being and our joy in it is not necessarily to be *conscious* of feeling these things. The feeling is usually only there as a state of mind, a mood, a tone to our existence. It manifests itself quite unconsciously in our vitality, in our sense of our own strength, power, and reality, in all our valuing of other things, of other people and of ourselves, and thus finally in our deep joy in these and in ourselves. This awareness of our own being and its feelings, this self-affirmation of our reality and powers, is in general what psychologists call "health," and it is, as psychoanalysis has taught us, the foundation for all our capacities both to achieve real relations to others and to be creative of value. And as with bodily health, we become conscious of it more often because it is not there than because it is. Of course, all of this may also become itself an explicit object of awareness, and we say, "My God, it's good to be alive!" One significant trait of this strength, vitality and joy in our being or existing, experienced by all of us at one time or another, is that it is *given*, it appears, it manifests itself in us suddenly and uncreated by us, even unevoked. We cannot call it forth by will, however hard we may try. We may say that in a strange way our bodies and we here can experience *ourselves* as secular analogues, so to speak, to religious "symbols," that is, as finite media of something ultimate that pulses through us, the power and wonder of life, of reality, of being itself. The ultimacy here experienced through our sense of

---

[10] One of the most profound philosophical expressions of this unity or identity—which here we are seeking to express—between actuality and value, that value stems from actuality since actuality is intensity of experiencing and *that* is also value, is found in Whitehead's philosophy. Cf., for example, *Religion in the Making* (New York: Macmillan Co., 1926), p. 100, and the discussion of value in *Adventures of Ideas* (New York: Macmillan Company, 1933), p. 320 ff.

our own being is evident in the fact that being, as it appears in us, is the ground of all our values, not *one* among the values of our life but their basis; in the fact that it and our sense of it are absolutely *given*, quite beyond our creation, our control or our determination; and finally that it appears *in* us as the basis of what we are, and not over against us as are other finite objects.

There can be little doubt that the concrete experience in which the power and wonder of existence and of life have most directly manifested themselves to mankind has been in the experience of birth, when through us and to us "being" originally appears. For this reason, fertility has always been one of the primary forms of the sacred in religion, manifesting as it does the unexpected, given, and essential power of life on which man absolutely depends, which he can in part direct, but which he can never originate or completely control by his own powers.[11] This experience of an ultimate, awesome, and yet wondrous power of life on which every value depends is, then, the explanation for a whole range of religious phenomena extending from sexual and birth symbols and rites through vegetation and agricultural symbols and rites, to the universal importance of feminine deities. It also may help explain the strange and awesome power of women in human life.

While postprimitive man knows he institutes the power of life in woman, nevertheless both sexes are deeply aware that it is in and through the woman's being, not in his, that the power of life waxes and appears in space and time. He can, to be sure, feel power *over* other objects from the outside through his finite strength and finite intelligence, and thus is the male sense of power more direct, obvious, but in the end always relative. Woman can feel directly within herself and so from within— and man knows this deeply—the ultimate power of life by which all creatures come, working through and in her, and thus in her

[11] Eliade's work makes plain this unity of motif that runs through the religious celebrations of the wonder of birth and of fertility not only in sexual symbols, but also encompassing all agricultural myths and rites and the crucial worship of the power of life manifest in the sacred tree. See *Patterns*, Chapters 7–9, especially pp. 244ff., 261ff., 306 and 309.

experience of herself as mother, she enjoys a closer touch with ultimacy of being, life, and power than he can ever muster in his own ordinary and secular activities.[12] Any person who has witnessed the birth of a child has experienced the wonder, terror, and ultimacy of that event, the strange way whereby the woman may be said to become a medium or "symbol" of that power, the "place" in time and space where it manifests itself creatively, and a man's quite external relation to this ultimate wonder. All the aspects of birth bespeak this experience of an ultimate power of life which works *in* and *through* the mother, not *by* her: the intertwined exultation and pain, the almost superhuman force that suddenly appears within her to expel the babe, and the certitude with which every mother asserts that this was the most wondrous, powerful, and meaningful experience of her life. It is no wonder that women feel such a crisis for their own sense of reality and of meaning when this capacity to transmit life, this intensely meaningful role as a "vehicle" of a transcendent and sacral power, is taken from them by incapacity or age. The serious impoverishment of the modern spirit—as opposed to all previous historical *Geists*—can be seen when we consider that this tremendous experience of the power and wonder of life, celebrated in all ancient cultures, is almost unavailable to modern men. In modern maternity hospitals, the woman is generally knocked out by anesthetics the moment labor begins, the husband is forced by the anxieties of the medical caste to remain outside, nervously poking butts in the father's crummy waiting room; and the attendants, who alone are witnesses of the "event," are inwardly technologists and no witnesses, forced by the requirements of their tasks to be aware of nothing but the practical medical problems involved in the delivery. This is not to denigrate the wonders of modern medicine in preserving both maternal and infant life. It is, however, to bemoan the almost total absence of

---

[12] The strange antipathy in the history of religion between the priest and the woman is perhaps clarified here: he, as the sole direct mediator of the sacred, finds a real rival not so much in the relativity of male power exemplified in the warrior and even in the chief, as in the directness and immanence of the sacred in and through the woman, who bears life within her.

this experience of the depths, power, and grandeur of the life we seek to preserve, an experience most directly present to us when in and through *us* the wonder of creaturely being appears. In seeking too desperately to "preserve" our life, and to keep it normal and unruffled by the incursion of strange experiences and events, we may easily lose all sense of its beauty and mystery, and so all real touch with its value. In any case, in numerous experiences of self-affirmation and of joy, and in special "hierophanies" of birth, our contingency manifests itself to us as a medium or symbol of that which is sacred; or, to put it another way, it is suddenly experienced against the horizon of ultimacy and infinity—at first as the creation of that infinity and then as the medium or symbol of an ultimate being which works in us, pulsates through us, and creatively realizes itself in our powers and acts.

There is, however, also an anxiety, a fear, a sense of the Void that is the correlate of this exultation. When it is not quieted, it may, and often does, overcome completely our natural joy in our given life. This is the fear that we may lose our existence, our power to be and to continue in being. We are all deeply if dimly aware that we do not finally control our own being, that all too easily something or some force can snatch our life, and the forms of security on which it depends, away from us. As the reality of our finite being was felt from the inside as strength and as vital joy, so here the *contingency* of our finite being is felt from the inside as anxiety.[13] In this experience, we "know" that our existence is given to us and not created by us; that, as our contemporaries have put it, we are merely "thrown into being," and so can as easily be thrown out of it by some chance flip of the powers that surround us; that, put in logical terms, there is nothing essential, necessary, or self-derived about us; and that, speaking practically, it is only by luck and good management that we can continue in being at all. Like its opposite number, the joy of

[13] The dependence of our discussion of both of these forms of "mood" or deep inner awareness on the thought of Paul Tillich (cf. especially *Systematic Theology*, Volume I, 189–198) and of Martin Heidegger (cf. *Being and Time*, pp. 172–182) is obvious.

existing, this anxiety about contingency is almost always felt only on the level of the dimmest sort of awareness as a tone of our being, and only at times bursts into consciousness as an anxiety or an emptiness of which we are explicitly or directly aware. Nevertheless, as with the joy in life, it can be there as a basic state of mind, not only qualifying as a private tone all that we do, but also causing us to do in our public behavior much of what in fact we do do. As the positive joy of our contingent existence appears when that existence is experienced against the dimension or framework of ultimate being working in and through it, so, whenever we feel our contingency threatened, the negative anxiety of contingency reveals itself against a similar infinite horizon, the infinite Void of insecurity. This Void or infinite horizon of ultimate insecurity and helplessness has been symbolized in religious history by the blind and yet all-determining figure of Fate. We can only understand the shape and character of our inner anxieties and so of our patterns of public behavior if we comprehend our contingency within this dimension or framework of the ultimate, both as the ground of our own reality and "rule" over our destiny, and as the unconditioned threat of Fate which, paradoxically, appears as that which rules over us. Thought about the contingency of all things, as we saw, more than anything else created the naturalistic view characteristic of secularity. Ironically, it is precisely our own contingency, when experienced in personal awareness, that reaches beyond itself to formulate an ultimate question, and thus in the most dramatic way opens up for us the infinite dimension, the unconditioned horizon, in which we exist.

In fact, to protect ourselves against these threats to our contingent existence is the most fundamental reason for the balance of our activity in the world. We say this because our ordinary behavior witnesses to the presence of an anxiety of contingency which can be understood only in relation to an awareness of this category of ultimacy. A threat to our existence comes to us always as an *ultimate* threat. Correspondingly, the human activity to protect our being is driven and so characterized by a dim awareness of the ultimacy of any threat to our security and our being, and this gives to our activity in the world its frantic character and its drive toward infinity. The experience of contingency, both positive and negative, uncovers a corresponding dimension of ultimacy.

In large part we act, to be sure, in order to survive, as do the animals. Naturalists see this fact clearly and ascribe it to the normal "will to live" of the animal world in relation to its environment. What they often overlook is the dimension of ultimacy involved in this threat when it appears in human existence, and which calls forth in man the need infinitely to buttress the security that guarantees his survival, i.e., to search not only for security from others but also for power *over* others—which form of power might, I suppose, be called the "male remedy" for our contingency, as birth is the female. The infinite search for power over what surrounds and so may threaten him overlays in man the relatively finite search for security and survival characteristic of the rest of the animal world. Man is not only conscious of threatening *things* and *beings* in his world; he also "has a world," an ordered environment within an infinite horizon. Thus he is vividly albeit unconsciously aware of the infinity of insecurity that threatens him from every corner of that world and that can cause the loss of his contingent being, and so he is driven to establish an infinity of power over other beings to protect his existence. Human contingency is felt by us against a background or horizon of ultimacy, which background appears positively in the experience of our own being and negatively in the experience of an infinite threat to our being. This is the way contingency is *experienced*, even by modern man—however it may be thought about or conceived in secular categories. And it is this framework of ultimacy within which contingency is appropriated inwardly that gives to the human quest for survival and so for power its panicky character, its endless striving, and its demonic possibilities—and so its peculiarly human and so dynamic character. In man the threat to life becomes an ultimate threat, and the will to live is thus translated into the will to power.[14]

[14] The most brilliant analysis of this significant shift from the animal's will to live to the human's demonic will to power which the category of "self-transcendence," or, as we have called it here, the "dimension of the ultimate," effects in man, is, of course, Reinhold Nie-

Thus, to take just a few of the endless examples, we seek material—which in our culture means financial—security not only against the immediate threats or perils to life such as hunger and cold. We seek also the power to guarantee for the almost infinite future the job or the status that gives us that security, and so our search for power takes on its strange character of infinity.[15] And even those of us in professional life who do not know the real feel of power—as have the warrior chiefs, the political leaders, the commercial barons of history—grasp for it in the strangest sorts of ways. For we are continually building defenses for our jobs and our careers—which in turn defend our security —by all sorts of political and public-relations maneuvers at the office, at the ministers' conventions, or on our faculty; and then we seek, if we can, to gain a name, a distinguished reputation, so that our status in our professional world, and thus our work and its value, will be secure for the future. Politely, intellectually, but bitterly this struggle "to be" goes on in the professional world as it does in the commercial and the political—and in each it has the endless character of infinity and the deadliness of ultimate stakes. Correspondingly, we each feel deep anxiety if anyone in our own professional world gains more of a name than we do, achieves a rank or an honor beyond what we possess, or in any other way moves closer to what we feel anxiously to be the

---

buhr's *Nature and Destiny of Man*, 2 volumes (New York: Charles Scribner's, 1941–43). For empirical material illustrative of this same point, see the author's *Shantung Compound* (New York: Harper & Row, 1966), a description of the struggle in an internment camp of ordinary "nice" people for space and for food, in which struggle both this dimension of ultimacy and the unrequitable fear of the threat of fate were particularly apparent.

[15] Following the lead of Augustine, Tillich emphasizes that one of the results of sin, i.e., the loss of the relation to God as the source of our being, our truth, and our love, is that man looks for this ultimacy and so for an unconditioned security, truth, and goodness in *things*, in the world around him. Since, however, no *creature* can provide this ultimacy, the search has an infinite and a frantic character, the essential character, says Tillich, of concupiscence. *Systematic Theology*, Volume II, "Estrangement as Concupiscence," p. 51ff.

"real" centers of power and security in our world.[16] Our infinite human hunger for wealth, prominence, and place is in large part an effort to amass power in some form or another so as to guard against the threat of Fate, that unpredictable force of destiny that can snatch from our contingent hands these guards for our security and so for our existence. The symbol of Fate is by no means unknown in sophisticated secular existence, even if it is disbelieved in by most learned secular men. For it balances our contingency, standing for that unconditioned power which threatens our contingent being and of whose reality we are at least convinced enough to counter it with innumerable significant actions. Fate is thus a verbal symbol for the fact that the relative powers around us—a rival, our boss, a statistical drop in market prices, or a frightening news report—become "symbols" or media of an ultimate and infinite Void, a Void that contains an infinite threat to our being and its meaning. Knowledge of this infinite dimension relative to our contingency is deeply present in all of us, though it is almost impossible precisely to explicate symbolically. For the fear of just this ultimate Fate is what leads us to grasp for an ultimacy of power against it.

Since, as essentially social beings, most of us are from the beginning aware that we cannot deal with Fate in all of its forms through our individual capacities alone, this security is by the majority of men socially maintained, and our activities in the community are in large part ways in which this is accomplished. The fact that we act in community is, to be sure, inescapable and aboriginal; but the *shape* that that activity takes, in our vocations in all their variety, in our political life, and in a great deal of our social activities, reflects this infinite drive to preserve our security. In this regard, the "breadwinner," the "patriot," and the "insur-

---

[16] After seeing the way the presence of such a prize as the Nobel prize in science (the mere fact it is, like Everest, "there") impinges on the consciousness, in fear and in hope, of every budding scientist—in envious competition in the younger ones, and in sadly resigned disappointment in the middle-aged—one who pursues his university work in the humanities can only be very grateful that there is no corresponding single symbol of success in his own area.

ance policy" are useful, and very secular, modern symbols of this effort in and through community to achieve and maintain personal security against fate: the one seeking economic wherewithal as a defense against one form of this threat; the next seeking united political and military security to stave off the threat of other groups and cultures; and the third a cooperative effort directed against those arbitrary "acts of God"—sickness, loss of job, and so on—that might remove whatever it is which guards us against the loss of our existence.

In this sense, most of the life of our secular world is devoted to this assuagement of this fear of the loss of our existence, and the infinite, frantic, grasping dynamic of that life receives its most fundamental tone from the anxiety that is its motivation. By this I mean a deep sense of the infinity of the Void against which our contingency appears, by which it is threatened, and so a sense of our consequent inability ever to guarantee our security to our satisfaction. Concretely, what we feel when we become aware of our contingency in confrontation with Fate is that, whatever amount of finite power we may have amassed by whatever means, it is by no means sufficient, and that we are consequently in the end helpless. This "knowledge" that here we have reached the limit of our finite capacities and powers, and that we still *want*, an awareness dimly present in all of us in such situations, causes when it becomes explicit, the panic that dominates so much of our history, and, when it remains implicit, spurs our infinite search for power. This awareness of the infinite or ultimate character of Fate and, correspondingly, of our limit, our ultimate incapacity, is at the heart of much "religious" awareness of the negative side of the divine, and it is surely a persistent character of the secular experience of our time.

This dim awareness of an ultimate insecurity against which we are essentially helpless is evidenced by the fact that in our worldly activity we are never satisfied with any finite level of security. We always want more, and having achieved a certain level of financial or social stability, we become anxious all over again if we cannot move on to a still higher level. What we are aware of here is not only the ineffectiveness of our individual efforts ultimately to protect this security, but even more that our aggregate, communal efforts are helpless against the power of Fate. Our real anxieties in history arise when we sense the relativity and contingency of the community that protects us, and then our social fanaticisms, far deeper and more dangerous than the individual ones, are born. This deep awareness of communal contingency comes to explicit consciousness in the business community when there appears the threat of a recession or an inflation, and then all the savings and securities of the wealthy, however great they may be, become suddenly problematical. Even the most potent symbols of security in a capitalist world, namely stocks and bonds, become useless when the whole context of financial interrelationships is in danger of collapsing. Those of us who are old enough chuckle at the memory of the walls of club locker rooms and lavatories papered with market securities made worthless by the crash of 1929. But the emotional, existential, and historical meanings of that experience of an ultimate communal insecurity were serious enough, as the suicides in our country and as the collapse of German culture ten years later, largely because of a similar but more extreme case in the inflation of post World War I Germany, indicated vividly. When a culture's security collapses, the men within it become aware of the ultimacy of the threat that faces their contingency, and the resultant panic is one of the driving forces of historical existence. This awareness also becomes conscious through the political crises of history, in a revolution, a war, or in some vast shift in social structure. For in such upheavals of the very structure of social order, every form of human security, political, vocational, military, and even personal, is threatened with dissolution. The powers that secure our lives are then themselves toppled, and Flux is truly king.[17] People are aware of this *possibility* of ultimate insecurity long before it occurs, and their frantic reactions of defense help to spread the process of dissolution. *That* awareness is the awareness

---

[17] Cf. *Shantung Compound*, for a description of the collapse of all their well-trusted forms of security and meaning which the British residents of China experienced at the close of the last war when the period of colonialism in Asia came to a sudden end, and they found themselves adrift and helpless in an insecure world in which they no longer had a secure or meaningful place.

of Fate, and of its ultimacy, and history manifests it continually.

That there is no human or finite guard against the fate that threatens our security, and that we know this below the level of direct reflection in our anxieties and fears, was ironically but clearly manifested to this writer in a TV program he was accustomed to watch a number of years ago. Sponsored by a well-known insurance company, this program dealt on occasion with analyses of the crises of our time. Before the program itself began, there came, of course, the commercial: against a picture of children and mother playing happily on the green carpet of a suburban lawn, the mellifluous voice of the announcer asked the viewer a probing question: "Do you wish to guarantee the health and happiness of these loved ones against *every* contingency? Then buy our package policy, and your security and theirs will be assured against *every* mishap." At this, the mellifluous voice would fade out, and the hard, informed, and realistic accents of Walter Cronkite began: "Now let me tell you just how serious is the present situation in Cuba!" And for half an hour he would scare the viewer to death with his portrayal of how precarious our hold was not only on peace, but even on the continuation of our form of civilization. At the midpoint, back would come the mellifluous voice, and in serene confidence its owner, apparently quite unaware of the implications of what Cronkite had just been saying, would repeat: "Do you wish to guarantee the security of your loved ones against all possible contingencies?" At the end of the program, as the picture on the screen of the secure ranch-style house in the midst of the green lawn faded from sight, this viewer had his own vision, that of the most pathetic man he could imagine: the man was standing alone in the middle of a bombed-out, suburban lane, waving that package policy.

In such moments of awareness, our fundamental human contingency, and the contingency of all that we men may make or create to protect us, become clear to us. An infinite or ultimate dimension has opened before us and we realize that there is simply no human guard against the infinite power of Fate. Our finite powers cannot answer the question our anxiety is raising: the threat of Fate and so by implication the horizon within which our contingency exists in the stream of history, is thus in that precise sense an unconditioned one, and an answer to this threat must likewise be unconditioned. In such situations, as we have sought to show, we have definite experiences, though admittedly negative in character, of what we mean by ultimacy and by sacrality, in which we are in such direct touch with an unconditioned dimension that our feelings and our behavior alike can be explained only within terms of a framework that is so delineated. We have experienced a threat to our being which clearly transcends the limits of our finitude, and we have sought in vain for a further, presumably also ultimate ground on which to stand—and have experienced then our failure to find that ground. And out of all this arises our experience of deep, historical anxiety and the temptation to panic and fanaticism is there. Put in the religious language of our tradition, we realize then that we are not and cannot be our own gods, the ground of our own being, or the source of its ultimate security and value. As the secular mood knows well, we are relative beings immersed in a course of history whose path we cannot control—for neither we nor anything human is absolute. But as secularism overlooks, in the midst of living out this immersion existentially—of actually being in a world whose course we cannot control—we experience the threat of this contingency and this relativity as an unconditioned one, as it is; and correspondingly, our anxiety has an ultimate quality. And inevitably we ask further, whatever our naturalistic mind-set may tell us, about an unconditioned security to answer this unconditioned threat of Fate, and secular though we be, we search for this level of ultimate security in all that we do and are, and in every political and social movement that appears in the arena of history.

Thus what the secular mind *knows* in its thought as our inescapable contingency—and formulates naturalistically—secular life *feels* as an absolute and unconditioned threat and so unbearable. All men dimly know this Void, for the worldly behavior of all of us is a continual reflection of this undertone of anxiety and insecurity. Only in terms of this dimension of experience can either the despair at the loss of security evidenced in the suicide rate of modern men and countless forms of escapist behavior, or man's demonic creations of false absolutes in nationalistic, racial, and other kinds of historical fanaticism be understood. If we seek to quiet this fear of a destiny we cannot control, and which *thereby* is hostile, by exerting our own power, then, as our country is (or should be) learning in Vietnam, we are embarked on an endless, fruitless, and fatal quest. For no earthly power is infinite or absolute, and if its anxieties drive it to try to control all of destiny, it will only hasten the appearance of those hostile forces that will ultimately triumph over it. If we seek to found our victory over fate in our own powers alone, we are all the more irretrievably lost—and *thus* are our own powers at this level incapable. Historical destiny reveals itself to us in our secular feelings, not in our secular thoughts, as an unconditioned Fate. And it raises the fundamental question of how, if this is so, we may love and affirm our existence creatively in its ultimate contingency and so its ultimate helplessness.

What is being sought here, the question that our anxiety and ultimate sense of insecurity are raising, is the question of an unconditioned security that rules these fates that rule over us, a ground for the now evident fragmentariness and helplessness of the life we do love—else we can hardly affirm it in courage and joy. In this very ordinary secular experience, we are looking for a God of the Fates, or to the Christian mind, for God the Creator and Ruler, though we may not know that at all. The provisional sense of the joy and security of life is universal—an effect of what a Christian consciousness would call "common grace." But once the inability of finitude to generate and maintain out of itself that state of mind has been deeply felt, only an awareness of an ultimate ground of existence and meaning that is more than the finite, and yet not the empty or demonic ultimates of secularity— of what Christian faith comes to call "God"—can cause that innocent sense of joy to return. Both to love our contingent life and at the same time to be indifferent to its inevitable loss, are difficult. Such an existence in both joy and courage, in ultimate indifference and yet passionate concern for living, is the first intimation of "grace" in secular life.[18]

[18] We have described the experience of contingency in its relation to the ultimate in very much the same way that Schleiermacher did,

A good many themes have been interwoven in the above discussion; let us, then, back off for a moment, take up a methodological question, and ask: "What is the form of our argument here; what is it that we are in fact maintaining in this analysis?" We have sought above all to show that the secular experience of contingency, both in its vast positivity and in its universal negativity, manifests itself as set within a dimension of ultimacy or of the unconditioned, and thus that man's experience of contingency, which is all that we here *directly* encounter (and so the only "essential structure" we can make an object of hermeneutical analysis), nevertheless points beyond itself to what we can only call a level, range, or horizon of ultimacy. And the immediate implication for language is that, if contingent man does continually experience this deep joy and this shattering anxiety, from which

---

except that he would have designated it all "feeling." Contingency, we have said, is something of which we are "aware," and in that self-awareness this experience raises for the "state of mind" or "tone" of our existence an unconditioned threat and forces us to find, or to create, an unconditioned answer. Contingency as an inward, felt, or dimly experienced qualification of our existence thus has an essential relation to ultimacy, and this relation is reflected in awareness or feeling. The most significant difference is probably that for us the feeling reveals the *negativity* of the experience of the ultimate fully as much as it does any positivity, an aspect implied by his thought but by no means so clearly recognized or emphasized by Schleiermacher. The cosmological proof attempts to express this intimate experienced relation of contingency to ultimacy in the vastly different mode of logical argument or the implications of thought. It fails as an argument because it does not realize the possibility of an experience of the *negative* absolute, the Void, within the natural awareness of contingency. As a result, it is impossible, without presupposing the category of belief or faith, to move from the given fact of experienced contingency to an assertion of a *positive* ground for contingency. The demonstrable relation of "natural" contingency to the dimension of ultimacy, as that relation is reflected in secular experience or feeling, can, in other words, take for the "natural" man either a negative or a positive form. It is only on the basis of a definite and positive experience of the sacred as *God*, and thus from the viewpoint of a particular stance, that this ambiguity is finally broken. Thus the final movement of the cosmological proof of God is based on the experience of an *answer* to the question of contingency, not on our "natural" experience of the question itself.

both his greatest values and his most destructive behavior patterns arise, then it is necessary to bring the light of symbolization and so the possibility of reflection to bear on this all-important region.

The argument has, moreover, had three separate elements, which have a kind of sequence of implication, but which are in form no "proof of God." The only demonstration intended here is the presence of the dimension or framework of ultimacy within ordinary experience and its implications for religious symbolization, and nothing more than that about the character, attributes, or objective reality of an ultimate, unconditioned, or sacred being. Nonetheless, here are the three elements:

1. Our own contingency appears to us, both in awareness of exultation and of crisis, as set within a framework of ultimacy and the tone of our self-awareness as contingent can only be so comprehended. Especially are the threats to our contingent existence experienced by us as unconditional threats; even if in a secular culture the presence of the sacred is not mediated to us, at least its absence is directly experienced. These threats raise on the level of life, if not of thought, the question for us of an unconditioned security. This question is answered by men in their frantic and often demonic search, even in a secular culture, for an unconditioned power or status to guarantee their security. Such a search, universal in man, is proof that he is aware of an unconditional threat of Fate and does look for an unconditional answer—though he may not know it consciously. These experiences of an ultimate and sacral ground of life, and of an ultimate Void that threatens life, are undeniable, and the questions they raise about an ultimate security are, therefore, significant questions. We are all aware of them in our experience, and covert symbols about them are used in meaningful communication in a host of ordinary secular situations, as well as in literary, dramatic, and universal religious discourse. There is no one who has not in panic or serenity, foolishly or wisely, in traditional or novel terms, sought for answers that are meaningfully related to these real questions, and so used some sort of symbolic systems with which to thematize these ever-present aspects of our common existence. Discourse in this realm, however presently impoverished,

uncoordinated, and even "nonstock," is thus part of ordinary life and so is obviously intelligible.

2. We have said that, since the experience is specifically one of our own limits, questions in this realm reach beyond the finite for an answer, and we have shown that no finite can provide a genuine sense of security at this level. Therefore, it is implied by this element of creaturely incapacity, as well as by the character of the experience itself as pointed beyond itself, as given and as beyond our control, that wherever a sense of security and joy in our being is known—and it is known universally in human life —there there is a dim but present awareness of what is actually ultimate, unconditioned, and sacred, quite beyond the level of finitude in ourselves and around us, what, in other words, religions have called the "divine" and Christians have called "God." The quality of ultimacy in the positive awareness of a fundamental security establishes by implication an unconditioned ground or "whence" of that same awareness, and the universality of the human experience of that ground. No proof of God is possible here because this experience, while universal, is by no means necessary or ineradicable, since in its place the Void can be experienced in life and no positive ground known at all. The ultimate as Void is as widely felt as is the ultimate as creative being on which we absolutely depend. In any case, this infinite ground of the experience of serenity may be apprehended even if a consciousness of "God," or any use of that symbol, is not present at all; specific forms of religious faith are not essential for this "natural" sense of security and joy in life. Such secular experiences of ultimacy and sacrality are aspects of what in theological language can be called "common grace" or "general revelation," since they are universally felt and (as we have also seen) universally threatened in all of human life.

3. Granted, finally, that the negativity of ultimacy, this Void at the depths or foundations of experience, is known in secular life, that contingency realizes in explicit consciousness its own ultimate helplessness in the flux of things, then "God" or an unconditioned answer *in some* form must be known explicitly for security to be again possible. Once the unconditional character of the Void—in that it represents an ultimate threat

to all forms of finitude—comes to self-consciousness, explicitly finite forms of security are no longer effective. In that case, either idolatry must result, the finite being raised to the level of the ultimate; or the ultimate itself must be discovered in and through the finite. Thus "faith," in the more special sense of an *explicit* awareness of the ultimate as "God," is a necessity called forth by the experience of the ultimate as Void. Religious faith in this sense is by no means either universal or ineradicable, for it is that which *answers* the emptiness and alienation resulting from the experienced loss of ultimate security and meaning. It is the *new* condition, after this awareness of loss, for the return of an original and innocent affirmation of life. As definitely neither necessary nor universal, the presence of faith in this sense depends on special kinds of experiences, and so cannot be derived or established by a secular analysis such as this.

     Speaking for the moment from a Christian perspective, that is, looking back from the context of a systematic theology, we may say of this prolegomenon to theology that it can be regarded as seeking to provide one element in a "secular" definition of God as well as to show the universal necessity and meaningfulness of religious language. Even if men do not know its source, to be aware of this "common grace," of a sense of joy and of security in their contingent existence, so that the Void is really conquered, is to know, in fact if not in consciousness, what faith names "God" as our universal Creator. The explicit belief of Christian faith in God our Creator is then, on the one hand, the experienced and explicit Christian answer to this very common secular question of the origin and security of our contingent being; on the other, it is the definite Biblical or Christian "name" by which we symbolize the origin of our existence universally experienced as affirmative. Speaking theologically, we are suggesting that the presence of God to all his creatures as the creative source and ground of their being and their life—a presence undeniable from the point of view of faith—is *apprehended* by them as the source and ground of their being whenever they experience in themselves this joyous and serene affirmation of their own contingency. To know our contingency as grounded beyond ourselves, and so to be serene in the face of this contingency, is to know, in life if not in reflection, he whom we Christians name "God our Creator."

If what we have said in the preceding section is a true description of aspects of our concrete experience, then implied in these experiences are a manifold of ontological conclusions about man's being. For reasons we have mentioned, our task here is not to develop an ontology either of our being or of Being generally. Nevertheless, before we go on to the next aspect of concrete experience that interests us in our search for the dimension or framework of ultimacy, let us draw out a few of the most relevant of these ontological conclusions. It is evident from our description that man is a being who experiences his being in the world as real and yet as contingent, and who feels or is aware of that being in the tonal characteristics of joy or anxiety. This awareness, we have said, is, on the one hand, the almost direct awareness of an ultimate threat to his being and instigates a search for an ultimate security. Likewise, his quite natural awareness of joy in the face of his contingency points by implication, if not in direct awareness, to the ultimate source of his being and doing. Clearly, the ontological condition for this situation of inner awareness of reality and contingency—so basic to all our valuing, feelings, anxieties, and ordinary behavior—is that man's being exhibits not *merely* a contingent reality. Rather, his existence must also be an existence characterized by self-awareness: he is aware he is there, he is "illumined" as Heidegger says, *erleuchtet;* his thereness is disclosed to and in him. He is not a thing, an object, but a subject, one who *is* in the world in terms of awareness and so state of mind, in terms of understanding and so of intelligence and knowledge.

Out of this ontological situation, of course, arises the possibility of the peculiarly human characteristics of our contingent being. We are aware that we are; we are aware that we are in a world, and that we are moving into a future; we can communicate with others; we can think, conceive, make symbols, create projections, and ask questions. And this awareness subsists both on the level of mood or state of mind, and on the level of symbolic, conceptual, explicit consciousness or thought. We are or exist in terms of our awareness, our decisions, our self-creation; our essence is in this sense our "existence." Thus our environment becomes a world, a temporal passage, a unity which we see as a whole and about which we can and must wonder, think, and ultimately master cognitively, and so into which we inevitably inquire. In our understanding of our world, furthermore, we are involved in the inescapable search for unity and coherence; correspondingly, our self becomes penetrated by self-awareness, by freedom, and by our projects into the future. Thus we *are* our projects, what we decide for the future. We are not just given, but called to become something by intellection and decision in relation to a model or norm, and we must understand ourselves and our life in some context of meaning that spans past, present, and future—for we exist in memory, in present awareness, and in future projects and meanings. Both cognition and valuing, plans and forecasts, and so science and freedom—and, of course, community as well—stem from this basic ontological structure of our being in the world. Man is man because in him resides a "logos," a principle of self-awareness, illumination, of communication and knowing, and of projection.[19]

This situation of illumination, as we noted, is a condition of our creative powers as men, and correspondingly, also the condition of many of our peculiarly human problems. For from it come our awareness of contingency and mortality, and so much of our creativity and our despair. Also from it arise our powers of understanding, conception, and judgment, which

[19] The relation of this discussion to the thought of Heidegger about Dasein in *Being and Time*, is, of course, obvious. See especially Part I, Chapter 5, "Being as Such." Since, however, we would define the ultimate category of being, insofar as we would use it, in terms of our *existence* and *contingency* as these were defined in the first section, as well as in terms of what we have called the "logos" of self-awareness and so of knowledge and decision, our understanding of being is quite different from that of Heidegger, who seems to us to draw a sharp line between the *existence* of all contingent creatures, and the "existence" of man in the sense of the *disclosure* of his existence to himself. For this reason, I do not agree that the symbol "God" is correlative with Heidegger's notion of being, unless speaking Trinitarianly, one is willing to drop the Father in total favor of a preexistent Son or Logos.

lead to science—and to the possibility of relativism and doubt. The powers of freedom and value, of becoming a self and all the human difficulties of morals and community, also find their roots there. And finally there is the problem of meaning and its relation to the future which is our concern in this section. Since man is as a being aware of himself and his world, he exists in terms of meaning. What he is and does is apprehended by him as set within the horizon or context of the world as a whole and the world as past, present, and future in which he exists. Because of this structuring of his entire world *as a whole*, man is fearful about his contingency, and thus he asks, whether he will or no, what all he is and does *means*, where it is all going, what its purpose is, and what is its worth. Past, present, and future are open for man's freedom because of this power of structuring his total world in terms of meaning. But by the same token, they are threatening to him as well. For the category of an ultimate meaninglessness is thereby a possibility and poses as deep a threat to man's being as does that of the loss of his existence.

We cannot merely do what we find ready at hand to do. The self-awareness of our being in the world in relation to the totality of things and to history means we must set what we do in some wider context of meaning that reaches out infinitely— that spans the past and the future. Inevitably we ask about the relevance of what we do to our own ends, to those we love, to the events around us, to the order of history in which we live, and to the future that is created by history. We search for *meaning* in our existence, and by this we intend the search for a context inclusive of historical space and time in which our life finds place and worth. As the contingency of man's being is seen to press toward an anchorage in a transcendent totality of being, so the fragmentary meanings of man's consciousness—both intellectual and existential—press toward a coherent and total system of meaning both for the truth he knows and for the historical meanings he enacts. We shall not here discuss the foundations and characteristics of inquiry and the search for validity, although they, too, require the same context of ultimacy. We are concerned here with the more existential meanings on which depend a man's vitality and worth, for they too, as fragmentary, are threatened by a void of meaninglessness, and so they, too, require an ultimate context within which to subsist creatively. Both man's search by inquiry for validity and his search through activity for meaning stem from the same character of man, namely that he is aware of himself and of his world, and thus is both forced and enabled to know the scheme of things entire and to find meaning for his life in that same total context.

We humans, therefore, need more than physical and material security, more than mere existence in life, if we are to be human. We need also what we are calling "meaning" if we are to live creatively and actively. Here the problem of meaning is existential, referent to life, rather than intellectual and semantic, referent to symbols and their usage. To have meaning in this existential usage is to have the sense that what we do, the life we live, the activities that make up our days, have or will in the future have some sort of value for us, for others, for the community, for the course of history, and so on. It is the sense that our life in its concreteness and its activity is worthwhile. This sense of worth has, in turn, two facets: first of all, that our activities have value in their present actuality, that there is joy and pleasure accruing solely to their doing, as when an artist *loves* to do what he does; and secondly, that they relate us to a meaningful future, they build for future moments of increased value, they create value, that they are instruments or means to future ends we find worthful. A sense of meaning combines a sense of the immediate joy of what we do with a hopeful projection into the future to be achieved by means of our creative activity. Both of these elements are important, though one or the other may be muted. Both depend upon our *eros*, our love or evaluation of something related to our particularity as supremely significant, whether it be our doing of what we do, or the future ends achieved by what we do.

Again, this feeling may exist unthematized and so unconsciously—we may not think about it or formulate it at all. This sense of worth is most directly manifest in the energy, physical, vital, intellectual, that we pour into a "meaningful" activity. Although we thus need not be *conscious* that we have "purposes" in our life or even of what they are, some purpose relating present and future through creative activity must be implicit, must be *felt* in our existence, if that existence is to be fully human. And by that is meant that we find ourselves involved, almost despite ourselves, in willing some activity, that we evaluate it as worthful, as creative of future values, and thus that it excites us and so draws out our enthusiasm and our powers. Thus meaning is immanent in all vital human life; some activity flooding our present with worth and joy, and building the future, grasps us as significant and worthful—be it our struggle with nature's elements in our work, our art, our profession or business, or working for our family, our community, or a social reform—or, as we are witnessing in our time, a revolutionary cause to create a new social content. And we respond to this experience of being grasped by meaning and by hope in intentional activity. If any of this sense of meaning is lacking, we dry up, the engine stops running, and we die inwardly. Meaning, and its corollary hope, provide the fuel that stokes the human machine.

There is a dialectical relation between the aspect of our human being concerned with meaningful activities which reach outward into the world and into the future and the one discussed earlier concerned with merely our "being" or existence in the present. The two can and must be distinguishable as different, and yet they are intrinsically related and mutually dependent. Can there be a *meaningful* existence if one just "is" in the present? Or is, as we suspect is the case, our humanity so dynamic and living in its fundamental character that it must express itself in some form of activity or work beyond itself into the world and into the future if it is to enjoy, be aware of, and appropriate its own present reality? This is by no means an unreal argument today, as the immensely significant hippie culture seeks to separate meaningful being from external, historical activity in the world. "Why not just *be?*" they ask, in persuasive rejection of our culture's emphasis on worth as solely achieved by "work" in society and for the future of society. As we shall see, the sense of the reality of our own being fades when we can find nothing to do with our powers—when, to use hippie language, we have no "thing" that is our own to do. This dependence on *activity* for our sense of reality and strength is, we suspect, not merely a

function of our activist culture, so that a totally leisured existence
is probably not a creative possibility. On the other hand, it is certainly true that present Western, especially Protestant and capitalistic, culture—as opposed to many another—has so emphasized activity, defined as work for the future, as the center of
meaning in life that the sense of the intrinsic value of being in
the present has almost totally vanished. The great middle class,
especially its executive and professional leaders—even those who
comment learnedly on this same theme—find it almost impossible
just to "be," and merely to enjoy some aspect of their present
being: food, talk, beauty, sleep, rest, or love. For many of us, all
meaning involves activity that builds something to be enjoyed
at some future time; it is *merely* intentional activity; its sole value
is as a means toward a further end. As Aristotle, or any sensible
inhabitant of the medieval culture, might have told us, however,
a mere means without ever an achieved end is literally the most
meaningless of all things. Hence a life of furious action devoted
to a future which, when it is finally present (say in retirement)
cannot ever, in any present, be savored or enjoyed—because all
worth is activity for the future—is literally a meaningless life.[20]

[20] This dialectical interdependence of being and activity, of
present reality and of active external meanings, is clearly related to the
whole problem of the "meanings" of male and female, and so the difficult question of the roles of each in any healthy adult life. Our own
feeling is that (*a*) the "meaning" of woman is uniquely and powerfully
related to the category of being and the re-creation of being; and correspondingly (*b*) male power is uniquely related to the creation of objective social, legal, and cultural meanings outside the self and its existence.
This does not mean that woman cannot adopt the latter cultural role, or
should not; or that man cannot or should not find meaning in "being"
and its creation. Both roles must overlap, as the sexuality in each of us
overlaps. What is wrong, I think, is when, as in extreme feminism,
woman sees herself entirely in the activist, culturally oriented role of
creatrix of objective cultural meanings through "work" in the world, as
career executive, politician, scholar, artist, writer, and so on, and imposes
either a subordinate or a subservient role on her wondrous and unique
power as creative vehicle of being and of life. This is, we feel, to sell
out to the male view of human value and worth entirely, on the good historical but poor philosophical grounds that the female role has led to
bondage. Consequently, it is also to understand the "meanings" of a
woman's life in the confined, activist terms of a later-day Calvinist,

Furthermore, it is almost certain that there can be no healthy appropriation of our own active powers, however magnificent they may be, without a prior acceptance and appropriation of our simple being, else all our self-feeling and self-love be based on our success in the world and not on an inward and felt appropriation of our own reality.[21] Thus, to sum up our dialectic, creative active meanings are dependent on a positive awareness of the present reality of our own contingent being, and the latter is realized as manifested livingly in the usage of our powers and activity directed outward in the world and forward into the

---

bourgeois, and professional culture—a culture which, as the hippies are pointing out, is constrictive and deadly to *both* male and female!

These lines of comment cannot be written without the further question being raised whether the ontological categories of becoming, activity, and process toward a future goal, which are so "modern" and have so clearly replaced the older Greek categories of being, rest, and eternity in the present, do not ironically reflect the triumph of precisely this Calvinistic, bourgeois, male and so activistically future-oriented culture over against a Catholic, feudal, agricultural, and possibly female one. Possibly one of the arguments for a return to some (admittedly dynamic) form of the category of *being* is in order to balance the total victory of activity and future goal-orientedness over presence and possession. The same set of questions makes me nervous at the *definition* of man as one who is "open for the future"; this too sounds too much like der Streber, or his Anglo-Saxon (or Semitic) counterpart, who cannot ever relax or enjoy himself in the lush present but must always be striving for something or other to be had in the evanescent future. The ultimate irony is, of course, that the professor who writes these wise comments about "being in the present" is striving to end his book in order to begin a new one!

[21] A most interesting (Calvinist?) denial of the category of "present actuality" in favor of activity with a total future orientation has appeared in a revolutionary rather than a middle-class form in Jürgen Moltmann's book *The Theology of Hope* (New York: Harper & Row, 1967). Here the authentic self is one *alienated* from its present self and from its cultural setting, and is thrust totally into the future (pp. 91 and 337). All appropriation of self-reality and of worth, and so all self-realization, is here eschatological, future, in the not-yet. We doubt that the total dislocation of the self, or of God, from the present into the future is psychologically, historically, or theologically sound, although its emphasis on the essential role of the future to both selfhood and faith is surely welcome.

future. And, let us note, both these aspects of our being are essentially social: we come to be and are in a community, and we can work creatively only in community, whether it be the wider context of culture and history, in the small withdrawn group of Haight-Ashbury, or in a separated community dedicated to a future revolution.

Returning, then, to our discussion of meanings as a sense of the value of what we do, whether in culture, out of it, or against it, in each case it is evident that meaninglessness, the despair or hopelessness that nothing is worthwhile, that there is no open future for us, makes it impossible for us to use our powers. For if we feel that nothing is important or significant— only our Cokes and a show now and then, or later only our alcohol and "trips"—then our life ceases really to relate to time at all and is correspondingly drowned in nothingness, and we cease, like the alcoholic or the junkie, really to exist at all. Whether we are participators in cultural life, hippies with our "thing," or revolutionaries creating a new heaven and a new earth, our powers, physical, artistic, intellectual, or practical, are of no use to us at all, and lie fallow if we cannot discipline and use them; and that disciplined and controlled use depends on a vivid awareness of the meaning and significance for both the present and the future of what we do that can energize and so organize these powers. Immanent purpose, the love of what we do as creative worth, gives power, creativity, and direction to our existence. It is a necessary ingredient to a life that is human. Its joys are among the greatest we can experience: the excitement and satisfaction of creative labor, in the house, in relation to the care and rearing of a family, in hard physical work with nature, in fashioning artifacts and goods for important use, in artistic and intellectual creativity, in helping to fashion a new and better community.

But, like our existence itself, how vulnerable are our purposes! The relativity and flux of all things, formulated intellectually with great elegance in secular philosophy, is *felt* in secular life as the relativity of all of our meanings. On the level of *existence* the experience of relativity, so creative of the naturalistic character of modern thought, raises precisely a religious question, namely the spectre of *meaninglessness*, an ultimate Void which we cannot easily stand. What is the significance of what we do in all this passage? Do not the march of time into the future and the infinite variety of things in the wide, wide world drown in nothingness the little that we can do? The farm one generation clears may decay and molder, and in the next the land may be covered with growth again; the family we build will itself pass away and be represented only by headstones in some forgotten cemetery in some unremembered place; the institutions or community we helped to fashion may be passed by and left stranded in decay in the ever-changing future shapes of our culture; the art we create and the books we write will one day gather dust instead of comments—and soon the whole network of our culture may disintegrate and be buried, like the works of Ozymandias of old. The very fluidity and mobility of modern life, which make new creations and new meanings possible, also infinitely increase the sense of their relativity and transitoriness. What does the creation of a family or a community mean as "works" when no one recalls where a grandparent or even a parent is buried, and when social change transforms in a generation the structures and so the values of our towns and cities? The infinity of the world, the passage of time, and the opaqueness of the future together threaten the meaning of what we are and do, for they prevent the fragmentariness of our lives from finding lodgment in some context of ultimacy that includes the world and spans the passage of time into the future. Without such a context of spatiotemporal ultimacy, relativity drowns out all our meanings.

The relativity of the total environment—natural, historical, and spiritual—in which man comes to be and lives, has been, we have said, one of the main creative elements of modern life, making possible the enactment of creative freedom and so the appearance of the new in history. No longer is there a sacred, changeless structure to things and events, and thus are they "set free" to become what they will in the passage of time. Correspondingly, an affirmation of the truth and the value of the relativity of all things to their passing context has been one of the essential ingredients of the secular spirit. One might think

that such a process of relativization would have a solely dampen-
ing effect on the modern spirit, as it surely did for the Stoics.[22]
On the contrary, this relativism has had a freeing effect on the
modern *Geist* and has, as much as anything, contributed to its
innate optimism. How is this possible?

The reasons, we feel, are twofold, the one sociohistorical
and the other ideological in form.

1. When a culture is waxing, an increase of fluidity leads
to an increase of opportunities for economic and social growth,
for new enterprises, for movement to higher social strata, and so
on. In such a sociohistorical situation, characteristic of a good
deal of post-Renaissance Europe and almost all of American history (except that of the post-Civil War South, and much of
twentieth-century New England), the relativity of social structures leads to an awareness of freedom and opportunity, and so
to optimism, rather than to an awareness of the potentialities of
meaninglessness, nullity, and futility.

2. Corresponding to this waxing or growing social situation appears a view of social process as both creative and progressive, as leading from real value and meaning to ever more value
and meaning in the future; and this can be regarded, or better
felt, quite possibly unconsciously, as a general law of things, a
structure helping to determine the unknown future toward increased value, presupposed and assumed as characteristic of reality itself. This belief in Progress, in the social process as a movement of value toward more value, has been, we believe, of in-
calculable importance with regard to the question we are here
discussing, namely the sense of the meaningfulness of what we
do. For this "myth," if we may respectfully so label it, set what-

[22] Cf. the following from Marcus Aurelius: "All things are the
same, familiar in experience and ephemeral in time, and worthless in
the matter. Everything now is just as it was in the time of those we have
buried." Marcus Aurelius, *Meditations*, Book IX, Section 14.

"Soon will the earth cover us all; then the earth, too, will
change, and the things also which result from change will continue to
change forever, and these again forever. For if a man reflects on the
changes and transformations which follow one another like wave after
wave, and their rapidity, he will despise everything that is perishable."
Ibid., Book IX, Section 28.

ever small works a man or woman might accomplish into a temporal framework of ultimate meaning, which framework in turn communicated to these fragmentary contributions a sense of lasting worth and invulnerable value. Whether a man cleared a larger farm, helped to found a new community, contributed to the establishment of a school, church, or communal government, enlarged his father's store, or the business he had started—whatever it might be, this work, however infinitesimal in the whole context of things and however feeble to guarantee itself in the face of the unknown future, was lent value, worth, and stability because it was apprehended as a small and creative addition to what was a growing realm of value, and in fact added its bit to the total movement of value accomplished by Progress. Very much as the belief in Divine Providence had, in the sixteenth, seventeenth, and early eighteenth centuries, given ultimate significance and secure meaning to the small works of Calvinist men, so for the increasingly secular men of the late eighteenth, nineteenth, and early twentieth centuries, belief in liberal society and its inevitable Progress resolved the problem of the inherent relativism and fragmentariness of all we do by setting these contributions into an ultimate context which was built into the very grain of things and so which would not pass away. The appropriation of what we do as meaningful depends upon a sense that it can be a part of an open future, that it contributes to what will be, and thus has significance despite its relativity—and that sense depends upon the ultimate context or structure of meaning that spans present and future. Such was Progress.

Elsewhere, in our discussion of the breakup of liberal theology, we have commented on the demise of the theory of Progress as one of the most important steps in the development of the mid-twentieth-century mind. The assumption that our culture is not only creative of value, but even more increasingly creative in a visible progress to a better state of things that will ultimately characterize all of history, has by no means fully disintegrated, especially as one moves into the Mid- and Far West, out of the urban setting and its intelligentsia—or as one probes the minds of many scientists and social scientists! But there can be little doubt that that assumption is far more precarious in the minds of all of us than it once was. That things will be better and in an American way may be something we still believe. But it must be *believed* now; it cannot be assumed, as it once was, as self-evident. We now feel our entire culture to be precarious, possibly mortal, and certainly relative to the onrush of historical forces. It might not last, it might be replaced, the future might contain a different social structure, with a vastly different set of goals and so a different scheme of values.

All of this has been *negatively* experienced in the first instance in the rise of Communism to a power situation comparable to our own; there has here arisen what is clearly a potent historical reality that was not like us and did not wish to be. While few of us believe that the future lies with them rather than with ourselves, still we can hardly deny that this is now a *possibility*, however small. The negative apprehension of the relativity and mortality of our culture and its values has, in the most recent past, been experienced even more directly and intensely by our culture through the more militant Negro revolutionary movements and, in a quite different fashion, by the hippie culture and the general phenomenon of youth's alienation. These are movements of great significance in that each in its own way is a studied and deliberate repudiation of the whole system of values and meanings essential to our liberal, democratic, and capitalistic culture. To the Negro militants, this society and its meanings are too oppressive and unjust to deserve further actuality, and they would as soon help to dismantle it as to try to be creative within it. In the view of those who prefer to withdraw, even though this social structure might last, it is meaningless, destructive of identity and of real life, and thus not creative of any value and *a fortiori* not creative of increasing value. Our time has, therefore, witnessed and felt the relativism of the meanings of Western culture in two guises: the external challenge of another set of values and structures which has revealed the precariousness and mortality of the context of meaning in which we live, and the internal challenge of a militant minority and of the dropouts who have questioned the inherent values which our culture has affirmed. Gibbon said that the fall of Rome was caused by the external victory of the barbarians over Roman political structures, and the internal victory of Christianity over the Hellenistic spirit. Our culture now feels, and we suspect has felt for a long time, even if it cannot or dare not conceptualize it, this same combination of external and internal threat to its life and consequently his own relativity and mortality. What is significant in this history for our present point is that, when the ultimate context of meaning within which the culture had existed creatively has begun to disintegrate, then within this now dissolving cultural whole even the small, proximate, and relative meanings that make up its concrete life themselves disintegrate and vanish. Apparently relative meanings cannot exist *as meaningful* unless they subsist within a historical horizon of ultimacy. And let us note that that horizon of ultimacy, a sense of the ultimate pattern and direction of history itself, appears with equal necessity whenever a revolutionary community challenges an established culture. For we revolt against an established system of meanings only in the name of some other scheme of historical ultimacy.[23]

Now the point is that the disintegration of this sense of progressive value has made many of those who still participate in modern secular culture aware—again on the level of feeling tone rather than of conscious reflection—that what they do in this historical context is so relative as to be infinitesimal in its importance. The loss of belief in Progress has removed from the secular its former foundation for the meaning of our works in a context of ultimacy. We realize in a new way that participation in social existence may not be creative of value for ourselves or for others, that the inevitable change of that social context does not always mean the growth of our values and accomplishments. Rather, active work in the world can be dead and pointless, and change can also be threatening, portending the decay and disappearance of all that we hold dear. For as we are now much more inclined to see, the towns, stores, industries, schools, hospitals,

[23] Whether this sense of the "open future" originally guaranteed by the Calvinistic belief in Providence, and then later by the secular belief in progress and in the material dialectic, can now be brought back by a reinvigorated Biblical eschatology is, it seems to me, even more dubious, despite Moltmann's valiant efforts to do so. Cf. *Theology of Hope*.

communities, reforms, etc., that we have helped in whatever
small way to further, will themselves decay—and the meaning of
what we did will vanish with them. In other words, when *this* is
the way our world and our work within it are apprehended, the
social context for our values is no longer seen to be ultimate,
and itself becomes a part of the relative flux. A really relative
change—where *nothing* in process remains—is directionless, and
a future created randomly or arbitrarily provides no grounds for
the meaning of what we do now.[24] That sort of total relativity is
felt as the loss of even our small meanings, as the anxiety of
meaninglessness. Our fragmentary meanings cannot exist except
in a context of ultimacy. As a result, it is easy and commonplace
in such a cultural milieu to wonder what is the significance of
what we do. How silly it seems to get excited about something
so relative and transient—our job, our creations, our particular
family, our activities, our contributions to this or that. An
abyss of meaninglessness yawns below us; an enervation comes
over us.

Such a sense of meaninglessness is at present common
enough on the assembly lines, in the large corporation offices, at
the teachers' desks, in small professional rooms, and in the ordinary homes of our land—not to mention the single apartments
and the ghettos of its urban life. And this Void of unqualified relativity and meaninglessness, too, we cannot stand. In many, this
state of mind takes the form of hopelessness and so of dull des-

[24] One implication of this analysis is to question the "total"
eschatological emphasis of Moltmann with regard to "hope" and so to
meaning in life. A future that is *totally* open is structureless, and thus
provides no basis for promise, no ground that my present actions—be
they revolutionary actions against culture or conservative actions to defend it—will bear fruit in that future. In such a case of *infinite* possibility, there is no hope, for the effect of present actions is devoured in
nothingness. As Whitehead realized, a creatively open future must have
a structural relation to present actuality; its possibilities must be limited
by past actualities and by present decisions, if that future is to give meaning and hope to our present activities. A *totally* new creation in the
future that *contradicts* the present (as Moltmann *seems* often to imply,
ibid., pp. 18, 100, 221), would make the present meaningless and
any creative action within it futile. Eschatology must be tempered by
Providence if either social or revolutionary action is to be meaningful
at all.

pair. And rather frighteningly, this inner despair of meaninglessness drains away our sense of our own reality and the reality of
the world in which we live. A self with nothing of worth to do
is an empty and increasingly unreal self; the lack of meaning in
its activities results in a sense of a lack of substance in its being—
meaninglessness points and drives toward nothingness. For when
there is nothing significant in our lives, existence becomes a
treadmill leading nowhere, a mere succession of rote acts; of
commuting in the subway, opening letters, making out orders,
typing someone else's correspondence, sweeping a floor, digging
a ditch, or tramping a street in hopeless bitterness—and then at
the end of the day eating another meal and brushing your teeth.
In a world of meaningless acts, there is neither self, world, nor
future. Our self takes on substance and strength from our intense
intentionality in relation to the world around us and the future
ahead of us, the *care* (or better, the *eros*, the love or desire) with
which we do what we do in that world and for that future. For
it is our activity in the world and for the future that challenges
and so marshals our powers of intelligence and will, forces us to
create, decide, dare, and persevere—and in these acts we become
real to ourselves. And correspondingly the world, or more concretely the community around us, which presents itself to us as
the environment for this intentionality, becomes real. When
there is no such *eros* and no future, and all we do is rote—
or convention—then self and world fade into grayness; there is
neither a coherent external realm nor a consistent open future
that calls out our powers, nor a self which can be a free, inwardly
determined center of activity and so of experienced reality. If
life is a mere succession of unrelated and insignificant acts, with
no inner telos and no strong bonds of community, then the inner
sense of one's own reality tends to disappear. Hume's world of
discrete impressions vacant of substantial selfhood[25] is *felt* whenever our life finds no meaningful relation between our activities
and our social and historical context, and thus affords no thread
of motivation holding the moments of life together.

   Meaninglessness, like contingency, when it is felt in all
its ultimate power, is a messenger of an ultimate Void, of terrify-

[25] Cf. David Hume, *The Treatise on Human Nature*, Book I,
Part IV, Sections 5 and 6.

ing nonbeing, and quite blankets out the apprehension of the relative, finite self, its world, its future, and the community within which alone it can really exist. The objective results of this descent into nothingness when no meaningful activity is possible or is available, are vast indeed. In the private world of the lower middle class, where what we do is someone else's business and has no meaning for us, there is inner despair, dullness, leading inevitably to disintegration of persons, family, talents and joys with the gradual erosion of hope: interior nothingness is the end of this road. In the proletariat of our society, given a communal and angry selfhood through oppression, the descent to nothingness reacts in another way and projects this ultimate Void in part inwardly in self-destruction but in the end outwardly into the objective social sphere. The community which refuses participation to this hopeless group is thus for them stripped clean of all value; it contains for them neither creative possibilities nor latent promises; it is oppressive, already dead and worthy to be eradicated—so let it burn. American culture, experiencing in the last decade for the first time the ultimate relativity and contingency of its own culture, has in the last year or so even more vividly confronted this ultimate Void in the midst of its urban life, the will to total violence and destruction of everything which America had considered to be valuable. Modern urban secular life thus feels the specters of relativism, of fragmentariness, and of nonbeing, in their most demonic forms; and it is also witnessing the demonic efforts of the privileged classes to protect at all costs their existence and their meanings against this abyss. If the self has no *meaning* through creative participation in a historical context, and if it has no hope for such meanings, then the destruction either of the self or of the social context follows inevitably. Thus injustice slowly but surely breeds destruction, and thus do the small social meanings with which secular life thought itself secure and content reveal themselves as fragmentary and precarious because threatened by an ultimate Void into which they can easily disappear.

In the end, the substance of the self and its activities are mutually dependent, as are the self and its world or the self and its community—for the self can only *be* when it acts meaningfully in a community for the future, and when it thus has a world and a future that offer to it an ultimate context of meaning for its life. This essential relation between the activity of the self in its social context and for its future, on the one hand, and its sense of reality, on the other, both of itself and of its world is, one might say, the existential and psychological reflection of the fundamental ontological doctrines of internal relations and of passage into the future, so significant, we have noted, in modern thought. An entity—in this sense a self—*is* in terms of its outgoing activities in relation to its world and to the future, and its reality disappears when these relations beyond itself to its world and to the not-yet themselves are reduced.

This is not to say that all in present society are suffused with either inward personal despair or dangerous social anger. There are millions who regard our culture as stable and secure; but even there the same problem of meaning arises in an acute form. In those who are fortunate enough to afford expensive pleasures, but who despite their surfeit—or because of it—have no meaningful purposes, the same inner emptiness or nonbeing appears as boredom. Again there is the basic problem that nothing in the self's world or its future captivates or enthralls and so makes life worth all the effort. But now this evidence of nonbeing does not so much drain out the reality of life in despair or anger as make it insignificant, a plaything, a series of pleasures but with no substance and no weight. Consequently, once again a real self, a real world, and a real future vanish. And so these fortunate but lost souls shuttle back and forth from insubstantial resort to resort, from yacht to ski slope, from this society to that, bored, restlessly searching for something exciting, and quite unable to enjoy their life that is suffused with nothing but enjoyment. They, too, have no hope for the future, for having tried everything and found it wanting, there is no "new" that is possible for them. This problem of boredom and of restless meaninglessness our affluent society (which before affluence had probably only added the modern toilet to the onrush of culture!) has had the distinction to discover for the first time as a mass problem, spreading rapidly into the middle classes. Heretofore, in ancient and European societies, it had been largely reserved for the aristocratic classes. Peasants always *knew* why they worked, namely to keep hunger from the door.

The answers which we see all around us to this Void of meaninglessness at the center of ourselves are, even in the upper middle classes, both significant and demonic. They, too, account for a good deal of the behavior that makes up our secular existence, a behavior we can neither understand nor deal with until we comprehend this need for an unconditioned context if there is to be meaning in our life. Certainly, the bottle and skipping from bed to bed are very popular answers to this Void—for something, anything, exciting must enter our life before we die! But, among professional and business groups, perhaps the most common answer, because the most socially admired, is to clutch after success or prominence. For success means significance, and a sense of our own significance assuages the aching emptiness that neither we nor anything we do have any importance at all. Thus we begin to push our way to the top of whatever world we live in, of the professional, the business, and the political worlds if we are male, and the social world of garden clubs and of bridge societies, Junior League and church socials, if we are a woman. In this process, we must push others out of the way since success is chary of its favors, and fame and distinction are isolated posts at best. And so we use others—ourselves, our friends, our colleagues, even our children—to get to this pinnacle, which ultimately means nothing. In the end we are alone, embittered, and forgotten; the meaning we have so desperately sought has, by the manner of our searching, evaporated away. This dismal process has been well documented in the literature and drama of our day, especially in the earlier films of Ingmar Bergmann.[26] Again the lesson is that the threat of the Void is an unconditioned one even among the privileged. Consequently, since we are creatures and cannot be our own gods, we have here reached the region of our limits, for we cannot *create* the meaning of our lives any more than we can create their security.

Meaning and an open future are almost the most precious

---

[26] Reference is here made particularly to the films *Wild Strawberries* and *Through a Glass Darkly*.

gifts which destiny can bestow on us—next to the power to love. And the power to experience and to actualize meaning is, like the joyous affirmation of existence, one of the main elements of grace in natural life. For it, too, has the same unconditional character and so presumably the same unconditional source. The meanings which generate our enthusiasm and so our active powers are, in fact, relative; but they must for us participate in an unconditioned element, an ultimate network of meaning,[27] which alone can overcome the threat of relativity that we have discussed. What we do must, despite its obvious insignificance and its fragmentariness, have some touch with what is not only significant for us but what is not in itself relative and subject to dissolution. In other words, our small meanings must participate and share in a context of unconditioned meaning. The need of an ultimate context for our historical meanings—theologically the need for Providence and eschatology if we are to act—is necessary for every sort of creative historical activity: for the man within culture who finds meaning in his work by participation in its creative activities, for the man creating a culture who sees ahead the ultimate progress his work is accomplishing, and for the revolutionary who can shatter one historical context only if he believes in the possibility of another one of ultimate significance, value, and staying power. Secularity understands this in practice if not in theory, for it has found precisely such an unconditioned meaning in its own most significant "myths" by which our culture has lived: in the myth of an inevitable progress of liberal history; in that of the dialectic of economic process of Marxism; in the recent eschatologies of the New Left, the Black Power movement, and even of the hippies; and among the bourgeoisie, in the splendor of one's own career, or in the eternal power and glory of the nation or race of which we are a part. Each of these "myths" tends toward what theology terms "idolatrous meaning," for, if they are made ultimate, they will only in the end lead to destruction or despair. But both the positive function and the demonic characteristics of these forms of surrogate ultimate meanings are present because these myths mediate to us

[27] Cf. Heidegger, *Being and Time*, sections 31 and 32, pp. 182–195.

a sense of an ultimate significance and value as the context or horizon within which the meanings which make possible our being as a self can subsist.

To realize at once the actual insignificance of our existence, and yet to be energized by the significance of what we are and do, is to incarnate an important element of the excellence or the authenticity of human life. And it is intensely difficult, as is any creative appropriation of our contingency and finitude. As the threat to our significance is ultimate and so overwhelming, so the answer is a sense of an unconditional meaning in which our fragmentary meanings may participate—and this sense we cannot create by ourselves without self-destruction. Thus the gift of a sense of the significance of what we do comes unearned, quietly, and without our bidding, for we cannot establish it. It is the condition and not the result of any of our willing and our action. As our contingent being and the values that stem therefrom were given to us and not created by us, since both were the basis of our activities and our desires and needs, so a sense of meaning is the basis, not the effect, of our willing and doing. We cannot change our willing and say to ourselves, "No, I shall love this and not that,"[28] "I shall from now on enjoy work and not find it pointless." Or, "I shall will for myself a new set of hopes for myself, for the world, and for history, and thus conquer by willing the enervating despair of my life." One cannot create in oneself a love of art, of writing, of creating things, or of com-

[28] Augustine expresses better than any other theologian this helpless inability to manufacture or to change our own meanings and loves: "For the specific gravity of bodies is, as it were, their love, whether they are carried downward by their weight or upward by their levity. For the body is borne by its gravity, as the spirit by love, withersoever it is borne." Augustine, *City of God,* Book XI, Chapter 25, p. 171. We are impelled by our love, and we cannot *will* to change our love; thus if we love the wrong thing, we are quite helpless; we cannot will what we only partly *want* to will: "But I, miserable young man . . . had entreated chastity of Thee, and said, 'Grant me chastity and continency, but not yet.' For I was afraid lest Thou should hear me soon . . . which I desired to have satisfied rather than extinguished. . . . With what scourges of rebuke lashed I not my soul to make it follow me. . . . Yet it drew back; it refused, and exercised not itself." Augustine, *Confessions,* Book VIII, Chapter 7, in *Basic Writings,* Volume I, p. 120.

munity, nor a passion for a new world. If one seeks to do this, one can do it only for the sake of a goal or a love already possessed—probably in this case as a means to the real end of being a success, prominent, effective, powerful, and so on. But then the cart is surely before the horse, art is loved in order to be a great painter, learning in order to be a renowned scholar, or justice in order to gain power, and the effort defeats itself. The love of something as worthful cannot be willed, but is the basis of all willing. It is therefore one of those givens in life on which our creativity and values are founded. For this reason, the experience of being given meanings and hope, of having our *eros* changed, recreated or born again, and of feeling the meaning for the future of what we do, as much as anything else has been that which has led men to speak of the Providence and the grace of God.[29] How was it that I, with these meager talents, landed here to do this work that I find so exciting and so filled with meaningful hope? For there is wonder here, that out of this entire nexus of relative, natural, genetic, historical, and cultural forces, and with all the mystery of the future, there is this place, this enthusiasm, these powers, and this sense of significance in a given task.

Meanwhile, the very common experiences of the loss of significance and of our inability to create it out of ourselves or by our own powers of will or mind manifest vividly the unconditioned character of the question of meaning. Our fragile meanings come to us in the context of ultimacy, which both supports their significance for us and, in its negative role, threatens that significance with nullity. For there can open up a Void of meaninglessness which we creatures cannot fill or which we seek to fill with great historical destruction.[30] The experience of most

[29] This is the point of Augustine's *Confessions*, namely not to tell about the bad things he did, but to confess and witness to the wonder of God's Providence that led him, usually *against* his own willing, to a life of increasing meaningfulness, and in the process changed his will to love.

[30] This is perhaps the point where our view disagrees most with that of Schubert Ogden. Like ourselves, Ogden argues that all meaningful cultural activity requires a prerational, unargued, often unaware confidence in the ultimate harmony or coherence of things which we may call "God"; hence every man, says Ogden, has "faith" as the pre-

men is that only when we know or are given a context of meaning greater than ourselves, when we lose ourselves in activities
which embody a significance that reaches beyond us and takes
its place in some horizon of ultimacy, can we know what the secular world seeks—the meaningfulness and the zest of life. And
only when our own causes, while related positively to an ultimate
meaning, are nevertheless seen not themselves to embody the
meaning of history—when there is, to speak theologically, an
"eschatological judgment" even on what we feel to be ultimately
meaningful, can the destructive role of meanings in history be
tempered. The relativism of modern experience, which is one of
the main ingredients of modern self-understanding and so of
secularity, appears in a different role in modern *existence*; there
it points beyond itself to the question of an ultimate meaning
in which our fragmentary lives find themselves completed and
fulfilled. The inevitable human question of meaning thus calls
for the theological answers of Providence and eschatology.

As in the case of the quest for an ultimate security, therefore, there are facets of what we have called "common grace"
known everywhere in human existence, i.e., everywhere where a
human life or a community of men vividly experiences on the
secular level the meaning and creativity of their own particularity. But when men become aware, through the relativity of what
they do and, through the uncertainties of the historical context
within which these activities must function, of the fragility of
all of their meanings, and stare at this Void, then only the awareness of an unconditioned context of meaning, of a purpose or

---

supposition of his cultural life. We agree that all *creative* cultural activities require some such confidence, and also that every form of "faith,"
even the most idolatrous, reflects the deep awareness of the divine Providence. However, what he seems not to envision as a possibility, and
what seems very real to me, is that men can lose precisely this ultimate
confidence in a final coherence, that the ultimate context of meaning on
which their activities depend can crumble, and so that despair and fanaticism are *real* possibilities in human experience. For his expression
of the "ineradicability of this confidence in the final worth of things"
—and so, one gathers, of the nonpossibility of despair and meaninglessness—cf. Ogden, *The Reality of God* (New York: Harper & Row,
1966), pp. 32–43, and 114–116.

telos in events that is not fragile and that transcends even what they come to love, can put meaning back into life. And thus arise both the idolatries of secular existence and its own deeper search for the reality of what we call "God." In this way, secular life moves inevitably into the realm of the religious if it is to remain life, and nature into the conscious awareness of grace if it is to keep its creative natural powers. A faith in that which undergirds our creaturely life and its meanings is a necessity for creative worldliness. And it is in terms of this faith in the ultimate context or ground of life's ordinary meanings, supporting and yet transcending each of them, that whatever Christian theology wishes to say about God's Providence and about eschatology is going to have relevance to our secular age. The doctrine of Providence, we may say, explicates the experienced Christian answer to a quite ordinary secular question, namely what is the mystery from which the meaning of my life in my history arises, from which the "new" in tomorrow's coming will arise, and so the ultimate context within which these fragmentary meanings of our daily lives, past, present and future, find their being as significant values and thus escape ultimate relativity? And eschatology provides the answer to the related question, if no visible value or meaning in life reveals directly or unequivocally the character of that ultimate context, how is that context of ultimate historical judgment and of hope to be understood symbolically?[31]

There is one more aspect of our creatureliness that adds fuel to our search for significance and reality, those two interrelated

[31] The point of our basic disagreement with the powerful thought of Richard Rubenstein appears essentially in this section, although the whole of Part II, emphasizing as it does the intimate and essential relation of the "given" to all forms of human meaning and value, is a studied answer to his views. In any case, in this part we have argued that any finite or partial meanings in life, "projects," if you will, which man wishes to retain, depend for their creative being in history on an ultimate context of meaning which only some form of the doctrine of Providence and of eschatology, and so implicitly of creation, will allow. Without the Lord of history, we are saying, Rubenstein's modern man cannot have his human meanings, any more than he can have his Jewish rituals.

goals of most of our endeavors. We are, whether we like it or
not, temporal. As secular thought has emphasized again and
again, we are in time; even more, time is in us. It propels us, to
be sure, into the new future filled with possibilities. But our temporality also pushes us out of time, ever more rapidly from ado-
lescence to youth, to adulthood, to middle age—faster and faster
across the stage of life. In a remarkably short time it will push us
quite off that stage into death.[32]

Temporality, then, like all the ontological structures of
our being, is essentially ambiguous. Grim though temporality
may appear when we thus ponder in consciousness its relation to
ourselves, our temporality is, however, by no means an unmiti-
gated curse, as if for us to be in time is to be merely doomed to
death. The dominant wing of modern thought, especially in
America, seems in fact to have seen only the positive side of
temporality, the way temporal passage opens out possibility, possibility of the new and the achievement of the new in the future.
Time is here viewed as correlated essentially with hope, since it
is the presupposition of benevolent change, of growth, and so of
the magic of unlimited possibility; it is, says one of the greatest
of modern thinkers, passage in time that prevents existence from
stagnation in the mediocrity of the actual, of the structure of what
has been, and it is time that impels it onward to further and finer
realizations.[33] This purely positive side of temporality we expe-

[32] The reality and supreme significance of the human experience
of temporality and of its term, death, even for a secular age, is, of course,
more markedly illustrated by the centrality of both these aspects of our
existence in existential thought, especially that of Heidegger. In fact it
is death as the main ontological implication of temporality that in Heidegger provides that context of ultimacy which makes authenticity possible. One might distinguish our view from his earlier one (on grounds
other than relative importance!) in that the *negative* ultimacy of temporality and death is for us balanced by the positive ultimacy of being
and eternity. His later period seems to move closer to this position.

[33] Whitehead, who understood relatively little of the demonic
or the meaningless in actuality, did have a fine sense of the ambiguity of
temporality. Passage was for him the condition of the movement into
novelty, and thus it provided, as we said in the text, the guard against
stagnation, mediocrity and fossilization due to a lack of intensity in experience. On the other hand, the final evil, as he said, was the passage of

rience quite naturally in our youth as our powers wax ever greater, as new experiences add their joys to the old, and as the sense of competence, potency, and the ability to create significance begin to appear and mature in us. Then change does seem to augur only growth and the wonder of newly actualizing possibilities. All this is natural and easy—for youth, and for a youthful culture where passage seems always to mean progress. And for this reason, the secular culture that knows only our temporality tends to make an idol of this period of life; and tries to pretend to itself that growth, youth, and progress are really all there is to being in time. If change is all, then we had best think positive thoughts about it; smile and smooth away the wrinkles! Thus regarding youth as the only normal and bearable period in life, our culture forces other stages to bend their own excellences to this limited model. It is a much sterner inward task to appropriate the joys of middle adulthood and older age than of our youthful temporality. Nevertheless, they are equally real: the sense of the richness of past experience; the earnest and serious concentration on the present moment and what it holds of enjoyment and creative possibilities; the balance that comes with having tried many things and learned a great deal; the inner freedom no longer to expect too much from life; and the serene courage to face the imminent passage into another, less vibrant and less creative stage of life.

Again, this essential passage of things is not difficult to contemplate intellectually in science or academic philosophy, and countless glowing treatises are written on the becomingness of things and their passage into the new. Far more difficult, even or perhaps especially for a secular age in which no eternity penetrates easily into time, is to appropriate with serenity and courage our own passage into mortality, and the passage of all that we value into an unknown future. For temporality combined with relativity means not only that we and our creative novelties re-

---

things out of actuality, the loss of achieved values when one entity replaced another. Thus in his eyes temporality did raise the question of eternity, as well as of historical meaning, and as a result, certain aspects of his Consequent Nature of God come into view. Cf. *Process and Reality* (New York: Macmillan Company, 1929), pp. 517, 523–530.

place those who preceded us, but also that others at some point take our place, and the place of all we hold dear. A temporality whose directions are all relative, in which there is no absolute dimension at all, augurs not just the maturing of our values, as classical culture knew well. *Radical* change in time bodes the loss of all our present values as well. Secular culture has been able to obscure the threat of temporality by hiding from itself the reality of the decay involved in passage, and by inserting into its concept of process a quite possibly unwarranted ultimate directedness toward the cherished values of that temporary culture.

Actually, like every other aspect of our finitude—our contingency, our search for meaning, and our freedom—our apprehension of time is fraught with both negative and positive elements. It is good but also fearful to be immersed in the strange passage from past to future, and this ambiguity has been universally experienced by mankind, and is also so experienced by a secular culture. As we noted before, modern man apprehends his temporality in very different ways than did primitive and ancient man, and for this we may be grateful in large part to the influence of his Biblical heritage with its emphasis on the creative activity of God in time and so on the possibility of the new in history. Thus, while ancient man resolved the anxieties of time by seeking to return to the original structures of things founded *in illo tempore*, modern man, Christian or non-Christian, looks to the open future rather than the originating structures of the past for the source of his courage and hope. Nevertheless, despite this significant difference between the modern apprehension of time and its predecessors, what is held in common in all ages is the problem of the ambiguity of time that every age feels in its own way.

While the future is for modern man the arena of possibility, of the new and of the better, and passage into it the condition of progress, inescapably the future is also unknown and quite beyond our control. Actually decay and death as well as new possibility appear in the future of each generation, and in the wider historical arena destructive possibilities threaten us as much as a potential utopia beckons. This ambiguity is experienced as anxiety about temporal passage, an anxiety both for ourselves as individuals and for the wider history in which we participate. It raises in all of us what we can only call the "religious" questions, first, of our mortality as individuals, and secondly, of the direction of temporal passage in social history—questions which we must all deal with in one way or another.

The felt awareness of our own personal temporality comes late, perhaps in the middle thirties. But once it is there, this awareness, like the awareness of the beating of our hearts, is never absent, and it continually threatens our sense both of our own reality and of our significance. On it depend a vast number of the inner anxieties and also the familiar public activities, both creative and stupid, noble and piteous, of our secular life. Our wives first feel it explicitly with the appearance of wrinkles; and they become coy about their age. But, more important for the secular economy, with this anxiety the vast cosmetics industry is born. Men feel it with the onrush of gray hair on their chins, seen nervously in the morning shaving mirrors. Thus begin the efforts of the aging alumnus to sow that last wild oat, and quite possibly much of the financing of private institutions of learning is, like the cosmetics industry, an important cultural function of the anxieties of a suddenly discovered temporality.

The awareness of temporality lodges permanently within us, however, with the sudden horrified intuition that we are no longer "a promising young man." One day we realize with a shock that our significance can no longer be understood in terms of potentiality, that golden realm of possible being where all kinds of significant achievements, and possibly even fame and distinction, are waiting in potentiality for our enactment. Rather, suddenly actuality takes over in our assessment of ourselves, and so unwillingly we are dropped into the mere present. With a shock we recognize that the significance of our life is to be limited to the range of what we are now, that whatever we may become will be on the same level of powers and of achievements, realized in the present—and, as we know well, *that* is very ordinary indeed. With that sobering thought follows its shattering corollary: as possibility has now been vastly restricted to present actuality by the passage of time, and as the present is mediocre at best, so the future is itself limited by the passage of time. Actuality as well as potentiality will one day cease to be; there is an absolute deadline on our total life, as there are now relative deadlines on term papers, on theses, or on professional assignments. Consequently, life's significance must be *now* if it is to be at all—and there will come a time when it will reside only in the relatively unreal memories of the past, as it now is confined to the ordinariness of the present. With this awareness of our mortality, of the limitedness of the time given to us, of the future, and so of possibility, and of our rapid passage from one of these stages to another, we are made to realize with a new force our essential insignificance. Previously, the mediocrity and frustration of the present were borne through the magic of future possibilities; but now we are made to look this present fully and realistically in the face as both ordinary and fleeting, and as the sole reality there is. Thus does the realization of our temporality add fuel to the problem of our significance, and together they challenge deeply whatever sense of reality and meaning our lives have been able to embody.[34]

   We cannot stand this knowledge that we are only animals that live and die, that both insignificance and death are together our lot.[35] So in the depths of us all there appear again an infinite Void and a driving anxiety. We must find something about us that will remain; we seek now not only for importance but for an

[34] Cf. the following from Augustine on the relative unreality of temporal things: "These days have no true being; they are gone almost before they arrive; and when they come they cannot continue; they press upon one another, they follow the one the other, and cannot check themselves in their course. Of the past nothing is called back again; what is yet to be expected is something which will pass away again; it is not as yet possessed, while as yet it has not arrived; it cannot be kept when once it is arrived." Augustine, in ps. 38:7, in Pryzwara, S.J., *An Augustine Synthesis* (London: Sheed & Ward, 1945), p. 91.

[35] The *combination* of the problem of mortality and of insignificance to form a radical experience of nonbeing is well illustrated by the following remarks, found in an interview for *Playboy* with the actor Richard Burton: "Nor is the actor [Burton] always frivolous; Tynan asks him if he is afraid of death, and Burton replies that it is not death so much as being forgotten which frightens him—'It is . . . the fear of being *nothing* that keeps me awake.' " From a book review by Kathleen A. McHale, of *Playboy Interviews*, in *Commonweal*, LXXXVI, No. 22 (September 29, 1967), p. 613.

importance that will last. And so we attempt to pile up fortunes, to make a name, to become in some sense important—to publish a book, *anything* to make our existence permanent and significant, to give it reality that will not vanish down the vast disposal of temporality.

Again, it is obvious that we cannot do this alone: the mortal cannot give immortality to the mortal.[36] No matter how high we build our monuments, or how hard are our bronze coffins, or how perpetual is the care we are promised by the friendly neighborhood mortician—at some point all of this, too, will pass away. There is no conquest of the ongoing flux from within that flux. Most of secularity can only bear this unhappy but obvious fact either by supposing a permanent and so ultimate direction to that flux which no evidence warrants and which its own sense of relativity rejects; or else, shutting its eye to the truth that temporal change means necessarily the decay of what is as well as the growth of what is to be, it ignores the hard truth that death as well as new birth are our mortal lot. Here, then, we encounter another negative "hierophany" of the dimension of the unconditioned: in the Void of mortality which nothing finite can overcome. And in the awareness of this Void, and the anxiety that is consequent upon it, the loss of eternity appears in secular experience. For with that loss we seek desperately to make our own mortal works and powers eternal, and that search penetrates into and influences almost every one of our ordinary secular attitudes and activities. The search here is for what will last, a temporal embodiment, so to speak, for some eternity transcendent to mere passage that has been lost, and an assurance about a directed structure of time in which both we and what we value will not vanish away into nothingness.

This question of a dimension transcendent to passage,

[36] This is a slight reworking of a famous phrase of St. Irenaeus, circa 190 A.D.: "For by no other means could we have attained to incorruptibility and immortality, unless we had been united to incorruptibility and immortality. But how could we be joined to incorruptibility and immortality, unless first, incorruptibility and immortality had [in the Incarnation] become that which we are?" Irenaeus, *Against Heresies*, Book III, Chapter XIX, Section 1.

what classically has been called "eternity," is, unlike the others, only fleetingly answered in our present experience for which becoming and finally death are the final terms. It can, therefore, be dealt with only by the most radical faith, accompanied by the most courageous if tenuous forms of speculation. That faith is founded, not so much on a direct experience of eternity, as on those aspects of grace that may be known here and now, namely the power and love of God evident in the course of our mortal life and believed to provide both direction and permanence to value within the passage of time. However, the presence of the question in our secular life is undeniable, evident in the vast industrial and commercial efforts to keep us young, in our frantic search for permanence, significance, and hope, and in our inner anxiety at death. Modern secular culture, sure on the surface that it has come of age and has no remaining religious problems, spends a good deal of its resources to hide the reality of death from its awareness—all totally unsuccessful. The Void without the divine eternity is ever with us, and an awareness of this Void is one of the characteristic features of the world's life.

To sum up this chapter, a "hierophany" and so an experience of an unconditioned dimension of existence is not at all absent from ordinary life, as the philosophies of secularism maintain. This dimension or framework of ultimacy appears *directly* in the awareness of an unconditioned Void, and a dim but powerful awareness of this negative context of ultimacy is the source of our common traits of fanaticism, frantic striving, meaninglessness and boredom, and terror at death and the future—an awareness that is thematized in our puzzled and often painful personal questions about life's meaning, and more formally in the literature that explores this range of ultimate questions. It is experienced *indirectly* in the joyful wonder, the creative meanings, and the resolute courage of life despite its obvious contingency, relativity, and temporal character; and this awareness of the power and meaning of life is thematized in one way or another in every positive philosophy of man, secular or otherwise, and in all of his religions. The human experience of being in the world and in time appears, therefore, to involve at its deepest levels more than what we usually call the world or temporality. It seems open to another, an infinite dimension; perhaps in terms of the dim awareness of anxiety and an unconditioned Void that is encountered in feeling, perhaps in terms of formulated questions about an ultimate security, meaning, and permanence in existence; perhaps in terms of a positive apprehension of the power and meaning of our existence which enables us to live with serenity and courage. This dimension at this level of our analysis is still undefined and unclear, though its character, as we have seen, is to us of the utmost significance, in fact of ultimate concern. For it appears as a Void that raises but may not answer all our ultimate questions about life, and produces in dim awareness the anxiety our ordinary life reveals; or it may appear as that ultimate mystery whose presence produces our existence and shapes its meaning, the "Holy Nothingness" which is the beginning from which we come, the inscrutable fate that rules over our meanings, and the dark end to which we go.

In any case, we have sought to show that secular experience contradicts secular self-understanding in the precise sense that the anxieties, the joys, and the tone of ordinary life reflect the context or framework of ultimacy. Such a context is specifically denied by a secular understanding proud that man has come of age in a cosmos essentially irrelevant to his being, his meanings, and his passage. But as did ancient man, modern man continues to live in this context of ultimacy. Thus he finds his life blessed at the most basic level by aspects of the given which establish his reality, found his values, make possible his meanings, and give him courage to face both the future and death. What is sacred in and to his existence comes actually not from his autonomy but from beyond himself as the source and ground of his autonomy. Conversely, what worries him most is not, we have suggested, so much the "problems" which his intelligence and technology can solve, but the continuing "mysteries" which reflect the transcendent context of his life: fate, meaninglessness, the unpredictable future, and death. Thus the fundamental traits of man's religious existence are as characteristic of modern secular life as they were of any life in the past: again it is the sacred that establishes and makes possible and of value the profane, and it is the sacred dimension that continually threatens all that man has built. To leave these supremely significant areas of our existence unsymbolized, unpondered, and so uncomprehended, is to leave secular life impoverished with regard to its real values, and vulnerable with regard to its real fears. Religious discourse is essential if secular life is to achieve a creative worldliness.

Speaking for the moment from a Christian perspective, we may say that the sense of the absence of God penetrates into every facet of life, giving to it those characteristics of the demonic, the tragic, and the empty so familiar to our history. Correspondingly, natural existence is also continually penetrated by divine grace, providing the basis for life's equally undeniable goodness, meaning, and confidence in the future. If we may put it this way, God, who transcends the secular, can yet be said to be apprehended in the secular in the sense that every significant joy and every compelling anxiety of ordinary existence reflect an apprehension of this dimension of the unconditioned, and the awareness of his presence or his absence.

4 / *The Dimension of Ultimacy in Secular Experience: II*

IN THE PRECEDING CHAPTER, our aim was to show how the ordinary experience of man, his secular experience of what we might call his "ontological" structures (his contingency, relativity, and temporality), points beyond the secular to a dimension or context of ultimacy. We argued that, because of this, religious language, which deals with this dimension, is an essential and creative aspect of secular culture. In this chapter we shall carry this analysis further, pushing now into those more uniquely personal, moral, and communal areas of our common experience to see again where it is that the dimension of the sacred reveals itself, and how it shapes our ordinary life. In this area we meet with the last of the key categories of modern secularity: freedom and autonomy. Again, in an analysis of how we live, as opposed to the way we think about ourselves, we shall see how this, too, points beyond itself to ultimacy.

As we gradually realize in maturing, we are blessed and also burdened with the gracious but strange gift of freedom. We are, whether we like it or not, saddled with a task in life, for the completion of which we are responsible: this task is creatively to find our own identity and to enact this identity insofar as we are able, through our own decision and power. It is for this freedom to will and to become ourselves that our secular culture, in almost all of its creative forms, has above all stood.[1] And in the

---

[1] Existentialism, of course, has been particularly associated recently with this emphasis on freedom and responsibility as the "es-

name of this principle of self-realization, secularity has been particularly critical of religion as representing external, authoritarian
standards that crush this freedom to be ourselves. While there
are many reasons why modern culture has been wary of an absolute or an unconditioned upon which man may be dependent, the
fear that in such a universe man's freedom to become himself
will be fatally compromised, is surely among the most important.

This freedom to be ourselves is not at all easy to achieve,
as we all somewhat painfully, and often expensively, learn. The
main reason is that we are inherently social beings so that our

---

sence" of man: "Man's essence *is* his existence" means in effect that man
cannot be man except through the realization of himself through inward
freedom; if he merely *is*, adapting his life to external or given standards
and authorities, submitting to historical models of man, receiving himself from the outside, so to speak, through the willing either of others
or of society generally, he ceases to "exist" as an authentic human. Nothing bespeaks so clearly the disappearance of absolute norms from history
as does this rejection in the name of authentic freedom and selfhood of
all *given* structures into which man must fit his life.

Clearly, however, other major strands of modern culture have
in their own way assisted the same theme of the radical autonomy of
human freedom: the requirement of *intellectual* freedom and so of the
right to doubt, question, and decide on the evidence, if one is to exist as
a mind, which characterized the whole Enlightenment and is now almost
the only "existential" element in modern naturalistic and positivistic
thought, oriented as they are to the sciences and to social liberties; the
emphasis on personal uniqueness and self-realization in the Romantic
movement, culminating, of course, in Nietzsche; and finally the entire
weight of psychoanalytic theory, affirming that psychological health is
almost to be defined as the power to affirm oneself over against the
external authorities of parents, society, and the Super-Ego. One can also
point to the significant Whiteheadian assertion that each entity finally
comes to realization through a self-creativity in freedom—in which it
is, in some way analogous to God, *causa sui*—as with existentialism a
powerful expression in contemporary ontology of this theme of self-
creation or freedom. In any case, however much the ontologies of many
strands of modern culture may vary, and however strangely some of
them may challenge in the name of determinism the reality of the freedom involved in this basic assertion (for example, many forms of naturalism), there is in modern thought substantial agreement that in one
way or another the essence of man lies in his freedom, his power and
responsibility for self-actualization and self-creation, if he is to be fully
human.

selfhood and therefore even our uniqueness come to be in community—perhaps the other major insight on which modern culture's view of man is based.[2] We become persons not through isolated self-achievement, but through our relations to other persons in the community of the family and of our social groups. Our inward existence as personal, free, and intelligent beings is as much an effect as it is a cause of our dialog with others, in being loved by them and loving in return, and in our communion with them through signs, symbols, and language expressive of shared experience.[3] Not only the fact but even more the character or the form of our personness is given to us through the social context of our life: from our family, our community or town, our country, and our wider cultural milieu. The fundamental way we

[2] One can see in the juxtaposition of these two fundamental modern affirmations of the autonomy and freedom of man, on the one hand, and the communal nature of man, on the other, the reason that Hegel, more than any other thinker, can rightly be called the father of Modernity. No previous thinker rejected so powerfully the oppressive and life-draining power of any transcendent over against man, the glory and in fact divinity of the unfolding of an unlimited human autonomy as the goal of human history, and the need therefore to think out reality in terms not only of deity but also of immanence and autonomy. And no thinker at the same time so clearly saw the historical, the communal, in effect the contextual, character of all human individuality and spirituality.

Both of these emphases—the personal uniqueness of each man, and his radical dependence on community for his inward nature—were major themes of Romantic philosophy. One finds them first expressed theologically in Schleiermacher, in his two basic categories: (1) each person must experience religion *for himself* (cf. *On Religion: to Its Cultured Despisers* [New York: Frederick Ungar, 1955], Second Speech); (2) the character of each person's inward experience and feeling is communicated to him from his *communal* context (i.e., the "race consciousness" of mankind), whether in religion that feeling be that of "sin" or of "God-consciousness" (cf. *The Christian Faith* [Edinburgh: T. & T. Clark, 1928], Sections 60, 71, 93, 94, 107–111, 121–125).

[3] The dialogic character of man, the fact that the I arises out of a man's relation to another Thou, is a discovery neither of the great Martin Buber, of social science, nor of modern psychology, but, surprisingly, of Hegel, and especially of his great pupil, Feuerbach. Cf. *The Essence of Christianity* (New York: Harper Torchbooks, 1957), Part I, Chapters 6, 8, and 9.

look at things, our standards and values, the very structures of our language and so of our thought processes, the shape of our feelings and desires, of our fears and our hopes—each of these takes its form from the social and historical context of our existence. Thus are we Southerners or Yankees, Americans, Christians or Jews, Western, twentieth-century, etc., and *not* Hellenistic Romans, Medieval Franks—or universal men! Our personal consciousness, and so the very mechanism, so to speak, of our freedom, is a social and communal, a historical, consciousness.

This communal basis for our personal identity is also an existential threat to its realization. The family out of which we come, and through whose love, care, and discipline we become a person, as often as not is the very group which resists most powerfully and subtly our freedom and independence, our personal discovery of who we are and will to be—as almost every school counselling appointment and every psychoanalytic session witness. The community whose customs, courtesies, attitudes, and standards form us, also resists our freedom to be ourselves and seeks to make that self merely another embodiment of its own common attitudes, habits, and appearance: clean-shaven and short-cropped, neat, buttoned-down, respectable, American, ambitious, churchgoing, and moral—as they define morality. In desperation, the stronger young person rightly revolts against this communal pressure on his freedom, and, possibly growing a beard, long hair, or becoming leftist, refuses to adopt the conformist, conservative, perhaps segregationist or nationalist standards forced on him. Or possibly he resists the conventional moral codes that seem to make him not himself, but a junior edition of what his parents and everyone else pretends in public to be like. It is a tragic fact of our existence in time, and inescapable, that we must resist those who love us and the community to which we wish to be loyal, if we are to become ourselves. Conflict with our community, distance from it inwardly in rejection of its conventional ways or, in extreme situations, outwardly in external withdrawal, is as necessary to the achievement of integrity as is participation.

No epoch in history has been so aware of this need as has the modern West, or so clearly on the side of those seeking freedom from conformism to the patterns of home and community to which we all owe so much. The development of personal selfhood has been the main burden of the most powerful secular voices of our time: of our literature and our theater, of the academic goal of freedom of thought and of individual expression, of existentialist philosophy, and of that most dominating influence on our cultural life, psychoanalytic theory. Perhaps no people in history have been so deliberately conscious of the values of unique individuality and selfhood as has the modern American, a consciousness embodied in his habits of child-rearing, his educational theories, his tremendous enthusiasm for psychoanalysis, and his literary and artistic productions. It is, therefore, an irony of social history, a symptom of the intractability of man, that this same culture should appear to the rest of the world as overwhelmingly "conformist" and lacking precisely in any traces of genuine individuality, and that the most potent social movement among us, the hippie revolt of the younger generation, is in reaction precisely against what to them is a culture totally lacking in the possibility of individual being. In their view, to participate in a culture explicitly geared to the development of individuality is ironically to lose all uniqueness and freedom.

This emphasis on personal selfhood enunciated by both our educational establishment and by those who revolt against it has great validity because no man can be creative of a meaningful existence unless there be in him facets of genuine inward freedom, unless what he is and does springs from himself, from the use of his own powers, evaluations, and decisions. This is valid for all the significant roles of human existence: that of craftsman, trader, businessman, doctor, teacher, artist, citizen; and certainly it holds in the more intimate roles of lover, spouse, parent, friend, and child of God. If in any of these communal roles and relations, what a man does is merely conventional, done because mother and father or others have done it, and because it is expected of him or forced upon him, then his thoughts, feelings, loves, and actions will have little worth or weight. No creative community with others, in the family, in friendship, or in the wider society, can be formed without the free, self-directing participation of the members of that community. Freedom and community are in tension but also inseparable, and no fully human existence can be possible without both.

The search for selfhood involves, we have said, the initial resistance to and the testing of, perhaps even the rejection of, the ways and standards of the various communities that form us. Because of this, many young people, rejecting the standards of their elders, and even some older intellectuals who once did so, have concluded that freedom means the necessary loss of *all* standards. Seeing the invaluable function that the modern relativizing of all moral codes has performed in the service of free and authentic existence, especially in the area of sexual behavior, they feel that freedom means that distinctions of value no longer exist and that all norms are thus rendered obsolete. Does not each society have its own parochial preferences; is there anywhere an absolute or universal value or standard; is it not true that in every society the absolutizing of its parochial values has always compromised freedom in the achievement of authentic existence—so the argument runs. Thus once again the genius of the secular spirit in the realm of thought has led to the seemingly inevitable terminus of relativism, and once again Flux appears to be king.

Relativism is, however, more difficult to achieve in human existence than many of its proponents realize. The arguments of those who point to the "reality" and the value of relativism themselves presuppose certain values and norms which are, for the purposes of the argument itself, assumed not to be relative, notably the values we have just been enumerating of freedom, self-expression, and communal relations structured in their light. What the modern moral relativists have done is thus to redefine authentic human existence in the light of a new set of values centering about freedom and self-realization, which inevitably relativize an older set of values, but which they by no means wish to relinquish or to find dissolved in the processes of social change. And so when confronted with either conservative or revolutionary forces which find no place for the values of personal freedom, these liberal intellectuals defend them as staunchly as any older generation defended their standards.

As this example indicates, freedom does not mean the loss of all standards, and a free society is not at all a society with-

out norms for the guidance, evaluation, and control of its behavior. What the modern emphasis on freedom and personal decision does mean is, first, that there are for us no norms which
are given an absolute authority over our decisions by social or
religious tradition; and secondly, as a consequence, that in a
pluralistic society we are involved in the task of self-determination through our own choice of norms. Of course, the values
among which we must choose are themselves mediated to us
through the communities of which we are a part; none of us is
the first in the line of human beings, and our standards, like our
existence itself, do not spring *de novo* out of our self-creativity.
Even the stance of existentialism, which emphasizes the total
self-creation of man through his own freedom, depends upon
a long, historical tradition in Western spirituality in which the
concept of self-determination through decision slowly matured.

Nevertheless, there is something new in the modern
Geist; and that is the requirement that each modern man faces of
choosing those values and norms by which he directs and evaluates his decisions, and in terms of which he judges both himself
and the community in which his selfhood realizes itself. Modern
Western man, Protestant, Catholic, Jewish, or secular, is not
bound by his past; he is not the passive and helpless recipient
from an absolute tradition of either his values or his sense of his
own place in the scheme of things. Whatever view of his life,
of its worth, and of its goals he receives from his community,
this he must appropriate for himself before it can be effective in
his own existence; and no secular or religious community can have
effective spiritual authority over him unless he chooses to exist
spiritually within it. Modern Western man is free from any *particular* set of values which are pressed upon him, by his church,
by the intellectual community, by the SDS, by the Rotary Club,
or by the John Birch Society. There are and can be no merely
given historical absolutes for him, and in *this* sense he has come
of age and is autonomous in a new way.

This is, we suggest, the deeper historical meaning of the
freedom defended at present by Western society; not the freedom
of an economic activity or even of the vote, though some form of
each is an implication of this notion, but the freedom to be crea-

tive of his own ultimate values, convictions, and style of life and so ultimately of the social matrix within which he lives. Both the communist East and the democratic West express a radical vision of the autonomy of man in history, only they express this in very different terms. The communist emphasizes *communal* autonomy over the demons of exploitation, want, inequality, and conflict through the control by the Party and its doctrine, acting for man as a whole, over man's social existence and through that control over history itself. The democratic Western vision of autonomy, which we have expressed here, emphasizes the freedom of each man in each community over traditional norms and customs of behavior, freedom from the control of outside political forces, and thus freedom through unfettered inquiry, new ideas, new goals, and personal decisions to vary creatively our norms and patterns of behavior, and through this experimental, pragmatic variety of response to conquer the external, historical demons of exploitation, welfare, and want. In each case, the "faith" of the community is placed squarely upon the powers of human wisdom and autonomy, through the Party or through the community of individuals, to move the social body progressively forward in history. Eternal, changeless, sacral patterns have in both been replaced by sacral powers of intentional change latent in man and creative of the historically new and the hopefully better.

If, then, Western man is on his own in the sense that he can now be creative of his own values and so of the social context in which he is to live, by the same token he is *not* free to escape the problem of norms and values entirely. If he is himself to guide his own life in freedom, he can do so only in relation to some view of human excellence which grasps him as an embodiment of authentic existence and in relation to some form of community which he finds creative of this style of life. Norms which structure communal life and so which participate in some mode of ultimacy are, we suggest, inescapable, even in modern autonomous culture.

The reason for this need for norms is that human freedom is embodied within an organic existence that is contingent, communal, or internally related, and temporal. Its acts of free self-determination do not arise out of nothing, creating themselves, their own world, and all their values *de novo*. Rather, freedom is the self-directing capacity of an organic life existing in time and in given interaction with its environment and in interrelations with others. It must, therefore, shape itself into the future and so over the continuing moments of time, and that shaping, both to create inner strength and integrity (without which acts of freedom are impossible) and to create enduring relations with other things and persons (without which it is quite unrealized and so empty, as we saw earlier), must follow some consistent pattern, some model or image of possibility according to which decisions are made and the open future actualized. There is neither self nor community, neither freedom nor relations—in fact there is neither a surviving organism nor a human reality—if there are only arbitrary, sporadic decisions and acts, momentarily evoked by a continually changing set of desires and values. Creative individual freedom, like creative community, requires a consistent and pervasive set of norms by which our lives are shaped over the moments of time. In other words, for there to be the actuality of free existence, of "existence" in that sense, there must be relevant possibilities that provide the norms or models by which a life is guided.[4] Thus are the often dim and unconscious, but also occasionally conscious, questions, "Who am I?" "What am I to become?" "What is it for me to be a man?" the most significant

---

[4] No philosopher has expressed with more clarity and insight this need for consistent, repeated, and so eternal forms if there are to be consistent, real individuals amidst passage than has Whitehead. What we have (following Kierkegaard) said about man's decisions over time and so of the human self and those relations to others that arise out of these decisions—as well as create them—Whitehead has said in his ontological analysis with regard to the relation of becoming to "eternal objects." Eternal objects are, for him, the forms that make possible order and novelty within the perpetual flux of becoming. Without these eternal objects or essences, no *endurance* of individual "things" or objects, and *a fortiori* no persons, would be possible; for the fleeting occasions achieve their temporal order by repeating in endlessly changing modalities changeless forms. Cf. the passage on change, endurance, and eternality in *Science and the Modern World* (New York: Macmillan Company, 1925), p. 121; or as he puts this in *Process and Reality* (New York: Macmillan Company, 1929), "In the philosophy of organism it is not 'substance' which is permanent but 'form'." p. 44.

questions that arise in individual life, for it is in terms of some answers to these questions about possibilities for man and so for us, about projects for our own future being, that our style of life is determined. And if we do not receive an answer to them ready-made from our parents, fraternity, local ethnic or national community—and so relinquish again our self-direction—we must find them and appropriate them for ourselves in some communal context of our own choosing.

The inescapability of standards is evident in any phenomenological analysis of an act of choice, whether that act be trivial or extremely significant for our future. At any point where we are free to decide—to go to this college or that, to go to the movies or to study for an exam, to prepare to be a doctor or to enter into business, to be with or marry this girl or not—our decision is, in the first place, itself inevitable. If we refuse to decide, time slips by, and in the end we have, through no decision at all, in fact decided something—but something negative. For the man who fails to choose a *particular* girl in the end in fact has chosen to be a bachelor—unless, of course, he is himself grabbed by an exemplar of modern feminine autonomy! But also involved in each of these unavoidable enactments of freedom by choice is the concurrent affirmation of a standard in terms of which deliberation evaluates alternatives and so in terms of which the choice is made. Some evaluation of significance and worth takes place in each choice of an activity or of a career: if I deliberate and then choose to study rather than to have a good time—or the reverse —I have affirmed an evaluation of significance for my life, held momentarily or permanently, consciously or unconsciously, but nevertheless there. Insofar as it achieves itself in an embodied action, freedom must have found for itself some direction or model, and it must identify itself with some community which expresses and embodies that stance or style of life. Whether in culture or without, in a vocation or in revolt, we cannot dodge the necessity for standards, models, and community if we are to be free and if our freedom is to be shaped in autonomy. To be itself, freedom points beyond itself to a standard or image by which it is directed and shaped, and inescapably that norm has for the freedom which it shapes the character of ultimacy and sacrality—for it is the source and foundation of our own existence as we create it, and of all value and good to that existence.

Of course, we should be clear that levels of our personality below what we can identify as conscious or deliberate participate in all of the most significant of our choices. In choosing and enacting our careers, in our relations to others, especially in love and marriage, in our most fundamental activities and attitudes in social and political matters, and in the general shape of our character, we are (fortunately) carried forward by forces far deeper than the intellectual assent to certain standards and the acts of conscious will in accord with those standards. In these cases, we may say that our conscious selves discover rather than create or decide upon the direction in which we are as a total self already going. There is destiny as well as conscious freedom in all that we do. Otherwise, there would be little organic unity to our being, little affect or love in our important relations, and little enthusiasm and drive (*eros*) in what we do. The notion of intentionality or freedom must, therefore, point to deeper levels than merely those of conscious choice or of intellectual assent if it is to express the phenomenological reality of significant choices and activities. And thus, in each act of centered freedom, our whole beings are involved if we are fully men.

Nevertheless, this does not mean that freedom is or can be devoid either of deliberation or of the standards or models which deliberation necessarily entails. I cannot make choices consistently and with full personal participation, and so *I* cannot shape my life creatively, without becoming in some measure clear about what those standards are, and without therefore willing them in personal awareness over the moments of time as new occasions for new decisions arise. Just as the basic direction of my life must participate in deeper levels than the conscious, so too it must "surface" into deliberation and so conscious decision. Those two sciences of man which emphasize the unconscious determinants of man's freedom, psychoanalysis and sociology, have as their *goals* the bringing of these determinants into the area of consciousness and so into the arena of free choice and intellectual determination. On the existential, if not on the theoretical level, the sciences of man all recognize that man to be man must exercise some form of conscious, deliberate control over his life and his actions. Thus, though we may never realize it, do we all shape ourselves in terms of some dimly discerned model embodying some evaluation and so hierarchy of significance, some picture of authentic man which grasps and holds our minds and wills, some style of life or ethical perspective which determines the use we make of our freedom because it provides the structure by which we choose.

On the deepest level, then, each person is faced with the question, "What *kind* of person do I want to become?" We are referring here not to the vocational question, mentioned earlier, namely the question of what sort of work or profession I should embark upon, but, supposing any sort of professional or life work, what style of life or mode of being as a person do I wish to embody with that vocation? This is the real import of the question, "Who am I?" We face this question with increasing intensity as we mature, perhaps first in school or in college, and our answer qualifies the total remainder of our lives. Is my model for real humanity the big shot, the brilliant, active, admired man, envied by all, popular, acclaimed? Do I find friends and participate in activities because I like *them* or because I want others to see that I am a popular and talented person? How easily this model mixes with Christian piety, on campus, in seminary, or in the ministry! Or again, is my image the righteous prophet—am I interested in helping others or in knowing myself to be righteous and being thought so by others? And let us note, if our model for our true self is one of these self-oriented varieties, then it matters little ethically what vocation we decide to pursue, whether it be that of the doctor, bond salesman, professor, minister, or revolutionary reformer—our goal will be that of the capable, successful, admired and distinguished man, and there will as a result be little inner integrity, real relations with others, or effective creativity in our life. Clearly, here there is little to distinguish this image, or style of life, from that encouraged by our culture's advertisements: portraying as a symbol of achievement and so of human excellence the elegant, powerful, graying man stepping with courteous indifference into his deep-blue Cadillac, or, alternatively, the lovely, gracious lady, supremely confident of herself, admired by adoring men and by an attentive husband, able to subdue any rival—and quite without love for a soul.

These and others like them are the important images of our culture, and we are all subject to them. They shape the way we use our freedom, for our decisions all down the line are tailored by their pattern. Thus they shape us. And when it comes to advancing our interests—to getting that Cadillac, that fur stole, distinguished professorship, or larger church—then these images and the values they embody will determine all that we do. A person's life is molded by the values he adopts because his decisions over the passage of time determine, in large part, who he is. And since each decision requires and obeys a standard—by which the decision for this or that is made—it is the standard that ultimately shapes who we are. Returning to our ontological theme, the consciousness of freedom in man, of the possibility and the necessity of self-creation through decision, has, it seems, implied once again the rejection of any metaphysical categories expressive of an independent, unrelated, and changeless substance (or essence) as the fundamental mode for understanding the self. Such a "substance" would be determined neither by choices over time nor by possibility (standards and norms for the self). Thus both those modern philosophies that emphasize freedom and self-creation, existentialism and process philosophy, also reject a given "substance" or "essence" of the self, and assert the crucial importance of future possibility or projects in the becomingness of our humanity.[5]

The gift of freedom thus requires a standard, a relevant

[5] It is interesting to reflect on the surprising similarity between existentialism, where there is no essence of the self but only a continuity of decisions illustrating an integrity formed by commitment (cf. Kierkegaard, Judge William's letters, in *Either/Or,* Part II [Princeton: Princeton University Press, 1944]), and process thought, where, since there is no substance, there only can be a continuity of form among serial occasions. In both of these views, the categories of form, possibility, norms, and commitment or aim are central because of the lack of "substance" or "essence" in the ontology—showing (*a*) how divergent forms of thought in the same cultural epoch reflect the same fundamental tendencies, and (*b*) how ethical and ontological matters inevitably interact with one another.

possibility for my freedom, a project, and insofar as I am really free to be myself, so much the more am I forced to find a model, an image of man's existence which I wish to embody. And, let us note, such a standard manifests the dimension of ultimacy of which we have spoken; it is sacral in character. In the first place, it functions as an ultimate for us. It determines totally the one life we have; to it we give our lives, in expectation that through it our lives will be fulfilled. Thus these images function in fact as kinds of surrogate gods in our existence, or at least as manifestations for *us* of the divine. For our god is whatever it is to which we give our lives, and from which we expect in turn to receive all our blessings.[6] If we make our important decisions on the basis of the image of the man in the Cadillac or in First Church, then that is for us a hierophany of the divine, for we expect—perhaps dimly and unconsciously, but very effectively—happiness and good fortune to come to us from a successful embodiment of this standard. Clearly if we should be wrong, if only unhappiness, emptiness, and isolation characterize an existence patterned on this model, then this deity will turn out to be only an idol, falsely worshipped. For the one life we live will have been determined utterly by this standard, and quite literally then be ruined. This *is* an ultimate concern.

Secondly, the adoption and active embodiment of this model requires a sense of the relation of this chosen self to the community, to the immediate historical context, and to the ultimate frame of history. To draw us to itself—however petty it may seem to be to others—this model must parade before us as

---

[6] Cf. Luther's well-known definition of what it is "to have a God": "A god is that to which we look for all good and in which we find refuge in every time of need. To have a god is nothing else than to trust and believe him with our whole hearts. As I have often said, the trust and faith of the heart alone make God and an idol. If your faith and trust are right, then your God is a true God. On the other hand, if your trust is false and wrong, then you have not the true God. For these two belong together, faith and God. That to which your heart clings and entrusts itself is, I say, really your God." Martin Luther, *The Large Catechism*, First Part, the First Commandment, found in the *Book of Concord*, translated and edited by Theodore G. Tappert (Philadelphia: Muhlenberg Press, 1959), p. 365.

an essential image of the nature of man and so built into the grain of history itself. It must have for us a significant place in the ultimate context of things, a pattern of what our human reality is and was meant to be—else it contains no promise for us and no power over us. To enact our freedom, therefore, we are driven to an ultimate dimension immediately, an ultimate standard for ourselves or our community and an ultimate view of our being in history. In all traditional cultures, as Mircea Eliade has taught us,[7] one of the most important functions of the religious language of myth has been to provide a setting of ultimacy for the sacral models by which cultures have patterned their significant acts and so their lives. Our culture, despite the ingression of freedom, is no different. And one of the most important uses of mythical discourse in a secular culture concerns the explication of these images of man by which this culture lives—whether it be the sacred king in the Cadillac, or the shaman in the scientist's white coat!

Again, in the inevitable use of our freedom, we encounter a manifestation of the sacred, some form of the ultimate, namely an unconditioned standard for our existence, the model which determines the concrete shape of what we are, and the ultimate context of history within which this model functions. Our self-understanding, expressed in images of man, is quite literally of

[7] Mircea Eliade notes that the sacred, which in primitive life always involves those originating forces which *in illo tempore*, at the original time, founded the world, its space and its creatures, also provides the models or exemplars with which and on which man patterns his behavior. No activity is worthful, no person real unless both are guided by the relevant sacred exemplars. "Every myth, whatever its nature, recounts an event that took place *in illo tempore*, and constitutes as a result, a precedent and pattern for all the actions and 'situations' later to repeat that event. Every ritual, and every meaningful act that man performs, repeats a mythical archetype. . . . But note that the majority of myths . . . constitute an *exemplar history* for the human society in which they have been preserved, and for the world that society lives in." Eliade, *Patterns in Comparative Religion* (New York: Meridian Books, 1963), pp. 429–430. One might say we are seeking to locate some of those secular exemplars that provide sacral patterns for the ordinary life of modern man in the world, for these traces of the sacred are no less important to us than they were to ancient man.

ultimate concern to us because these models help to determine
the character of all we do, and to create the weal or woe of our
own life. A secular culture that provides no means for consistent
and intelligent discourse about these all-important symbolic
forms that guide and shape our freedom is one that, believing
fully in autonomy, will nevertheless proceed to enact that autonomy blindly and unintelligibly.

Here for our freedom, in our inescapable commitment
to some style of life by which our selfhood becomes itself and
measures itself in its community, is probably our first brush with
the sacred.

It is, further, worth noting that amidst all the variety of
models of authentic humanity that proliferate in our culture,
when the most thoughtful of our secular intellectuals offer us an
image of authentic manhood, and try with perhaps the most
modern empirical methods to picture the "mature" human, there
is surprising agreement with regard to their common answer.
For almost all, the model of human excellence—sometimes assumed, sometimes clinically proved—is that of a free self-determination from within, motivated and shaped by love for
those around us.[8] As we have noted, individual personness comes
to be out of the polarity of self-realization in community; so,
enacting the same theme, human nature fulfils itself in excellence when that polar structure of entity and relation is actualized
by an inward freedom whose character is outgoing love to others.

This model of authentic humanity offers to us perhaps
the one point where secular goals and aspirations have made
close contact with traditional Christian norms. For clearly the
picture of the Jesus of the gospels has been historically operative here, shaping the self-understanding of Western culture
away from images of the indifferent wise man, the passionless
intellectual, or even the prudent and just man of power, toward
this model, well-nigh now universally accepted among thoughtful people. The freedom of Jesus *from* the pressures of tradi-

[8] Cf. especially Erich Fromm, *Man for Himself* (London: Routledge & Kegan Paul, 1949), and *The Art of Loving* (New York: Harper's, 1956).

tion and convention and *for* the welfare of others, his freedom from self-concern and his corresponding creative concern for all who approached him, this combination of inner integrity and outgoing love, has engrafted itself onto our culture's consciousness and so been recognized far beyond the bounds of the Church as the true measure of our humanity, the form in which the ultimate mystery which is the origin of our being claims us for itself.

We know, if we know anything at all about these ultimate questions of our existence, that in these terms alone can we find our true selves. In all the mystery of existence, with its emptiness, evil, and doubt, this surely is clear: we find ourselves when, like him, we love ourselves enough to be free, and yet when we also can lose ourselves for others as he did. For this reason, the ideal or norm of integrity, with which this discussion of freedom began, culminates in an entirely different set of norms, those of love and justice, the requirement *to* my integrity that the self, if it is to *be* a self, give itself to its neighbors in love and in the fundamental respect of the neighbor's integrity and rights.

In this sense the radical theologians are right: In Jesus our freedom does find its rightful Lord, he who provides us with a model of individual authenticity and of social community, the image and symbol of our self-understanding which we did not (at least historically as a race) seem to have been able to find on our own. Strangely, it is the Lord on the cross who gives to the world which put him there the only model for its own fulfilment. For we may well ask, can such an authentic measure of ourselves be found amidst our own wayward and shifting desires, our false starts and self-centered images of perfection; or is it writ large in our ambiguous social environment and the many empty or one-sided models that that environment offers to us?

In this sense, too, we can affirm the long tradition, stemming in modern religious thought from Kant and ultimately from the Reformation, which finds the essence of humanity in the moral sense or the conscience, and our central relation to the sacred in the call of moral responsibility to others.[9] To be sure, to limit our relation to the sacred to this category of moral obligation, and so to regard the essence of true humanity as the moral control of desire and the denial of the innate life and desires of the self is, as has often been noted, to create a legal, often repressive, and ultimately heteronomous form of spirituality— as if the vitalities and joys of selfhood in and of themselves were "evil" and only became "good" when the self was morally smothered and sent on helpful errands by obligations beyond itself. As we have urged, the sacred initially appears as the basis of the reality, the activities, and the meanings of the self, its community, and its world; it functions as the ground of the *reality* of each individual and of its innate, loved meanings as much as the sanction of the creative moral relations of individuals to one another. Healthy and moral relations thus become possible only when the self and its meanings are affirmed as well as obligated, loved as well as denied—i.e., when the sacred is seen as manifesting itself in the categories of life, of being, and of *eros*, as well as of duty, obligation, and self-denial. Or, to put this point in doctrinal terms, creation and providence (and ultimately grace) must be balancing emphases to the category of the divine moral law. Nevertheless, with these clear qualifications to this tradition which roots the religious solely in the moral, we must agree that the true life of the self is found only when it knows and molds itself by some moral ideal above itself, and further only when it can realize creative social rela-

---

[9] Cf. this from Ebeling, continuing this Lutheran-Kantian tradition: "And the only responsible talk of God is that which aims at the place where God and the world meet as it were in a mathematical point. That place is the conscience. Because responsible talk of God aims at the conscience, the world necessarily also becomes a question when talk of God stands in question . . . For as conscience man stands between God and the world." Gerhard Ebeling, *Word and Faith* (Philadelphia: Fortress Press, 1963), p. 356. Perhaps one can say that the law or conscience is the most intimate touch man has with the divine—until he knows the Gospel. Unless, however, the power and life of God as creator and the rule of God over events as Providence are *also* a part of the "point where God and man meet," God and religion can only become heteronomous to the autonomy that is to become "moral" through the conscience.

tions to others. And this realization in turn requires a moral control of the self over itself, a qualification of its natural desires in the direction of self-abnegation, and above all a concern for the welfare of others to balance the overriding concern we each have for ourselves—when, as we have noted, love and justice balance the norms of integrity and freedom. Thus, however true it may be that ultimately self-love is involved in all authentic humanity, granted the tendency of our freedom to love itself inordinately, the true self is a *moral* achievement, and is more often found by self-denial than by a simple self-affirmation. Consequently, we do understand God more truly when we know him not only as the ground of the self's strength and power, but also as "good," that is as righteous will, as the source of the moral law, and as judgment on evil.

To sum up, when we ask, "Who am I?" the most secular because the most human of questions, we are again searching for an ultimate, in this case an ultimate model by which our freedom is to shape itself. In our search for an answer to this moral question that our self-determination raises, we encounter this lord, and in his terms we find what seems to be the will of our destiny for us to become. In this prolegomenon, the ground has been prepared—through the secular search for an ultimate standard, model, or style of life—for us to understand the meaning of the religious symbols of the righteous will of God for us and of the divine moral law for our life. Correspondingly, a clearer delineation of the divine mystery from which we arise, now in the more personal terms of an unconditional moral will and intention, begins to be possible in theological discourse. The vagueness of the sacred as the ground of our being and as the context of the meanings of our temporal existence is partially dispelled by this moral manifestation of the sacred in relation to our freedom and its search for authenticity. The sacred now *obligates* and *judges* us, as well as empowers and threatens us; its mystery, as well as its clarity, is paradoxically thus increased as we come to know ourselves as obligated. For the essence of the sacred as the ground of obligation is, as always, its unconditional character, unconditional in its requirement on us, and unconditional in what it demands of us. To know ourselves as

obligated—and no serious person fails in some part to apprehend *this*—is to know perhaps the most direct and inward of
all human experiences of the ultimate and the unconditional.
For, as anyone who has asked himself, "*Should* I resist the draft
in this war?" knows, he has neither created, nor can he by willing dispel, this ultimate requirement of obligation which he
feels. And he is also unhappily aware that neither the anthro-
pologist nor his analyst can protect him from this unconditional
and inescapable judgment of conscience, of the moral law, and,
strangely, of his own integrity.

But now the paradox of our self-knowledge reverses itself. In
knowing ourselves at last as obligated, we now find we quite
cease to understand ourselves. For as both our personal and our
communal or historical experience witness, our freedom is the
strangest of our powers, and in its exercise we seem to cease
even to recognize the self we thought we knew. Our minds seem
freely able to attach themselves to an ideal, and our wills to decide firmly to enact it; we determine to have "character," to be
loving rather than hostile or irritable persons, to forget our selfish and wayward ambitions, to accept and love the neighbors
around us, and to help with all our powers to reform the world.
If we be Christians, the Lord on the cross becomes our Lord,
and we seek to incarnate his freedom, his weakness, his avail-
ability for others. All of us who take our existence seriously, and
certainly all present young Christians who are captivated by the
will to love and serve in the world, have had such experiences
of dedication to an ideal. It runs like fire through the present
college and seminary communities: commitment to an image of
the selfless, suburbanless, prophetic mission practically defines
our present *Geist*. And often we think, and even are taught, that
this is all religion is—or as the radical theologians put it, this is
what the substance of being a Christian is, namely to commit
ourselves to an ethical perspective or style of life, to dedicate
ourselves to reform or to revolution, to try to "become like Jesus
in the world."

Actually, however, this is precisely where the deepest
problems of human self-realization, far from reaching their end,

only really begin. For the model seems to refuse incarnation; it remains "over there," unembodied in us, outside of us—and we remain much as before, dedicated, yes, but untransformed, inauthentic, and now divided against ourselves. And it is only on this deeper level that we can understand either the mystery of our own freedom or how we might become more like Jesus in the world. Something in ourselves, that we perhaps did not know was there, prevents our enactment of this image; we seem unable, perhaps even strangely unwilling, to become what we thought we really wanted to be. Among many descriptions of this situation, secular and religious, St. Paul's is still the most searching: the good I would I do not, the evil that I would not, that I practice; there is a law in my members that wars against the law in my mind, and I am helpless to enact the law (or the model) I cherish. And he concludes[10] that because of this inner bondage, the law alone, dedication to a model or image of human authenticity, cannot save us and in fact kills us. Our valuations by our minds and our dedication through our conscious wills are not enough, for however hard we try, they do not represent the actual balance of forces in our real world.[11] This is

[10] Rom. 7.

[11] For this writer, one of the major fallacies of Whitehead's otherwise profound interpretation of life lies just here, and the same problem runs through most of the theologies that are too strictly dependent on his vision. He assumes, as do almost all Pelagian thinkers—including most of the radical theologians—that the underlying will of the entity, represented ontologically by the subjective aim, is a pure and uncompromised aim toward value, toward, that is, that particular possibility of intensity of experience relevant to that occasion. This is, of course, what we consciously feel our own aims to be and are sure that they are; and Whitehead's age assumed that this optimistic assessment of our own will's benevolence and adherence to value was correct. What experience continually reveals, however, is that while the conscious level, so to speak, of our subjective aim *is* toward values, nevertheless within that aim itself there is an antithetical principle that frustrates and despoils our establishment of the values we claim, a principle that in fact rebels against the possibility presented to us by the primordial nature of God for realization. Our problems, then, are not only those of weakness, indecisiveness, mediocrity, and transience, as he and his age assumed; they are rather that we continually, actively distort the possibility of the moment and thus fundamentally despoil the harmony of

surely our most common experience of ourselves, and of movements, secular or religious, in history.

Or, to be more honest, it is our most common experience
of *others*! It is perfectly evident to all of us that these others do
not live up to their ideals. We may see this in our roommate or
a professional colleague telling us about his cherished goals.
How blindly he interprets himself by his own ideals—as prophet,
as servant of the Lord, as merely helping others—and refuses to
see the hostility, the ambition, and the self-centeredness that so
clearly color his every action! Only in rare confidential moments,
filled sometimes with relief, sometimes with despair, lubricated
possibly by midnight beers, does he admit this other side either
to us or to himself. Secular wisdom, as opposed to secular philosophy, knows this to be the pattern of our general behavior. It
is common knowledge, universally assumed by all who pretend
to know the world, that in our economic striving, our political
allegiances, and our group loyalties, we are motivated by self-
interest; and every statistical survey of voting habits bears out
this universal tendency of our values and opinions to follow the
directions of our interests. In each of these areas, the men who
dominate the real world, the advertisers, businessmen, real-es-
tate agents, judges, politicians—and even social scientists—
never question but that our behavior is dictated by our self-interest rather than by our proclaimed ideals.[12]

---

process rather than merely adding to its increment. There is, in other
words, a seeming cancer in our actual, existing subjective aim of which
his "essentialist" view of process is apparently not aware.

For cultural as well as theological agreement with this somewhat jaundiced view of the actualities of our existence—if not the potentialities of our essence—one can appeal not only to Paul, Augustine,
Luther, Kierkegaard, and so on, but to many modern writers who repeat,
some in despair, some in resignation, and some in a strange joy, this
theme of our bondage to an evil in our wills which we do not wish to
will; Camus, *The Fall* (New York: Knopf, 1957); Golding, *The Free
Fall* (London: Farber and Farber, 1959); and Miller, *After the Fall*
(New York: Viking Press, 1964), being merely three examples which
explicitly use the ancient Biblical symbol to interpret this most secular
of experiences.

[12] For an empirical validation of these facets of man's life, see
Gilkey, *Shantung Compound* (New York: Harper & Row, 1966),
Chapters 5–8 and 14.

This other, darker side of our freedom is clearest of all to each of us when we come into conflict with other social groups. In the first place, we always hold that *they* are "free." No sociological, historical, or psychological causes determine our hated neighbors! Such necessitating causes would function as excuses for them, and so we reject such explanations. On the contrary, we are convinced that they *chose* their odious action, and that thus they acted purely from malevolence or from a freely willed self-interest. Determinism, "reasons" beyond our control, always explain *our* failings, but never the evil our enemies perpetrate on their victims. Furthermore, we see clearly how another political party or class in our own society, another racial group, another nation, or another cultural complex such as communism represents, acts (freely) for self-interest rather than from moral conviction. In their case, it is perfectly plain to us that *their* proclaimed ideals are just "expedience," "politics," "propaganda," and that what really motivates them is not at all the idealism they proclaim, but a cross between self-interest and a lust for power. But we ourselves? We are interested in being servants, in the good life for all, in peace and justice, in helping the other fellow.[13] We judge ourselves in terms of the ideal images we cherish, and others in terms of the rude character of their actions. As Paul remarked, "We know nothing against ourselves," and everything against our neighbor.[14] Thus, in this

[13] One may say that the only way in which President Johnson and the adherents of the New Left resembled each other is that each saw his person and his role on the field of history as that of a large Boy Scout, eager only to help others who are in need, and so full only of good will toward mankind in general.

[14] It is particularly ironic that many social scientists, discoursing "objectively" about "man," illustrate Paul's view that we judge others differently than we judge ourselves. On the one hand, the laws of human behavior which they find as a result of their studies presuppose this universal self-interest of mankind. Nevertheless, when they philosophize about man's nature and destiny, they enunciate a view of man as moral and rational which the presuppositions and the conclusions alike of their scientific studies continually belie. Most books of the sciences of man, in their "scientific" sections, portray man as determined by economic, political, social, and ethnic forces that determine his behavior along lines strictly devoted to his own well-being and security and that of his group, and that make his ideals epiphenomenal at best. But in their "prophetic"

combination of self-deception about ourselves and of hostile interpretation of others, we, too, defy our own model and so illustrate the same human problem all over again.

If the vast laboratory of man's history, secular or religious, illustrates any one general truth, it is that human freedom, however creative it may be, is not simply a freedom capable of choosing and then following its own ideals. Despite our best intentions, we do do something else; what we do gets corrupted and ends up sadly different from what we had intended; an evil that was not part of our purpose—or of the purpose we told ourselves was ours—appears from nowhere as an aspect of what we have done. For our human lot is filled with bitter tensions

---

sections at the ends of their books, when they discuss human destiny and the possible uses social scientific knowledge can offer toward the eradication of human evil and the improvement of the human situation, these same authors tend to see man as rationally motivated by their own liberal ideals of general well-being and social progress. The reason for this contradictory estimate of man probably is that when they look at man in their scientific inquiry, they are regarding the behavior of *others*, and are thus very realistic about the disparity between actual behavior and proclaimed ideals. When, on the other hand, they speak of man's possibilities in the future, they tend to look within themselves as liberal scientists at their own goals, motives, and commitments to their own ideals—for it is usually the "scientists" as rational inquirers and manipulators that provide them with their model of modern man and so the basis for their hopes for a better world. Seeing there in themselves the image of the objective inquiring scientist, they go on to describe man's possibilities in terms of this flattering model taken from their own experience of themselves, and so, quite naturally, they become idealistic and optimistic about the future. Like most of us, they think of "man" in relation to two different models of performance. When we think of the others, we see man's tendencies to use ideals for his own benefit; when we think of ourselves, we tend to view man optimistically in terms of the goals we consciously cherish. Few books of evolutionary or social science put these two models of man together. It would complicate the "science" of the early sections if the *freedom* presupposed in their hopes for the future were put into the development of man from the beginning; and it would dampen their hopes expressed in the last part if the *self-interest* assumed at the beginning were to be thought as a continuing element of the human problem. Thus many of these authors illustrate rather than illumine the baffling human tendency to judge others in a much more realistic way than we judge ourselves.

and destructive conflicts between persons and between groups—each side knowing nothing of "bad intentions" but on the contrary being sure of its own virtue and morality. This complicates endlessly our creative relation to culture and the role of our human autonomy in history. For it means, on the one hand, that every culture, created by the ambiguity of this freedom, is sinful and sick, always and in part, and thus, speaking theologically, under the judgment of God and of our judgment if we be Christians. But it also means that we, too, are under judgment, and that the only man who can be a faithful prophet against the sin of the world or a creative reformer of its ills is one who sees that the community of sin includes himself, his directing revolutionary group, and even the shape of the new world he envisions in his protest.

Empirically our wills seem quite free to choose an ideal, but although nothing prevents us but ourselves, we seem unable to enact it. Something gets in the way, we corrupt our model for some other purpose; we turn it to our own use; we seem helpless to become what we want to become, or what we claim to ourselves and to others that we are.[15] However much we determine to be a loving person and to bring in a clean new world, we find ourselves more interested in being thought loving, and in being secure and powerful in that new world. And so we, too, corrupt our ideals, and with them the future as others have the present—and hardly know we are doing it. Every empirical analysis of human community or of history's revolutions will reveal this ambiguity of freedom, and so the relevance to our secular life of theological discourse about man.

There are latent here a host of relevant religious symbols. When we seek to *enact* our image through our personal and communal acts of will, the sacred manifests itself in our

[15] Again Augustine best illustrates this inability of the will to control or to direct itself: "The mind commands the body, and it obeys forthwith; the mind commands itself, and is resisted. . . . For the will commands that there be a will—not another, but itself. But it does not command entirely, therefore that is not which it commands. For were it entire, it would not even command it to be, because it would already be." Augustine, *The Confessions*, Book VIII, Chapter 9, in Oates, *Basic Writings of Augustine* (New York: Random House, 1948), Volume I, p. 122.

existence continuously and in innumerable forms. First of all, another ultimate besides that of the sacred model has appeared in secular life, the tendency to make ourselves and our interests ultimate, to give unconditioned commitment to the well-being of oneself and one's group. This is what theological language has called the "demonic" or "idolatry." This tendency to give to the creaturely an unconditioned loyalty presupposes a dimension of ultimacy; it is universal in secular experience and is the basic factor corrupting every culture's life and so the life of history itself.

This strange, unguessed dimension of the demonic in ourselves is closely connected with another aspect of our own reality that heretofore we had in all likelihood not realized was there. Up to this point we had probably experienced ourselves as made up of needs, desires, and emotions on the one hand, directed or controlled, or potentially so, by our rational minds through our conscious wills, on the other. Such is our initial picture of ourselves—and such is the picture presented to us by most academics who ponder life's mysteries in the undisturbed quiet of their studies or laboratories. But now in our actual existence, a new reality has appeared: what we can call the "total self," the concrete unity of these factors, an existing organism in interaction with other organisms, and concerned above all with its own security and well-being. That total self is not simply driven by desire—for what it feels it needs and wants is seen by its mind as well as felt by its instincts. Nor is it pure mind—for what it wills and does is neither as rational nor as moral as the logic and the ideals it pretends to affirm. It is a unity of organic life and spirit, of contingent bodily needs and universal mind and moral aspiration. But it is that existing unified self that dominates each of these "faculties" or aspects, expanding its needs and desires to infinity, and using its rational and moral powers to justify its own restless striving after security and well-being. Whenever that self is threatened, therefore, as it continually is in the jostling and interaction of life, it defends itself and its own with all its faculties and powers. Its will becomes a will to its own security, power, prestige, and glory—even to a glory based on its virtue and distinction. And for this reason it is unable to affirm with all its power the model or ideal it thought it cherished with its mind, because it is in bondage to its own well-being.

Man's basic problem, therefore, is not just a matter of the achievement of freedom or autonomy, of acquiring an enlightened mind and a devoted will which can then control through affirmed ideals a rebellious instinctive nature. Rather man is to be seen as a totality, a unified being made up of body and of instincts, of consciousness and of subconsciousness, of intelligence and will, all in baffling and complex interaction. And it is that total psychophysical organism, that total existing self in its unity, which determines whether the higher powers of mind and of will are going to be used creatively or destructively. Ironically, the existing self reveals itself, not to psychological or to philosophical introspection—as Hume amply demonstrated—nor to the behavioristically inclined observer. It reveals itself in experience only in actual social and political intercourse, in living rather than in thinking or inquiry, when the actual self manifests a living existence that defies its own apprehension of its essence or of its ideals. And the mystery of this total self in its freedom and its bondage to itself can be explicated, again not by philosophy or science, but only in the broken language of religious symbol and myth.[16]

---

[16] Paul Ricoeur makes this point repeatedly: Only in terms of religious symbols and myths can the *concrete*, actual character of man's being be thematized, as opposed to his essential potentialities which are available to rational metaphysical or eidetic analysis. "Still more fundamentally, the myth tries to get at the enigma of human existence, namely the discordance between the fundamental reality—state of innocence, status of a creature, essential being—and the actual modality of man, as defiled, sinful, guilty. The myth accounts for this transition by means of a narrative. . . . Thus the myth has an ontological bearing: it points to the relation—that is to say, both the leap and the passage, the cut and the suture—between the essential being of man and his historical existence. . . . By its triple function of concrete universality, temporal orientation, and finally ontological exploration, the myth has a way of *revealing* things that is not reducible to any translation from the language in cipher to a clear language." Ricoeur, *The Symbolism of Evil* (New York: Harper & Row, 1967), p. 163. Very much the same position with regard to the function of myth in relation to the "mysteries" of transcen-

It is in the uncovering of that total self that the dimension or context of ultimacy in human existence appears in its most crucial form, here that the intrinsic religiousness of man manifests itself most clearly. For this total self exists as a unity in terms of its own ultimate commitment; this commitment is that deepest spiritual center of a man's life—what has been called by Reinhold Niebuhr a man's ultimate faith (or idolatry) and by Paul Tillich his ultimate concern—which provides for his life its final security and meaning, which determines and shapes therefore his characteristic and most significant acts and behavior patterns, and to which he gives his ultimate love and devotion.

As we noted in our discussion of the problems of contingency and meaning, every man has such a spiritual center of security and meaning. It gives to existence a feeling of invulnerability and to his activities a purpose and significance, and thus provides his existence with stability, coherence, and direction. If anything should happen to this center, a man feels that his life is radically insecure or totally incoherent, that its pieces fall apart into unrelated bits and that it is totally vulnerable to the threats of fate and of meaninglessness which beset him. Existence then degenerates into a series of events and actions that lead nowhere, produce nothing, and so mean nothing; and as we have seen, this, in turn, leads to a sense both of panic in the face of threatening powers and of the unreality and the unrelatedness of the self, its alienation from itself, from others, and from its world.

These centers of ultimate concern vary greatly. For many men, the preservation and advancement of their own power—financial, political, military, or social—may be what provides them with a sense of security and meaning. Such men will feel

---

dence, of freedom, of sin, and of history, was taken by Reinhold Niebuhr in his works (cf. especially *Nature and Destiny of Man* [New York: Scribner's, 1941–43]), Volume I, and "As Deceivers Yet True" in *Beyond Tragedy* [New York: Scribner's, 1937]); and by the author in Chapter X of *Maker of Heaven and Earth* (New York: Doubleday, 1959). This point forms one of the most telling criticisms of the use of the univocal and precise language either of science or of metaphysical speculation as fundamental for theology.

radical anxiety in the threats of insignificance and unreality until their own position and wealth are advanced to a point where they appear that they cannot be threatened by competition. For others, it may be their job or profession—music, art, scholarship, or science—for which they will sacrifice anything, because from it they receive the meaning their life knows. Still others find this sense of security and meaning in the status of their families or of their social group, such as their class, nation, race, or church, through whose wider success and prestige their own transient and precarious security and fragmented meaning gains status. Thus do the ultimate concerns or "idolatrous absolutes" which we create out of our own anxiety as contingent, relative, and transient creatures move out of the private and interior sphere into the public and historical arena to render demonic the social, economic, and political forces of history.

Three things should be noted about these centers of human concern. First they are "ultimate," unconditioned, or sacred in the precise sense that to them an unconditional loyalty is given transcending every other loyalty as the foundation of all others; a man will do anything, sacrifice anything, and if necessary think anything to protect and foster them, for they are the basis of all else in his life. They function as gods, and to them we have what can only be called a "religious" relationship. Secondly, these are *hidden* gods for most of us; our proclaimed ideals provide us with our own self-understanding and with the picture of ourselves which we wish others to share with us. But underneath them and determining the use we make of them is this other god, a deity who in one way or another represents our self and our interests. The fundamental bent or commitment of the total self in all of us is inward, turned toward our own welfare and that of our own group. The paradoxical character of man's existence, his love of nobility and claims for virtue, side by side with his capacity for cruelty and conflict, reflect this duality between the law in our minds and in our members, the god we proclaim and the self-oriented ultimate we really worship. It is this experienced disruption between the ideals we cherish and the idols to which we are actually devoted that gives secular meaning to the traditional theological categories of the demonic

and of sin as alienation from the real self, as idolatry and as
pride, and to the experience of God's judgment on this quality
of our being.

Thirdly, we should note that the ethical issues of secular
social living and so of the wider patterns of history are the outward expression in action of these deeper, more inward ultimate
commitments. Thus religion is not divorced from secular or historical existence, but lies in its very center. For the ultimate loyalties of men are assuredly a religious concern: those things, be
they gods or idols, to which men give their final love and commitment manifest the undeniably religious element of a man's
existence, whether he considers himself secular or not. And it is
what we can only call the "religious" worship of a finite creature—that creature being one's own life or that of his group—
that in the end causes the disruptions and conflicts of society.
When in history an ultimate concern is directed to some partial
or limited interest, we can scarcely avoid inhumanity toward
those outside that interest. Thus the secular, moral problems of
selfishness, greed, and dishonesty, the intellectual problems of
bias and of ruthless competition, and the social problems of
racial prejudice, inordinate privilege, tyranny, and aggression,
are altogether the result of the deeper religious problem of finding in some partial creature or group the ultimate security and
meaning which only the creator can give.[17] Once again an anal-

[17] Reinhold Niebuhr has made this connection between the spiritual or religious sin of pride and the social sin of injustice transparently
clear: "The Bible defines sin in both religious and moral terms. The
religious dimension of sin is man's rebellion against God, his effort to
usurp the place of God. The moral and social dimension of sin is un-
justice. The ego which falsely makes itself the center of existence in its
pride and will to power inevitably subordinates other life to its will and
thus does injustice to other life." *Nature and Destiny of Man*, Volume I,
p. 179.
    "Wherever the fortunes of nature, the accidents of history or
even the virtues of the possessors of power, endow an individual or a
group with power, social prestige, intellectual eminence or moral ap-
proval from their fellows, there an ego is allowed to expand. It expands
both vertically and horizontally. Its vertical expansion, its pride, involves
it in sin against God. Its horizontal expansion involves it in an unjust
effort to gain security and prestige at the expense of its fellows." *Ibid.*,
p. 226.

ysis of freedom, now as fallen and so as guilty freedom, has led to the requirement of justice as absolute and normative for man. One might say that, because freedom is in bondage and did *not* lead to real or creative autonomy, so freedom demands justice as its own absolute requirement. In this case, therefore, the norm of justice appears not as a "call" or as a "lure" but as a judgment on our almost inevitable, but never necessary, tendency to be unloving to our neighbor and so to construct and support in history a social order that incarnates injustice.

Thus are culture and history essentially ambiguous creations of sin as well as of grace and human creativity, and able and fit to die as well as to live. And thus does the sacred manifest itself as now opposed to, in radical judgment on, human life. The will of God *for* us has become the judgment of God *on* us. The divine call to action, self-creation, participation, and service in the world has become the condemnation of ourselves and our community, a judgment of uncleanness and decay in ourselves and in our world. The ultimate is experienced as negative in a new way: not as Void but as condemnation.[18] Correspondingly, our sacral role becomes that of prophet and radical reformer—except as the final experience of this sacral negation, the corruption is known to include us as well as the society we judge and seek to change.

[18] Perhaps the most vivid and direct Biblical experience of the presence of God is the prophetic experience of an impending and almost present holiness that threatens to demolish the guilty one to whom the appearance is given, whether this be communicated in the more direct vision of Isaiah in the temple, or in the reception of the Word for the people by Amos: "In the year that King Uzziah died, I saw also the Lord sitting upon a throne, high and lifted up, and his train filled the temple. ... And one [of the Seraphim] cried unto another, and said Holy, Holy Holy is the Lord of Hosts. ... Then said I, woe is me, for I am undone; because I am a man of unclean lips, and I dwell in the midst of the people of unclean lips." Isaiah 6:1–5. "Hear this Word, ye kine of Bashan, that are in the Mount of Samaria, which oppress the poor, which crush the needy, which say to their masters, bring and let us drink. The Lord God hath sworn by his Holiness, that, lo, the day shall come upon you, that He will take you away with hooks, and your posterity with fishhooks." Amos 4:1–2. "Woe unto you that desire the day of the Lord! To what end is it for you? The day of the Lord is darkness and not light." Amos 5:18.

This religious dimension at the center of human life, giving to it both its self-sacrificial and its demonic character, permeates our personal, communal, and political existence. The presence of this dimension, more than anything else, renders false any purely secular account of man's problems and hopes. For secular theory there are and can be no ultimates in existence; but secular existence continually produces and acts and lives by surrogate ultimates. At the very moment man declares himself most proudly to have "come of age" and so to be free at last of religion, he falls prey to some new personal, political, or racial idolatry which plunges his social life again into turmoil, renders history ambiguous, and so darkens his hopes for the achievement of authentic meaning. Speaking theologically, man's freedom allows him to misuse the gifts of providence; the divine becomes over against us, and its realization only in the future, not in the present. Just as the innate goals of autonomy, enacted by a self, call for their own balancing in the moral requirement of justice for the other, so our historical hopes, enacted by ambiguous, self-centered selves, call for an eschatological dimension in order that there be any hope at all in history.

It is the dynamic centrality of this ultimate concern, directed to some finite, contingent, and transient creature, which produces those forms of anxiety about our existence, about the meaningfulness of our activity, and about our death, which we explored in the last chapter, and consequently those distortions of our freedom and of our ideals discussed in this one. Man is a contingent, temporal creature, organic and yet free, who exists essentially in communion with others and who must cohere his fragmentary and insecure existence around some ultimate concern, lest it fall apart into unreal bits and he cease in fact to be as a man. This dimension of ultimacy is what makes him human and his communities possible. It is, for an analysis of secular existence, what raises the painful questions of the Void and of idolatry in his life; and it is, from the point of view of Christian faith, what starts him on the search for God. Theological discourse can begin to make meaningful the traditional categories of "faith," and of the lordship and sovereignty of God, insofar as it conceives them as answers to these secular questions of an ultimate concern and an inescapable search for an ultimate security and meaning in existence; in the same way it can make intelligible the myths of sin and of the fall in relation to our very real and universal experiences of a fault which is neither our true nature nor our own deepest intention.

The presence of the sacred and ultimate as condemnation—God's absence as creative love and his presence as wrath, to use Luther's language, is deeply felt in secular experience, especially at the moment. It is one of the most universal of human experiences: we all know inside culpability and fault, and outside injustice, oppression, and conflict. And we know their results: guilt, isolation, alienation, and broken community, each immensely destructive privately and publicly. Consequently, a new kind of search for the ultimate on which we depend appears: not this time for an ultimate security or meaning in existence, nor even for a standard by which to live. Rather, it is outwardly a search for an authentic world or social order, a kingdom manifest in history and so for a historical ground for hope. Inwardly, it is a search for the ability to accept ourselves, to feel solid and real and creative again, for the power to become what we wish to be, and above all, for the capacity of reconciliation, to reestablish community, to love, and to hope for a better world.

Much might be said about the necessity for secular life of these outward symbols of historical transformation and hope, of what in theology are called "eschatological" symbols;[19] we shall approach this complexity through the inner problems of our ordinary life, for here too an ultimate expressible only in religious symbolization appears. The search for self-acceptance and the power to reestablish community is spurred by two to-

[19] There is no question that the emphasis in Moltmann and Metz on the eschatological promise of Christian faith and so on the future is well warranted both because of its clear Biblical prominence and its relevance to historical and so to modern man, and also to the fact that it has been almost universally ignored except among Adventist groups. However, we feel this necessary emphasis of Christian hope must, in order to be Biblical, intelligible or creative, be set within the wider framework of the creative, judging, and redemptive presence of God both in the past and in the present—as we have sought here to do.

nalities of our life that are both universal and destructive. These are, first, the sense of alienation, of being disunited at the core of our being from our real selves and isolated from others on the one hand, and, secondly, the sense of guilt, of unworthiness or unacceptability, on the other.

Like most of the other forms of self-awareness or self-consciousness which we have described, alienation and guilt or unworthiness do not for various reasons always surface into full consciousness. Nevertheless, they are, I believe, there as deep tones or modalities in our dim understanding of ourselves, and they, too, shape a great deal that we feel, think, and do. Their universality in human experience is attested in many ways: by the prevalence in almost every form of religion of myths and rituals for reconciliation and for the expiation and purging of stain, of sin and of guilt—through sacrifice, offerings, acts of atonement, "scapegoats," etc.; through their continual restatement in every form of literature concerned with the understanding of man; and perhaps most clearly in modern experience, through the steady prominence of experiences of alienation and of guilt in psychoanalytic sessions.

Of course, as the psychoanalysts have pointed out, a sense of alienation from oneself, of isolation from others, and of guilt or unacceptability, like all other central aspects of our experience of ourselves, often appear in very neurotic and abnormal forms. Nevertheless, the fact that in a neurotic person alienation, isolation, and guilt take neurotic forms, does not at all mean that *all* experiences of them are caused by neurotic structures, and therefore will or could disappear with psychological help in the achievement of "normalcy" or "health." Sexuality, too, always takes neurotic forms in neurotic people; nevertheless it is regarded as an essential and not a deviant aspect of universal human reality, and so our sexuality is by no means treated as a mere function of the neurosis. It is not, in other words, expected to vanish with the last session on the couch—and if it did, the analysand would be well advised to start his sessions all over again! The sense of alienation and guilt are, unhappily, all too normal among us. In fact, by common consent, if a man is quite unable to feel any guilt or remorse for what he has done, he is by no means regarded thereby as "healthy"; on the contrary, it is precisely for this lack of what we call "conscience" that he can be legally declared by the psychiatrists themselves to be psychotic. Perhaps we could say that the normal sense of alienation and guilt, that sense which reflects in self-awareness the universal pattern of being human, appears when we deny, as we all do, our own freely chosen or at least deliberately affirmed standards and models, and when in so doing we have effected a real break in our significant relations with others. Such an experience of an uneasy conscience is a sign of health, and any sane analyst would be frightened to death if his therapy removed it. He realizes in practice, if not always in theory, that his function is to separate this sort of real apprehension of alienation and guilt from their neurotic forms, and thus to bring the patient into touch with his own ethical and so social reality.

These experiences of inner duality, uneasiness, and even uncleanness are, then, quite universal among us, accompanying the likewise universal tendency of man to love himself more than he should. If our ultimate commitment to the parochial gods of our own making reveals an alienation from our "true selves"—as we like to say—our sense of guilt at this experience of alienation demonstrates that that true self is not entirely destroyed, but remains there intruding itself into our awareness in terms of this uneasiness and this bad conscience. In any case, both our private and our public life reflect these negative experiences because a great deal of what we feel and do, as individuals in society and as communities on the stage of history, is shaped by the search, on the one hand, for the power to accept ourselves and the confidence to affirm our own being once again, and on the other to experience again a sense of unity, integrity, and creativity in our personal being and of reconciliation with others in our now broken community.

The experiences we have briefly described as alienation and guilt are among the most destructive we can know. A sense of inner disunity and self-betrayal, which we have called "alienation," drains away our self-awareness of our own reality and of our own powers. Sensing the ineffectiveness of our own conscious ideals and wills, we feel ourselves to be unreal and empty

among a world made up of solid, weighty people who *do* do
what they intend. A sense of uncleanness at our inability to do
what we feel we should, adds further to this alienation from
ourselves and from others. We become even more separated by
distaste and by rejection from the now empty person we find
ourselves to be; we do not like even the remaining but stained
reality we find in ourselves, and so there is no sense left of a
personal identity or being which we can or wish to affirm or
which we dare to relate to others. A man who cannot accept and
love himself as real and as worthy enough to affirm his own
being in feeling, thought, and act, cannot even be moral, let
alone selfless and loving of others; and feeling himself unreal
and unclean, he apprehends himself only as separated from the
real, strong, and good people around him.[20] Like a solitary ghost
that continually flits away from his own insubstantiality, he is
always escaping, he is never really there in feeling or in centered
activity—and what he does is done automatically, passively, because required from the outside, and so lacks all strength and
effectiveness, and makes real relations with others impossible.
The only real affects or feelings that are possible in this situa-

[20] Rubenstein expresses very well the isolation from all real community which an unrelieved sense of guilt always incurs: "Few guilts are
as difficult to bear as the feeling that the individual in his transgression is
entirely isolated from his peers. One of the most terrible aspects of the
sense of guilt is that it tends to isolate the deviant, cutting him adrift from
the community and fellowship of his peers. Since all human beings are
in some measure guilty, we would be a 'lonely crowd' indeed, were it
not for the knowledge that our guilt is no dark peculiarity which isolates
each of us from our fellows." Rubenstein, *After Auschwitz* (Indianapolis: Bobbs-Merrill, 1966), pp. 97–98.

For this reason, he argues powerfully and rightly for the need of
a religious community in which this self-betrayal and guilt are recognized, dealt with, and so relieved; and so which restores both the sense
of personal reality and integrity, as well as an experience of community
with others in the same situation. It is, unfortunately, true that the same
needs drive men into the idolatrous communities that bedevil the social
existence of man, and in turn often render even religious communities
cruel and intolerant of those outside them—unless they contain, as central to their ethos, some "prophetic" sense of criticism on their own
demonic possibilities, a judgment which Rubenstein's God seems now
unable to make.

tion of alienation and guilt are those of resentment and hostility at the reality, power, and creative activity projected upon others, that always stem from this situation of unreality and self-hatred. But the moment his hostility appears, it compounds the problem of alienation from the self and from others, as well as of guilt, and so this feeling, too, is pressed far out of the reach of awareness because it further isolates us from everyone else.[21]

The most frequent resolutions, achieved with immense relief, come, on the one hand, through understanding the self in terms of neurotic idealized images of the self,[22] or on the other, socially through participation in the more normal but infinitely destructive idolatries of our community. As the chaotic social history of our time well illustrates, commitment to some cause of race, class, or nation, will often give back a sense of reality, healing, and community to disintegrated and isolated selves. Our human story fluctuates back and forth between an idolatry and pride by which we raise our causes, our groups, and ourselves to the level of ultimacy and by which we achieve a sense of reality and community, and a disintegration and self-destruction in which we find in ourselves only nonbeing, stain, isolation, and hopelessness. Truly man is caught between heaven and earth,

---

[21] As we noted in an earlier chapter, there has been a distinguished tradition of thought, culminating in Altizer and Norman O. Brown, that has associated the feelings of emptiness and resentment or hostility with *transcendence*, with the belief in a deity that drains the self of its reality, its worth, and thus its relations to others. We would agree with much of the analysis of this debilitating process, as our text shows, but we would insist that this tradition has laid the blame in the wrong place—as usual—that is, on God rather than on ourselves. As we have argued here, the source of our sense of unreality, isolation, and helplessness is not the divine—which in terms of forgiveness and reconciling power is just what we lack, but our own alienation from ourselves and from others. This tradition is, in other words, far too sanguine about man, picturing him as a good guy able to affirm himself in power and to love his neighbor in sacrifice were it not for the entry of the transcendent onto the scene. There is no evidence at all for this strange fiction, and a great deal against it—not the least being the continuing reality of alienation, isolation, and guilt in an almost totally secularized culture.

[22] See especially Karen Horney, *Our Inner Conflicts* (New York: Norton, 1945).

402 NAMING THE WHIRLWIND

between an idolatrous being and the ultimate abyss of nonbeing, and his life swings back and forth between these two destructive ultimates. Our most fundamental searches, then, as transient fallible creatures, are for an ultimate commitment in terms of which our contingency may be anchored against disintegration and unreality, and for an ultimate acceptance and reconciling power through which this inevitable process of self-rejection and inner disunity can be stopped and reversed into creative community with others. While psychoanalysis directed to individuals can help a very great deal on some important levels of these problems, it cannot answer these full needs with regard to the total self which has freely and autonomously, and not neurotically, encouraged self-betrayal and unacceptability, and which must therefore deal with these real, and not fancied, distortions of its actual existence in the world. And while participation in creative social causes directed to healthy social change can surely provide a valid sense of reality, purpose, and commitment to individual life, nevertheless as we have sought to show, if such movements are entered into idolatrously as ultimate answers to our deepest religious questions, then they can only exacerbate and not relieve our problems. These two modern "secular" answers are not capable of dealing with the religious issues of the reality, meaning, and reconciliation of the self in community; these are problems in secular life that transcend the capacities of secular answers.

It is commonly said that to modern men the most meaningless traditional religious symbols are those of atonement and justification, since there is in the modern consciousness no experience of stain or of sin, and so no felt need of being cleansed, renewed, or "being made right again" with God or with anyone else. If that is so, it is because the meaning of these symbols as answers to our very common experiences of alienation, isolation, and guilt has not been spelled out. For modern life is as much qualified and shaped by the search for personal reintegration and innocence, and for the healing of our broken communities, as has been that of any other age. What else explains the almost universal response to the healing arts of psychoanalysis; our frantic moral claims of innocence in almost all aspects of our communal existence; and our continual flight into racial and political communities which, on the one hand, absorb and subvert our hostilities and at the same time give to them a cleansing moral justification? The need for *religious* justification and reconciliation is surely not explicitly felt among us; but much of our lives and our wealth is spent in the search for psychological, moral, and social forms of the same necessary blessings.

The writer realized anew the universality of this search for innocence and reconciliation when one day he sat in a New York City bus in front of two ladies, one of whom was regaling the other with a story of a quarrel she had just had with some third person who had been, apparently, a close friend. It was clear that the quarrel had hurt the lady; its devastating effects on her sense of personal self-confidence, integrity, and of important communion with others were evident in the emotional tone that covered every sentence and which obviously inspired the long recital. One hardly needed to hear *what* was being said, for the *way* it was said revealed all the important aspects of the recital. When she repeated to her listener what her antagonist had said to her ("And so *she* said to *me* . . ."), the tone was hard, unyielding, hostile, and aggressive—hearing *those* remarks said in *that* way, no one could blame the teller for her angry reaction (in fact, I said to myself at that point, "Even St. Francis would have taken affront at *that!*"). Then when she repeated what *she* had said in reply ("And so *I* said to *her* . . ."), the tones vastly altered; now they were quiet, infinitely tolerant, reasonable, and reconciling—no one could take offense at *those* reconciling remarks, or possibly misconstrue that outgoing warmth. The tones themselves unmistakably proclaimed that the blame for the angry explosion and the break in community, with which the quarrel had ended, lay entirely with the other lady, and that the raconteuse had been, in this situation—although manifestly innocent and the embodiment of love itself—deliberately misunderstood, unfairly and gratuitously insulted, and then brutally rejected by a ruthless, hostile foe. Obviously the emotional *point* of the story was to establish, both to the new friend who was listening and, above all, to herself, the blamelessness of this lady in the situation in which she felt momentarily disunited in herself, fairly

guilty, and suddenly socially isolated and alone. This long recita-
tion (all the way from 122nd Street to 79th) was a vast effort
to make the self acceptable again to others and especially to itself, and to establish alliances amid seriously broken community.
Both efforts were futile, as her listener's neutral, wary, and un-
committed comments made clear, and as her own obviously
continuing sense of guilt evidenced. How could she convince
herself of her innocence when she herself had created this interpretation of past history, because she already knew herself
to be partly to blame!

The listener, of course, smiles at the two ladies, recalling
that they are neither seminarians nor theologians dedicated to
loving others. But needless to say, these efforts by editing, by
reinterpreting and rewriting the past, and by apportioning the
hostility and aggressiveness elsewhere, are not confined to West
Side ladies on a New York bus. They appear in the way all of us
recount crises in our personal relations with others. And in almost every relation between groups that social history shows, the
same frantic effort to establish its innocence and to assure its
love of community appears in blatant form.

Conflicts in personal and in wider communal relations
represent moral failures, and, as with this lady, they hurt. They
also are universal in secular experience. They destroy both the
communities essential to our life, and the self-acceptance necessary to our existence as a self in community. Our universal
efforts to prove our innocence are directed, on one level, to re-
grouping and consolidating the forces of community in which
we participate—as the woman sought to elicit the support of her
listener, and as nations wish to be supported by their allies and
by the neutral onlookers to their dubious activities. But on the
deepest level we are seeking to justify ourselves to ourselves; we
are searching for an acceptance of ourselves that *we* can accept
and on the basis of which we can live further with power and
confidence. For only then can we feel whole rather than alienated
and unreal, and can we overcome the terribly debilitating effects
of a consciousness of guilt. An authentic self must know itself
as ultimately innocent and so as acceptable, despite its very evident lack of both; and like all the most significant requirements

of our humanity, this appropriation and healing of our inner derangement is very difficult indeed.

The futility of such efforts to generate the power to accept ourselves and to recreate community is apparent: the others never accept our doctored accounts, and we who have censored and edited them, are deeply aware that they are by no means the whole truth.[23] Nor does it finally help if this acceptance by which we can accept ourselves comes from Mommy and Daddy, from their later surrogates, or even from our fellows: our friends, or our national, racial, or religious communities, however full of grace their love, forgiveness, and acceptance may be. In the first place, these immediate communities of acceptance are all too apt to share in and so to enlarge the conflicts that beset our communal life; in being accepted by our community we may be impelled into a wider and deeper conflict. But more profoundly, in receiving our own deepest acceptance from these others, we again lose our integrity and freedom, for the basis of our spiritual existence is thus surrendered to others, and our final independence is forever gone. Again, integrity is achieved and preserved not only by community, but also by distance and separation as well. Finally, even the analyst can do this important task for us only temporarily, in the context of the session—and not for our continuing life as a whole. We seek for an ultimate acceptance by which we can live, yet one which neither we nor the humans around us can generate.[24]

[23] This futile dialectic of deception of the self and of others has, of course, been most clearly elaborated by Reinhold Niebuhr: "The desperate effort to deceive others must, therefore, be regarded as, on the whole, an attempt to aid the self in believing a pretension it cannot easily believe because it was itself the author of the deception. If others will only accept what the self cannot quite accept, the self as deceiver is given an ally against the self as deceived." Reinhold Niebuhr, *Nature and Destiny of Man*, Volume I, pp. 206–207.

[24] It is at this point that the optimism of humanism most tragically breaks down. It is of the essence of this faith, first and most powerfully expressed by Feuerbach and now represented by Hamilton, that the community of one's fellows can do all that "God" was supposed to have done. This optimism forgets the ultimacy of the framework within which all human acts occur. Other men can, says Feuerbach, forgive us so that we accept ourselves. This forgets we search here for an *ultimate* justifica-

Again the dimension of ultimacy has appeared in human existence at its deepest personal center. We call this *ultimate* because the need for acceptance is unconditioned, if the self is to be at all; because this acceptance constitutes and recreates the self from beyond itself; and because the acceptance that is sought has in two senses an unconditioned character. First, it is unconditioned in its knowledge of what we really are—only an acceptance that knows us through and through and yet loves us is worth anything. This is one reason that both religious absolution following confession and psychotherapeutic acceptance have such healing force: both come after a thorough airing of all that has caused the alienation and guilt. And secondly, it must be unconditioned in its acceptance of us: whatever you are or have done, you are loved. As our common experience continually validates, both the innocence that is demanded by our search for acceptance, and the forgiving love which resolves the issue—in Christian terms, both the law and the gospel—have an unconditioned character, else the healing for which we search cannot begin. For us to accept and love ourselves unqualifiedly and so creatively—whatever we are—we must be loved and accepted unqualifiedly, and yet by an acceptance that we know to be valid, neither based on ignorance nor sentiment, one that knows both our guilt and yet still loves us. Again the finite—the self itself, the human friend, parent, or analyst, even the wider community itself—cannot answer this question or resolve this search without deluding us, on the one hand, or destroying our freedom, on the other. For what we need is not an acceptance based on the assurance of our innocence, as we might now tell ourselves; what

---

tion with no ambiguity and therefore one which we can accept, that can reconstruct and empower the self. But all communities are as ambiguous as are individuals; and *their* acceptance as a basis of the self's acceptance of itself compromises the integrity and freedom of the self far more than does deity—as all totalitarian experiences show. To receive *this* from man, then, is not to find but to lose the self. It is clear that here the humanist is not speaking of historical, actual man in all his fragmentariness and his ambiguity, but his mythical image of Man and Community, benevolent, selfless, and ideal. They thus have not at all dispensed either with deity or with religious language; they have merely tried to squeeze them ineffectively within the good but frail and wayward creature man.

we need is forgiveness, i.e., a recognition of the guilt we know full well to be there, and then an awareness of a reconciling power that can both reintegrate our alienated self and our broken relations with others. Put in terms of Christian discourse, we are in all of this secular activity, common to the life of all of us, searching for God as forgiving and justifying love and as healing and sanctifying grace—though we may not be at all aware of this, and may see no possible relation of these older symbols heard in church to the problems in office, club, and family kitchen, as well as in our social and international conflicts, that worry and unnerve all of us.

And Christian witness would add that we will not be whole again until we find the unconditioned love, forgiveness, and re-creative power of God—though we cannot pretend to have established that through such an analysis of our ordinary life as this. It is probably by now clear, however, that only on the basis of having experienced our own fallibility and fault, and subsequently having discovered a healing acceptance of ourselves, that we can have a prophetic role *against* others in the world and *for* the oppressed therein, a role that is not hostile but creative. When we, too, have been forgiven for our sins, we may more hopefully embark upon becoming like Jesus to our neighbor in the world. Thus the cross is not only a sign of the negation of the world, but also necessarily a symbol of the negation of the virtue of the prophet himself!

Continuing for the moment further concerning the character and shape of Christian commitment and belief, we can say that it is especially in relation to these ultimate questions discussed in this chapter, "Who am I?" and "How can I be whole again?" that Christian existence has structured both its piety and its self-understanding. As a form of religious faith, it is based on the experience of answers to these two universal and quite secular human questions. And thus as a religion it has always been most centrally concerned with issues of morality and of community, of responsibility, of personal identity, of sin, of forgiveness, and of reconciliation between men; or, put in terms of doctrines, it has been more interested in the issues centering around the covenant, the community in history, the law and the gospel than those issues arising out of creation, providence, or eschatology; and more concerned with the character of the will of God toward man, with his judgment and love, with justification and sanctification, than with the modes of God's cosmological or ontological activity. And for the same reason, it has classically been Christocentric, or better, Christomorphic.[25] For in the Christian answer to these questions arising from our freedom, from our need of a model or image for our individual and communal style of life, and from our sin, the role of Jesus has been absolutely central.

The role which Jesus plays in the Christian answer to these personal, moral, communal and so historical problems changes as we move deeper and deeper from issue to issue. When our self's creative freedom was seeking to form itself, and so was in search of an ultimate standard or model for itself, he then appeared, as we saw, as embodying that style of life for which both our personness and our essential relation with others in community and in history called. As we noted, this role as model for ethical commitment was all that radical theology would allow. But experience shows that our deepest problems arise precisely in connection with this role. When we determine to "become like him," a free man for others, we find that in fact we cannot and the familiar sense of helplessness, unreality, guilt, and isolation "under the law" result, now in a Christian rather than in a secular context.

At this point, his role changes for Christian experience. Here he embodies more than merely what we ought to be—he seems to reach out toward us and to deal creatively with what we actually are. He communicates the forgiving love and the healing grace of God to us. For when we look at him as the community presents him to us, read his words, ponder again his acceptance of the wayward people who come to him, gaze at his death and its meaning for the community, and above all share in the spirit of the community which arose with and from him in its worship and its ritual, something happens in us and we experi-

25 The word "Christomorphic" is owed to Richard R. Niebuhr in his thoughtful and illuminating book, *Schleiermacher on Christ and Religion* (New York: Charles Scribner's Sons, 1964).

ence a new acceptance. Through him, as Christians have always said, is mediated to us the forgiving love of God, a forgiveness that accepts us unconditionally, and so through which we are re-united to ourselves again. And with this experience within the community, as Christians have also said, comes a sense of a new life, a new power again to love ourselves and to relate to others, to live once more toward this model of a freedom qualified by love. *Now* in grace his freedom is "contagious" and the beginnings of authentic life are again possible for us.

Thus in the Christian experience of an answer to these ultimate questions, the healing love and power of God are mediated to us through the figure of Jesus.[26] We know it is God who is at work in this experience because no man in the distant past could so communicate to us in the alienated present the healing self-acceptance and the power to affirm and realize our own freedom. If he is to do this in and to us, and, as even the radical theology witnesses, Jesus does this in Christian experience, then some power that underlies him and did not die with him, and now works anew through the present community in us, some power that transcends his passing and continues as the ground of our fleeting present, must come to us through this lordly figure of the past. And only the forgiveness and grace of the source and ground of our life can heal us without destroying our autonomy and freedom; if we are dependent at all for our personal being on something beyond ourselves, on a lord of any sort, it must be on God the creator of our free self that we depend, lest we lose our humanity all over again. Neither the categories of nature nor of historical community contain such an experienced power, nor express the ultimacy that is inherent in both the devastation of its absence and the blessing of its presence. Only the symbol of God, pointing as it does to the tran-

[26] The movement of the figure of Jesus from that of a model to a parable of God's activity is well put by Frederick Herzog: "Jesus' life as a whole is a parabolic directive—not merely the prophetic office or his office as a king. Jesus' life is a parabolic directive in the sense that he is an embodiment of God's rule. His life is a parable of *God's order.*" Herzog, *Understanding God* (New York: Charles Scribner's Sons, 1966), p. 126.

scendent, the everlasting, and the unconditioned character of this love and this grace, can properly thematize in reflection that of which we are here aware in our existence.

We can, perhaps, say that a central part of what it is to be a Christian is to experience in these ways a unifying answer to all these common questions we have here begun to delineate. It is to know that the mysterious power from which our existence comes, and the mysterious destiny on which the meanings of our active lives are dependent, are to be understood as the *same* power and meaning that accepts, loves, and heals us through Jesus of Nazareth. In the love communicated to us through him, we know at last more clearly who or what it is that has created us and that rules our destiny. The mystery on which we depend, the "Holy Nothingness" that is the beginning, the middle, and the end, takes its shape, becomes "God," in the figure of Jesus Christ. Thus does he become "our Lord," and the center of both our freedom and our existence, and thus do we begin to know of whom we speak when we say the word "God."

The experience of the sacred and so our knowledge of what Christians name God are not separated from our secular life and its values. The sacred is dimly but universally experienced by all men everywhere as a source of that life's power and joy, the source of its meaning and structure, and finally wherever that experience is known, as the sole ground of that life's healing.[27] And thus, in our Christian language about God, we can begin to talk of him in secular terms—though by no means without difficulty—as the creator and ruler of our existence and above all as the father who in love comes to us in Jesus who is the Christ.

[27] Again Herzog, even though a hermeneutical theologian, seems to agree with us about the universality of the awareness of God, even if what is experienced is not universally *known*: "We are describing man's awareness of being as a primordial ontological experience and not as the result of a logical argument from the finite to the infinite. It reflects an immediate encounter with Being beyond our own being and the being of the world. Being beyond our own being evokes our awareness. However, man does not immediately *know* what he senses. It is exactly at this point that the hermeneutical problem begins for theology. Theological hermeneutic must stress that the immediate experience is not instantly known as God." *Ibid.*, p. 38.

What is a meaningful area of discourse, a meaningful language game? Surely whenever vivid and universal ranges of experience can be indicated, out of which significant and universal questions—reflected in universal symbols, in behavior, and in persistent structures of ordinary speaking and of thinking—arise, there is an area of significant discourse. If to ask about the ultimate security and meaning of life, if to wonder about who we are and what we are to be, and if to realize the ultimate insecurity and contingency of our existence, our need for ultimate values, loyalties, wholeness, and reconciliation, and to search in life and thought for answers to these questions, represent universal and intelligible questions, then answers which relate directly to these same questions are meaningful.

The "unintelligibility" of such discourse to a secular age stems neither from the lack of such questions and answers, as we have tried to show, nor from the semantic unintelligibility of religious language, as Donald Evans and others have shown. It stems rather from the basic *answer* of a secular age, which we outlined earlier, namely the apprehension that the environment of man is merely contingent, relative, and temporal and that all questions of meaning relate to human autonomy and to nothing else. Our emphasis on "the meaningfulness of the given" in life, the intertwining of the given with human meaning, is a part of an answer to this. And another part is our attempt to show that secular life, whatever its claims for itself, resolves these same problems in many "religious" ways: by means of its own myths of nature, race, progress, and autonomy, its own surrogate gods of wealth, power, fame, and distinction, and its own secular means of self-realization, healing, and reconciliation. Ours is a culture which explicitly finds the religious dimension meaningless. In actuality, our secular life is saturated with religious elements, impoverished because they are inarticulated and so unexamined, but nevertheless, as we have argued, these sacred elements are as basic to our life amidst the profane as they were to any traditional religious culture. If, then, currency and significance within ordinary cultural life establishes the meaningfulness of a language game, and if, as we have argued, one of the significant meanings of "the meaning of a symbol" is its relevance to and necessity for the thematization of aspects of ordinary experience, then the meaningfulness of religious discourse has been well established by this analysis. Of course, neither the semantic meaning of the language game, its ontological meaning, nor the intentionality of individual symbols in relation to the system of symbols in which they operate can be dealt with in this prolegomenon. But their possibility is, we believe, dependent on the primary relation of symbols to ordinary experience which we have sought to demonstrate.

The area or region within which religious discourse functions concerns those ranges of experience which we have called the "dimension" or "context" of the ultimate or the sacred. This region of experience provides the "situation" within which this type of language makes sense and communicates, and within which its own forms of validation, as we shall see, take place. This is an area of experience, of questions and of thought, quite familiar to secularity, as we have tried to demonstrate, and it forms the region within which most of our literary and dramatic creativity moves. What is spoken of and referred to in those areas, in its presence and in its absence, makes a vast, essential, and observable difference both to the private and the public character of secular life. Let us note that, in arguing the meaningfulness of this type of language, we have made no appeal to traditional "nonsecular" assumptions, either to a religious faith-event in relation to revelation, or to an ultimate harmony or order within the system of things that forms the basis of metaphysics.

We have spoken directly so far only of the general area with which religious language has to do, the region within which this language game functions intelligently and meaningfully. In this general region, of course, all sorts of specific things may be said, points of view taken, and symbols used. In this dimension of experience, which concerns the dim horizon of ultimacy within which we live, we may make negative as well as positive statements; we may discover and thematize only a Void, and affirm that no answers arise here at all; or we may find an answer and develop this range of language on its basis. In either case, we are using what we call "religious" discourse, for we are discoursing either in negative or in positive terms, either in terms of mere questions or of experienced answers, about the ultimate and unconditioned context of our life. To argue, then, that religious language is meaningful, is not to argue either that there is a God or that he has characteristics which Christians wish to affirm of him. Ours has been a phenomenology of religious apprehension within secular life; it has not asked or answered questions about the "reality" or the ontological structure of the ultimate or the sacred that "appears" there. It has sought only to show that it does appear, and how and where it does appear. Only indirectly and, so to speak, in brackets have we made positive or "Christian" reference to God or to doctrines about him.

This has been an ontic prolegomenon to theological discourse, not an example of theological discourse—although as we shall see, this prolegomenon will function very importantly in any theological language that follows upon it. A prolegomenon, in other words, is just that: it prepares for Christian theological discourse by establishing the meaningfulness of religious discourse in general in relation to experienced characteristics of human existence in the world, and thus by providing for the meaningful and relevant use of the specifically Christian symbols in a secular age. It can neither establish by itself the truth of that faith nor even provide the symbols within which that faith expresses itself.[28] Our final question is, then, on what other grounds or sources is Christian theological discourse based if, as we have just said, it is not based exclusively on this prolegomenon, and how, in that case, are we to conceive of their interrelation with one another?

---

[28] Our effort to create a prolegomenon is in aim, if not in content, not unlike that of Father Rahner's *Anthropologie*: "Eine solche 'fundamentaltheologische' Anthropologie, wie wir sie in ihren äusserste Umrissen durchzuführen suchten, ist die eigentliche Religionsphilosophie. Was wir trieben, ist eine Anthropologie, insofern wir vom Menschen handelten; ist eine 'theologische' Anthropologie insofern wir den Menschen begriffen als das Wesen, das in Freiheit in seiner Geschichte auf die mögliche Botschaft des freien Gottes zu horchen hat; sie ist eine 'fundamentaltheologische' Anthropologie, insofern dieses Selbstverständnis, das der Mensch von sich hat, die Voraussetzung dafür ist, dass er die faktisch ergangene Theologie überhaupt zu hören vermag." Karl Rahner, *Hörer des Wortes* (München: Kösel-Verlag, 1963), p. 208.

5 / Christian Discourse
about God

I N THE FOREGOING, we have sought to show that religious
language, which concerns itself with what we have called the
"dimension" or "context" of ultimacy, is meaningful since it
explicates situations in experience which all of secular life shares.
But we have admitted that, within this meaningful but quite
general language system, all sorts of things, both negative and
positive, can still be said and so all sorts of symbols used and
affirmed. We have not, in other words, raised the questions of
the reality or nature of what appears, and so of the truth of any
particular symbolic forms within this sort of language. Ours has
been, in a modest sense, a phenomenological analysis of the experience of the unconditioned since it has bracketed questions
of reality, of explanation, or of validation and has sought an
"eidetic" reduction of experience to certain general forms centering about our contingency, our relativity, our transience, and
our freedom. In another sense, it has been an analysis of language about the unconditioned, of the "situations" in which the
use of this language takes on meaning, makes sense, and so communicates to others. As far as theological discourse about "God"
goes, as a result of this analysis we know only that, in man's
being in the world, he finds himself in an essential, creative, but
also potentially threatening relation beyond himself and his
world, a relation that manifests the qualities of ultimacy and
unconditionedness, but which from the point of view of general secular experience can reveal as much a Void, a final mean-

inglessness, and the possibility of false ultimates as it does an almighty power, meaning, and love. Clearly, therefore, merely to have found and spoken of this dimension or context of ultimacy by analysis is not yet to speak of God as Christians are traditionally wont to do, or to speak of what in theology we can or should call "faith." Also, it is plain that we agree with the general import of both the phenomenological and the linguistic currents of modern philosophy that a philosophical analysis of ordinary human experience and language, an anthropology, can take us no further beyond immediacy than this. How, then, does Christian discourse about *God,* or affirmations about *what* appears, the positive form of God-language, proceed? Above all, how can a positive theology based on a specific faith, a particular historical tradition, and a particular cluster of symbolic forms participate in the secular meaningfulness we have sought here to exhibit? How is a secular and yet a Christian theology possible?

We recall that, for language philosophy, analysis can only point to the possible situations or experiences where sentences might be used and propositions verified; philosophical analysis cannot in and of itself validate any propositions within the language game it analyzes. Thus philosophy of science investigates the usage of words, formulae, models, etc. in the special sciences, but it tells us nothing about the validity of particular scientific hypotheses and so of the nature or reality of the "objects" of scientific inquiry. For validation of particular scientific hypotheses, and so for knowledge about "the world," we must turn to the special sciences which are based on direct experience, which formulate hypotheses and then proceed to test them. In much the same way, our prolegomenon has sought to analyze the situations within experience to which religious discourse or God-language applies, and so to point to some of the kinds of possible experience in which questions in this area arise and so in which answers may be found. We have shown *where* in experience a particular apprehension of the sacred has appeared and, in general, the sort of language applicable to it. But the prolegomenon itself, finding in human experience such a varied apprehension of the dimension of sacrality, cannot move beyond the issue of the meaningfulness of religious language to that of the validity of particular systems of symbols. The reason is that a definite answer to the universal human questions of existence, meaning, death, value, and reconciliation must be received, a particular way of viewing these issues affirmed, for such particular symbols to appear, that is to say, a definite apprehension of the sacred is required in order that there be specific, particular symbolic forms of religious discourse and out of them assertive propositions capable of validity or invalidity. Symbolic thematization of the "reality" encountered within the region of experience we have delineated is rooted in and expressive of *particular* experiences of this dimension of life, and with that we move out of the "neutral" area of prolegomenon into that of positive theology, expressive of a certain apprehension of the sacred and so correlated to a certain, definite tradition of symbolic forms. It is, however, within the same range of experience we have called the "dimension" or "context" of ultimacy in which particular apprehensions of the sacred appear and so particular answers to the sorts of questions we have explicated earlier are received and known.

Now the relation between our "knowing" of answers and the particular sets of symbolic forms in which they are couched is a complex matter, but one essential to the questions of the sources, the task, and the authority of theology. First of all, it must be admitted that the reception of such a manifestation of the sacred, of what we are calling an "answer," partakes of two different levels of apprehension which generally accompany and supplement one another, but which in special circumstances may exist apart. When such separation occurs, we are faced with the dilemma of a secular society whose spiritual existence is thematized by no coherent religious symbols and whose traditional religious symbols appear empty and meaningless. On the one hand, the apprehension of the sacred, or reception of an answer, can frequently subsist merely on what is called the "existential" level: the level of feeling, of mood, of dim emotional awareness of the self in its world—as a confidence in life, a sense of worthful meaning, an apprehension of and commitment to

certain values, a sense of unity and reconciliation, and the courage
to face death. Such basic experiences and tonalities are universal
in secular life, and are, as we have argued, experiences of a
sacred reality and power which Christians would call "God."[1]
From the vantage point of Christian faith, one may say that these
experiences are known in the Word for what they *really* are, i.e.,
as the work of "God," but it is also important to say that such
experiences of the sacred, or of "God," are not confined to the
Word—else God's activities be separated from our ordinary human life. On this first level, the sacred seems to speak "silently"
within us, to illumine unheralded and uncommented upon, our
being in the world with courage, vitality, meaning, and authenticity. Cases, especially in a secular culture, are common in which
no explicit symbolic expression seems to mediate or to accompany this silent speaking. It is no surprise that a secular culture
which experiences frequently this creative "given" wonders what
the use, function, or validity of these sorts of symbolic forms
might be. It is, however, the case that even such silent affirmations have their own roots within the traditional symbolic forms
of the community, and that the possibility of these affirmations is
dependent on that community's traditional apprehension of the
world and of man latent within those "religious" forms but now

[1] Ebeling expresses powerfully this reception of an answer as an
"illumination" that enlightens anew our being in the world, and so transforms it. He seems, however, in contrast to our view, to confine these
"Word-events" or hierophanies of the sacred to the hearing of the Word
in Scripture about Christ—which creates all the difficulties both for secular life and theology that we have outlined. "But actually we live on
the reality that is disclosed to us by language, and on the immense wealth
that is handed down to us, and on which our speech draws. Language
opens up the space to us in which the events of the word can take place.
. . . And when the event of the word is an extraordinary one, it is
creative of language, i.e., it creates new possibilities of addressing and
understanding the reality which approaches us, and becomes the source
of light which can again and again lighten up the darkness of existence.
. . . When God speaks, the whole of reality as it concerns us enters language anew. God's Word does not bring God into language in isolation.
It is not a light which shines upon God, but a light which shines from
him, illumining the sphere of our existence. If God's countenance shines
upon us, the world has for us another look." Gerhard Ebeling, *The Nature of Faith* (Philadelphia: Muhlenberg Press, 1961), pp. 188 and 190.

so deeply presupposed in the life of the culture that their necessity and even their presence is unrecognized.

In order, therefore, that such silent apprehensions of
being originate or that in the long run they be maintained in a
culture's life, there must be a second level, namely one of symbolic thematization. Just as theological symbols are empty without existential apprehension, so no "meaning" is or can be apprehended within experience as a whole without symbolic forms
through which that totality and our place in it is structured and
thematized. Symbolic forms expressive of those silent, deep,
existential apprehensions of our being in the world are thus
essential. In the first place every apprehension of the world is
"historical" in essential character, that is, it is particular, from a
vantage point, starting somewhere, in some particular experience
of some aspect of the totality of things that has communicated
to man its power and structure—and that particular apprehension
of things is communally borne. It is *here*, in *this* place, through
this finite medium as expressive of ultimacy, and thus in *this*
community, that the sacred has manifested itself. That means
that, with this affirmation of a definite starting point in space-
time, each community also affirms those symbols, verbal, mythical and ritualistic, and their accompanying norms, expressive of
that particular starting point in a finite medium. Each of us as
individuals, moreover, receives our answers to these questions
through the symbols and patterns borne by the community—a
nation, a colloquium of scientists, a party, or a church—in which
we spiritually exist. The mythical language of a community discloses to us the structures of ultimacy in which our community
lives, and through these symbols the face of ultimacy manifests
itself to us. Thus particular symbolic forms, carried by a community and a tradition, are the essential media of each human
apprehension of ultimacy and so of our creative answers to
ultimate issues.

Secondly, men must think and conceive what they feel if
they are vividly to apprehend it, fully to appropriate it, and especially if they are communally to share and perpetuate it. A
fundamental point of view, a particular apprehension of the
ultimate context in which we exist, cannot, therefore, become

creative or be transmitted unless it has appropriate, consistent, and relevant symbolic expression. Symbols illumine, structure, bring to light, and reveal to us the tonal characteristics of our felt being in the world.[2] In the long run, there are no existential answers that do not include some symbolic expression, which in turn had its origin in a definite, historical apprehension of the ultimate character of things. In the experience of an answer, then, there is both the level of silent, re-creating illumination of ourselves, our world, and of the symbolic horizon of our being, and there is the level of symbolic conceptualization and expression which makes this apprehension possible, communal and permanent, and gives the possibility of reflection and so of rational ordering and inquiry to the important issues of existence.

If this analysis is valid, then in a secular as in religious cultures, fundamental *answers* to ultimate questions, embodying a definite point of view with regard to man's being in the world, stem from concrete and often particular experiences, expressed symbolically and borne communally. However universal their scope, various their form, or "rational" and objective their character—be they explicitly philosophies or theologies—alternative standpoints or stances in human life originate within special experiences in life in which some basic clarification or illumination of our ultimate questions, expressing itself in the form of some appropriate symbolic system, has been received and transmitted historically. Here the general region of religious discourse has been specified through some particular "experience" and so in definite symbolic forms. With this specification, the question of the *validity* of each definite cluster of symbols arises for the first time—for now claims are made about the nature and structure of what is apprehended. And generally the questions of validity are answered in the terms of criteria derived from and expres-

[2] Cf. this comment from Eliade: "The important part played by symbolism in the magico-religious experience of mankind is not due to the convertibility of hierophanies into symbols. It is not only because it continues a hierophany or takes its place that the symbol is important; it is primarily because it is able to carry on the process of hierophanization, and particularly because, on occasion, it is *itself* a hierophany—it itself reveals a sacred or cosmological reality which no other manifestation is capable of revealing." Mircea Eliade, *Patterns in Comparative Religion* (New York: Meridian Books, 1963), pp. 446–447.

sive of this central core of the community's spiritual life.[3]

This appearance of an experienced answer and its symbolic forms, set within a community and a definite historical context and tradition, brings into view for specifically religious discourse the second, positive form of God-language, namely *theology* as the systematic reflection on the meaning and validity of the symbolic forms of a given religious community, from the point of view of one who shares that community's faith and life and so seeks responsibly to express its religious ethos. Our purpose in this concluding chapter is to understand some of the formal elements of this sort of language, the language of positive theology per se, in relation to the discussion of religious discourse in general that has preceded. In order to do this, we must note several implications for theological discourse of what we have found religious language in general to be.

The first implication for theology of our analysis of reli-

[3] As Eliade says: "Each must be considered as a hierophany inasmuch as it expresses in some way some modality of the sacred and some moment in its history; that is to say, some one of the many kinds of experience of the sacred man has had. Each is valuable for two things it tells us; because it is a hierophany, it reveals some modality of the sacred; because it is a historical incident, it reveals some attitude man has had towards the sacred. . . . Every hierophany we look at is also an historical fact. Every manifestation of the sacred takes place in some historical situation." *Ibid.*, p. 2.

The same general principle, that every experience of the Whole comes through some particular finite medium in some particular historical situation, and thus is given its *particular* form, was laid down carefully by Schleiermacher: "If thus the direct, inward expression of the feeling of absolute dependence is the consciousness of God, and that feeling, whenever it attains to a certain clearness, is accompanied by such an expression, but is also combined with and related to, a sensible self-consciousness: then the God-consciousness which has in this way arisen will, in all its particular formations, carry with it such determinations as belong to the realm of the antithesis in which the sensible self-consciousness moves." *The Christian Faith* (Edinburgh: T. & T. Clark, 1928), paragraph 5, postscript. For this reason, every religion is "historical" and "communal," the forms of religious experience being determined by the forms of communal feeling or self-consciousness passed on in the historical tradition. Tillich expresses much the same view in his notions of originating revelation through a miracle, and dependent revelation through the symbols stemming from that original constellation. *Systematic Theology* (Chicago: University of Chicago Press, 1951), Volume I, p. 126ff.

gious language is double-edged, limiting the scope of religious statements while granting them their own legitimacy. If religious discourse is meaningful as explicative of man's experience of ultimacy, in relation to which he finds himself in all facets of his being, then it is meaningful as a form of discourse *only* in that relation. It has to do solely with the relation of the finite to its unconditioned and sacred ground, not with the relations of the finite to other events and entities within the space-time nexus. Objectively, its contents are confined to the various relations of creatures to their creator, and only derivatively and indirectly to the relations of creatures to one another (as, for example, in ethics). Subjectively, its language is confined to questions and answers of ultimate concern to the existence and meaning of the creatures, and not of proximate or limited concerns. Thus such language involves uniquely and inevitably elements of self-involvement or commitment. This means that, wherever religious symbols are used as explanatory of the relation of finite events to one another, they are misused and their meaningfulness—and so, of course, any validity propositions using them may have had—vanishes.[4] Thus religious symbols are not transferable di-

---

[4] This point, that religious truth has reference to "transcendence" (or to depth) and not to "matters of fact" is common, as we noted, both for liberal and for neoorthodox theology: Cf. Reinhold Niebuhr's distinction of primitive or literal myths versus permanent myths ("The Truth in Myths," in *The Nature of Religious Experience,* ed. J. S. Bixler [New York: Harper & Brothers, 1937]), and Tillich's distinction between mythology and "broken myth" (*Dynamics of Faith* [New York: Harper Torchbooks, 1957], pp. 48–54. See also *Systematic Theology* [Chicago: University of Chicago Press, 1957], vol. II, pp. 37, 38, 151, 152). Ricoeur stresses this same point: "That is why we must never speak here of demythization, but strictly of demythologization, it being well understood that what is lost is the pseudo-knowledge, the false Logos of the myth, such as we find expressed, for example, in the etiological function of myth. But when we lose the myth as immediate Logos, we rediscover it as myth." And, "It must be well understood *from the outset* that, for the modern man who has learned the distinction between myth and history, this chronicle of the first man and the first pair can no longer be coordinated with the time of history and the space of geography as these have been irreversibly constituted by critical awareness. It must be well understood that the question, where and when did Adam eat the forbidden fruit? no longer has meaning for us." Paul Ricoeur, *The Symbolism*

rectly into the context of the language systems of the physical or the social sciences, or even of anthropological or historical inquiry, which legitimately for their own purposes presuppose the sufficiency of explanations dependent on finite factors alone. For this reason, most of contemporary theology is correct in requiring that all religious myths and symbols be understood as "broken", that is to say, as recognizing that, while religious discourse may be significant of our situation *vis à vis* the ultimate reality with which we have to do, its symbols and myths cannot be taken "literally," as direct statements explanatory of facts or events observable in the space-time continuum. Propositions in religious language thus do not replace or conflict with propositions in the special sciences. Religious discourse is thus symbolic and not literal in form, and symbolic of man's relation to the unconditioned and the sacred on which he ultimately depends for the existence and the meaning of his life. Since philosophy, at least in its speculative-ontological forms, deals with both the relations of the finite to the finite (for example, in questions of cognition, substance, causality, space, time, and so on), and the relations of the finite to its ultimate ground (Nature, Being itself, Reality, Process, etc.), its language not only contains elements clearly outside the realm of what we have called "religious discourse," but also elements that participate in that realm. Thus metaphysical or ontological philosophy has always enjoyed an ambiguous, paradoxical, hostile yet dependent relation to theology, a relation that is neither one of total disrelation nor one of identity. Some of the implications of our discussion for this relation between metaphysics and theology will occupy us below.

The "other edge" of the first implication of our definition

---

of Evil (New York: Harper & Row, 1967), pp. 162 and 235. One of the few illiberal, and unwise, elements in Karl Rahner's thought is his effort to preserve the Adamic myth not only as *religious* discourse about the situation of man in relation to the eternal, but as historical, factual discourse about a first pair who began the human race and did a certain unfortunate deed. Cf. Karl Rahner, *Theological Investigations* (Baltimore: Helicon Press, 1961–1967), Volume I, Chapter 8, "Monogenism."

of religious language—namely that it is expressive of our experiences of ultimacy—is that in order to have religious meaning, this language must be in fact multivalent in form; that is, it must express *ultimacy* whenever it speaks, as it always does, also of the finite. Thus religious discourse inescapably moves towards transcendence, absoluteness, and ultimate sacrality, even when it speaks—if it be speaking *religiously*—of some nether god or godlet. No historical discourse about *merely* finite objects or persons, however moral or significant, can be religious discourse. Nor, if there be literary talk about what was once religious myth, historical or aesthetic talk about someone else's idols or sacred emblems, or, let us note, strictly philosophical talk about finite and so largely comprehensible deities, is there a religious use of language. Thus has philosophy or ontology a strange, paradoxical role in religious discourse. As we noted, insofar as the abstractive language of philosophy carries the mind beyond the level of concrete or ontic objects in space and time, beyond "phenomena" to universal structures and relations on the level of ontology, philosophical language helps to raise religious discourse to the level of ultimacy appropriate for it. Historically, therefore, philosophy has properly functioned to "demythologize" older forms of religious speech, and in a new cultural situation to make them more "religious" by raising language to the level of transcendence and ultimacy beyond that of the phenomenal plurality of personal beings.

On the other hand, the requirements of coherence and intelligibility in philosophy set limits to this creative role in religious speech, for they move its characteristic discourse in the direction of a system of univocal language. Here all that is discussable is spoken of in the terms of one set of categories used in the same way throughout the scope of experience—as, for example, in Whitehead's thought, God and "the least puff of existence" illustrate the same set of terms and concepts, and so are conceived to be similarly "in the grip of process." Thus frequently the God described in philosophical terms is set within a system of coherence (Process and its categorical structure) by which he is made intelligible to us on the one hand but which transcends and limits him on the other. Again, when this happens, religious speech is apt to vanish, for whatever is ultimate, unconditioned, and underived lies elsewhere, namely in the necessary and universal categories of the philosophical system and of the Whole which it reflects, rather than in the finite figure of God. Religious language, and so its symbol of God, requires that some significant mode of ultimacy or absoluteness be latent within the object to which the symbol is applied, that the sacred transcend, and infinitely, the finite in and through which it appears. By the same token, however, since the sacred to which the language refers appears *in* the finite, illuminating and transforming it, the continuous relatedness of ultimacy to the finite is *also* implied. The result is that the concept of an unrelated, utterly self-sufficient absolute is more of a philosophical than it is intrinsically a religious category. Thus religious language, in a way that arises out of its multivalent form, is essentially paradoxical: it is referent to ultimacy and absoluteness, but through finite media. Either to talk *merely* of ultimacy—in a philosophical or mystical mode—or to talk *merely* of finitude—in a pseudo-scientific or a metaphysical mode—is to lose religious speech.

The second implication of our analysis is that it is with these special apprehensions of the sacred and their accompanying symbolic forms that for the first time the question of the *validity* of religious statements arises. To clarify this point, let us return to that rough but helpful parallel found in the relation between the special sciences as forms of knowing and modern philosophy of science as an analysis of scientific language, which may help us to comprehend further the movement from prolegomenon to positive theology. As modes of *knowing* in science and in common sense (because their propositions can be tested and so verified or falsified in relation to experience) are in relation to linguistic philosophy, as the analysis of the *meaningfulness* of the general language forms of science and of ordinary discourse; so in turn are special apprehensions of the sacred and their accompanying symbolic systems, as modes of "knowing" the context of ultimacy in which we exist (and so as making true or false statements about the sacred, and validating these in relation to

the experiences which give them rise), to such a general phenomenological analysis of the meaningfulness of religious discourse as we have conducted. Thus, according to this analogy, the
question of the *validity* of religious statements arises only in
relation to some particular tradition of symbolic forms, based on
a specific apprehension of the sacred, and making specific claims
about the reality and nature of the sacred, and *not* in relation to
a discussion of the general character of religious discourse as
such. If all religious language is declared to be *ab initio invalid*,
we may be sure that such a verdict stems itself from some deep
intuition, naturalistic in symbolic form, of the ultimate structure
of things according to which reality is claimed to be of such a
nature that any category of ultimacy or of sacrality is *ipso facto*
in error. That religious discourse can, except on the now dis-
credited terms of some such criterion as the verification principle, be called *ab initio meaningless*, we have, we believe, suffi-
ciently disproved by our efforts so far.

Let us turn, then, to those special apprehensions and their accompanying symbolic systems to uncover their characteristic forms
and so their implications for the development of an appropriate
theological method. The modality of the dimension of ultimacy,
the sacral context of our being in the world, is, we have said, always known through special apprehensions and their characteristic symbolic forms, and thus known within the historical tradition of a particular religious community. The word generally used
in the history of religions for such a manifestation of the sacred
through a definite set of symbolic forms and received by a particular historical community is "hierophany";[5] because, however,
we intend to relate these phenomena to theological method, we
wish to use the traditional theological word "revelation." "Revelation," as we use that word in the context of this secular prolegomenon, is that definite mode of experience in which a particular
answer to these ultimate questions that arise in relation to all
secular life manifests itself, is received, and so "known." We are
thus giving a "secular" ground in ordinary experience for the

[5] Cf. Eliade's careful definition of this term, *Patterns*, pp. 2–14.

theological conception of revelation, as we have sought to do for the other major doctrinal affirmations of the Christian faith.[6]

Revelation so defined is universal in human existence. This we know because its results, on the level both of dim awareness and of symbolization, are universal. Everywhere men have symbolized the meaningfulness of the given; they have affirmed and celebrated the life that is theirs in its meanings, and possessed in some form a sense of worth, value, and reconciliation—and everywhere also these positive affirmations have been accompanied by a deep sense of the threat of the Void to the reality and value of life. Correspondingly, symbolic answers, latent in all human awareness although received always in a *particular* natural, social, and historical context, are universally symbolized and thematized in the omnipresent religious life of man—and rationalized in other, more "secular" communities into the bases of man's many philosophical visions. General revelation, we are saying, is the mode in which the universal presence—or sense of absence—of the unconditioned and the sacred enters into human awareness. This always occurs in definite, particular—socially and historically conditioned—forms of experience, and through definite historical symbolic media peculiar to that community, and it always thus results in some quite definite form of an answer to

[6] One might say that we are here giving a secular or general definition of the concept of revelation, following out a suggestion made by Schleiermacher in his well-known discussion of revelation: "Accordingly, we might say that the idea of revelation signifies the *originality* of the fact which lies at the foundation of a religious communion, in the sense that this fact, as conditioning the individual content of the religious emotions which are found in the communion, cannot itself in turn be explained by the historical chain which precedes it. . . . And thus it becomes difficult to avoid a widened application of the idea, to the effect that every original idea which arises in the soul, whether for an action or for a work of art, and which can neither be understood as an imitation nor be satisfactorily explained by means of external stimuli and preceding mental state, may be regarded as revelation." Schleiermacher, *Christian Faith*, paragraph 10, postscript, pp. 50–51. Assuming as he did that all fundamental points of view in existence, and so the foundations of any cultural life, stem from an apprehension of the sacred as reality, meaning, value, and end, we have ventured thus to secularize this definition as an attempt religiously to comprehend the origin of basic cultural forms.

these universal problems. General revelation is always and in each case special revelation.

It is, then, in definite experiences within some historic tradition that the truth of particular symbols and symbolic systems within the general range of religious discourse becomes evident to the experiencer. Every philosophy has ultimately such an historical and existential root, expressing in coherent, systematic order the symbolic forms of its cultural time and place; and correspondingly, every theology stems explicitly from the tradition of religious apprehension and of symbolic conceptualization from which the theologian writes. For example, in the special case of Christian language, propositions about "God" ultimately derive from the historical continuum which is the religious life of the Christian community. This derivation occurs both on the existential level—for here the Christian God is known; and on the symbolic level—for here the divine is known in terms of *these* symbols. Accordingly, it is within the terms of *that* life that such propositions are verified insofar as they are validated at all. The experiences that originate and so validate Christian propositions are, therefore, historical experiences in two senses: (1) they are historical in the life of an individual, they happen *to* him and *in* him in some definite experience or set of experiences of clarification, illumination, and renewal; (2) they are historical in the wider sense that they occur within the "space" of a definite community, and so of a communal and historical tradition, bearing definite symbolic forms within which the individual finds this experience and so himself.

We speak of revelation in this sense largely to emphasize, as did Schleiermacher, the *given* character of this experience of an answer and its symbolic explication; the fact that we have not discovered it but rather received it; and thus that we have not derived it from our ordinary experience either by inferential logic or argument but found it manifesting itself to us. We do not question, of course, that an experience of an answer to questions concerning the ultimate nature of things comes to us *in* experience. Otherwise, it could never be known. Our point is that, during the course of the flow of experience which *before* had been confused, empty, pointless, or threatening, there has been an en-

lightenment, a new sense of the reality, worth, and goodness of
one's being, an experience of clarification, and an assurance of
wholeness and healing—thus one's being is illumined, stabilized,
and strengthened. Being speaks in and through us here, as Heidegger intimates; our existence is "enlightened," or, in the pithy
language of our times, "we are turned on." And hence for us the
occasion or context for that experience, and so the symbolic forms
through which it was received and in which it is conceptualized,
become vital for our understanding of ourselves, our destiny, and
the world. But it is equally clear that such an answer or, as we
have put it, such an apprehension of the sacred, while occurring
within experience and through its finite media, is not a simple
part of ordinary experience, in logical or causal continuity with
other aspects of experience, a part of the passage of things we experience every day, and therefore able to be simply "discovered"
by us by the usual methods of either common sense or sophisticated inquiry.[7] For, as we have intimated all along, what is apprehended here is some facet of ultimacy or the unconditioned,
something which transcends the observable capacities of the finite, since it answers questions raised precisely by the finite which
the finite could not answer. Through a finite medium or "symbol," whether it be a natural object or objects, the cosmos in part
or as a whole, a community's power or history, or even a person,
an ultimate or unconditioned reality, power or meaning has manifested itself. The content of all religious discourse—whether in
primitive religions, in advanced religions, or in those secular
religions of human autonomy on which modern culture is based
—represents an apprehension beyond the possibility of the facts;
it is given and received, because it manifests the depths of reality,
its ultimate structures and tendencies, often obscured on its surface; and thus it is expressed in the symbolic religious language
of multivalent images and myths. Such knowledge, though appearing through finite media and in the world of ordinary experience, seems to come into experience from beyond its usual

[7] "The sacred is qualitatively different from the profane, yet it
may manifest itself no matter how or where in the profane world because
of its power of turning any natural object into a paradox by means of a
hierophany." Eliade, *Patterns*, p. 30; cf. also pp. 23–24, 216, 447.

range. For these reasons, we wish to use the word "revelation" when we speak of the origins of religious symbols of all sorts, whether in explicit religious traditions or in secular life generally.

The question that faces us at this point is a very complex and controversial one. Granted, the reader may say, that *religious* symbols do seem to arise from experiences such as have here been described—special, transcendent, illuminating, healing experiences, about which there can be little objectivity or rational argument but only confession and description—what has this as a serious epistemology to do with secular experience and secular culture? Surely the day of sacred hierophanies through stones, sky, trees, and snakes is gone—and hopefully those through clan, tribe, and race; and by "secular" we certainly mean in part that the older certainties of a revelation on Sinai and even at Pentecost have faded as well. What, then, does secular thought about life, concerned though it may be with what we have been calling "ultimate questions," to do with the category of revelation, even general or universal revelation as so described? Some significant *continuity* between religious apprehensions, on the one hand, and secular or philosophical points of view, on the other, must be demonstrated if this clearly "religious" category is to have secular relevance; where, then, does that continuity lie?

To answer this question and so to justify a secular use of the category of hierophany or revelation, involves the explication of a theory of the sources and grounds of ordinary human thinking, especially of philosophical thought, only a sketch of which can be given here. In general, this position reflects the Augustinian and, in modern times, the existentialist traditions that the fundamental form of thought is correctly expressed by the phrase: *Credo ut intelligam.* In other words, according to this tradition some form of "faith," in the broadest *secular* sense of that word, namely as a basic attitude or viewpoint that is argued from and not argued to, and so which arises mysteriously out of experience itself, lies back of all our creative thinking. Most recently this position has been elegantly elaborated by Paul Ricoeur in terms of the phrase "The symbol gives; but what it gives is occasion for thought, something to think about."[8] In terms of our thoughts here, this means that the significant presuppositions of all secular thinking, philosophical, scientific, and ordinary commonsense thinking, are tacit, assumed within specific communal traditions, consequently held to by conviction and belief, and thus are not themselves the products of, nor capable of being made precisely intelligible by, rational inquiry and discursive thought themselves.[9] Insofar as they can be expressed at all, therefore, they are conceptualized symbolically, as examples of precisely the sort of language game we have been elaborating here. The symbols of religious discourse express that which eludes discursive thought both because it is too concrete, too close to the actual in all its paradoxical and fluid mystery, and because it *founds* our relations of inquiry into the actual. It is through symbols that we illumine that context of ultimacy within which our being in the world and so all our thought about the world and ourselves take place; and all philosophical speculation, science, and ordinary thought depend upon and express that general context. As Ricoeur says, a level of symbols precedes and lies back of all forms of gnosis. If this be so, then the origin of these primary symbolic forms in concrete experience—in what we have called "hierophanies" or "revelation"—is extremely relevant for all aspects of secular inquiry and thought. We shall only deal with this large subject in terms of philosophy and its presuppositions.

It is widely recognized by philosophers that the presup-

---

[8] Ricoeur, *Symbolism*, p. 348. Ricoeur goes on: "The symbol gives: a philosophy instructed by myths arises at a certain moment in reflection and, beyond philosophical reflection, it wishes to answer to a certain situation of modern culture. . . . Understanding of symbols can play a part in the movement toward a point of departure. . . . The illusion is not in looking for a point of departure, but in looking for it without presuppositions: A meditation on symbols starts from speech that has already taken place. . . . It wishes to be thought with its presuppositions."

[9] One of the most informed and powerful exponents of this general position is Michael Polanyi, cf. *Personal Knowledge* (London: Routledge and Kegan Paul, 1958) and his new volume, *The Tacit Dimension* (Garden City, N.Y.: Doubleday, 1966).

positions of any system of thought are not subject to proof, i.e., that one cannot consistently derive one's basic principles of reality and intelligibility from any thinking prior to them. They must, therefore, arise elsewhere. Now, these principles are essential if thinking is to begin at all. Thought is reflection upon and discrimination within a broad spectrum of awareness and of feeling which is as yet relatively inchoate, thematized only in terms of the broad symbolic patterns of a culture's life, and yet pregnant with all the significant categories and dimensions of reality. No thinking which coheres this manifold into some thematized order can function purely passively in relation to this varied and vague given of experience. It would not know where to look: to dreams, to sense, to rational ideas, to facts (and what *are* the facts?); and it would not know what to do with what it found there when it looked—and no form of *knowing* would result. On the contrary, cognitive thought deals actively with the vast "buzzing chaos" of experience—i.e., it "knows"—through those aspects of the total given which are already considered to provide the most significant clues to what is real; and it deals with those chosen aspects of the given according to certain principles which are already affirmed to lead to intelligibility. Thus out of the totality that is given, the mind, in order to proceed at all, must affirm some form of "fact" taken to be an indisputable clue to reality, and, in order to proceed with these given data, it must affirm some procedure, some relation of logic to experience or reality, according to which that reality can be made coherent. All thought is thus "theory-laden." It grapples with the stuff of experience in terms of a presupposed pattern of judgment as to what is real and what is intelligible in that manifold, and it selects its data and coheres them according to these assumed principles.[10] Every philosophy, therefore, assumes at its beginning a principle of reality and a principle of intelligibility. These are not the *results* of

[10] A most interesting and illuminating confirmation of this thesis that all thought is "theory-laden" if it is to proceed at all has come in the studies of the history of science of Stephen Toulmin and Thomas S. Kuhn. For the first, see *Foresight and Understanding* (New York: Harper Torchbooks, 1963), pp. 38–82; for the second, cf. *The Structure of Scientific Revolutions* (Chicago: University of Chicago Press, 1962).

its thought about experience; rather, they are its *presuppositions.* Philosophical thought is not so much the root by which self-evidence is achieved, as it is the explication and unfolding, in the face of all the facts, of affirmations which have come to be regarded by the thinker during the course of his actual living as self-evident.[11] Thought follows and symbolizes life, not the reverse; direct experience or awareness—and the symbols in which that is explicated—precede rationality and cannot be created by it.

Now, if we ask where these ultimate principles of thinking originate, we suggest that (*a*) in most men they arise directly out of the cultural *Geist* which provides for the majority of us the ultimate presuppositions about our being in the world, namely our attitudes about its reality, its order, and the relations of our minds to that order. But (*b*), if we ask where *these* arise, we can only say that in exceptionally creative individuals new attitudes to reality do appear, and that in such persons these attitudes, whatever they may be, are generated on that relatively inchoate but weightier level of experience where the creative self as contingent and fragmentary confronts the existential problem of its being in the world, and seeks to make sense, order, and meaning out of its position there. And they arise because that person has experienced an illumination, a sudden apprehension or seeing which brings reality and order into the chaos of life.

Men are faced with a confusing mass of events in which they are involved, an infinity of facts which they must understand, with inherited theories which they must consider, and with decisions which they must make. Thus they are forced, alone or

----

[11] "All knowledge, we feel, must be built up upon our instinctive beliefs; and if these are rejected, nothing is left." Bertrand Russell, *The Problems of Philosophy* (New York: Henry Holt and Company, 1912), p. 39. "Thus philosophical reflection is not the cause of that ultimate, comprehensive decision which determines the manner of a man's life and purpose, but rather its effect and expression. So understood, my philosophy represents the result of my efforts to give a carefully articulated, objective, and all-inclusive account of life and reality as they appear to me from my point of view, an effort sustained by my desire to commend my point of view by demonstrating that it is one from which it is possible to see life steadily and to see it whole." J. Langmead-Casserley, *The Christian in Philosophy* (London: Farber and Farber, 1949), p. 193.

in concert, to undertake the necessary task of unifying this chaos
into an ordered coherence, for without some unity, coherence,
and meaning to this initial confusion, individual existence would
not be humanly bearable and man could neither think nor act.
Men can find this intelligibility only if some illumination, some
insight with regard to the questions of reality and order are given
to them; and in response, if they determine in some deeply voli-
tional act, some profound "Yes" of awareness, to stand somewhere, to regard something within this welter as real, and to hold
to some principle of order. Just as man cannot act as a human
without first affirming that something is of value—be it only not
to act at all or only to enjoy life—so he cannot think at all amidst
all the welter of events and facts if he does not affirm as a presupposition, and therefore ultimate for his thought, something
from out of this given to be real and some means amongst all
those possible by which this real can be organized into a coherence that satisfies him. Even in thinking, man confronts an ultimate which is the ground, both existential and logical, of his
thinking. The principles upon which any philosophy is founded
are themselves prior to the resulting philosophy and come from
the philosopher's cultural tradition or from his own response to
the existential predicament in which as a human being he finds
himself. The basis, therefore, for any speculative ontology is the
reception in experience of a "revelation" of the ultimate order
of things, a revelation which is not so much the result of speculative thought as its ground. Philosophy is the courage in which
this faith is measured against every conceivable fact and every
conceivable rejection.[12]

  We thus propose as at least one relation of religious discourse to philosophy the view that, when one inquires into the

[12] As Ricoeur says: "A philosophy that starts from the fullness of
language is a philosophy with presuppositions. To be honest, it must
make its presuppositions explicit, state them as beliefs, wager on the
beliefs, and try to make the wager pay off in understanding." *Symbolism*,
p. 357. See also Toulmin's category of the "limiting questions" that lie
back of any ultimate cultural activity of man, and which must be answered
by faith in terms of religious forms of discourse. *An Examination of the
Place of Reason in Ethics* (New York: Cambridge University Press,
1950), chap. 14.

prerational basis of any philosophical thought, the ultimate convictions about reality, order, and value on which it is founded, one is then entering the realm of religious discourse or of religious symbol. Here discursive speculative thought has reached its limit, since it is now dealing with its own presuppositions. And we are proposing that both in form and in substance these presuppositions are "religious" in character, since they concern the ultimate structures of things and of our thinking, and are received in special experiences of "revelation," and are discussed only in terms of the language game we have called "religious discourse."[13]

Throughout our discussion we have pointed to the present problematic of metaphysics, the evident fact that confidence in the speculative capacities of reason has disappeared in our time. We are now ready to suggest one explanation of this cultural development. If the confidence in the power of reason to explicate an ontological structure of things depends upon a

[13] "What the metaphysician does, therefore, is to construct a theoretic model drawn from analogy from some form of intellectual or spiritual relationships which he judges to be especially significant or important. . . . And at the creative point of experience there comes an inevitable power of positive response; the thinker finds himself saying, 'yes,' freely with his whole being. I do not believe that any of the great metaphysicians have cast round looking for some interesting idea on which they might be able to construct a theory. They have been charged with a sense of the importance and significance in some spiritual or intellectual experience, and the excitement of this has driven them on to attempt to give intelligible form to other vague reaches of experience with reference to this basic thought." Dorothy M. Emmett, *The Nature of Metaphysical Thinking* (London: Macmillan and Co., Ltd., 1949), pp. 197–198.

"So understood, metaphysics is a search conducted throughout the length and breadth of our experience for the most pregnant and revealing analogies. The search is guided and motivated by fundamental judgments of value, or existentialist self-affirmations, which express and betray the intrinsic personality and moral and spiritual situation of the metaphysician himself. . . . A metaphysical scheme, according to this doctrine, is an analogical picture of reality. The analogies are drawn from that realm of human interest and experience which the philosopher regards as most decisive and revealing." Langmead-Casserley, *The Christian in Philosophy*, pp. 223–224.

deep prerational and so experiential sense of an ultimate order pervading all of process, then what is lacking is precisely such an existential awareness, in the intellect if not in the viscera, of that ultimate order. A sense of the unconditioned ground of order has been as absent from our secular experience as has that of the unconditioned ground of meaning and of love. Thus just as theological language about God has been impaired through secular experience, so has metaphysical language about an ultimate order. And correspondingly, just as theological language about God can begin, not by assuming *ab initio* the meaningfulness or validity of its religious symbols, but only by unearthing the grounds in ordinary experience for these symbols, so metaphysical or ontological language in theology must start with the foundational experiences of order in ordinary experience—with that "revelation" of the ultimate order which grounds thought— if such language is to be possible today. A modern theology using metaphysical or ontological discourse itself depends upon a contemporary reception of the revelation of such an order if it is to be possible; such a theology will only be intelligible and valid if those grounds are established by some such prolegomenon to metaphysical language as our own in this volume.

It is, then, in direct and quite special experiences of illumination, clarification, and release, received in and interpreted through some important communal tradition in which the recipient participates, that the fundamental principles, convictions, or presuppositions of each particular type or brand of thought take their rise. And from these principles flows all our thinking, shaping and determining both the form and the conclusions of our philosophies. The process of philosophical thought, then, validly begins with that point in personal and historical experience where intelligibility itself has begun, where the light in our otherwise confused experience has dawned. For some thinkers this illuminating experience has been in the community of science and its proximate clarities, for some in ethical experience and its values within the wider democratic social context, for others in social or political experience or some strand of the historical development of their cultural community, for others more directly and specifically in religious experience in some religious community. And from this level of special personal experience mediated through wider communal experience, the different viewpoints even of secular philosophies as well as of theologies stem, for here the basic questions of each of us are answered and so our fundamental convictions about the character of reality and about its intelligibility take their start and so receive their ultimate form. If in philosophical thought this methodological principle means we start our thinking where in experience and in symbolic explication our ultimate principles have appeared, in all forms of positive theology making statements about ultimacy, it surely means that thought should begin with the point where the sacred has been known, with the direct experience of an answer, with the concrete reception of the revelation of ultimacy and so with its appropriate symbols.

The first important implication for method of these principles of reflective thought at this level is that there is no essential difference in *form* between the philosophical thinking which explicates a fundamental "metaphysical vision," and so results in metaphysics (or, we believe, *any* form of philosophical analysis—for all are based on some ultimate vision of this sort), and the theological thinking which explicates the fundamental vision of things received in the religious experience of a specific community and so is expressive of what we ordinarily call "faith." In the one case, the central illumination and clarification of the manifold confusions, anxieties, and questions of existence, has come within some special community in secular life, perhaps in the scientific, the mathematical, the academic, the artistic, or the political community; in the other, it has come through one's participation in a religious community or tradition where, it is held, a Word is heard and a presence met in terms of which all the rest of life then becomes meaningful. In both cases, because they have led to this experience of illumination, and thus have made possible the process of thinking at all, the symbolic forms, the standards, the goals, and the criteria of the community in which the experience occurred are presupposed as determinative for thought. A naturalistic, rationalistic, or positivistic philosopher quite naturally makes ultimate the symbolic forms, the criteria of truth, and the values of the scientific and democratic communities in which that thinker spiritually exists. In the same way, most Christian theologians appeal to the symbolic forms, criteria, and values of their own Christian tradition. In each form of thought, personal experience of clarification and release, apprehended within some communal tradition and its forms—what we have chosen to call a "revelation" of the ultimate ground of reality and coherence—makes possible our thinking and thus sets for each of us those ultimate principles of reality, truth, and value in terms of which we answer the fundamental questions of our common life. The fact that most thinkers of an epoch, and certainly of a given civilization, exist in many of the same communities and therefore share these same proximate experiences of clarification and release (for example, all of us participate, more or less, in the artistic, scientific, and democratic or political communities of our society), accounts for those common assumptions that make conversation and joint action possible, and that give to a historic epoch its own particular shape and form. The fact we each find our ultimate standpoint in a different way, different communities within our culture, or even in different cultures, makes for the vast difference of points of view which the philosophical and theological thought of an era exhibit. In philosophy as in theology, ultimate viewpoints vary as one moves from community to community, and in both, while there is an unlimited possibility of fruitful discussion, there is no possibility either of disproof or of final settlement. No community is universal, and no point of view reflective of the communal presuppositions of its time and place is universal. And all find their roots in the existential experiences of clarification, illumination, and release that take place in special communities.[14]

[14] There is little question that there *is* a frustrating aspect to traditional philosophy, a trait despaired over unto death by linguistic philosophers, namely the fact that in the development of philosophy no issue seems ever to be settled, but the same arguments go on interminably, and that therefore no *accumulation* of cognitive results, as in science (or *supposedly* in science, as Kuhn sees it, *Structure of Scientific Revolutions*), is ever possible. (For examples of this despair, see R. M. Rorty, *The Linguistic Turn* [Chicago: University of Chicago Press, 1967], pp. 4–5, 8, 14, 153, where it is regarded as a "scandalous fact" that philosophers cannot specify common criteria for settling their issues.) To many linguistic philosophers, the reason for this "scandal" is that the questions traditionally asked and so the problems discussed—since they are not settleable—are not genuine questions, but rather result either from confusions of ordinary language or a misuse of ordinary language—some

The second implication of these methodological remarks is that proof in philosophy or theology is secondary. As Whitehead said, proof in philosophy means "given certain presuppositions about reality, such and such conclusions are thereby implied."[15] What is proved is always derivative from principles prior to itself, and thus deals with the relatively unimportant. Clearly, then, to prove basic principles is impossible, since it is these that must be assumed in order that the process we call "im-

kind of "bewitchment of grammar." It is, we agree, undeniable that traditional philosophical issues are and can never be "settled." However, it is the even worse "bewitchment of science" that has caused these philosophers, possessing, apparently, a vast inferiority complex, to conclude from this that the discussion of traditional philosophical issues was a tragic mistake. For this shows not only a misunderstanding of traditional philosophy but also of science. The "unsettleability" of philosophical issues derives rather from the character of the range of experience with which philosophical thought has sought to deal, and so from the type of language, and consequently the forms of meaning and validity, that result. These issues concern the ultimate bases or horizon of man's being in the world and our thinking about it. Thus, (1) different viewpoints on these issues are inevitable, granted the vast difference of historical and cultural loci for thought, *and* the very different experiences of and attitudes toward life that different individuals inevitably have. (2) The character of these issues as "ultimate" means that they are better understood as "mysteries" to be at best symbolically clarified rather than "problems" to be solved once and for all. Above all, since these discussions concern the *foundations* of thinking, and therefore also the foundations of all inquiry and testing, they cannot themselves be submitted easily to any neutral mode of validation. Thus they are not subject to the same natural verification or falsification process as are scientific hypotheses, which can assume an agreed-upon mode of validation as authoritative. One good reason why philosophy is not science is that intrinsically it raises questions about itself, about knowing itself, which science in its relative innocence never raises. (3) Finally, since these issues and the ranges of experience where they arise are inevitably "there" and are of the utmost importance, it is better to apply, insofar as one can, reasonable discourse to them, than to flee from them because they are not matters of fact—and thus to leave them to blank unreason and to unthinking custom. Nothing is so unclear in the otherwise clear analytical movement as its understanding of what sorts of language traditional philosophy was composed of, and consequently nothing is so wide of the mark as the reasons *they* give for their own dogmatic reactions against all such forms of philosophical discussion.

[15] Whitehead has put this point in the following magnificent

plication" may begin. Thus, we would argue, philosophical thought moves *from* its own basic principles found in our existence within historic community; its function and role is to disclose what these basic points of view mean and imply, and all it can say at the end is: "Look, is *this* not the way things truly are?"[16] Thinking about the ultimate structure of things explicates

---

passage: "Unless proof has produced self-evidence and thereby rendered itself unnecessary, it has issued in a second-rate state of mind, producing action devoid of understanding. Self-evidence is the basic fact on which all greatness supports itself. But, 'proof' is one of the roots by which self-evidence is often obtained. . . . In philosophical writings proof should be at a minimum. The whole effort should be to display the self-evidence of basic truths, concerning the nature of things and their connection. It should be noted that logical proof starts from premises; and that premises are based upon evidence. Thus evidence is presupposed by logic; at least it is presupposed by the assumption that logic has any importance. Philosophy is the attempt to make manifest the fundamental evidence as to the nature of things. Upon the presupposition of this evidence, all understanding rests. . . . It follows that philosophy, in any proper sense of the term, cannot be proved. For proof is based upon abstraction. Philosophy is either self-evident or it is not philosophy. The attempt of any philosophic discourse should be to produce self-evidence. . . . The aim of philosophy is sheer disclosure." A. N. Whitehead, *Modes of Thought* (New York: Macmillan Company, 1938), pp. 66–67. Cf. on the same point, Edmund Husserl, *Ideas* (New York: Collier Books, 1962), pp. 204, 210, and 211.

[16] The important *cognitive* aspect of our human powers, our power to think and to know—in practical life, science, and philosophy—has only briefly been a subject of our discussion in this work. It has, we believe, the same unconditional basis as do the other facets of our existence in the world, our contingency, meanings, values, and freedom. For thought and certainly knowing cannot begin unless there is present an unconditional commitment to the truth, unless some understanding of reality (what the "facts" are) and of the order of things are presupposed —as we have argued above—and unless the mind, in affirming that it *knows* (as it must do if it is to claim a cognitive act) has experienced the unconditioned character of our proximate judgments. Thus there is, to us, an experience of an unconditioned dimension contained in all thinking, and an experience of the loss of that foundation in all really radical skepticism and doubt. To show this is, however, the subject of another treatise. It is relevant here because, if it is a sound view, it implies that the legitimate use of the symbol "God" in philosophical theology can only be referent to this unconditioned *ground* of scientific and philosophical thought, and not to any demonstrated or hypothetical *product* of or *inference* from these autonomously conceived enterprises.

some answer to our most fundamental questions arising out of our being in the world. Such thinking does not move *toward* its own final principles, for without them, it could not begin to move at all. Thinking in ontology and in theology explicates or discloses, it does not establish, the fundamental convictions and viewpoints about reality which it represents.

The third and final implication of these methodological principles is that, in philosophical theology, the ultimate and the sacred, that to which the symbol "God" refers, cannot be proved, lest this symbol contradict its own intention, its own meaning and function in the language game of religious discourse. Since proof is secondary to more fundamental presuppositions, a god who is proved is reached indirectly through implication from other, more ultimate principles or certainties, rather than itself functioning as the ultimate ground of our being in the world and so, of course, of our thinking as one aspect of that being. Such a god is thus a prisoner held by and hidden behind principles of thought more basic than himself. In our analysis of a philosophical proof of god, we found that every god of natural theology is established as "real" by the categories of a metaphysical system; if he is thus dependent on them for his reality and intelligibility, he can hardly then transcend those categories once he appears on the scene. As the ground of *his* being for our thought, the metaphysical categories, and the ultimate coherence of things they illustrate, are more ultimate than he, so it is they that determine his nature and functions and not the reverse. The real ultimate or sacred, then, in such natural theologies is not the god that reason discovers by implication, but the ultimate coherence of the universe, or of process itself, which reason presupposes for its metaphysical vision. God may be an important factor in that coherence, and so implied by it; but it is the rationality of the totality of things, far transcending any finite god and expressed in the metaphysical system of categories itself, which is "god" in the phenomenological or linguistic sense of that word which we have uncovered. This is one reason that the gods of the philosophers seldom have any religious sense of the holy or the sacred about them. Phenomenologically, these philosophical factors are not functioning as "gods" at all, that is, as the ultimate grounds and limits of

what is; rather are they subordinate deities, demigods, in relation
to the *real* "high god" which is the rational coherence of all
things. And it is in relation to the high god of coherence alone
that most metaphysical philosophers express their most cherished
dogmas and have performed their own religious and cultic rites!

Our analysis has shown that religious discourse and so
religious symbols have meaningful usage with regard to a certain
area or dimension of experience, namely with that which limits
us, that which grounds, determines, and ends our finite existence,
and grounds as well the courage, the coherence, and the meaning
which we may find within that existence. Religious symbols, and
preeminently that of God, are meaningful, therefore, as thematizing answers to our ultimate questions; in symbolic form, they
thus express, if they express anything at all, that unconditional
answer which is essential if we are to live with serenity, intelligibility, meaning, courage, and love in the face of our contingency, relativity, temporality, and the ambiguities of our freedom.

With regard to the question of the ground of thinking
and cognition, therefore, and so to that of science and philosophy,
religious symbols, if they are to have any relevance at all, are
meaningful only as explications of that ultimate or unconditioned apprehension of and so faith in the coherence and intelligibility of things in which science and speculative philosophy
itself are founded. Thus a philosophical use of the symbol "God"
makes sense *only* if that symbol thematizes or has reference to the
ground of ultimate coherence which the philosophy itself presupposes, if God is explicated as the source of that coherence rather
than merely as a finite exemplification of it. But if God be the
source of ultimate coherence, and so the object of the philosopher's faith in which his speculation begins and by which it
proceeds, God cannot be proved or established by that speculation itself, nor even subjected univocally to the categories of the
reason he founds. For then, as we have seen, the god the philosopher tries to prove ceases to be the unconditioned basis of
philosophical explication itself and becomes merely its conditioned product, understood by rational criteria and metaphysical
categories, and established in relation to some other ultimate and
so to some other god. Since the *meaning* of religious discourse

lies solely in the fact that this discourse thematizes that relation to the ultimate by which we live, think, and value, a philosophical use of religious symbols that will make intelligible rather than unintelligible their legitimate religious usage must have reference to the unconditioned, transcendent, and ultimate ground of our thinking itself, and not merely to a product of its exercise. To subsume religious language under a metaphysical system, and to attempt to ground its meaning and intelligibility there, is thus *not* to make it intelligible, but precisely to threaten whatever intelligible use it may have.

This basic rule of theological method has often been overlooked by philosophers more concerned with explicating the coherences in existence which thought can envision than with the religious and existential issues of the deeper bases of their own faith in coherence. Thus, presupposing confidently this faith in ultimate coherence, they were indifferent both to the problems of its origin and also to the problem of a subservient god derived from their own more ultimate philosophical principles. For example, one thinks of the case of F. H. Bradley, who used the symbol God only in relation to a principle subordinate to his philosophical absolute,[17] and that of A. N. Whitehead, whose god is subordinate to the larger process and so to the metaphysical categories explicative of that process.[18] When such philosophical thought is applied directly into the theological domain, or, better put, when theological discourse is translated directly into the ontological structures of such a metaphysical system, confusion is apt to result—for two gods are now present,

---

[17] Cf. F. H. Bradley: "God is but an aspect, and that must mean but an appearance, of the Absolute." *Appearance and Reality* (Oxford: Clarendon Press, 1946), p. 397. Cf. also F. H. Cleobury, *God, Man, and the Absolute* (London: Hutchinson & Company, 1947).

[18] Cf. Whitehead, "Actual entities . . . are the final real things of which the world is made up. There is no going behind actual entities to find anything more real. They differ among themselves: God is an actual entity, and so is the most trivial puff of existence in far-off empty space. But, though there are gradations of importance, and diversities of function, yet in the principles which actuality exemplifies, *all are on the same level.*" *Process and Reality* (New York: Macmillan Company, 1929), pp. 28–29 (emphasis added).

that which grounds the philosophical principles of the system itself, and the religiophilosophical entity or godlet derived from them. To be sure, a god who is proved by prior philosophical principles is not necessarily divested of his deity; but, as in a faculty with two deans, he has a difficult time at best fulfilling his rightful role!

Philosophical thought, therefore, can neither derive its own basic principles by its own process of philosophical proof, nor, for essentially the same reason, if it is meaningfully to use religious discourse and symbols, can it derive the God of which it might wish to speak by those processes of proof. As its own presupposed principles provide the dimension or context of ultimacy for its own thinking, so the symbol "God" points to that most general context of ultimacy within which all our being in the world and so all our thinking take place. Thus, in all philosophical theology the philosophical elements are dependent on the religious elements in two important ways: (a) on the presupposed principles of thinking whose origins lie in "revelation" or its secular correlate, that is in existence, in existential and in communal experiences of ultimacy, and thus in some cluster of religious symbols expressive of that experience. (b) Insofar as this philosophical theology seeks to elucidate and express a specific religious faith, it is dependent on those traditional symbolic forms through which it seeks to enact a positive theological position. The trick of philosophical theology is, in short, to achieve without "cheating" a unity between the "secular" but ultimate presuppositions of its thinking (a) and the religious symbols of ultimacy derived from its explicit religious tradition (b).

We wish to propose that a meaningful philosophical usage of religious symbols will, as Paul Ricoeur says, see these symbols as giving rise to our thought and to further opportunities for thought, that is, as providing the foundations for philosophical thought and, through it, for all of man's cultural activities. Thus in connection with the question of philosophy itself, philosophy will use religious symbols to uncover the foundations of its own assumptions and procedures: the symbol of God, or specifically that of the divine Logos, will function as the source of the principles of reality and intelligibility with which philosophy itself works. Philosophical discourse about God as the ground of coherence and so of thinking thus points beyond itself to theological or religious discourse about God if it would understand its own roots. Theology, in its turn, depends upon philosophy, for in order to explicate the full meanings of its symbols, it must move beyond itself into philosophical ontology, for part of the "meaning" of its symbolic content can only be explicated in terms of ontology. On the other hand, the positive role of theology for philosophical inquiry is primarily that of exploring the existential foundations of that faith in an ultimate coherence and intelligibility with which a given philosophy begins. This faith is not the product of philosophy but its presupposition, and it arises in some form of direct illumination or clarification, some relation to an unconditioned ground of coherence—and it is *this* that we have called "revelation" as the point in our existence in community where the unconditioned manifests itself to us. In *this* sense (and only in this sense), metaphysical philosophy is founded on revelation, the general and universal manifestation of the sacral and ultimate ground of being and order to human awareness in the passage of life. Religious intuition in experience, and the theologies that explicate these experiences of revelation, do not, therefore, only provide *data* for autonomous philosophical criticism and elaboration—as most philosophers of religion argue. Perhaps, more significantly, they explicate the grounds of any philosophical elaboration whatsoever. And so again we are led back to the category of "revelation," understood secularly, as the ultimate ground for thought.

There is another reason we have wished to call the point where positive God-language begins "revelation." This is that, while our experiences of the sacred always come to us, as we have shown, in connection with our awareness of the finite—of its contingency, its fragmentariness, its transience, its freedom, and its disruption, isolation and guilt—nevertheless the *answers* to these questions raised by finitude clearly do not have their origin solely there. They are for us in that sense special experiences, rooted more deeply than are our other experiences of the ordinary sequences of events, things, and persons in the visible world of immediacy. The sacred, the numinous, what we have called the category of the "ultimate," has appeared everywhere in human life and in connection with all sorts of experiences. But when men have become aware of it, it has never felt like ordinary experience, as if it were merely a part of the ordinary sequence of natural or historical events. In all of religion, the sacred, while experienced in and through the profane, has not been experienced as a part or even an inference from the profane; and, accordingly, experience of it has been demarked as a special kind of experience.[19] No religious tradition understands itself as having invented or even discovered its fundamental symbols; rather, phenomenologically they are always seen to have been "given" to that tradition. In that sense, religious discourse and revelation are essentially tied to one another. Part of the essential quality of this experience—and so the essential form of its language as symbolic or multivalent—is the character of ultimacy that appears in it and that points the recipient beyond the normal sequence of finite things to their source, beyond the proximate coherences of life to their ground. Consequently, in coming from beyond the finite which we understand in our accustomed ways, such answers appear to us as a revelation of what in ordinary experience has remained quite mysterious and hidden within the ambiguity of things, something that we feel we could not even have uncovered or discovered, but that has through and in itself manifested itself to us.

This mysterious and yet *given* character of the experience in which religious and so theological language begins has also been made manifest by our analysis of secular experience, its crises and the ultimate questions that these crises can raise. In locating the area in which God-language has meaningful usage, we found this area to lie where the creature experiences his own limits, and in experiencing precisely these limits, he asks the

[19] "Further, while a hierophany presupposes a break in religious experience (for there always exists, in one form or another, a *breach* between the sacred and the profane, and a *passage* from one to the other —which breach and passage constitute the very essence of the religious life) symbolism effects a permanent solidarity between man and the sacred." Eliade, *Patterns*, p. 447.

question which reaches beyond the creaturely—a question about an ultimacy that the creaturely cannot itself provide. The questions raised at this level—questions of an ultimate security, order, meaning, value, sovereignty, acceptance, and eternity—are raised precisely by the contingency and the helplessness of the finite itself. Since, moreover, these questions are raised by the essential character of finitude *as finite*, finitude can by itself at this level only generate questions; it cannot provide answers, and this is precisely what the experience itself communicates to us. It asks about an ultimate, about that which it itself is not. And this character of the experience is evident from the experience of our lack of control on the situation that gives it rise, from the helplessness of our finite capacities, and from the givenness of the answer. And just as the questions derive directly from our contingency or creatureliness, so in each case the answer that is called for has an essential ingredient of ultimacy or unconditionedness that no creature can possess or create. And by that is meant that the answer precisely grounds, founds, makes possible, and limits the powers which we as creatures possess. An answer here, therefore, if one is here at all, is one *from* transcendence *to* finitude, from that which in *not* sharing in these dependencies of the creature is itself *more than* creaturely. When we ask, "Is our existence grounded on an abyss or on being, on what is to us nothingness or on God?" only some manifestation of the character and form of this transcendent ground of our life can answer us, not further information about the dependent creatures around us.

At this level, therefore, we are dealing with mystery and hiddenness in which our usual thought processes find themselves dizzy if not incompetent. As Whitehead insisted, full clarity of philosophical vision and thought cannot extend beyond the coherent system of finite things, and so beyond that system there is for our philosophical reason mere blankness.[20] And the empirical naturalists, the early phenomenologists, the positivists, and most analytic philosophers have progressively hardened this same prin-

[20] Cf. Whitehead, *Process and Reality*, pp. 5–6, and *Science and the Modern World* (New York: Macmillan Company, 1925), pp. 249–250.

ciple to say that thought cannot move beyond the level of the immediate experience of finite things or structures at all. Thus since, as we have seen, these answers (and even, as we have suggested, the above philosophies that explicate some answers) come from beyond the area where experiment and argument by rational implication are possible, they are less discovered by us than given to us; if they are there at all, they are "revealed" to us. One conclusion, of course, frequently drawn from this mystery and hiddenness characteristic of answers at this level, is that, while they are, apparently, "there" and important, we should nonetheless not talk about them at all.[21] But, as we have argued, we do talk about these obscure and yet significant elements of experience all the time, and in fact we have to, since, on the level of awareness and behavior, we live continually in terms of such answers. If secular life in all of its facets manifests the presence or the absence of the transcendent, and reflects this dimension in a multitude of anxieties and behavioral forms, it is far better to reflect on that mystery as intelligibly as we can in terms of consistent symbols than irrationally to leave this area in silence, where it remains uncomprehended and so quite uncontrolled.

Our point that knowledge of God has, in this sense, a transcendent source and is not to be discovered easily on the surface of life, has been more than verified by the modern mood of metaphysical modesty. For, as we have seen, what is peculiarly characteristic of this mood is that it has pushed its questions about ultimate principles precisely to these limits of thought, and has at the end of this process found no answers available. Conscious that modern man "waits for Godot," i.e., that modern man asks these ultimate questions with great seriousness but can find no answers, the contemporary spirit has searched throughout ordinary experience for some clue to an ultimate coherence and mean-

---

[21] Wittgenstein, in the *Tractatus Logico-Philosophicus* (London: K. Paul, Trench, Trubner and Co., 1922), p. 189, put this position in its classic modern form: "Of what cannot be said, thereof one must be silent." As Michael Polanyi has pointed out throughout his writings, however, most of what we do is based on a "knowing" which cannot be "said clearly or indistinctly", and that to ignore in silence this tacit dimension of knowing is to leave the most significant bases of experience and of our activities blind.

ing—but, as in that Becket play, all that has been found at this level are only the Void and the Absurd, or, as the naturalists and positivists put the same thing, the Meaningless. To our generation, however provisionally meaningful it may seem, the immediate surface of life apparently reveals no coherence or rationality secure enough to provide speculative thought with immanent grounds for finding answers to these pressing questions. This is not for our age an obviously rational, harmonious, or coherent world, and so one in which thought can move from immediate experience to ultimate certainties. Beyond the immediate has yawned, for our time, the Void—and that experience of ultimate nothingness, whether in its naturalistic, existentialist, or positivist forms, has called a sharp "Halt" to all our efforts to discover by autonomous reason a secure order evident within ordinary experience. Speculative philosophical thought based on a faith in ultimate coherence and meaning, as its present almost total dependence on some religious tradition or other shows, can only reappear when, through some existential contact with the ultimate ground of all creaturely being and order, a sense of coherence is given to us again. Thus philosophical rationalism, too, begins with a special apprehension of the ultimate order of things. When the current emptiness of the ultimate Void has, through direct experience, become for us "God" instead of nothingness, when the absurd has become a dimly trusted coherence and meaning, when an ultimate meaninglessness and blindness has for intuition taken on the lineaments of order and even of love—then, against the linguistic retreat from all speculative thought and against existentialist despair, speculative ontology may be able to begin again. The possibility of a philosophical theology depends upon the *givenness* of an answer to these questions of ultimate coherence, which it is almost impossible, in our skeptical age, to create, a givenness that can only be denominated by the words "religious experience" or "revelation," and which can be explicated only in terms of the symbols of religious discourse designed to deal with the ultimate context or framework of things.

Let us admit, then, that if we are to talk of *answers* to our ulti-

mate questions; if we are to make or imply claims or assertions
about what is ultimately real, true and good in the system of
things; if[22] we are to speak *theologically*, and not just phenomenologically, about the sacred or "God," or philosophically about
a coherent Process or even of Nature; if we are to use *any* form
of positive, assertive religious discourse, whether in philosophy or
theology, we cannot remain merely at the level of description or
analysis—whether it be linguistic analysis of our word usage, phenomenological analysis of immediate experience, or metaphysical
analysis of the universal structures of general experience. A *break*
must appear at this point in the course of the argument of our
prolegomenon; a *new* and a *particular* assumption must be made,
an assumption based on some special experience of the ultimate
nature of things. The "new" must enter underived from the analysis that has gone before, because as we have seen, (*a*) any positive answer to an ultimate question is always correlated with and
so can be balanced by a corresponding 'No' as another possible
answer, and so consequently, (*b*) the affirmation of the answer
always depends on the particularity of concrete special experiences where something has *entered* the ambiguity of life to clar-

[22] We have used the word "if" here because two contemporary
ways of doing "theology" or talking of religion seek, illicitly we believe,
to avoid making such claims. The first type, realizing the difficulty and
the presumption of speaking of *God*, seek only to speak of the Bible, of
Christ, of proclamation, of faith, or of the eschatological event—as if any
of these had *theological* meaning without an implied God. The linguistic
meaning of the Arian controversy was surely that any *theological* statements about the Christ-event, or about Revelation, are in some way statements about God, and thus statements about the ultimate nature of reality. The second way to avoid this sort of claim about "what is the case" is
by studying other people's religions: their myths, rites, models, and hopes
in the history of religions. By this means one can, in a secular age, where
to claim anything to be true in these areas is difficult, still be in close
touch with religion and a religious view of things without making any
wager about what is actually so. As Luther said, however, a man can
neither live nor die on another's faith (first Wittenberg Sermon, in
Works of Martin Luther [Philadelphia: Muhlenberg Press, 1943], Volume II, p. 391), nor can one even understand what religion is by such
objective study alone. Thus inescapably statements must be made and
claims asserted about the character of reality—either if we are to live with
our own faith and hope, or to understand with our own mind.

ify, re-create, and redeem it, and not on the general character of
universal experience. For it was that general character of common
experience itself which, in appearing essentially ambiguous and
problematical, had previously given rise to such questions. Something that had not been found by an analysis on the level of creaturely interrelations, where the ambiguities of finitude still remain, and so where the possibility of ultimate doubt and despair
still appear, must have been added that the creaturely could not
itself provide. What is *new* here is the experience of an answer to
our questions that concern the finite itself, and that means that, in
some way, the transcendent has in fact been unveiled for us or
appeared to us. The possibility of such an awareness, such an
unveiling or revelation in a secular age, is the most crucial step
of the argument with the secular spirit in all its forms. For if
the sacred is *not* apprehended thus somewhere in experience,
through awareness or revelation, then the Void *is* all; and, as a
consequence, Christian God-language, though meaningful, remains only a possibility for another world, and unreal or invalid
in this one, its symbolic forms based on no real experiences and
no real transformation. But if the sacred is known there, then
an answer is received, the divine obituary is premature, and God-
language that is both meaningful and validatable can be derived
from these experienced answers. No proof here is possible; in this
situation, speech naturally takes the form of confession and conviction based on the acknowledgment of this sort of experience.
And at *this* level, whether in philosophy or theology, no other
answer than this is possible with regard to questions of validity.

This does not mean, however, that theological thought is
either irrational or incoherent, or that criteria of validation are
quite inoperable at these levels of discourse. Theology stands
under the same criteria as any other form of thought of this general type, namely that it provide an internally coherent and widely
applicable scheme of general symbols or categories which, while
founded on some particular form of experience, can illuminate
any other area of general experience. As we saw, each viewpoint
of the nature of things, whether philosophical or theological, can
only argue that, in its terms, the general contours of experience
are brought into a more intelligible order than in any other

scheme—and to establish this capability of universal explanation is incumbent on any system. But beyond this, there is little possibility of either demonstration or disproof. Ultimate principles of explanation can be debated; but since they involve, as we noted, assertions of a different logical type than are factual ones, they can be neither conclusively verified nor falsified. Finally they depend, as we said, on their power to describe and illuminate the experience that we all share; and one moves from one system or viewpoint to the other, insofar as such a move has intellectual grounds, because of the success or failure of each in this task of illuminating what are taken to be the most crucial and universal factors in ordinary experience. Validation at this level of thought is tricky and not easily comprehended or interpreted. But a viewpoint dependent on special experiences of what is called "grace" is no different in principle—either in its requirements or in its legitimacy—from one based on an experience of the vitalities of life, on cognitive endeavors of intelligence in the laboratory, on particular forms of social experience, or on an intuition of an ultimate coherence in existence as a whole—for, after all, as we have argued, each of these fundamental experiences is itself the gift of that unconditioned ground in which we live and move and have our being. Naturalistic forms of metaphysics can no more be established than can any other. Their obviousness to their defenders and to great numbers of their adherents in our day merely shows that they are explications of the texture of general experience as our widespread secular mood experiences that texture, though, as we have argued, they are not without significant omission and so, according to one of the criteria of philosophical or theological truth, they are not without error.

Just as, therefore, the claim of the *meaningfulness* of discourse about God depends upon establishing the close relation of an answer to the ultimate questions all humans ask, so the claim of the *validity* of any particular form of God-language rests in the first instance upon the assumption that an answer at this level has been given and experienced. The presence to our experience of such a given answer in secular life corresponds precisely to what in theological language we refer to when we use the category of "revelation" and speak of its "reception in faith." In positive theological discourse, this category expresses the conviction that the knowledge of this answer depends upon God's initiative in crossing that Void. Or, to put this point better, God has unveiled to us through that Void his presence here with us all the time, as the foundation of every creative aspect of our creaturely life, but a presence hidden for us as long as we existed purely in terms of the creaturely and tried to ground our answers to ultimate questions on our creaturely capacities and powers alone. Initially to Christian faith, God is the Void seen in a new light: while to our secular inquiry our existence seemed based on nothingness and incoherence, to the new gaze of faith it reveals itself as grounded in the divine reality, coherence, meaning, and love.

This experience of a sacred beyond and in the profane, of an unconditioned behind and within the contingent, of an ultimate order behind and within the ordinary sequences of experience, and an eternal good beyond and within the ambiguities of our life, is as old as mankind and is, as we have argued, present, at least in dim awareness, wherever man is fully man. Consequently, the reality of what has been called in theology a "general revelation" of the transcendent in one form or another is manifested in all creative human life and in all religion—as is the terror at what we have called the "Void." There is hardly any form of religion that fails to share our general thesis that the secular has no ultimate foundation except through and in the sacred, and that despite this pervasive presence of the divine, the latter cannot be known except in the special places, the particular symbols and experiences through which it reveals itself to us and which are treasured and communicated through time in the historical community of a particular faith. In this sense, as we noted, the category of "special revelation" is implied rather than contradicted by that of general revelation. From its particular and historical starting point every form of thought, secular or religious, expands outward to encompass, if it can, all of experience.

For Christians, this category of special revelation, providing particular, unique, and normative form to what is known in general revelation, is of course essential. While Christians recognize that God has made himself known elsewhere, nevertheless, the place where their faith has begun and so where their discourse about him starts, has been with Jesus Christ and with the historical community and the tradition that leads up to and then stems from that event. Here for us, in this community which has known God as the answer to life's deepest problems, the sacred has become real to us, for here God has entered our experience as its saving force and ground. The "verification" of all we say about God occurs, first of all, then, in the life of faith lived by that community, and from that living experience springs the usage and the reality of its particular forms of God-language. That verification in Christian existence must be supplemented, however, by a continuous awareness of the relevance of these symbolic forms to the deepest questions of our ordinary, secular life, and by the power of the viewpoint thus created to interpret and illumine every facet of our widest experience. Finally, the meaningfulness of this language, while apparent to this community that knows God in its faith and so interprets its day-to-day life, is not restricted to the bounds of that community. For this language game is intelligible as a coherent and relevant answer to the deepest questions that existence raises in all men everywhere.

Christian theology, then, as the positive explication of the faith of this community and so of the meaning for our day of the originating and traditional symbolic forms of its life, is based on those special experiences of God's activity and presence which we have called "revelation." How, then, does its thought proceed and how is it related to the analysis of human experience we have outlined? Only a fully developed systematic theology could provide an adequate answer to these questions; and so in these comments, which are still essentially a prolegomenon to that effort, a merely formal answer will be given. This answer is important, however, if we are to make good our claim that a secular theology is possible, one that genuinely speaks of God as the Christian tradition has done, and yet one that speaks in the accents and concepts of a secular age.

Two factors are significant in such a theology, one of them a secular question, the other a Christian answer. First of

all, in our life in the world, we find that inevitably certain questions, which we have called "ultimate" questions, arise from our
situation as human creatures. We exist, we celebrate that existence, and are ultimately concerned about our security; we know,
we celebrate that knowledge, and are concerned about its status;
we search for meanings, we are vital in their presence, and are
concerned about the meanings that grasp and often elude us; we
are free, and must choose and actualize values; we find ourselves
judged and guilty, and are concerned for forgiveness, wholeness,
and reconciliation; we face death and are concerned about this
ultimate threat to our being and value. These quite secular joys
and anxieties are the issues with which Christianity has sought
to deal. There are no specifically "religious" problems that are
real; each facet of the Christian gospel deals with the concrete
issues that man's being in the world raises for him. If this gospel
provides any valid answers at all, it provides answers that are
relevant to these secular celebrations and these secular problems,
and to no others. Christian faith is, therefore, formally one answer among other possible ones to the questions which secular
existence raises for man—if we take "questions" in *both* its
positive and its negative form, as pointing to some ultimate
source of our powers for joy as well as to some ultimate threat to
them. Thus the meaningfulness of Christian theology to men
of any age depends entirely on the correlation that is established
between the experienced bases and the felt crises of actual life,
and what the gospel has to say to them.[23] As we have reiterated,
while the *validity* of positive religious discourse and the *reality*
of its object are inescapably based on "faith" as the apprehension of the sacred in and through the profane, nevertheless, its
meaningfulness cannot rest only on that slender "religious" basis
of the faith experience and its certainty. Then it becomes isolated

---

[23] As these remarks indicate, this writer feels that one of the most
creative, and universally illustrated, contributions of Paul Tillich to theological discussion has been his "method of correlation" between the questions which ordinary existence raises and the answers which the Christian
message provides. See Tillich, *Systematic Theology*, Volume I, pp. 59–
66. The dependence of the thoughts here expressed upon those of
Professor Tillich will be evident to anyone familiar with his work.

from profane life and empty. Rather we insist that the sacred is apprehended in and through the structural elements of secular life, and if its symbolic explication is to be *meaningful,* religious symbols must be understood as answers to the questions of ordinary life.

Now, this formal equation between secular questions and Christian answers implies that, just as each aspect of the Christian message has been received existentially in relation to a question embodied in our existence, so in Christian reflection each theological symbol, each facet of Christian theology, each "doctrine," is to be understood, reflected upon and clarified in relation to that same question which human existence in the world had raised. Christian theology attempts to specify in terms of consistent categories and concepts what we *mean* when we speak about that on which our existence as Christians rests with regard to life's deepest problems and in relation to all else we know and think. But, as we noted earlier, meaning results from an interaction of experience and symbol, and thus the *meaning* of religious symbols is, in the first instance, found in relation to the experiences which they thematize and bring to expression and clarity. What theological doctrines mean, therefore, is first of all elucidated by relating the traditional symbols of a community to those experiences which we have found them to illumine.

For example, if we wish to state theologically what we mean in Christian faith by the symbol of "God the creator," this is to be done by interpreting that symbol as an *answer* to our "secular" questions about our own contingency; for that is how this symbol has functioned meaningfully (or "religiously") in this community. If it has not so functioned, it may have been affirmed as "true," but we can be sure it had little meaning and so little illuminating or healing power. Correspondingly, what we mean by faith in and symbolic affirmation of God's providence is to be understood theologically only in terms of its status as an *answer* to the questions of meaning which secular life, both individual and social, raises. What we mean by the symbols of divine forgiveness, mercy, and love is theologically shaped insofar as they are symbols expressive of an answer to the common secular problems of self-acceptance and the search for an ultimate forgiveness. We cannot understand meaningfully the theological symbols of creation, providence, eternity, the divine love, or eschatology unless we understand and conceptually structure them in relation to our experienced problems of contingency, meaning, mortality, freedom, and guilt. The task of theology is thus, on the one hand, to thematize the ultimate questions that existence raises, and, on the other, to explicate conceptually, in the light of these questions, the Christian answers to them. Doctrines take their shape as answers to the problems uncovered by an analysis of secular existence. Thus do they participate as answers in the meaningfulness of the universal questions to which they are relevant. The felt or experienced *meaning* of religious symbols, i.e., its relation to experience, is made possible by this careful correlation of the structure of the symbol to the secular experience to which it provides, for Christians, the answer.

The other crucial factor contributing to the shape of a meaningful Christian theology is the historic Christian community where these answers have been known or received through the symbolic forms of that community. This community has represented in its scriptures, historic symbols, worship, and the other elements of its common life an attitude toward existence generally and toward its ground, toward man and his destiny, toward our obligations one to another, and toward past, present, and future time, which we call "the Christian faith." This attitude receives its basic imprint from the figure of Jesus Christ, who has been taken, amidst a variety of doctrinal affirmations, as that man in history who manifests to us who we are to be if we would be whole, and, through the character of his whole life and death, what is the fundamental will and intention of God for us and for time itself. When, therefore, the Christian in his effort at personal self-understanding asks the most fundamental of ultimate questions—Who am I? What is the force that has thrown me here? Where am I going? What is the ultimate worth of it all? and, What force is it finally that determines our destiny and the destiny of my future, since I know that I do not do that for myself?—his answer is shaped essentially by the symbolic forms

of the historic Christian community, centering as they do around
this figure of Jesus and what he reveals of the nature of things
to us, an answer mediated through the community, its spirit, and
its life. The historic witness of the Church, in all its manifold
variety, but concentrated in this luminous figure presented to us
in the documents around which this community has gathered, is,
then, the other factor out of which theology arises. For it is in
hearing this event read, proclaimed, and reexperienced, and relating the symbols there presented to his own secular experience,
that the Christian finds the answers to the secular questions which
qualify and determine his day-to-day existence. Christian faith is
lived in the world, but the Christian *is* in the world as one
qualified and shaped by his relation to God through Christ. Correspondingly, Christian theology speaks in the world's language,
as an answer to the questions that the world's life raises; but it is
a speech shaped fundamentally by the symbolic answers found
in the historic community of faith where the nature of the reality
with which we must ultimately deal is known.

After a prolegomenon examining secular experience with
regard to ultimate or religious issues, therefore, the next task of
theology is the elucidation of the structural meanings of its own
traditional symbols and myths. Here again, phenomenological
method, more akin to that devised in the history of religions,
may be of help to us. For what is needed is, in essence, an "eidetic" inquiry into the meaning of each symbol, myth and rite,
as they function in the system of symbols expressive of that faith.
Such an inquiry, elucidating the gestalts of historical doctrines,
should begin with the Biblical materials, continue through their
historical interpretations in the tradition, and by eidetic reduction distill the essential elements of these symbols' "meanings"
from these materials. Such in fact has become in our age the role
of Biblical and of historical theology for constructive or systematic theology, that is, to provide an authentic and clear insight
into the meaning, the eidetic structure, of the symbols of this
community's traditional faith and life. We must stress again,
however, that because Bible and tradition can no longer function
as direct and infallible authorities for Christian thought, such
eidetic meanings are not *sufficient* for meaningful religious or

theological affirmations. However clearly and accurately they may
be delineated by historical study and intuitive insight, the eidetic
meanings of Biblical and traditional symbols remain inert and
lifeless unless their relation to our own concrete, ordinary, and
contemporary experience is also delineated. To say, in Biblical
theology, that such and such was believed by the Jewish people,
is one thing; to say in constructive theology, "This *we* believe to
be true," is an entirely different thing and requires for its meaning and its force that the Biblical symbol be *understood* in the
closest relation to contemporary experience. The eidetic phenomenology of historic symbols in Biblical and historical theology
must be complemented by a hermeneutical phenomenology of
contemporary *secular* experience. Their combination into a unity
of symbolic meaning and of actual experience is the first achievement of a constructive or systematic theology, of which the second is the elaboration of its philosophical implications into the
fields of epistemology, of ontology, of historical understanding,
of ethics, of psychology, and of social structures.

We are now, perhaps, in a better position to make sense
of the problem of the validity of religious or theological discourse, and thus it is time to discuss criteria for this mode of language. We agree essentially with Stephen Toulmin's helpful
discussion of criteria: they are, he says, related to and determined
by the larger activity—scientific, moral or religious—in which
the speech functions, and the criteria pertinent to that activity
are to be discovered by asking what sorts of things are relevant
as arguments for one action or another (in morals), or one sort
of religious symbolization or another (in religious language).[24]
What sorts of arguments do we use in proposing a theological
viewpoint; what sorts of things function as "warrants," as a good
brief, as persuasive reasoning in religious discourse? In the following brief discussion of this subject, we propose three "warrants," or kinds of arguments relevant to reasoning in this area.
None proves or establishes a religious point of view or interpretation; for such proof is impossible with regard to this sort of

---

[24] Stephen Toulmin, *An Examination of the Place of Reason in
Ethics*, pp. 84–85; cf. his more extended discussion in *The Uses of Argument* (New York: Cambridge University Press, 1958).

linguistic activity. But reasonable argument is possible with regard to proposals in religious discourse, and these are its criteria: (1) the relation, or more precisely, the fidelity of the symbols and their interpretation proposed, to the symbolic forms of the community and the tradition out of which the theological proposal emanates, and whose spiritual life it seeks to express symbolically; (2) the relation of the religious symbols proposed, and the interpretation offered of them, to concrete common secular experience, especially those positive and negative experiences that lead to ultimate questions, and the scope of such existential issues that this interpretation illumines and clarifies; (3) the intelligibility it provides as a basic and fundamental point of view in relation to other issues of human being and culture: to science, morals, art, politics, etc.—the universality of its scope and applicability as generating illuminating categories for the whole of life. Thus traditional depth, existential concreteness, and width of intelligibility are the criteria of a theological point of view, of a system of religious symbols; we shall briefly enlarge upon these, beginning with the requirement of "tradition."

The first criterion for a valid theology is that any theological statement be a consistent expression of the symbolic forms of the historical community within which the answers are received, experienced, and comprehended through the media of the faith. Theological symbols, such as creation or providence, have not only "felt" meanings in terms of our ordinary secular experience; for felt meanings, however relevant and existential, are blind without symbolic interpretation. Rather, if they are to function as communicating a definite answer to an ultimate question, the verbal symbols of a particular religious tradition—both with regard to their individual character (for example, that of Creation or of Incarnation) and with regard to the larger system of symbols within which they gain their meaning (for example, in medieval or in Reformation systems of thought)—must have an essential structure of their own, a unique gestalt, an integrity and a logic which has objective status, and which gives to that system of symbols that characterize a particular religion or point of view its "essence" and differentiates it from other religions and points of view. Particular symbols, and especially systems of symbols, say something definite and particular about ultimate issues, which, though never clear and distinct, has a unique essence and so can be delineated; and this uniqueness of each particular symbolic form increases when it enters the whole system of symbols in terms of which an entire religious perspective is expressed. It is because of this definiteness and uniqueness of structural meaning that the symbolic forms of a community *can* be mediatory vehicles of a definite or special form of experience which can provide an answer to an existential question, and an answer sharable in speech, in narration, in kerygma, witness, and reflection alike among a community and a tradition. The appropriation of a symbol both existentially and conceptually, and correspondingly for a symbol to "have meaning," involves, therefore, an *interaction* between the objective gestalt or structure contained in the symbols and the felt meanings of common experience. It is through the intentional structure of the symbol that the unconditioned is experienced, and thus are the felt meanings of experience clarified, illumined, and healed. The first criterion of a valid Christian theology relates, therefore, to those essential—although potentially abstract—"meanings" of the traditional symbols creative of the community's life. Correspondingly, the choice of the symbolic content of a theology and the interpretation or usage of these symbols in theological construction is, in part, to be validated by reference to the original Biblical symbols with which the community began, and the history of their interpretation, their "meaning for" the community which has treasured them. In this sense, every valid theology must justify its own categorial structure of thought first of all in relation to the central symbolic content, eidetically abstracted through historical study, of the Biblical materials and the tradition of life and of reflection which have made up the Church's history. This symbolic content must, to be sure, be reexpressed and reworked in the light of the conceptuality of each age; nevertheless, the first requirement is that a contemporaneously relevant theology express the integral structure of the community's attitudes toward God, the world, history, and man, and thus reflect in its time this community of faith from which the answer has been received.

As we have urged throughout, however, such traditional meanings of a historic symbol, however elegantly elaborated, are empty unless they relate to the stuff of ordinary and contemporary life. Definite symbolic structures, we have said, have meaning only insofar as they thematize the felt experience of the life of the people *for whom* they have meaning. Thus the second criterion for an adequate theology is the relevance of its symbolic content to the deepest problems and issues of human existence as an age experiences those issues, i.e., to the questions of contingency, relativity, temporality, and freedom. For the Biblical and traditional symbols of the community *have* use and, therefore, meaning only as answers to these questions. A theology is to be tested, in the second place, by its relatedness, its relevance, its correlations of symbolic answers to the actual questions of our existence.

This second criterion of relevance to *contemporary* existence is essential for all modes of constructive or systematic theology. For such theology in effect does not ask merely about the "eidetic" meanings of traditional symbols for our revered predecessors in the faith—whether at Sinai, in Jerusalem, at Antioch or Wittenberg. Rather inescapably, if it is to do its work, it must ask about their meaning and validity *for us,* for our time and in our cultural and historical situation. Systematic theology is the effort to understand *our* existence in terms of Christian symbols; thus necessarily, if it is to have a religious function, it seeks to express the meaning and validity of these symbols in relation to the actual world in which we as contemporary men live and think, and in terms of which, as we remarked at the outset, our views of reality, of truth, and of value—and so our sense of meaning—are forged. It is here, in the present world, that we exist and so in which we pose religious questions. If, therefore, symbols are to speak religiously to us, to communicate answers to our own ultimate questions, they must speak to and in this contemporary situation. The corollary to this criterion, then, is that a relevant and "true" theology must be intelligible in terms of all else that is known to be true in our time, and thus to the deliverances of the sciences—physical, social and historical—in so far as we accept and live by those deliverances. In this sense an appropriate "demythologizing" process, appropriate to the scientific Weltan-schauung which we actually accept as valid, is inevitably an aspect of any systematic theology which will be meaningful and true for us. If important symbols are not so interpreted in the light of our contemporary view of things, we may be sure that they do not function *religiously,* providing transforming answers to our own most pressing problems, but at best only nostalgically, reminding us of a day when they were meaningful and real to other people.

Thirdly, as we have said, such a symbolic system, mediat-ing historic symbols to contemporary questions, is to be tested and validated by its width of relevance and its adequacy of ex-planatory power. As a total view of man's being in the world, it should provide categories able to illumine at the deepest level each of man's fundamental interactions with his world, his fel-lows, and himself. From it should flow intelligible presupposi-tions or axioms for all of man's creative cultural expressions in social existence, in inquiry, and in the arts. This extension of theological symbols into the totality of human concerns depends, of course, on the elaboration of a "Christian philosophy," in which the primary religious symbolism concerning God, man, time, and the world is extended into more general ontological categories capable of elucidation in relation to all other special fields. A theology that is incapable in this sense of ontological elucidation in the widest philosophical terms is insofar "invalid." The community in the midst of which theology functions, and presumably the theologian himself, are meanwhile participating in and profiting from the full range of cultural existence, politi-cal, moral, scientific, and artistic. For this reason alone, that com-munity and its theology should be responsible that its own most fundamental symbolic forms provide an intelligible framework for its own life in this wider world. It is, we believe, an impor-tant element within the Christian's conviction of the "truth" of his beliefs that he affirms as well that it is in terms of Christian symbols that the most intelligible foundation can be discovered for the total cultural life of man. Thus it is a part of the task of any theologian that, as best he can, he seek to elucidate this wider intelligibility.

Thus tradition, Biblical and historical, contemporary existential experience, and scope of cultural relevance form the criteria for the assessment of the validity of a theology, and of the set of symbols which it seeks to explicate and interpret. We should recall, however, that, with regard to religious language, any experience of and so claim to validity is an *involved* experience and an *involved* claim. The threefold function of a religious symbol, and so its sole meaningful usage, is, we have said, to point beyond the finite referent of which it is a sign to the sacred and the ultimate that is there manifest; to "disclose" through this manifestation the ultimate ground and meaning of our life, and to answer through this manifestation the ultimate questions and crises of life; and lastly, to provide models and norms by which our freedom, individual and cultural, can guide itself. Each of these three functions presupposes our participation in the symbol as a vehicle of the ultimate and the sacred. If the symbol is to *be* religious for us and so meaningful at all, it must communicate to us an ultimate sacrality that grounds our life, rescues it, and directs it. This *is* its meaning, and the only meaning it can have; and to experience this meaning is to experience the validity of the symbol itself. For in the end, a religious symbol is "true" if it becomes for us a medium of the sacred, and it becomes "false" when that communicative power vanishes. Thus, however important the more objective criteria of tradition, contemporary experience, and width or scope of relevance may be, religious symbols are not validated by these means, for such objective testing communicates no sacral presence to our existence. Religious symbols function as religious symbols and so are known to be true only by those to whom they communicate a religious meaning, i.e., an awareness of an ultimate ground to life's passage and an ultimate answer to life's crises. And such a communication to us inevitably either effects or else presupposes an existential involvement in both the questions that are being asked and the answers that are being received.

A "secular theology," then, will seek to apprehend and interpret secular existence, both creative and ambiguous, through the means of the symbols of its Christian faith. Correspondingly, it will understand the symbolic forms of that faith in the terms of these evident characteristics of man's ordinary life. A relevant theology is man's existence seen in the light of Christian faith, and a relevant faith is one whose symbols are understood in the light of man's ordinary existence—neither one can be comprehended meaningfully without the other.

For secular existence is, as we have shown, unintelligible on its own terms. It cannot understand the facets of ultimacy that suffuse its life; its creativity in the midst of its tragedy betrays it into either optimism or pessimism, its vitality and autonomy beguiling it into naïveté, its relativity and temporality into despair. These secular elements of existence remain dark and inscrutable on any other terms—and a good theology must point this out. Conversely, the historical symbols or doctrines of faith have no meaning unless this relevance is established throughout their elaboration, and unless their own intrinsic meaning grows out of and is understood in terms of the powers, ambiguities, and crises of ordinary life.

We can, then, perhaps summarize the most important elements in our discussion of Christian discourse about God in the following way.

All religious talk, we have argued, is talk about the ultimate and the sacred as it appears in ordinary experience, that is as it appears in and through the finite, in its experience of itself, of its being in the world and its being in time. Religious discourse is thus *symbolic*, talk about the finite but with regard to its ground, its limits, its ultimate structures, its resources of healing and renewal, and its bases for hope. It is not, therefore, directly talk about God; we cannot know him as he is in himself, and in any case such talk would have no experienced base or content and so would be meaningless. It is talk about the divine *as* it appears in and to us in our experience of finite things as contingent, relative, temporal, and autonomous beings; it is talk about creatures, others and ourselves, as the sacred appears in them. Thus and only thus is it meaningful language, language about a region that is definite to all of us because it is experienced by us all. It is not talk about heaven, but about earth—with regard to its ultimate and sacred ground and limits. Correspondingly, Christian talk about God is language about this ultimate and sacred dimension: our ground, limit, meaning, judge, and resource, in terms of Christian symbols. And those symbols in turn reflect and express those points where *this* apprehension of the divine was manifested in a particular community's life through *those* finite events, persons, media, and symbols. Again, we are talking about the ultimate and sacred dimension of our contingent, relative, transient, and autonomous being; but, as Christians, we know what that ultimacy and sacrality *is*, and so talk about it, as it has manifested itself in *this* history, and so as it is apprehended, conceived, and responded to in and through *these* media and *these* symbols. Thus we use the "Biblical" and "Christian" verbal symbols of creation, providence, covenant, law, judgment, gospel, forgiveness, and new age—and so on—as means with which to conceive the ultimacy and sacrality that appears in all of existence. "God" is this sacred understood in these symbolic terms; Christian God-language is language descriptive of the ultimate which grounds and limits us, but that ultimate apprehended and understood through these symbols.

Again, however, we should be clear, we are talking symbolically as we have defined and used that term. Our direct referent is *not* the divine as it is in itself, or even "God" as he can be imagined or pictured by means of revealed symbols. Such language "about God" quickly loses its touch with experience and so its meaning for us. Rather is our language multivalent, language *about* the finite with regard to what appears in and to our experience, the ultimate or sacral dimension there, but understood in terms of these symbols. Thus the symbol of God as creator refers not to some pictured absolute, but only to the ultimate and sacral ground of our contingency as that ground is apprehended by us in and through our contingency. Providence refers to the ultimate and sacral context of our life's and our history's meaning; judgment refers to the ultimate norm embodied in Jesus by which our life is evaluated; forgiveness refers to the ultimate love resident in him as a man and which accepts us in and through him—and so on. These are not doctrines about a being called God, but doctrines about the creaturely as the sacred manifests itself in and through the creaturely. The *way* we understand the divine in each of the above is very much shaped by the unique "meaning" or structure of the symbol; it is a *Christian* apprehension and understanding. But *what* we understand through these unique symbols and so in this unique way is the appearance of the sacred in and through the finite, and not the sacred by itself.[25]

Symbols in religion are, in the first instance, creatures, men or events through which the sacred acts creatively and manifests itself to men. Correspondingly, the verbal symbols of reli-

---

[25] Cf. the following from Schleiermacher: "Any proclamation of God which is to be operative upon and within us can only express God in his relation to us; and this is not an infra-human ignorance concerning God, but the essence of human limitedness in relation to him." *The Christian Faith, op. cit.*, paragraph 10. And, "All attributes which we ascribe to God are to be taken as denoting not something special in God, but only something special in the manner in which the feeling of absolute dependence is to be related to him." *Ibid.*, paragraph 50.

The dependence of our view of our knowledge of God and so our language about him on Schleiermacher's view is obvious. There is a difference, however, between that "romantic" view and views characteristic of our own age, namely that whereas they assumed that thematization and so symbols could be drawn out of feelings (see above), we do not. Rather, we see feelings, experience, or meaning as an interaction of symbols and life. Thus are our Christian experiences, apprehensions, and meanings a *combination* of our existential situation with its forms of awareness, and the symbolic systems with and through which we apprehend that situation. And thus is that experience, *qua* Christian, shaped fundamentally by the symbolic content—not only by the "spirit"—of the community. In this, we might claim, we approach Calvin, who, believing that God transcends all our talk of him, averred that he has "lisped with us his children" and given us symbols with which to speak correctly of him. For example: "For who, even of the meanest capacity, understands not, that God lisps, as it were, with us, just as nurses are accustomed to speak with infants? Wherefore such forms of expression [i.e., the Biblical, anthropomorphic symbols] do not clearly explain the nature of God, but accommodate the knowledge of him to our narrow capacity; to accomplish which Scripture must necessarily descend far below the height of his mystery." John Calvin, *The Institutes*, trans. John Allen, Book I, Chapter 13, paragraph 2 (Philadelphia: Presbyterian Board of Christian Education, 1936), vol. I, p. 138. "For, since our infirmity cannot reach his sublimity, the description of him which is given to us, in order that we may understand it, must be lowered to the level of our capacity. His method of lowering it, is to represent himself to us, not as he is in himself, but according to our perception of him." *Ibid.*, Book I, Chapter 17, paragraph 13, vol. I, p. 249.

gion, about which we here speak, are *symbolic* precisely in the sense that they are talk about the finite — creatures, history, men, communities and so on—with regard to their ultimate ground, limit and hope. And the symbol "God" is the way this community, with its experiences and symbolic forms, has apprehended that sacral ultimacy across the entire range of its existence, but centering its delineation of that apprehension on that final event in which the ultimate that is our origin and destiny has manifested itself—in Jesus who is the Christ. In this sense, the task of systematic theology is that of uniting or joining conceptually the Biblical symbols about *God*: as creator, ruler, Judge, Father, Redeemer and Reconciler, with our understanding of *ourselves* as "symbols" through which the sacred appears; for example, of understanding *God's* creation in terms of *our* contingency and its ground. To speak *only* of God is empty; to speak *only* of ourselves is pointless. To talk meaningfully of God is to talk of our existence in contingency and freedom in relation to its divine ground, judge, and redeeming resource, understood symbolically in the terms of our community's life. This by no means answers all our questions about intelligible symbolic language; but at least it relates religious discourse to concrete and contemporary experience without sacrificing either its Biblical or traditional content, its transcendent reference, or its possibility of intelligible ontological and cultural explication.

Our fundamental thesis in this chapter has been that the Christian awareness of God grows out of the wonder and the ambiguity of the ordinary life of man in the world, but that it is an awareness that is finally brought to conscious and definitive form by the central experience of illumination and renewal that comes in the community that witnesses to the Christ. For all of us, this original awareness is *there*, at once elusive and real, absent and present, threatening and reassuring, as the fundamental ground and tone to our ordinary existence—until the knowledge of "faith" illumines and clarifies in part, but only in part, this ever-present mystery. The Christian continues to live, therefore, amidst both the ambiguity and clarity of this situation—for faith clarifies but by no means removes the ambiguities and the threats of our natural existence. Our Christian existence participates in both the worlds we have delineated—that of ambiguity, doubt, and the Void, and that of confidence, meaning, and reconciliation. Finally, from this characteristic situation of Christian life in the present, the strange religious symbols of the immanence and the transcendence of God, on the one hand, and of eschatology, on the other, begin to make sense. We can understand the symbol of the *immanence* of God as the source of our being and meaning in terms of the common, universal, and secular experiences of the reality, wonder and joy of life, of the coherences that experience offers to our inquiries, and of the universally apprehended meaningfulness of life's tasks. Correspondingly, we can understand the symbol of the *transcendence* of God through our continual experience of the elusiveness of that security and meaning, in the experience of the radical relativity of our truth, and in our sense of alienation from forgiveness and from the power to love—of all of which our secular friends, as well as we, are so very much aware. Above all, we can know the divine hiddenness in the Void of insecurity, despair, doubt, guilt, and death, which every human faces—even Jesus himself in his cry from the cross. The transcendence of God is initially experienced in the Void, which is the first terrible face of the divine that, at least in a secular culture, man knows. But then in the joy and acceptance of our contingent being, of our relative life, and of our death, and in the achievement of relative meaning and truth, of love and of community despite our fragmentariness, the renewed immanent presence of God is also known, and we begin to be aware of who that ultimate reality is—and the promise of an end in which God will be all in all takes on concrete, experienced meaning. The beginning of faith then appears in the awareness of the sacred in the profane, of joy and wonder in the midst of insecurity, of meaning and truth in the midst of the meaningless, and of life in the face of death, and it culminates with our understanding and affirmation of their ultimate unity in God.

This dialectic of immanence and transcendence, of hidden presence to all of life and of absence from it when we look for him is, of course, not all of God that we can know, or that the Christian community has believed itself to know. It is only a beginning. "God" here remains perhaps real, deep, but vague and elusive—the mysterious, sacral power from which life comes and which rules our destiny, and the eternity from which we are now separated. When Christian experience and thought move beyond this point, and in the light of those more personal and moral questions raised by our freedom and by our relations to others in community and in history, begin to know the love and acceptance of God in his long relation to his people and especially in the figure of Jesus, then we can say we begin to know the sacred more directly as it is, we begin to know "God." And that knowledge will reflect back on all that has been experienced of the ultimate on the other levels of our existence, shaping our answers to life's dilemmas and so shaping the theological symbols with which we comprehend ourselves, our destiny, and the sacred itself. Then the mysterious source of our being, the dim ruler of our destiny, and the opaque eternity into which we are finally to move, become illumined for us through the law and the love shown in Jesus Christ, and we can begin haltingly, but with some sense of meaning and of certainty, to speak of "God." But that the presence of God is real in secular life, and that our dependence on him makes us search for him even in our most worldly affairs, is true, and thus begins the possibility of knowing the reality of God and of speaking of him in a secular age. Our Biblical symbols, the treasured vehicles of our community's life and faith, can be understood as meaningful and asserted as valid as forthrightly in our secular existence as in any other age— but only if we retain, both in our thought and in our existence, a lively sense of their relatedness to our ordinary secular life.

Index

Word, problems with in hermeneutical theology, 198–199; problems
with in neoorthodoxy, 95–99
Word-event, 191*n*.
World War II, 91
Worldly involvement, 24, 173; of
radical theology, 114–115; tragic
dimensions of, 173–174
Worldly value system, 153–154, 168f.

Wren-Lewis, John, 111*n*.
Wright, G. E., 86*n*., 92*n*.

Youth, 357

Zeus, 298
Zorba, 70*n*.
Zoroaster, 151